Insurance Contract Analysis

Insurance Contract Analysis

ERIC A. WIENING, CPCU, ARM, AU
Assistant Vice President
American Institute for CPCU

DONALD S. MALECKI, CPCU
President
Donald S. Malecki and Associates, Inc.

First Edition • 1992

AMERICAN INSTITUTE FOR
CHARTERED PROPERTY CASUALTY UNDERWRITERS
720 Providence Road, Malvern, Pennsylvania 19355-0716

Foreword

The American Institute for Chartered Property Casualty Underwriters and the Insurance Institute of America are independent, non-profit, educational organizations serving the needs of the property and liability insurance business. The Institutes develop a wide range of programs—curricula, study materials, and examinations—in response to the educational requirements of various elements of the business.

The American Institute confers the Chartered Property Casualty Underwriter (CPCU®) professional designation on those who meet the Institute's experience, ethics, and examination requirements.

The Insurance Institute of America offers associate designations and certificate programs in the following technical and managerial disciplines:

Accredited Adviser in Insurance (AAI®)
Associate in Claims (AIC)
Associate in Underwriting (AU)
Associate in Risk Management (ARM)
Associate in Loss Control Management (ALCM®)
Associate in Premium Auditing (APA®)
Associate in Management (AIM)
Associate in Research and Planning (ARP®)
Associate in Insurance Accounting and Finance (AIAF)
Associate in Automation Management (AAM®)
Associate in Marine Insurance Management (AMIM®)
Associate in Reinsurance (ARe)
Associate in Fidelity and Surety Bonding (AFSB)
Certificate in General Insurance
Certificate in Supervisory Management
Certificate in Introduction to Claims
Certificate in Introduction to Property and Liability Insurance

The Institutes began publishing textbooks in 1976 to help students meet the national examination standards. Since that time, we have produced more than seventy-five individual textbook volumes. Despite the vast differences in the subjects and purposes of these volumes, they all have much in common. First, each book is specifically designed to increase knowledge and develop skills that can improve job performance and help students achieve the educational objectives of the course for which it is assigned. Second, all of the manuscripts of our texts are widely reviewed prior to publication, by both insurance business practitioners and members of the academic community. In addition, all of our texts and course guides reflect the work of Institute staff members. These writing or editing duties are seen as an integral part of their professional responsibilities, and no one earns a royalty based on the sale of our texts. We have proceeded in this way to avoid even the appearance of any conflict of interests. Finally, the revisions of our texts often incorporate improvements suggested by students and course leaders.

We welcome criticisms of and suggestions for improving our publications. It is only with such constructive comments that we can hope to improve the quality of our study materials. Please direct any comments you may have on this text to the Curriculum Department of the Institutes.

Norman A. Baglini, Ph.D., CPCU, CLU
President and Chief Executive Officer

Preface

This text was written to meet some of the educational objectives of CPCU 1—Ethics, Insurance Perspectives, and Insurance Contract Analysis—one in a series of national examination courses leading to the professional designation CPCU, Chartered Property Casualty Underwriter. CPCU national examinations are administered twice-yearly by the American Institute. Educational objectives, review questions, and other study aids are provided in the CPCU 1 Course Guide, a companion volume that is revised annually, which is published by the American Institute. Although it usually is used in conjunction with the CPCU 1 Course Guide and other assigned texts, the authors recognize that *Insurance Contract Analysis* might also be adopted for other purposes. This text does not depend directly on other texts for support. However, it does presume a basic understanding of property-liability insurance coverages and insurance regulation.

This volume examines the nature, content, and interpretation of property-liability insurance contracts. It includes a detailed analysis of the types of information typically found in insurance contracts, as well as external factors that must be considered when insurance contracts are analyzed and applied. The first chapter sets the stage by describing the nature of insurance contracts as legal documents and introducing some fundamental principles of insurance. Chapter 2 describes the structure of insurance policies and describes an organized approach for reading these documents. The next chapter explains the important role of the common insurance policy provisions, found in most insurance policies, that are so commonplace that they often are overlooked.

For coverage to apply to any given party, that party must not only have an insurable interest in the loss but also be a party insured under an applicable contract of insurance, points explored in Chapter 4. Chapter 5 makes it clear that the loss must involve an insured event and analyzes the elements that comprise an insured event. When an insured event involves loss to an insured party with an insurable interest, the amount of recovery under an insurance contract may be established by considering policy limits and loss valuation provisions (Chapter 6); coinsurance, deductibles, and other loss-sharing provisions (Chapter 7); and multiple sources of recovery, including but not limited to other insurance (Chapter 8). Finally, insurance policy analysis is not limited to the clear language of written provisions printed within the policy. Chapter 9 examines a number of external factors that are also taken into account.

This approach to insurance contract analysis evolved from years of experience with not only CPCU 1 but also other CPCU courses. Both authors have been directly involved in writing and editing previous editions of CPCU 2, 3, and 4 texts. This text reflects many evolutionary changes in the insurance business, as well as direct and indirect feedback from thousands of CPCU candidates and their course leaders, from exam committee members, from graders, and from those who took CPCU examinations. Especially helpful in defining the needs to be met by this text were the suggestions over the years of the national Curriculum Liaison Committee of The Society of CPCU. Plans for this text were also profoundly influenced by many hours of discussion among members of the CPCU Curriculum Revision Committee of the American Institute. These staff discussions and the input of many outside advisers led to some fundamental changes in the CPCU curriculum that further affected the nature and content of a first CPCU course and the texts it would require. The writing of this text was a team effort, and it is no exaggeration to say that every single page has been affected by the work of several authors, contributing authors, reviewers, and editors.

G. William Glendenning, Ph.D., CPCU, not only drafted the original manuscript for Chapter 8, but also provided a final review of the manuscripts for every chapter in this text. Many improvements and refinements are the direct result of Bill's work on these semi-final manuscripts. Bill was an author of both editions of *Principles of Risk Management and Insurance,* Volumes I and II, the text previously used for CPCU 1.

George E. Rejda, Ph.D., CLU, drafted the original manuscript for Chapter 4. George also served as a co-author of *Insurance Perspectives,* another text assigned in CPCU 1. An experienced author of insurance textbooks, he has served as a co-author of *Personal Insurance,* a text used in the IIA Program in General Insurance. George is also the author of *Principles of Risk Management and Insurance,* published by

South-Western Publishing Company, a popular college insurance text, now in its fourth edition.

Bernard L. Webb, CPCU, FCAS, MAAA, who wrote the original manuscript for Chapter 7, is no stranger to CPCU textbook writing. He has been a co-author of four editions of the text for CPCU 5 and has frequently served as a contributing author for other CPCU and IIA courses.

This textbook also benefited from the groundwork laid in previous CPCU 1 texts by C. Arthur Williams, Jr., Ph.D.; George L. Head, Ph.D., CPCU, ARM, CSP, CLU; Ronald C. Horn, Ph.D., CPCU, CLU; and G. William Glendenning, Ph.D., CPCU. Even though the words have changed and the material has been updated, many of the concepts first formalized in that previous work are preserved in this successor text, as are the titles of several chapters.

We are grateful to the following people who reviewed the manuscripts for major portions of this text: Michael L. Averill, CPCU, Vice President, The Home Group; Paul A. Baiocchi, CPCU, AMIM, ARP, ARM, President, American Association of Insurance Services; James E. Brennan, CPCU, CLU, CIC, Professor/Consultant, University of Connecticut; Marlin Y. Evans, CPCU, ChFC, CLU, Auto Division Manager-Mid South Region, State Farm Insurance Companies; Arthur L. Flitner, CPCU, ARM, Director of Curriculum, American Institute for CPCU; John A. Reiner, CPCU, Assistant Vice President-Product Development, Crum & Forster; Dennis J. Ryan, CPCU, AU, Corporate Training Coordinator, PHICO; and Jerome Trupin, CPCU, CLU, Trupin Insurance Services.

We are also grateful to the following persons who shared their expertise in specialized areas related to topics covered in Chapter 8: Thomas J. Clarke, M.Ed., Secretary/Treasurer, Arbitration Forums, Inc.; and Joseph P. Decaminada, J.D., CPCU, CLU, ChFC, Senior Vice President, Secretary and Counsel, The Atlantic Companies.

In addition to the reviewers listed above, James J. Markham, J.D., CPCU, AIC, AIAF, Director of Curriculum, General Counsel, and Ethics Counsel; and Karen Porter, J.D., Assistant Director of Curriculum, both of the Institute staff, took time from their busy schedules to review portions of this text.

The Institute's Publications and Public Relations Department completed this text under severe time pressure. Their many years of experience, their unflagging devotion to quality, and their attention to detail are reflected literally from cover to cover.

Although this is a new text, it is not too early to begin thinking about the next edition. We invite CPCU students and other readers to send us their comments and criticisms in order that we might improve future editions.

We are deeply interested in the usefulness of this text as a learning device. Accordingly, we welcome constructive comments on how we might improve our presentation. Any text may contain oversimplifications and factual errors—especially if facts have changed since the text was written, as is almost a certainty in such a dynamic field as insurance. Although we have tried to anticipate and minimize such problems, we invite readers to call our attention to any that they may discover. Comments may be addressed to the Curriculum Department of the American Institute.

Eric A. Wiening
Donald S. Malecki

Contributing Authors

The American Institute for Chartered Property Casualty Underwriters acknowledges with deep appreciation the help of the following contributing authors:

G. William Glendenning, Ph.D., CPCU
Professor of Risk Management
Temple University (Retired)

George E. Rejda, Ph.D., CLU
V. K. Skutt Professor of Insurance
University of Nebraska

Bernard L. Webb, CPCU, FCAS, MAAA
Professor Emeritus of Actuarial Science,
    Risk Management, and Insurance
Georgia State University

Table of Contents

Damages or Other Penalties Assessed Against the Insurer ~ *Compensatory Damages; Punitive Damages for Bad Faith; Penalties Under Unfair Claim Settlement Practices Acts*

Summary

CHAPTER 1

The Insurance Contract

Insurance involves special relationships among insurers and insureds. These special relationships are formalized through insurance contracts—legally enforceable agreements. Following a brief examination of the insurance relationship, this chapter examines the nature of insurance as a contract and examines the two fundamental principles underlying the insurance relationship—the principle of indemnity and the law of large numbers.

THE INSURANCE RELATIONSHIP

The insurance relationship bears some resemblance to other personal and commercial relationships; yet it differs in some noteworthy respects. Like other personal relationships, insurance could not succeed if it were based solely on legal procedures. Good faith and fair dealing are essential. Like other commercial relationships, the insurance relationship is built upon a contract that defines the expectations of the parties.

On its face, insurance seems to involve an inequitable exchange of unequal values. A typical insured pays a premium to an insurer and receives "only" a conditional promise in return. Unless or until an insured event takes place, the insurance company will not be called upon to fulfill its promise. In the short run, the typical insured expects to pay premium dollars to the insurer and receive few, if any, loss dollars in return. Even over the long run, an insured should expect to pay more in premiums than will be received back in payments for loss.

Despite this superficial appearance of inequity, most insureds enter voluntarily into insurance relationships. They would not do so unless they regarded the insurance relationship as "fair" or, at least, legitimate.

1

Insureds are willing to participate in the seemingly unbalanced insurance relationship because they understand certain basic characteristics of insurance: Many parties facing risks of loss provide the funds that are used to pay for the losses suffered by relatively few. Each insurance buyer hopes he or she will not be among the few who suffer major losses, but each is willing to provide a portion of the funds for the benefit of those members of the group who do suffer insured losses. Each insured is willing to participate by contributing an amount of premium proportionate to the amount of risk he or she brings to the group.

Insureds usually do not contract directly with a few other insureds to form a risk-sharing group, but they enter into insurance contracts with insurance companies. These insurers also form similar contracts with a large number of other insureds, thereby serving as intermediaries to facilitate the efficient and manageable pooling of risks. The participation of a large number of insureds is important for both (1) making an accurate projection of losses and (2) generating adequate funds to pay for those losses. Insurance companies must project losses accurately so they can charge a fair premium to each insured, relative to the risk, and yet earn profits in the long run. If insurance companies were unable to earn profits, most would have no incentive to engage in the business of insurance.

As explained in a later section of this chapter, the "law of large numbers" enables insurance companies to project losses with a substantial degree of confidence when a large enough number of exposure units are involved. An insurance company can then charge each insured a premium that is adequate both to cover expected losses and to enable the insurance company to earn a profit.

Insureds are willing to pay premiums if they believe their money is used to make whole—that is, to indemnify—the relatively few who suffer losses. Each insured who is made whole has not received a windfall. Rather, the insurance mechanism has restored each insured who suffered a loss to the condition he or she would have been in if no loss had occurred. The fact that different insureds require different sums to be made whole is widely regarded as "fair," because all are given the opportunity, not to gain, but to be indemnified in the event of loss.

If certain insureds were actually to profit from insurance claims, other insureds would likely feel cheated. They too might try to profit, and the insurance mechanism might ultimately break down. Insureds will continue to regard insurance as a "fair deal" only if insurance is preserved as a mechanism that provides indemnification of losses, and not profits. The principle that people should not profit from their insurance, otherwise known as the *principle of indemnity*, is essential to insurance. The principle of indemnity is examined in detail in a later section of this chapter.

Insurance contracts bring together large numbers of appropriately grouped insureds and provide for indemnification of the losses suffered by the few. The individual insureds need not know one another—as a practical matter, individual insureds normally could not organize a large enough number of other insureds to make the insurance relationship work. Insurance companies, on the other hand, form a workable pool of exposures by entering into similar insurance contracts with a large number of relatively homogeneous customers.

The Role of Written Contracts

Insurance is transacted through written contracts, rather than oral ones. Even though oral insurance binders are valid, a binder could not readily be interpreted unless it were understood to refer to some type of written contract.

The general law of contracts does not require insurance contracts to be in writing to be valid. Although most state insurance regulations require written contracts, there is a more fundamental reason for using written contracts. There is almost always a period of time between the formation of an insurance contract and the need to perform under the contract—a delay between the time when a policy is effective and the time when a loss occurs. Because an insurance agreement can be complex, it is best to record all details of the agreement when it is formed so there can be no misunderstanding later. After a given loss has occurred, the financial interests of the insured and the insurance company obviously differ, and neither party could be completely objective about the terms of their agreement if it were not in writing. A written agreement reduces the chances of a misunderstanding.

The Role of Written Form Contracts

Preprinted form contracts are widely used in the insurance industry. The use of preprinted forms in other contexts, such as form leases or form purchase orders, often can be thoughtless and inappropriate, defensible only on grounds of expediency. In contrast, the use of form contracts in insurance serves to establish and support the essential characteristics of insurance. The use of the same standard forms among all homeowners, for example, creates a homogeneity, which allows insurance companies to apply the law of large numbers to homeowners insurance policies. Without standard forms, variations in coverage might be too great to group insureds reliably for statistical purposes.

ELEMENTS OF AN INSURANCE CONTRACT

People buy insurance to obtain the insurer's contractual obligation to provide financial protection. An insured may bring legal action against an insurer that has failed to live up to the promises in the insurance contract. As with other contracts, an insurance contract is effective because its provisions can be enforced through the courts.

In general, a contract is a set of agreements that are legally enforceable. The terms of a contract are formed by the mutual agreement of the parties to the contract. Usually, one party proposes certain contract terms, called by the law an *offer*, and the other party accepts those terms, an action called an *acceptance*. Many contracts require substantial negotiation before an agreement is reached. Once an agreement is reached, the agreement has the legal status of a contract because of consideration. *Consideration* may consist of performance of certain actions, a promise to perform, or giving up certain rights. Consideration must be given and received by each party to a contract. Contracts in which there are an offer, acceptance, and consideration are legally enforceable, as long as there is no defense such as illegality, fraud, duress, or incompetency. In general, contracts need not be in writing, although they often are written to prevent misunderstandings.

To be enforceable, an insurance contract must have the same essential elements as any other contract. That is, it must be true that the parties entered into an *agreement* consisting of a legally binding *offer* and an *acceptance* of that offer. *Agreement* must exist between parties who are *competent* to contract, and it must be a genuine agreement or assent. There must have been legally sufficient *consideration* to support the agreement. The contract must have a *lawful object or purpose*.

A contract that meets all of the above criteria is valid and *enforceable*, and a legal remedy is available if the contract is breached by either party. (For example, a court may order a party to perform its duties as specified in a contract or require a party to pay damages for having breached a contract.) An agreement that does not meet these criteria is *unenforceable*—the legal system will not enforce its terms or provide a legal remedy in the event of a breach. A contract may be unenforceable because it is void or voidable.

- *Void.* A void contract never had any legal existence. Even though the parties may have gone through the exercise of making a contract, no contract has legally been made because some essential element is missing. Either party may choose to ignore the agreement.
- *Voidable.* A voidable contract legally exists, but its existence is tenuous because it can legally be rejected, or *avoided*, at the option of one or both of the parties.

It is not required that an insurance contract be in writing; oral insurance contracts will be enforced.

Most insurance contracts meet the essential criteria stated above. However, there are situations in which an insurance policy may be unenforceable. If an insurance policy is unenforceable, an insurer can deny its liability under the policy, leaving the insured without the expected recovery.

An unenforceable insurance contract must be distinguished from one that has been canceled, or one under which the breach of a condition leads to a denial of coverage:

- *Cancellation.* To *cancel* an insurance policy is first to acknowledge that it *is* a legally valid contract and then to terminate it according to its own contractual terms. Insurers' rights to *cancel* insurance polices are limited by various state laws. However, an insurer normally may *deny coverage* under a property or liability policy at any time on grounds that it is unenforceable.
- *Denying coverage based on breach of policy condition.* If an insurer refuses to pay a loss on the grounds that the insured breached a policy condition, the insurer is *not* claiming that the policy is unenforceable. Rather, the insurer is strictly enforcing the provisions of a valid contract and alleging that the insured has failed to comply with those conditions.

Agreement in an Insurance Contract

The first condition for a legally enforceable contract is agreement to rights and obligations by two or more parties. Without agreement, there can be no contract. Agreement is reached when one party makes a specific *offer* and the other party makes specific and genuine *acceptance* of the exact terms of that offer.

An *offer* is the expression of a promise that requires some action on the part of its intended recipient to make an agreement. The party making the offer is the *offeror*, and the party receiving it is the *offeree*. The essential elements of an offer are as follows:

1. The offeror must express, by word or conduct, an intent to enter into a contract.
2. The terms of the proposed contract must be sufficiently definite.
3. The offer must be communicated to the offeree.

An offeree who receives an offer may accept it, reject it, or make a proposal that differs in some way from the original offer. Such an alternative proposal is a *counteroffer*. A counteroffer is a rejection of the original offer, and it therefore cancels the original offer. The counteroffer constitutes a new offer originated by the party who was originally the offeree.

Acceptance occurs when a party to whom an offer has been made either agrees to the proposal or does what has been proposed. An acceptance must meet three requirements:

1. It must be *made by the party to whom the offer was made.*
2. It must be *consistent with the offer.* That is, the acceptance must conform in substance to the exact terms of the offer; if it does not, it is not an acceptance but a counteroffer.
3. It must be *communicated to the offeror by appropriate word or act.*

Most insurance is sold through producers who solicit business for insurers, take applications, and sometimes prepare and issue policies. The complex relationship between insurance companies and those acting as their agents is the subject of agency law and is beyond the scope of this discussion. In brief, however, an insurance agent acts on behalf of the insurance company he or she represents.

Offer and Acceptance.   Do insurance agents identify prospects for insurance and attempt to sell them insurance, or do agents attempt to induce prospects to purchase insurance? Is the agent *making* an offer to sell insurance or *accepting* offers to buy insurance? The answer depends on the situation.

The Insurance Application.   As a general rule, an agent who contacts a prospective insured, hoping to sell an insurance policy, is considered merely to be *soliciting* offers. The actual *offer* is made when the applicant signs a completed application and sends it to the insurance company through the agent. If the insurance company later issues an insurance policy strictly in accordance with the application (offer), this policy issuance constitutes *acceptance* and thus consummates the *agreement.*

If the insurance company issues a policy that does not completely conform to the application (the initial offer), then the policy is considered a *counteroffer* that requires specific acceptance by the applicant.

The Policy as an Offer.   In many insurance transactions, the applicant submits an application, without paying any premium, simply to determine whether the application will prove acceptable to the insurer. In such a case, the applicant has not made an offer. If the applied-for policy is issued by the insurer, the policy constitutes an offer by the insurer. If the policy is accepted by the insured and the premium is paid, the offer and acceptance are concluded.

Communication.   As with contracts in general, communicating the offer to the offeree is essential. Also, a policy is not a binding contract of insurance until its acceptance has actually been communicated to the offeror or to the offeror's authorized agent.

Many insurance transactions are handled through the mail. In such cases, an insurance contract is consummated when the acceptance is actually *mailed*, not when it is received. So, for example, where issuance of a policy by the insurer constitutes the offer, the act of mailing the premium in response to that policy (offer) constitutes acceptance.

Oral Contracts. Oral applications and contracts are common in property and liability insurance. In life and health insurance, however, written applications and contracts are used universally.

Modern business practices often require that immediate insurance coverage be available. To meet this need, property and liability insurance agents often are given authority to "bind" coverage immediately on behalf of the insurance company. For example, a woman phones an insurance agent who knows her and asks him for immediate theft insurance on a $5,000 item of jewelry she has just purchased. The agent might reply, "You are now covered for $5,000 by Insurance Company A." Insurance Company A is bound by this oral agreement just as certainly as if a written policy had been issued.

When an insurance agent has orally bound coverage, it is sound business practice to issue a written "binder" confirming the details of the oral agreement as soon as possible. However, the contract is enforceable without a written binder.

Even though the courts will enforce oral contracts of insurance, there are strong reasons written contracts are preferable. An "insured" under an oral contract may honestly exaggerate or dishonestly falsify the terms of the oral agreement—lawsuits involving oral contracts often come down to one person's word against another's. Questions may arise regarding the events insured, the insured object or premises, the amount of insurance, the name of the insurer, and other matters. Courts may resolve these issues based on previous dealings between the parties, customary practices, and statutory requirements.

Genuine Assent. A contract that appears to be valid may be unenforceable if the consent of either party was not genuinely given and it is determined that the parties failed to reach the legally required agreement. An innocent party whose actual assent was lacking may avoid the contract. Absence of genuine assent might possibly be found under circumstances where any of several factors can be proven:

- Fraud is involved.
- A mistake was made by either or both parties.
- Duress was used.
- Undue influence is shown.
- Innocent misrepresentations have been made.

Most litigation relating to the enforceability of insurance contracts has involved questions of genuineness of assent. Like other contracts, the insurance contract is subject to the rules concerning mistake, fraud, duress, and undue influence. In addition, the insurance transaction must be free of concealment or misrepresentation by either party, either of which could create a lack of assent resulting in an unenforceable contract. Concealment and misrepresentation are discussed later.

Many of the thousands of insurance policies issued every year contain mistakes. Mistakenly worded insurance policies may be remedied by court interpretation or by reformation.

Court Interpretation as a Remedy. When a legal action is brought because an insurance policy is unclear or ambiguous, the court may attempt to interpret the policy. For example, where the language of a property insurance policy does not clearly provide or exclude coverage for a given property item that has been damaged, the court will most likely determine that coverage exists.

Reformation as a Remedy. The court may act to "reform" or change a formal contract so that it conforms to the true intention of the parties. The remedy of reformation is granted only upon proof of mutual mistake or of mistake by one party of which the other party was aware. It will not be granted for an error of one party unknown to the other. If clear and convincing evidence of the true intent of the parties is produced, a court of equity will reform the policy to conform with the intent of the parties.

If an insurance company denies a loss for an insured whose policy shows a different address for the insured property, an action for reformation may be maintained. It would be the obligation of the insured to provide evidence that both parties intended to insure property at the location where the loss occurred.

Competent Parties to an Insurance Contract

The parties to a contract must be legally capable of entering into an agreement. A contract may be voidable by any contracting party who was not competent at the time of agreement. The parties involved in forming an insurance contract, who must be competent, generally include the insurance company, the agent, and the insured. Sometimes, however, no agent is involved and the applicant deals directly (in person, by telephone, or through the mail) with an insurance company employee.

Insurance Companies. Insurance companies obtain their legal authority to do business from the states where they are formed, and they normally must be licensed to conduct business in each state where they operate. State regulations may also impose some restraints on insurance companies' rights to conduct business.

An insurance contract that is outside the corporation's authority may still be enforced against it. Suppose an insurance company mistakenly issues a policy using a contract form that has not yet been approved in a state. The insurer has exceeded its authority; however, the insured will still be permitted to hold the insurer to the contract. The insurer will not be permitted to set up its own wrongdoing as a defense to an action on the contract. (The insurer most likely would be fined for using the contract and enjoined from using it further—at least until it is approved.)

Insurance Agents. Agents' competency to enter into a contract has seldom been raised as an issue. Perhaps this is because authority to act as an insurance agent is controlled by state statute and administrative regulation. To assure the basic competency of agents, each state administers tests to prospective insurance agents before issuing agents' licenses.

Insureds. Unless the insured can prove that he or she was incompetent by reason of insanity, minority, or intoxication, an insurance contract may not be avoided by reason of incapacity. As a practical matter, insureds who wish to void an insurance contract rarely raise the issue of competency because the same effect can always be accomplished simply by exercising a cancellation right or ceasing to pay insurance premiums.

Consideration

A contract is not enforceable unless it involves legal "consideration." Most contracts involve agreements in which one party is saying to another, in effect, "If you will do this for me, then I will do that for you." The "thing" each person asks the other to do in this exchange is that person's consideration. In other words, consideration is a thing of value exchanged for something else of value. The consideration necessary to make a promise enforceable may consist of paying money, or it may be giving a promise in return, performing an act, or giving up a right to do what one is legally entitled to do.

Like any other contract, an insurance contract requires that there be valuable "consideration" by both parties.

- The insurer's consideration is its promise to indemnify the insured upon the occurrence of an insured event.
- The insured's consideration is its payment of the premium—or its promise to pay the premium.

In property and liability insurance, actual prepayment of the premium is not strictly required for the contract to be valid. If the premium has not actually been paid, the courts will readily find an implied promise to pay the premium. Suppose the insured fails to pay the premium before the outset of the policy period (as is common), and a claim materializes during the policy period but before the premium has actually been paid. The insurer is not likely to prevail in this situation if it takes the position that the contract is unenforceable based on failure of consideration.

If the insured has failed to make a premium payment when due, the insurer can take steps to cancel the policy for nonpayment of premium. If the initial premium has never been paid, the insurer might cancel the policy "flat," meaning that the policy was never in effect because it lacked consideration. *Flat cancellation* for nonpayment of premium is problematic. As a practical matter, it is generally not feasible to cancel a policy "flat" after an insured loss has occurred. The insured would normally be willing to remit the premium (assuming the premium is less than the loss), even if the premium payment is late. And it would be against public policy to permit insurers to deny every claim arising before the initial premium is paid. While it is not appropriate or desirable for insurers to provide "free" insurance, that is exactly what can happen in certain situations. For example, if there is a period of time before the first premium must be paid to avoid cancellation, the insured can either enforce a claim arising during this period or, if no claim takes place, permit the policy to lapse or to be canceled flat for nonpayment. While the insurer may have a right to collect the premium earned during this limited time period, if often is difficult to collect and usually not worth the effort.

Careful underwriting, billing, and collection procedures by insurers and their agents should minimize this problem. Yet, business practices often make it necessary to place insurance in force before the details of billing, collection, and production of a written contract can take place. Also, some statutes require that buyers of some types of insurance be able to rescind a contract during a limited cooling-off period, typically ten days. During this time they may examine the policy to see whether it lives up to the claims advertised by a sales representative or advertisement, or they may decide their interest has lessened since the time they heard the sales pitch.

Legal Purpose

To be enforceable, a contract must serve a legal purpose. When either forming or performing the agreement constitutes a crime or a tort, the contract is illegal. For example, a contract to murder a person is clearly illegal, and any such contract would not be enforceable. No court would insist that a murder be performed or that payment be made for one that was performed.

The courts may consider a contract to be illegal if it is against the law or against public policy (as defined by the courts). For example, most gambling agreements are illegal contracts and therefore unenforceable by the courts. An agreement to pay a bribe to a government official in exchange for receiving a government job would not be enforced by the courts because such activities are against public policy.

Insurance contracts must involve a legal subject matter. Courts will refuse to enforce any insurance contract that tends to injure the public welfare or is illegal, and it is against public policy to issue such contracts. Contracts that tend to increase crime or violations of the law are invalid.

For example, some states prohibit liability insurance coverage for *punitive damages* on the basis that punitive damages are punishment intended to discourage wrongdoing by assessing monetary damages against wrongdoers, and that a person is not actually punished, nor is wrongdoing discouraged, if the damages are payable by an insurance company. The opposing viewpoint holds that punitive damages meet the requisites of a commercially insurable exposure—among other things, they can be completely unexpected or unintended from the standpoint of the insured, and the random nature of punitive damages awards makes it desirable for insurance protection to be available.

Child molestation is another area in which concerns about legal purpose have been raised. In some states, convicted child molesters have sought protection against civil suits under the liability portion of their homeowners policies. A number of states have enacted laws declaring that there is no coverage for such incidents.

Property insurance coverage on illegally owned or possessed goods is invalid. Property such as cocaine may not legally be possessed by most people, and property insurance covering such goods would be void and unenforceable. However, where it appears that the insurance is simply incidental to an illegal purpose, then the contract will still be enforceable. A fire insurance policy on a building in which illegal gambling or prostitution is carried on will still be enforceable, notwithstanding the illegal activity.[1] (Of course, business income coverage for illegal gambling or prostitution would be against public policy.)

SPECIAL LEGAL CHARACTERISTICS OF INSURANCE CONTRACTS

Previous sections of this chapter discussed principles of contracts in general and then examined the ways in which these general contract principles apply to insurance contracts. In addition to the legal characteristics it shares with all other kinds of contracts, insurance has a number of special legal characteristics that will be discussed here. It is not that insurance is treated differently than other contracts are, but that insurance contracts have certain characteristics that not every other contract has.

Insurance Policies Are Personal Contracts

An insurance policy is a personal contract because it protects not property, liability, lives, or health, but people. Moreover, the identity of the people it insures is highly relevant to the insurance company. Insurance companies are interested in preserving their rights to select insureds with whom they are willing to enter into contractual agreements and to reject others.

This concept has important ramifications. For one thing, an insurance company underwriter may carefully evaluate the personal characteristics of the person(s) applying for insurance. The insurance company has an obvious interest in avoiding moral and morale hazards[2] by declining to issue insurance policies to people who present unacceptable hazards. This important underwriting goal can be achieved only when the underwriter knows the identity of the insured.

If owners of insurance policies could freely transfer the policies to other parties, the insurance company would find itself legally bound to contracts with persons to whom it might never have issued policies in the first place, and the nature of the risks insured might be substantially different from the risks the insurer was willing to accept. Because insurance is a personal contract, most property and liability insurance policies contain a so-called *assignment provision* stating that the policy cannot be assigned (transferred) to another person without the consent of the insurance company. It would be possible, for example, for George to sell his property to Martha and also assign his insurance on that property to Martha, *but only if George's insurance company agrees to the assignment.* As a practical matter, the assignment provision is rarely exercised. Usually the buyer arranges his or her own insurance on exposures acquired from another party.

Some states have passed statutes requiring that insurance companies accept all applicants for auto insurance. While promoting insurance availability, this approach limits or removes insurers' rights to select the persons they will insure.

Insurance Policies Are Unilateral Contracts

Bilateral means two-sided; unilateral means one-sided. Most commercial contracts are bilateral—each party makes a promise to the other party that is legally enforceable. If either party breaches the contract, the other party can sue for damages for breach of contract or insist that the contract be performed.

Insurance contracts are said to be unilateral because once the contract is formed, only one party, the insurer, has made a legally enforceable promise—the promise to pay covered claims. It is true that the insured must continue to pay premiums if the policy is to be kept in force, but the insured generally cannot legally be *forced* to pay renewal premiums. Nor can the insured be forced to comply with other policy provisions. Insurance policies typically include provisions imposing certain duties on an insured—for example, the duty to report claims to the insurance company. The insurance company cannot technically force the insured to perform such duties. However, an insured who fails to perform duties imposed by the insurance contract may find subsequent claims denied by the insurer on the basis that the insured has breached the contract, and the courts may uphold the insurer's denial.

Insurance Policies Are Contracts of Adhesion

Contracts of cohesion are drafted by both parties to the contract. In contrast, a *contract of adhesion* is prepared by one party, with the other party having no alternative but to accept or reject all the terms. Most insurance policies are clearly contracts of adhesion. The wording in most insurance contract forms is drafted by the insurance company (or a service organization), and the same preprinted contract forms are used for many different insureds. Since it is the insurance company that determines (or selects) the exact wording in the policy, the insured generally has little choice but to "take it or leave it." The contract might, perhaps, be altered by the use of supplementary forms or endorsements, but the wording in these documents also normally is chosen by the insurer. In most cases, the person who wants insurance has no practical choice but to "adhere" (stick) to the contract drafted by the insurer.

This clearly creates an unbalanced situation. The insurer has more opportunity than the insured to delineate the specific terms of the policy. To offset this imbalance, the courts have ruled that any ambiguities or uncertainties in an insurance contract of adhesion are to be construed *against the party that drafted the agreement—usually the insurer.* If there is any reasonable room for doubt in interpreting a policy, it will be interpreted in favor of the insured. The reasoning is that the insurer theoretically had an opportunity to express its intent in clear and unequivocal terms.

If a policy provision can be interpreted in more than one way, it will be interpreted in the way that favors the insured. A policy provision that can reasonably be interpreted in more than one way is deemed to be ambiguous regardless of the original intent of the drafters. Whether or not a policy provision is ambiguous is ultimately a question of fact for the courts to decide. If the courts decide that it is ambiguous, then it is ambiguous.

In some cases, usually involving larger commercial insurance buyers or unusual situations, both insurer and insured play a role in drafting an insurance contract. In such cases the doctrine of adhesion may not be applied if it is presumed that both parties had an adequate opportunity to review the wording of the contract and equal expertise in doing so. This and related concepts are explored further in later chapters.

Insurance Policies Are Conditional Contracts Involving the Exchange of Unequal Amounts

An insurance policy is a *conditional contract* because the insurer has to perform only if certain conditions are met. Specifically, an insured event must take place *and* the insured must fulfill other conditions of the policy. If no insured event occurs, no performance can be required of the insurer. Of course, absence of an insured event does not mean the insurance has been worthless. The insurer's promise to pay "if needed" exists even if the "need" never develops.

Insurance contracts involve an exchange of unequal amounts in the following way: The premium paid to the insurer by each insured for a particular policy is not expected to exactly equal the amounts to be paid by the insurer in fulfilling its contractual obligations to that insured.[3] Some insureds may have major losses, while others may have minor losses or no losses at all. It is intended, of course, that there is a close relationship between the amount of premiums paid by all insureds and the amount paid for claims to or on behalf of all insureds.

Insurance Policies Are Contracts of the Utmost Good Faith

The nature of insurance requires complete honesty and disclosure of all relevant facts between the parties. All parties to an insurance contract are expected to be ethical in their dealings. That is why insurance contracts are referred to as contracts "of utmost good faith" (in Latin, *uberrimae fidei*).

The *Insurance Consumer's Bill of Rights and Responsibilities*, shown in Exhibit 1-1, summarizes the expectations of parties transacting insurance in good faith. Every insured has a right to rely on the insurance company to fulfill its promises faithfully, even if the insurance company is obligated to do nothing until some years in the future when a claim finally becomes payable. An insured may bring a legal action against an insurance company that it believes has acted in bad faith, and the courts have imposed severe penalties against insurers in cases where bad faith claims have been sustained.

Likewise, the insurer has a right to expect that the insured deals in good faith (see the *Bill of Responsibilities* portion of Exhibit 1-1). The test of good faith is failed whenever an insurance buyer conceals or misrepresents material facts, and an insurance company may be released from a contract if it can demonstrate concealment or misrepresentation by the insured.

Concealment. Concealment has been defined as failure to disclose known facts or as "silence when obligated to speak." The prevailing view is that the insured is obligated to reveal only material facts, and that a contract can be voided by the insurer only if the insured's concealment was material and intentional.

A *material fact* is one whose disclosure would have influenced the insurer's decision to accept the application. Whether the *insured* considers a given fact to be material is not the determining factor; only a judge or jury can ultimately make that decision. The courts agree that any fact that is specifically asked about is material. For example, failure to disclose relevant information in answering specific questions on an insurance application provides strong evidence of concealment, which may give the insurer adequate grounds for avoiding the contract on the basis that there never was a meeting of the minds.

Not only must the concealed fact be material; the concealment also must be *intentional.* Intent to defraud exists only when the insured knowingly and in bad faith fails to disclose a material fact.

Misrepresentation. Because it is an absence of information, a concealment obviously does not appear in writing, but a misrepresentation often does. *Representations* are statements made by an applicant for insurance concerning the loss exposure. They are intended to induce the insurer to enter into the insurance contract. They may be oral or written and may be in papers not connected with the policy contract. Representations precede and accompany the execution of the contract they are intended to induce. They are collateral to the contract and are not matters about which the parties contract.

For example, an auto insurance applicant may accurately or inaccurately represent that she has had no traffic tickets or accidents. This representation is an inducement to the insurer to issue an auto insurance policy, but the representation is not the subject matter of the insurance contract.

A *misrepresentation* is an incorrect or false statement of a past or present fact relating to the insurance or the subjects of insurance. A misrepresentation has the legal effect of allowing the insurer to declare the contract voidable if it is (1) false, (2) relied upon, and (3) material.

Exhibit 1-1
Insurance Consumer's Bill of Rights and Responsibilities

The Insurance Consumer's Bill of Rights and Responsibilities is your guide to fair insurance practices, protection of your insurance dollars, and honest, reliable representation. Take it with you when you interview an insurance agency, and make sure your agent reads and agrees with its principles.

Preamble

We pledge to support these principles as a first step in creating greater understanding of what consumers should expect in buying and using insurance, and to define clearly the responsibilities expected of consumers in return. Using these goals as a yardstick, consumers, agents, and insurers will be able to measure progress as we work together to build the best possible insurance system for the American people.

Bill of Rights

The Right to Protection

The right to purchase insurance that meets your needs, regardless of where you live or work, priced fairly according to your specific risks, without regard to race, color, or creed.

The Right to Be Informed

The right to have your policy printed in clear, easily readable type and written in understandable language; the right to have policy provisions explained to you accurately before purchase; the right to be told in advance, if possible, when the price or terms of your policy are to change, and why.

The Right to Choose

The right to be offered available options for protection; the right to enough time to adequately consider your purchase; and the right to make an informed choice of the coverage that best meets your needs for quality protection, fair value, price, and personal service; the right to a competitive marketplace where several insurance companies compete for your business.

The Right to Be Heard

The right to have a voice in major decisions that affect you, whether made by insurance companies, insurance agents, or insurance regulators; the right to prompt and constructive replies to suggestions and inquiries; the right to be informed about and participate in consumer organizations that are involved in insurance issues.

The Right to Redress

The right to prompt settlement of just claims; the ability to have access to third parties for mediation and to have access to a responsive state insurance department for further redress.

The Right to Service

The right to be treated with dignity, honesty, and fairness; the right to receive prompt and fair attention to claims, policy changes, and inquiries; the right to be served by an insurance professional who strives to provide you with the best insurance value.

Bill of Responsibilities

The Responsibility to Be Informed

The responsibility to understand the concept of insurance, to read each insurance policy and attempt to understand its terms and, when lacking understanding, the responsibility to seek answers from an insurance professional.

The Responsibility to Help Control Losses

The responsibility to minimize risk through safe driving, loss prevention, vehicle and home maintenance, and caring for your health.

The Responsibility to Report Accurate Information

The responsibility to file insurance applications and report claims accurately and in a timely manner.

The Responsibility to Keep Updated and Accurate Records

The responsibility to maintain in writing the name, address, and telephone number of your insurance agent and your insurance company, and all policy numbers and vehicle make, model, and identification numbers; the responsibility to maintain an updated inventory of household possessions.

The Responsibility to Comply with Policy Provisions

The responsibility to comply with the specific conditions outlined in your policy, including paying premiums on time, cooperating with insurance companies when they defend your claims, and reporting changes that may affect your coverage.

The Responsibility to Report Fraudulent Practices

The responsibility to report to law enforcement and insurance authorities any questionable practices by insurers, agents, consumers, auto body shops, doctors, lawyers, or any other parties seeking to defraud or circumvent the insurance system or consumers.

Reprinted by permission of National Association of Professional Insurance Agents and Consumer Insurance Interest Group.

The common law distinguishes between a *misrepresentation of fact* and a *misrepresentation of opinion*. A misrepresentation of fact may allow avoidance of a contract if material, while a misrepresentation of opinion may render a contract ineffective only if material and fraudulent. For example, if an insured, in applying for a fire insurance contract, misstated the age of the building by several years, it is not likely that such a mistake would have been material to the exposure. In addition, if the statement were only an estimate of age, it would be mere opinion.

Misrepresentations (as well as representations) refer only to statements at the time the contract is made. Promises that conditions will exist during the term of the contract may involve warranties or conditions, but not representations.

To be grounds for avoiding (making void) an insurance policy, a misrepresentation must be of a material fact and it must have been relied on by the insurer. If the insurer does not rely upon the representation, even though the representation is false, the insurer does not have grounds for avoidance of the policy.

Misrepresentation of facts, ideas, and circumstances can assume many forms. It can be difficult to determine when a representation becomes a *"mis*representation" sufficient to justify avoidance of an insurance policy. Courts take the position that representations are to be construed liberally in favor of the insured; representations are required only to be substantially true in the opinion of the courts. Even though a representation is not literally true, it is not a misrepresentation if it is substantially true. Whether an objective fact that is inaccurate is substantially true depends upon its materiality to the argument. The test of materiality, in turn, hinges on whether the contract would have been made if the truth had been told.

Most Insurance Policies Are Contracts of Indemnity

Indemnity may be defined as compensation given to make the person whole from a loss already sustained.[4] Under a *contract of indemnity* the insured is entitled to payment only if he or she has suffered a loss and then only up to the extent of the financial loss he or she actually incurred.

Insurance is a contract of indemnity when the amount the insurer pays is directly related to the amount of the insured's loss. A contract of indemnity does not necessarily pay the full amount necessary to restore an insured who has suffered a covered loss. Most insurance policies contain a dollar limit and other limitations and provisions that may reduce the total amount of recovery.

Contracts of indemnity are intended to support the *principle of indemnity*, a fundamental insurance principle discussed under the next heading of this chapter. Briefly, the principle of indemnity states that *the insured is not supposed to profit from an insured loss.*

Most insurance policies are considered contracts of indemnity. However, some insurance arrangements, notably most life insurance contracts, are *valued policies* rather than contracts of indemnity. With a valued policy, the insurer agrees to pay a preestablished dollar amount in the event of an insured loss. For example, in a life insurance policy with a $100,000 face amount, the insurer agrees to pay $100,000 upon the death of the insured. When paying a life insurance policy claim, no attempt is made to replace the dollar value of what the insured was "worth" at the time of death. Another example of a valued policy is the (misnamed) hospital indemnity policy, which pays a specified amount, such as $100 per day, while the insured is in the hospital.

Some property insurance policies also may be considered valued policies—notably those on antiques or one-of-a-kind objects for which it would be difficult to establish an objective value at the time of the loss. Suppose, for example, a person owned one of the few Tucker automobiles ever made. Such a vehicle would probably be insured on a valued basis. That is, the insured and the insurance company would agree on the value of the vehicle and the insurer would issue a policy reflecting that value. If the car should be totally destroyed, the insurance company would pay that valued amount without having to attempt a post-loss appraisal of the almost-one-of-a-kind vehicle.

The distinction between contracts of indemnity and valued policies is useful to the student of insurance, and that distinction is preserved in this text. However, some authors view all insurance arrangements as contracts of indemnity. Robert E. Keeton and Alan I. Widiss explain their reasoning as follows:

> [Some] writers suggest that it is . . . appropriate to classify life insurance policies as contracts of indemnity because the insurance proceeds are usually provided to a beneficiary who has sustained a loss of some benefits as a consequence of the decedent's death.

> *Observations*

> The most accurate conceptualization of insurance arrangements is to observe, first, that neither life insurance nor any other form of insurance is invariably a pure indemnity contract; second, that all forms of insurance are subject to the influence of the principle of indemnity; and third, that the influence of the indemnity principle is less pervasive in some forms of insurance, such as life insurance, than in other forms of insurance, such as property insurance. In other words, although the characterization of insurance as an indemnity contract is useful as a statement of a tendency or as a generalization, it is not always a reliable guide when answers are sought to specific problems of insurance law.[5]

THE PRINCIPLE OF INDEMNITY

Perhaps the most fundamental of insurance principles is the principle of indemnity. This principle underscores one of the most basic tenets of insurance—that the role of insurance is to put insureds back into the same financial position they enjoyed before the occurrence of an insured event, but insurance is not intended to enrich them unjustly.

The *principle of indemnity* is the concept that insurance contracts should confer a benefit no greater in value than the loss suffered by an insured.[6] Stated in the negative, the principle of indemnity means simply that *a person should not profit from an insured loss.*

Notice that the principle of indemnity does not say that the insured must be "made whole." Less-than-full recovery may take place because of deductibles, limits of insurance, or other limitations on recovery. When insurance provides a benefit equal to only a part of the financial loss, the principle of indemnity is not violated. Questions may be raised, however, in situations where an insured could be overcompensated.

Reasons for the Principle of Indemnity

The principle of indemnity serves two related purposes:

- It prevents insureds from profiting because of their insurance.
- It reduces the moral hazard by removing the profit incentive.

Moral hazard is a condition that exists when a person may try intentionally to cause a covered loss or may exaggerate a covered loss that has occurred. As used by insurance practitioners, the term "moral hazard" sometimes refers to a defect or weakness in human character. Often, however, it is applied not to people but to overinsurance on property or other situations that might tempt people to cause or exaggerate insured losses from which they might benefit. For example, there are all too many cases in which a buyer simply cannot be found for a failing business or an unwanted item of property. An insurance company that has agreed to restore the lost values (in effect, to "buy" the property), if a covered item is destroyed by a covered peril, may present an irresistible temptation to the desperate businessowner or property owner.

Clearly, it is undesirable to tempt insureds by promising to pay a dollar amount that vastly exceeds the property's true value to the insured. Overinsured property may create moral hazards because it presents the property owner with a financial incentive for "arson for profit" (or similar destructive acts not involving fire).

Defining the Extent of Covered Loss

Insurance policies inevitably contain provisions intended to clarify how the amount payable by the insurer will be determined after an insured event takes place. Valued policies simply state the dollar amount that the insurer will pay upon the occurrence of certain conditions (such as the death of the insured or total destruction of covered property). Contracts of indemnity, however, describe a method by which the extent of the covered loss will be measured.

- In property insurance covering direct damage or destruction of property, it is necessary to state how the value of the damaged or destroyed property will be determined.

- With time element insurance, it is necessary to clarify the extent to which lost income or extra expense is reimbursed.
- With liability insurance, it is necessary to clarify the extent of the insurer's obligations.

In any case, the goal is for the terms of the insurance contract to precisely and unambiguously explain just how the insured will be indemnified—restored, but not enriched.

Direct Damage Property Insurance. The traditional approach to property insurance, and one that is still used in many policies, provides coverage for direct property losses on the basis of the property's "actual cash value." This approach is designed to put the insured into approximately the same financial position after the loss as immediately before it.

Actual cash value often is simply defined as "replacement cost minus depreciation." *Replacement cost* is the current cost of restoring the damaged property to pre-loss condition using new materials of like kind and quality. *Depreciation* is an allowance for wear and tear and economic obsolescence.

Actual cash value takes into account the effects of both economic inflation (which tends to increase some property values over time) and depreciation (which tends to reduce most property values over time). For example, Sally bought a newly constructed house for $150,000 (not including the value of the land). Today it would cost $225,000 to build an identical new house—this is the current replacement cost. However, Sally's house is not a new house, and some quantitative measure of its depreciation must be factored into the determination of its actual cash value exclusive of land. In this example, the replacement cost of the house *increased* by $75,000, but depreciation has *decreased* its value by, say, $25,000, giving the house an actual cash value of $200,000.

If Sally were to insure her house to its full value "on an actual cash value basis," she would purchase $200,000 of insurance, and she would collect up to $200,000 in the event of loss to the house. Before a total loss she has a house worth $200,000; after the loss she would have $200,000 in cash.

Actual cash value insurance presents a theoretical ideal—it would make Sally whole, but she would not be enriched. Notice, however, that Sally would have to spend, not $200,000, but $225,000 to have another identical house constructed on her property. From Sally's viewpoint, the actual cash value insurance has not made her whole. Further detail on actual cash value and other approaches, notably replacement cost insurance, will be discussed in Chapter 6.

Business Income and Extra Expense Insurance. Business income and extra expense losses generally are covered on the basis of the loss or expense actually incurred. For example, business income insurance provides coverage on the basis of the actual (net income) loss sustained by the insured during a period of business interruption. Detailed policy provisions, beyond the scope of this chapter, explain how that amount will be calculated.

Extra expense insurance provides coverage for expenses actually incurred to avoid or reduce a suspension of business or to reduce a business interruption loss.

Homeowners insurance policies include coverage for additional living expenses, defined generally as expenses over and above normal living costs incurred because the insured cannot live in the home while it is being repaired following direct property damage by a covered cause of loss. Recovery is on the basis of expenses actually incurred.

Liability Insurance. Liability insurance policies typically contain an agreement to pay all sums that the insured becomes legally obligated to pay as damages because of bodily injury, property damage, or other covered offense(s). Most liability insurance policies also state that the insurer will pay defense costs actually incurred in litigating or settling the claim, as well as other specified expenses that are incurred.

In this way, the insurer's obligation is limited to the actual extent of the insured's legal obligations. The insured's legal obligations (the amount the insured is legally obligated to pay as damages) are determined either by the court or by an out-of-court settlement to which the insurer consents. Losses are paid on behalf of the insured, and related expenses are paid, but the insured is not overcompensated.

Exceptions; Technical Violations of the Principle. Several practices or requirements appear to violate the principle of indemnity. Replacement cost insurance, as previously explained, is one example. Other important examples are valued policies and valued policy laws.

Valued Policies. As explained earlier, the insurer issuing a *valued policy* agrees to pay a preestablished dollar amount in the event of an insured loss. For example, in a life insurance policy with a $100,000 face amount the insurer agrees to pay $100,000 upon the death of the insured (barring extenuating circumstances). No consideration is given to how much the insured was "worth" at the time of death.

Valued policies are also used in those accident insurance policies that promise, for example, to pay $5,000 upon the loss of sight in one eye. In property insurance, valued policies are used to insure articles such as antiques, paintings or other objects of art, and cargo in transit, whose value would be very difficult to determine following a loss. This problem is overcome by stating the value of the insured object in the policy, a value to which both insurer and insured agree. In the event of a total loss to an insured object, the insurer pays the insured the valued amount given in the policy.

The amount payable for a partial loss may be determined by policy provisions or, if the policy does not clearly address the issue, by court interpretations. Some courts have based the valuation of partial losses on a percentage of the agreed value for total losses. Other courts view the agreed value as solely a device for setting an upper limit on the insurer's liability and hold that partial losses should be paid on the basis of actual cash value, repair cost, replacement cost, or whatever other valuation standard may be in the policy.

Valued Policy Laws.   Many states have valued policy statutes that apply to insurance on real property. Typically, such statutes require a property insurer to pay the full amount of the policy if the insured property is totally destroyed by a peril specified in the statute and covered by the policy. Stated differently, in case of a total loss to insured property, the insured recovers the face amount of the policy—regardless of the property's actual value. Many such statutes apply only to dwellings and other *buildings*, and then only to the perils of fire and lightning.

Many valued policy statutes were enacted in the nineteenth century to keep insurers from overinsuring at high premiums and then questioning the values in the policy after a loss occurred. Valued policy laws encouraged insurers to investigate the value of insured property when initially issuing a policy. Presumably, the insurer has an opportunity to inspect a building before insuring it, and the insurer therefore has the opportunity to determine its value. As a practical matter, however, many buildings are not physically inspected before they are insured. Inspecting individual buildings increases an insurer's underwriting expenses. It often does not make good business sense to incur the costs of inspecting a building that seems completely acceptable based on other available information. Like other decisions, the decision not to inspect is occasionally a bad one: Some buildings are overinsured, and some of them create moral hazards. Given the inflation rates of recent times, underinsurance has more often been a problem than overinsurance, but exceptions certainly exist.

In a state with a valued policy statute, when a building is *totally* destroyed by fire, the insurer usually must pay the policy limit. However, most valued policy laws permit the insurer to settle *partial* losses on the basis of their actual cash value at the time of loss—or, if smaller, the costs of repairing or replacing the damaged property with property of like kind and quality. Some of the laws stipulate that payments for partial losses are to be a percentage of the agreed value, with the percentage corresponding to the degree of damage to the property.

For partial fire losses, some laws even bar the insurer from applying deductibles or coinsurance provisions.

The Principle of Insurable Interest

A person has an insurable interest if the occurrence of an insured event would cause financial loss or injury to that person. *Insurable interest* may be defined as the kind of exposure to financial loss a person must possess in order to have *legally enforceable* insurance coverage. So, whether or not a person has a legally insurable interest depends on the relationship between that person and the property, life, or event in question. If the relationship exposes the person to possible financial loss, and the relationship is not unduly remote, it is sufficient to support an insurable interest.

The principle of insurable interest supports the principle of indemnity by providing that insurance benefits will be available only to people whose relationship to an insured event would cause them to suffer a financial loss, and then only to the extent of that loss. Unless the insured has an insurable interest, the courts will not force the insurer to pay a claim to, or on behalf of, the insured.

The insurable interest requirement supports the principle of indemnity in only those insurance contracts that are classified as contracts of indemnity. Most life insurance contracts are valued policies that pay a stated amount upon the insured's death, and they are not considered contracts of indemnity. Thus, supporting the principle of indemnity is not relevant to life insurance. Likewise, the insurable interest requirement does not enforce the principle of indemnity in those property or health insurance contracts that are written on a valued basis. Valued policies could violate the principle of indemnity if the amount paid were to exceed the actual loss, but insurers deal with this problem by underwriting controls and by policy provisions that tend to prevent overinsurance.

The discussion in this chapter is limited to the general principle of insurable interest. A detailed discussion of specific types of interests insurable in property and liability insurance appears in Chapter 4.

Insurable Interests Versus Loss Exposures. The law defines an insurable interest much as a risk manager might define a loss exposure (a set of circumstances that presents a possibility of loss). The person or entity exposed to loss has an insurable interest in the circumstances that present the loss possibility.

However, a legally insurable interest is not necessarily the same thing as an insurable loss exposure. Many financially significant loss exposures (such as those resulting from "business risks," or from wear and tear) are not commercially insurable. Furthermore, each insurer normally has the right to accept or reject applications for insurance based on its own underwriting standards.

Keep this distinction in mind. When discussing *underwriting* criteria, the term "insurable" refers to an exposure that is both eligible and acceptable to the insurance company. However, when discussing insurable interests, "insurable" should be viewed in a *legal* sense. Even though an insurable interest exists, an unacceptable applicant may not be "insurable" by underwriting standards. And even if an insurance policy has been issued, it cannot be enforced by a party who has no insurable interest in an insured event. Whenever possible, questions of insurable interest should be resolved before the policy is issued. To avoid situations in which a claim must be denied based on a lack of insurable interest, both the insured and the underwriter should try to avoid entering into an insurance contract unless they are certain that an insurable interest is involved.

Insurable interests are treated differently in (1) life and health insurance and in (2) property and liability insurance. Although this text emphasizes property and liability insurance, the principle of insurable interest becomes clearer when both approaches are examined.

Insurable Interests in Life Insurance. In addition to the insurance company, a life insurance contract involves four distinct relationships:

- The *applicant* who applies for insurance
- The *policyowner* or *policyholder* who owns the insurance policy
- The *insured* upon whose death the insurance company will pay benefits
- The *beneficiary* or *beneficiaries* who will receive the death benefits from the insurance company upon the death of the insured

The applicant and the policyowner usually are the same person, and the policyowner may also be the insured. For example, John applies for life insurance covering his own life, and John names his wife Mary as the beneficiary. John is the owner, the applicant, and the insured. As another example, Matthew purchases life insurance on the life of his son Mark, and Matthew names himself as beneficiary. In this case Matthew is the applicant, the policyowner, and the beneficiary, but Mark is the insured.

Policyowner Is the Insured. It probably would be stretching a point to say (as some people do) that a person has an insurable interest in his or her own life. The insured does not really suffer a financial loss from his or her own death (or at least does not survive to claim any compensation for the loss). The truth of the matter is simply that the question of insurable interest does not come up when a person purchases life insurance on his or her own life. Subject to the insurer's underwriting rules, an applicant for life insurance on his or her own life can purchase as much life insurance as he or she can afford. A person who applies for insurance on his or her own life generally can name anyone as beneficiary.[7]

While the law imposes no upper dollar limit on the amount of life insurance a person may purchase on his or her own life, there are practical limits. The insured-policyowner must be willing to pay the necessary premiums, and insurer underwriting practices would tend to deny the purchase of excessive amounts of life insurance. Also, the insured-policyowner is most likely to name a beneficiary who has some financial interest in his or her life.

Policyowner Is Not the Insured. An applicant who purchases insurance on the life of another person must have an insurable interest. The courts want to be assured that the insurance is not likely to provide a motive for murdering the insured. Most courts presume that family members have insurable interests in the lives of others who are closely related to them by blood or marriage. While there are variations in different jurisdictions, the following is generally true:

- Each spouse has an insurable interest in the life of the other
- Each parent has an insurable interest in the life of a child and a child in the life of a parent
- Brothers and sisters have insurable interests in each other's lives
- Grandparents have insurable interests in the lives of their grandchildren

Mutual insurable relationships may also exist between any two family members, even if they are distantly related, or between any two unrelated individuals if one is financially dependent on the other. The economically dependent person has an insurable interest based on the financial support that presumably would have been received from the other person had he or she lived. The person providing the support also has an insurable interest in the life of the dependent, in terms of recouping the costs of having provided that support.

Many business relationships give rise also to insurable interests in life insurance. Among the insurable interests recognized and commonly used to support the purchase of life insurance are the following:

- The interest of an employer in the life of a key employee
- The interest of a creditor in the life of a debtor
- The interests of both a partnership and the individual partners in the lives of each working partner

Each situation clearly involves the possibility that the business entity will suffer substantial financial loss upon the death of the insured.

Before issuing an individual life insurance policy to an applicant-beneficiary who is not the insured, many insurers will require the written consent of the proposed insured. Consent of the insured normally is not required (1) in group life insurance, (2) when one spouse applies for individual insurance on the other's life, or (3) when a parent applies for individual insurance on the life of a parent's minor child.

When Insurable Interest Must Exist. With life insurance, the insurable interest is legally required to exist only at the inception of the policy. This general rule has no practical effect in cases where the beneficiary has an insurable interest in the life of the insured, both at the time of the policy's inception and at the time of the insured's death. But it becomes highly important when personal situations change so that the policyowner has an insurable interest at inception but, at the time of the insured's death, that insurable interest no longer exists.

One result is that life insurance obtained on a spouse during marriage remains valid and enforceable after a divorce. Likewise, an employer may purchase an insurance policy on the life of a key employee and receive benefits from that policy even after the employee resigns, as long as the policy remains in force.

The major reason why the insurable interest requirement in life insurance has to be met only at the inception of the policy is that life insurance contracts typically are not contracts of indemnity but valued policies that pay a stated sum to the beneficiary. The principle of indemnity would be difficult to apply to life insurance because of the lack of precision inherent in measuring the economic value of a human life. Also, the courts generally believe that the objectives of preventing gambling and reducing the possibility of murder are met by requiring an insurable interest only at the inception of the policy. Further obscuring the issue, some modern life insurance policies are sold primarily for their investment value to the insured, the death benefit to the beneficiary being only a secondary consideration.

Insurable Interests in Health Insurance. Insurable interests with health insurance policies depend on whether the policy in question is a valued policy or a contract of indemnity.

Valued policies agree to pay stated sums, regardless of the amount of loss, if an insured event occurs. The insurable interest requirements for these policies are basically the same as those applicable to life insurance. That is, the insurable interest needs to exist only at the inception of the policy, it is normally the applicant-beneficiary who must have an insurable interest, and the persons who have insurable interests in health insurance are essentially the same people who would have insurable interests for life insurance purposes.

Contracts of indemnity are written to pay, up to the policy maximum, no more than the insured's actual loss. For health insurance policies of this type, the insurable interest requirements follow the rules that apply to property and liability insurance, as explained later. In general, it is the insured who normally must have the insurable interest at the time of loss. The insured may satisfy the requirement by having, at the time of loss, a right to income (for disability income insurance) or a responsibility to pay medical expenses (for medical expense insurance).

Insurable Interests in Property and Liability Insurance. Insurable interests in property and liability insurance have several characteristics:

- It is the insured who must have an insurable interest.
- The insurable interest must exist at the time of loss.
- Diverse relationships give rise to insurable interests.

The Insured Must Have an Insurable Interest. The two parties who enter into a property-liability insurance contract are the insurer and the insured. Obviously, it is the insured who must have an insurable interest in order to have a contract that can be legally enforced against the insurer.

Insurable Interest Must Exist at Time of Loss. Except by statute in a few states, property-liability insureds are not required to satisfy an insurable interest requirement at the inception of the policy. While insurers routinely impose the requirement as a matter of underwriting practice, the law generally requires an insurable interest of the property-liability insured only at the time of loss. This is in keeping with the view that most property and liability policies are designed to indemnify the insured for loss actually sustained. The courts will not violate public policy by requiring an insurer to unjustly enrich a person by paying a claim to an insured party who had no insurable interest at the time of the loss.

Many Relationships Involve Insurable Interests. Many relationships create or give rise to insurable interests in both property insurance and liability insurance.

A property owner has a rather obvious insurable interest in owned property. However, the notion of insurable interest is not restricted to property "owners." Many rights beyond pure ownership also create valid insurable interests in property.

Insurable interests in liability losses are somewhat less obvious. However, it has been clearly established that *any entity has an insurable interest in any event that may result in liability for that entity.* Insurable interests based on potential legal liability do not depend on whether the insured has any legal or equitable title in property, but on whether the insured may be charged in court with liability for damage or injury stemming from an insured event. If a claim arises, its existence

Chapter Notes

1. James J. Lorimer, Harry F. Perlet, Frederick G. Kempin, and Frederick R. Hodosh, *The Legal Environment of Insurance*, 3rd. ed., vol. I (Malvern, PA: American Institute for Property Liability Underwriters, 1987), p. 140.
2. A *moral hazard*, as discussed later in the chapter, is a condition that exists when a person may try intentionally to cause a loss or may exaggerate a loss that has occurred. A *morale hazard* is a condition that exists when a person is less careful than he or she should be, knowing that insurance will respond in the event of a loss.
3. This statement may not be true in the case of a cash flow insurance plan, usually involving large commercial insureds, in which the earned premium is directly related to the insurer's claims and expenses during the policy term.
4. Henry Campbell Black; *Black's Law Dictionary*, 4th ed., 1968, p. 910.
5. Robert E. Keeton and Alan I. Widiss, *Insurance Law*, 1988, pp. 141-142.
6. Keeton and Widiss, p. 135.
7. Questions occasionally develop in situations where insurance might be considered a wager or where it might provide an inducement to commit murder. For a more detailed discussion see Keeton and Widiss, pp. 181-195.

CHAPTER 2

Reading an Insurance Policy

The word *policy* is derived from the Italian *polizza,* a written contract that furnishes evidence of, or creates, a legal obligation. Although the Italians did not use *polizza* only for insurance contracts, the term "policy" has been carried into the English language as a name for the insurance contract. Partly because of this origin, some scholars have speculated that written insurance contracts had their origin in Italy.[1]

Early U.S. insurance policies were simple contracts written by insurers who knew their insureds well. Most insurers confined their operations to a relatively small geographical area and to insureds with whom the underwriters were familiar. Insurance was sold primarily through home office employees, without the assistance of agents or brokers. A typical fire insurance policy was extremely brief, including little more than the description of the property, the amount of the coverage, the period of coverage, and a premium citation. Insurance operations were characterized by individual underwriting and mutual understanding between insured and insurer. The importance of the insurance lay not so much in the wording of the written policy as in the understanding between the parties as to what they sought to achieve.

As insurance grew into a larger, more sophisticated business, simple contracts and marketing methods began to bow to complexity. The prosperity experienced by commercial fire insurance, for example, brought on increased competition and more creative marketing systems. The result was a decentralization of underwriting activities, a lessening of firsthand knowledge in the underwriting selection process, and marketing through producers who often were significantly detached from the home office of the insurer.

Selling and servicing policies in expanded geographical areas added further challenges, because the property being insured or the damage caused by each loss was not readily available for examination. Insurance companies recruited agents in various communities to sell and service insurance policies on their behalf. While local agents alleviated some of the difficulties that distance had created, they also created some new problems. An insurance company could not supervise the honesty of the agents or determine whether the out-of-state insurance applications contained accurate information. Moreover, the physical separation of the insured from the insurer left insurers more subject to moral and morale hazards. To address these problems, insurers issued policies filled with provisions designed to protect insurance companies from unwittingly accepting undesirable business and paying unjust claims.

Unfortunately, many policies were filled with restrictions, exclusions, exceptions, small type, confusing sentences, and undefined terms. Insureds often found they could not collect on their policies because of unseen exclusions buried deep in the fine print. Insurers found it hard to negotiate claim settlements because their policy conditions had become nullified, or otherwise modified, by widely differing court decisions.

As early fire insurance developed in the mid- to late-1800s and early 1900s, each insurer generally developed its own independent fire insurance contract. A general lack of cooperation among insurers in terms of developing a common form, or even guidelines toward a generally acceptable agreement, led to a hodgepodge of insurance contracts with resultant consumer confusion. Not surprisingly, the insurance industry was increasingly viewed with suspicion.

Since insurers developed their own contracts without reference to any common wording, fire insurance contracts were often ambiguous. Problems often developed in interpretation of coverage, in litigation, and in settlement of losses involving dual coverage. The need for more uniform fire policies that were both simpler and shorter became increasingly apparent. A long series of slow developments reached their climax with the 1943 New York Standard Fire Policy which, for almost four decades, was used in nearly all states in all policies providing fire insurance on buildings and contents. Despite its name, the 165-line standard fire policy was not a complete contract of insurance that could stand on its own. It was a foundation module supporting other attached documents that specifically described covered property, additional covered perils, and other relevant conditions.

The 1943 Standard Fire Policy was a major milestone in terms of policy standardization, and its widespread use led to consistent and predictable legal interpretation. However, like other policies of its day, it is not a paragon of clarity when compared with today's standards of written communication. For example, the first sentence of the policy itself reads as follows:

IN CONSIDERATION OF THE PROVISIONS AND STIPULATIONS HEREIN OR ADDED HERETO AND OF the premium above specified, this Company, for the term of years specified above from inception date shown above At Noon (Standard Time) to expiration date shown above At Noon (Standard Time) at location of property involved, to an amount not exceeding the amount(s) above specified, does insure the insured named above and legal representatives, to the extent of the actual cash value of the property at the time of loss, but not exceeding the amount which it would cost to repair or replace the property with material of like kind and quality within a reasonable time after such loss, without allowance for any increased cost of repair or reconstruction by reason of any ordinance or law regulating construction or repair, and without compensation for loss resulting from interruption of business or manufacture, nor in any event for more than the interest of the insured, against all **DIRECT LOSS BY FIRE, LIGHTNING AND BY REMOVAL FROM PREMISES ENDANGERED BY THE PERILS INSURED AGAINST IN THIS POLICY, EXCEPT AS HEREINAFTER PROVIDED,** to the property described herein while located or contained as described in this policy, or pro rata for five days at each proper place to which any of the property shall necessarily be removed for preservation from the perils insured against in this policy, but not elsewhere.

This 229-word sentence illustrates why the Standard Fire Policy was sometimes characterized as a "least read best seller." One of the best-selling writings of all time, the Standard Fire Policy was read by few people, and it was understood by even fewer.

In other lines of insurance, the degree of standardization among insurers depended on a variety of factors. Policy language was based on the writing style used in other legal documents. Insurers were reluctant to discard existing wording that had been interpreted by a variety of court decisions over a period of years; there was a legitimate concern that neither the insurer nor the insured could be certain of the meaning of innovative policy language that had not been tested in the courts. Although coverage modifications were made from time to time, sometimes in response to adverse court interpretations of existing language, there was an understandable reluctance to replace policy language that worked—even if it was not easy to understand.

The situation began to change during the 1970s for a variety of reasons. As coverage evolved over the years, provisions in the attached standard forms increasingly superseded many of the provisions in the Standard Fire Policy. Seeming contradictions between the Standard Fire Policy and the attached forms made the complete insurance contract increasingly difficult for both consumers and practitioners to read and interpret. Moreover, standards for written English shifted as the language evolved. Society became more interested in concise, pointed expression than with complex, precisely crafted verbiage. There was a legitimate concern that consumer documents communicate clearly to people with limited English language skills. And there were increasing instances in which the courts interpreted policies based on the "reasonable expectations" of a policyholder who could not possibly be expected to wade through extensive and obtuse phraseology to understand his or her policy. Too, there was the "consumer movement" in general, through which consumers began to place more demands on the organizations providing consumer services.

Insurers have responded to these changing demands by developing insurance policies that are somewhat easier to read, but some older-style policies still exist—especially for the less common or more sophisticated lines of insurance. And claims based on earlier policy editions will be litigated for many years to come.

Today's insurance practitioner encounters insurance policies in a variety of styles. Many ocean marine insurance policies continue to use language several hundred years old. At the opposite extreme are some "user-friendly" insurance policies that become almost chatty. Many policies present a compromise, using simple sentences to present the complex concepts inherent in insurance.

Insurance regulations in a dozen or so states require that personal lines insurance policies meet specified readability requirements. A National Association of Insurance Commissioners (NAIC) model regulation for personal lines insurance specifies a minimum score of 40 on the Flesch Reading Ease Test, scored by the following method:

1. For a policy containing 10,000 words or less [sic] of text, the entire policy shall be analyzed. For a policy containing more than 10,000 words, the readability of two 100 word samples per page may be analyzed instead. The samples shall be separated by at least 20 printed lines.
2. The total number of words in the text or sample shall be divided by the total number of sentences. The figure obtained shall be multiplied by 1.015.
3. The total number of syllables in the text or sample shall be divided by the total number of words. The figure obtained shall be multiplied by 84.6.
4. The sum of the figures computed under (2) and (3) subtracted from 206.835 equals the Flesch Reading Ease Test score.
5. For purposes of this Section, the following procedures shall be used:
   a. A contraction, hyphenated word, numbers, and letters, when separated by spaces shall be counted as one word;
   b. A unit of text ending with a period, semicolon, or colon shall be counted as a sentence;
   c. A syllable means a unit of spoken language consisting of one or more letters of a word as divided by an accepted dictionary. Where the dictionary shows two or more equally acceptable pronunciations of a word, the pronunciation containing fewer syllables may be used;
   d. At the option of the insurer, any form made a part of the policy may be scored separately or as part of the policy.

In addition, the policy must not be in less than ten-point type and "shall be written in every day [*sic*],[2] conversational language, consistent with its standing as a contract. . . . Short sentences and a personal style shall be used wherever possible. . . . Technical terms and words with special meaning shall be avoided wherever possible."[3] A similar model regulation, not widely adopted, exists for commercial lines policies, although it provides that Flesch scores lower than 40 may be accepted by the insurance commissioner.

Readability attempts have been humorous at times. One early "plain English" policy completely avoided any reference to "insured" or "named insured." Instead, the insured business was identified in the policy declarations page as "you." As a further modernization, the insurance company used "amendment" in place of the traditional term "endorsement." Soon after this policy was introduced, it became necessary to develop a method to modify the policy to cover additional parties, usually done by adding an "additional insured endorsement." To remain consistent with the vocabulary of this super-simplified policy, the insurer had little choice but to develop a so-called "additional 'you' amendment."

Despite the fault that can occasionally be found, the untold time and effort invested in policy simplification have greatly improved the clarity of modern insurance policies. Insurance students are among those who benefit from the results, as it is much easier to read, understand, and learn the coverage of simplified policies. A disadvantage is that many policies now contain phraseology that has been untested in the courts, and the ultimate interpretation of some policy provisions is therefore uncertain.

PHYSICAL CONSTRUCTION
OF INSURANCE CONTRACTS

Insurance policies are assembled in a variety of ways. This section of the chapter deals with the arrangement of an insurance policy as a physical document, explaining the function of each of the written instruments that is likely to be found in, attached to, or incorporated by reference into any insurance policy.

A number of words may be used to describe the various sheets of paper or documents in an insurance policy, and the terms are not consistently used by insurance practitioners. Following are some general guidelines:

- *Policy*—technically, the complete written contract of insurance. The term also is used when referring to any document forming part of an insurance policy, as in "What does the policy say about such-and-such?" (In some contexts the term occasionally is ambiguous because "policy" also refers to a practical philosophy, as in the saying, "Honesty is the best policy." Insurers may refer to a business practice as their "underwriting policy.")

- *Insurance contract, or "contract"*—generally, means the same thing as "policy." "Contract" is sometimes used to emphasize the legal nature of the insurance agreement, which may encompass agreements outside the written policy itself.
- *Monoline policy*—a policy covering a single "line" of insurance (see below), or part of a single line.
- *Package policy*—generally, a policy covering more than one "line" of insurance (see below).
- *Line of insurance*—the term "line" apparently originated with the various lines, or horizontal rows, on the Annual Statement that must be submitted to ("filed with") state insurance regulators by an insurance company. The Annual Statement contains the following lines:
  - Fire
  - Allied lines
  - Farmowners multiple peril
  - Homeowners multiple peril
  - Commercial multiple peril
  - Ocean marine
  - Inland marine
  - Medical malpractice
  - Earthquake
  - Group accident and health
  - Credit accident and health
  - Other accident and health
  - Workers compensation
  - Other liability
  - Auto liability
  - Auto physical damage
  - Aircraft
  - Fidelity
  - Surety
  - Glass
  - Burglary and theft
  - Boiler and machinery
  - Credit
  - International
  - Reinsurance

Except when referring specifically to the Annual Statement, the term "line" often is not applied rigidly to these categories, but is loosely used to refer simply to different types of insurance.

What is categorized as a "line" in any situation may depend on the reason for distinguishing among the coverages.

● *Form*—generally, one of the major documents within an insurance policy. In some cases, one form is the entire policy except for a declarations page.

● *Endorsement*—a document modifying the coverage of one or more forms. Many endorsements are relatively small, sometimes containing only a few lines of print. Others may be several pages long. In life and health insurance, the term "rider" is used instead of endorsement, but it means the same thing. Most endorsements are preprinted, but manuscript endorsements are also commonly used to adapt a policy or form to address a particular need or situation.

● *Coverage part*—one or more forms that, together, provide coverage for a line of insurance.

Self-Contained Versus Modular Policies

A self-contained insurance policy might be compared to a dress in a woman's wardrobe—a complete-by-itself overgarment that may sometimes be decorated with jewelry or accessories. A modular insurance policy is more like a mix-and-match ensemble—a jacket might be combined with matching slacks or skirt and one of several contrasting blouses. Like a dress, the ensemble might be embellished with jewelry and accessories.

Self-Contained Policy. A self-contained insurance policy is a single, complete-by-itself document that contains all the agreements between the applicant and the insurer. A single, usually standard, contract identifies the insurer and the insured, the subject matter of the insurance, and the amounts, terms, and conditions of coverage. Endorsements are occasionally used to add optional coverages. If the self-contained policy is compared to a dress, then the endorsements may be compared to the jewelry or accessories that customize it for special occasions.

A self-contained policy is appropriate for insuring loss exposures that are essentially the same from insured to insured. For example, private passenger auto insurance typically is provided in a self-contained policy that is used to insure all an insurer's individual auto policyholders throughout a state—and maybe even in several different states. When needed, a rental reimbursement endorsement or a towing and labor endorsement might be added.

Modular Policy. Like a woman's clothing ensemble, a modular policy is made up of a mix-and-match set of components, designed around one basic piece (such as a jacket) with several available pieces intended to be used in various combinations. Often a single document—sometimes called a "policy jacket"—includes conditions, definitions, or other provisions that apply to, or match, all other documents used with it. This item may also be referred to as a "common conditions form."

Many inland marine policies use the modular approach. Take, for example, a contractors equipment floater covering a contractor for loss to a backhoe described in the declarations. In addition to the declarations, the complete policy might contain two other documents—one form contains "common provisions" that apply to all the insurer's inland marine policies, and another contains provisions that apply specifically to insurance on contractors' equipment.

The modular approach is commonly used in commercial insurance. Exhibit 2-1 illustrates the structure of an Insurance Services Office (ISO) commercial package policy. Every policy contains (1) common policy conditions and (2) common declarations. If one line of insurance is covered, the policy is completed by adding the necessary forms to make up that "coverage part." For example, if "commercial property" insurance is provided, the " 'commercial property' coverage part" includes a "commercial property" declarations page, the necessary "commercial property" coverage forms, and a " 'commercial property' conditions form." This combination of documents would be a "monoline policy." It is a complete policy covering one line of insurance—"commercial property."

An advantage of this modular approach is that several lines of insurance can be handled with a single policy. The resulting combination is not a "monoline policy" but a "commercial package policy." For example, a commercial package policy providing commercial property and commercial general liability coverage would be constructed from the following documents:

- Common policy conditions
- Common declarations
- "Commercial property" declarations page
- "Commercial property" conditions form
- "Commercial property" coverage form(s)
- "Commercial property" causes-of-loss form(s)
- Commercial general liability declarations page
- Commercial general liability coverage form(s)
- Any applicable endorsements

Similarly, crime, boiler and machinery, inland marine, auto, or farm coverage could be added—all within the same "commercial package

Exhibit 2-1

Components of the Commercial Package Policy (CPP)

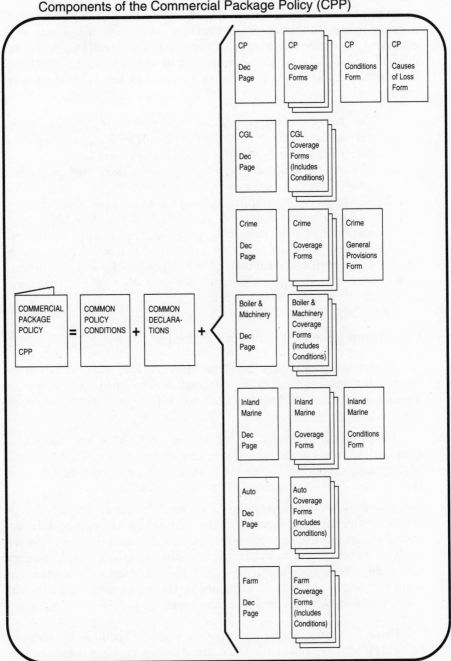

policy." Endorsements might be added as applicable to modify the various forms comprising the "commercial package policy."

The various coverages do not *have* to be combined in a commercial package policy. Similar coverage could be provided with separate, self-contained "commercial property," commercial general liability, crime policies, and so forth. However, as compared with self-contained policies, the modular approach to policy construction has the following advantages:

1. Carefully designed, coordinated, and dovetailed provisions in the various forms minimize the possibility of gaps and overlaps that might exist when several monoline policies are used.
2. The use of consistent terminology, definitions, and policy language makes it easier to interpret coverage.
3. Fewer forms are required to meet a wide range of needs.
4. Underwriting is simplified, since much of the same basic information that must be analyzed applies to all lines of insurance.
5. Adverse selection problems can be reduced when the same insurer writes several lines of insurance for the same insured.
6. Insurers often give a package discount when several coverages are written in the same policy.

Preprinted Versus Manuscript Policies

Preprinted policies are developed for use with many different insureds. A manuscript policy, by contrast, is developed for one specific insured—or for a small group of insureds with a common unique coverage need.

Preprinted Policies. Most insurance policies are assembled from one or more preprinted forms and endorsements. Insurers may adopt standard policies, also used by other insurers, or they may develop their own so-called "nonstandard" policies.

Standard Versus Nonstandard Policies. Insurance service and advisory organizations, such as ISO and the American Association of Insurance Services (AAIS), have developed standard insurance forms that are made available for use by individual insurance companies. Because they are widely used, standard forms provide benchmarks ("the standard approach") against which nonstandard forms can be evaluated. Much of the material in this text describes the coverage provisions of standard forms.

Some insurance forms also contain wording required by state or federal statute. (At times, the statutory wording has been prescribed by legislators who are not familiar with conventional insurance terminology; this can create ambiguities and can conflict with other, standard policy provisions.)

Many insurance companies have developed their own preprinted contracts, especially for high-volume lines of insurance (such as auto or homeowners) or for coverages in which an insurer may specialize (such as recreational vehicle insurance). These are referred to as *nonstandard* contracts, because policy wording and content may vary from the provisions used by other insurers or from those developed by insurance advisory organizations. Note that a nonstandard policy is not the same thing as a substandard (inferior) policy. In fact, many nonstandard policies contain coverage enhancements not found in standard policies.

Use of Preprinted Forms. Quantities of preprinted forms are kept in the filing cabinets or supply room of the insurance company office where policies are assembled and issued. Whenever a policy is issued, the contract itself is created by preparing a declarations page. The declarations page indicates the form number(s) and edition dates of the company's form(s) that apply, and a clerk gathers the form(s) needed and staples it or them to the declarations page to assemble a complete policy.

When an insurer uses preprinted forms, it generally is not necessary for the insurance company and its producer to keep in their files a complete duplicate of each policyholder's entire policy. All that is filed is the declarations page—and what is actually filed may be a computer record rather than a sheet of paper. Details of applicable coverage can be obtained, whenever necessary, by examining copies of the preprinted forms referenced in the declarations. Of course, the policyholder does receive a complete written contract.

In today's automated world, computer files sometimes replace a stock of paper forms and endorsements, especially for forms and endorsements not often used. Single copies are then printed out on a high-speed printer when a policy is prepared.

Resolving Ambiguities. The wording of preprinted forms and endorsements is carefully chosen by the insurer (or it is developed by a service organization and then adopted by the insurer). Applying the doctrine of adhesion, mentioned in Chapter 1, the courts will tend to interpret any ambiguities in policy language in favor of the insured who did not have an opportunity to choose the wording in the policy. The doctrine of adhesion is discussed in greater detail in Chapter 9.

Manuscript Policies. The word "manuscript" comes from Latin roots for hand and write. Today, final copies of insurance policies seldom are handwritten. However, a policy may be specifically drafted or selected for a particular need. An example might be products liability coverage on a manufacturer of cardiac pacemakers.

The final policy language may be the result of negotiation among an insurer, an applicant, and an insurance agent or broker. Some policy provisions may be copied from standard policies, while other provisions are specifically drafted or selected for that one contract. As a whole, a manuscript policy is generally a "one-of-a-kind" document. A manuscript policy might be used for more than one insured in some situations, as when it might be developed to meet the specific needs of a particular association or group of businesses.

Creating a manuscript policy involves a considerable amount of time and effort, to say nothing of the skills involved in writing an important, precise, legally enforceable contract. Manuscript policies are mainly used for large businesses having unique exposures and substantial bargaining power.

Resolving Ambiguities. The wording of a manuscript policy generally is developed through the joint effort of the insurer and the insured. Both parties have an understanding of what they wish to accomplish, and agreement is reached on the specific words that are used to express that understanding. When contract language was developed by both parties, the two parties are likely to be placed on equal footing if it becomes necessary for a court to interpret ambiguities in the contract.

Collateral Documents

The preceding paragraphs have described the basic formats of insurance policies themselves. Several other documents may become part of the insurance contract, either by being physically attached to the policy or by being referred to within the policy. Examples include the completed application for insurance, endorsements, the insurer's bylaws, the terms of relevant statutes, and other miscellaneous documents.

Completed Application. A written application is always used for some types of insurance but rarely required for others. Instead, coverage may be requested orally, in person or by telephone. An authorized representative of the insurance company also may create an oral insurance contract by immediately binding the requested coverage.

For types of insurance that are relatively complex or involve complex underwriting or rating, the insurer typically requires a written application. Even when coverage is bound based on an oral application, the insurer may require follow-up completion of a written application for subsequent underwriting and rating.

An application is certainly important for underwriting and rating purposes, and it contains information that must be reproduced in the declarations of the policy when it is issued. Beyond these obvious points, a written application is legally significant because it contains the representations made by the applicant to obtain coverage. An insurance contract may be voidable if the applicant's statements contain misrepresentations. The insurer may best be able to have a policy declared void on the basis of misrepresentation in the application when the application is made a physical part of the policy. Some statutes and court decisions stipulate that the written insurance policy must incorporate all the agreements between an insurer and an insured.

In some jurisdictions, statutes explicitly require that any written application be made part of the policy for some types of insurance. This is a common requirement with life insurance, presumably because the applicant often is the insured who obviously is not around to dispute with the insurer about a death claim. If a required written application is not attached to the insurance policy, the policy remains valid and the insurer loses the right to have the policy declared void because of false statements in the application.

Endorsements. An endorsement (called a "rider" in life and health insurance) is a provision that adds to, deletes, replaces, or modifies another document that is part of an insurance policy. Endorsements are not necessarily labeled "endorsement"; "policy change," "addition," and "amendment" are among the terms that may be used. Or an endorsement may have only a descriptive title, such as "Loss Payable Clause." Regardless of its label or title, an endorsement may be identified by its function of modifying another document.

An endorsement may be a preprinted, computer-printed, typewritten, or handwritten line, sentence, paragraph, or set of paragraphs on a separate sheet of paper attached to other documents making up the policy. While it is rarely done with standard, preprinted policies, an endorsement may even take the form of a handwritten note in the margin of a basic policy, form, or coverage part, dated and initialed by an insured and an authorized representative of the insurer.

Thousands of standard endorsements are available to meet the needs of insureds. In addition, "all-purpose" endorsements are available; these are little more than blank sheets of paper with headings, on which special agreements between the insurer and insured are entered.

An endorsement may contain information in the nature of declarations (such as correcting the spelling of an insured's name or naming an additional named insured), definitions, insuring agreements (such as identifying additional types of property for which coverage is provided), exclusions (such as identifying types of property for which coverage is *not* provided), conditions (for example, modifying the cancellation provision to conform with a state statute), and miscellaneous provisions (such as a loss payable clause). It may also replace or modify any of these provisions in the form to which the endorsement is attached.

As noted, endorsements often are intended to modify a more basic policy form. This means that the provisions in an endorsement often are different from the provisions in the basic policy to which it is attached—which can raise questions when it comes to interpreting an insurance policy. In general, an endorsement takes precedence over any conflicting terms in the policy to which it is attached. Moreover, a handwritten endorsement supersedes a preprinted or typewritten one. These rules of interpretation are based on the logical reasoning that alterations of the agreements between insurer and insured—especially handwritten alterations—tend to more accurately reflect true intent than do other, preprinted policy terms.

Sometimes, however, a statute or ruling requires that a particular policy be fully standardized, that it contain specified words or ideas, or that it not contain provisions prohibited by law. For example, there obviously can be underwriting reasons for wishing to exclude coverage under an auto insurance policy for one particular driver, and this practice is permitted in some states. However, a state might prohibit insurers from using auto insurance policies with a named driver exclusion because such an exclusion tends to subvert the goal of assuring a source of recovery for injured accident victims. If a policy in that state should contain a named driver exclusion, which fails to comply with the law, the policy usually would be interpreted by the courts as though it did comply with the law, and the excluded driver would have coverage.

Insurer's Bylaws and Relevant Statutes. In certain circumstances, it is important that the bylaws of the insurer or the provisions of pertinent statutes be incorporated into an insurance contract. For example, the insureds of mutual and reciprocal insurers typically have some rights and duties associated with the management of the insurer's operations, and these rights and duties must be specified in the policy.

Policies providing workers compensation insurance or auto no-fault insurance are among those that typically provide benefits specified by state statute. The relevant statutes usually are not printed in the insurance policy, but the insurance policy incorporates the statute by reference. For example, the standard workers compensation policy includes the following provisions.

We Will Pay

We will pay promptly when due the benefits required of you by the workers compensation law.

Workers Compensation Law

Workers Compensation Law means the workers or workmen's compensation law and occupational disease law of each state or territory named in item 3. A. of the Information Page. It includes any amendments to that law which are in effect during the policy period. It does not include the provisions of any law that provide nonoccupational disability benefits.

"Information Page" refers to the declarations page of this particular policy.

Insurer's Rating Manual. Insurance policies sometimes incorporate the insurer's rating manual (or the insurer's rules and rates, whether found in the manual or elsewhere) not by including the entire manual, but by referring to it in the policy language. For example, the commercial general liability policy contains the following provision:

Premium Audit

We will compute all premiums for this Coverage Part in accordance with our rules and rates.

Although the rules and rates themselves do not appear in the policy, they become, in this way, part of the contract. The applicable rules and rates often have been approved by insurance regulators as part of their normal rate regulation and contract regulation activities.

Miscellaneous Documents. Subject to statutory or regulatory constraints, insurance policies may incorporate virtually any documents. Some of the more frequently used miscellaneous documents include premium notes, inspection reports, and specification sheets or operating manuals relating to safety equipment or procedures.

A *premium note* is a promissory note, accepted by the insurer in lieu of cash premium payment. In most jurisdictions, the premium note and the insurance policy are considered separate obligations—one is a loan and the other is an insurance contract, and each is independently enforceable. In these jurisdictions, it is not important that the premium note be attached to the policy. However, in some jurisdictions a premium note is not enforceable by the insurer unless incorporated into the policy for which the note constitutes payment of premium. Usually this is done by attaching to the policy a copy of the note.

In some situations, an insurer and an applicant might agree that the coverage provided by a particular property or liability insurance policy is conditioned on the use of certain procedures or safety equipment. For example, a set of operating instructions or a manual of specifications can be incorporated into the policy by reference and used to define precisely and conveniently the agreed procedures or equipment.

It has become increasingly common for states to require insurance companies to provide a "notice to policyholders," informing them of significant changes when an insurance policy is revised. In other cases, insurers are required to furnish policyholders with documents summarizing the coverage options available to insureds and choices that must be made. These informational documents generally are not part of the policy contract as such.

PROPERTY-LIABILITY INSURANCE POLICY CONTENT

Taken as a whole, a typical insurance policy appears formidable. Yet, like most other writings, an insurance policy is nothing more than a combination of headings, words, phrases, sentences, and paragraphs. In combination, these components, called *policy provisions*, constitute the distinctive agreements that collectively make up each unique insurance contract.

This section of the chapter explains the types of provisions contained in an insurance policy. Every property-liability insurance policy provision can be placed in one or more of the following categories, depending on the purpose it serves:

1. Declarations
2. Definitions
3. Insuring agreements
4. Exclusions
5. Conditions
6. Miscellaneous provisions

Insurance policies are designed to communicate, in writing, the details of an agreement between the insurer and the insured. Policies usually contain several "Sections," or "Coverages," and often a variety of headings and subheadings. Like the chapter numbers, chapter titles, headings, and subheadings in this textbook, subdivisions and labels help organize the policy and make it easier to read. However, the important information lies within the text, not in the headings.

Many insurance policies include sections that actually are titled "Declarations," "Definitions," "Insuring Agreement," "Exclusions," or "Conditions." Although labels such as these generally describe the major information found in that portion of a policy, they do not necessarily describe every provision under that heading. As illustrated later, a section labeled "Definitions" may well include provisions that actually serve as exclusions, and definitions of policy terms are sometimes found within a section labeled "Exclusions."

The discussion that follows is not intended to describe the labeled sections of an insurance policy, but rather the characteristics of individual policy provisions regardless of the policy section or heading under which any specific provision is located.

Declarations

The term "declarations" arose because this is the portion of the policy containing information that was "declared" by the insured on the application for insurance, along with the insurance company's "declaration" as to what coverage it provides. In practice, insurance policy declarations typically contain not only information that has been "declared," but also other information unique to a particular policy. For reasons of efficiency, insurers attempt to minimize the number of sheets of paper that must contain typewritten or computer entries unique to one particular contract. As much as possible, policies are designed so that all such entries can be placed on the declarations page. Therefore, a policy's declarations may be the only sheet, or sheets, of paper unique to that particular policy.

Typically found in insurance policy declarations are the following items of information:

- The policy number
- The inception and expiration dates of the policy
- The name of the insurance company
- The name of the insurance agent
- The name of the insured(s)
- The mailing address of the insured
- The physical address and description of the covered property or operations
- The numbers and edition dates of all attached forms and endorsements
- Dollar amounts of applicable policy limits
- Dollar amounts of applicable deductibles
- The names of persons or organizations whose additional interests are covered (for example, a mortgagee, loss payee, or additional insured)
- The premium

Declarations often are computer-printed. In some cases the computer enters unique information, such as the insured's name and address, into a blank space on an otherwise preprinted form. In many cases the entire declarations page is printed by a laser printer that prints all information in a single pass.

Sometimes forms or endorsements within a policy also contain information that qualifies as declarations. For example, an endorsement providing glass coverage might contain either a typed description or a diagram of the covered glass. In recent years, insurers generally have tried to develop forms and endorsements that do not require declarations-type information to be entered. When specific entries are necessary, forms are designed so that they can be made by computer; for example, the usual text-oriented computer can more readily handle a narrative description of glass than a diagram or sketch.

Declarations are not necessarily labeled "Declarations." In the standard NCCI Workers Compensation and Employers Liability Policy, the label "Information Page" is used instead. Individual insurers may use different labels or put no title whatsoever on the piece(s) of paper serving as the policy's declarations.

One related term requires some explanation, because it is less often heard now that photocopy machines and computers have replaced carbon paper and manual typewriters. It used to be more common for insurance companies to furnish their agents with blank insurance policies that could be issued on the spot in the agent's office, after the agent (or an agency clerk) wrote or typed the necessary information onto the front page of the policy. Carbon copies of this sheet of paper provided a file copy for the agent as well as a copy for the insurance company. Each agent had a carefully guarded serially numbered supply of blank forms, and a carbon copy of every completed form was promptly forwarded to the insurance company *reporting* what policies the agent had issued that *day* and providing the information necessary for billing, underwriting, and claims purposes. This initial policy declarations page, containing all the information unique to a new policy, was referred to as a *daily report*, or *daily*, a label that might also be preprinted on the "Daily Report" itself.

Definitions

Many words and phrases are assigned a special meaning in the insurance policy where they appear. Some policies use **boldface** type to distinguish words and phrases that are defined elsewhere in the policy. More recently, there has been a trend toward using "quotation marks" around defined terms rather than putting the terms in boldface. Quotation marks are generally more compatible with the use of computer-prepared documents (some printers do not print in boldface), and it is sometimes difficult to distinguish boldface from regular type in photocopies or documents prepared with a variety of printers. Some policies use Capital Letters or *italics* to identify terms with special meaning, and others simply define terms that are used in the policy without highlighting them when used.

Many policies or forms contain a section titled "Definitions," which generally defines terms used throughout the entire policy or form. Sometimes a "Definitions" section appears near the beginning of the policy where it serves to clarify terms that will be used. A "Definitions" section may instead appear at the end of the policy where it serves as a glossary.

Definitions also may appear in the middle of a policy, where they may or may not be labeled as "definitions."

Many modern policies refer to the insurer as "we" and the named insured as "you," and such personal pronouns are used extensively throughout these policies. "You" and "we," together with related pronouns such as "us," "our," and "your" often are defined in an untitled preamble to the policy rather than in a definitions section as such.

Examples. The commercial general liability form provides several examples, because it contains definitions in the preamble, in a glossary-like section, and within the policy itself.

Definitions in Policy Preamble. The complete preamble to the commercial general liability coverage form is shown below. The first paragraph, which merely contains an instruction, is a miscellaneous provision, and the second and third paragraphs are definitions, although they are not labeled as such. The fourth paragraph is another policy-reading instruction that deals with definitions, but it is not itself a definition; it is a miscellaneous provision.

> Various provisions in this policy restrict coverage. Read the entire policy carefully to determine rights, duties and what is and is not covered.

> Throughout this policy the words "you" and "your" refer to the Named Insured shown in the Declarations, and any other person or organization qualifying as a Named Insured under this policy. The words "we," "us" and "our" refer to the Company providing this insurance.

> The word "insured" means any person or organization qualifying as such under WHO IS AN INSURED (SECTION II).

> Other words and phrases that appear in quotation marks have special meaning. Refer to DEFINITIONS (SECTION V).

Glossary-like Definitions Section. The "Definitions" section is the last section of the CGL policy form quoted above, in which fifteen definitions appear. As in many other policies, the definitions here are in alphabetical order, beginning with "advertising injury" and ending with "your work." One of the shortest definitions is that of occurrence:

> "Occurrence" means an accident, including continuous or repeated exposure to substantially the same general harmful conditions.

As this definition also illustrates, insurance policy definitions do not necessarily use the formal style of dictionary definitions. The word "occurrence" is defined in part with a near-synonym, "accident." Since "accident" is not defined, its everyday dictionary meaning is assumed. However, the "occurrence" definition goes on to indicate that "occurrences" include not only those events generally considered accidents, but also certain events of an ongoing or repetitive nature. Accidents are "occurrences," and some things that are not accidents also are "occurrences." This particular definition, brief as it is, has been the subject of extended discussion and litigation over the years. It is not always easy to agree on whether a specific act or series of acts constitutes one or more occurrences, and large sums of money sometimes depend on the ultimate outcome of the dispute, determined by the courts.[4]

Definitions Within the Body of the Policy. As mentioned, definitions sometimes are located within the body of a policy, without necessarily a "Definitions" heading, boldface type, quotation marks, or capital letters. This approach sometimes is taken when a term is used in only one portion of a policy or where it has a special meaning that applies to only that one portion. For example, the commercial general liability policy contains a so-called (but unlabeled) pollution exclusion that refers to pollutants. (The word pollutants is not capitalized in this form, nor is it offset by quotation marks or boldface type.) The final paragraph of the pollution exclusion, shown below, is actually a definition of the term pollutants (as well as a partial definition of the term waste, which is used in defining pollutants).

> Pollutants means any solid, liquid, gaseous or thermal irritant or contaminant, including smoke, vapor, soot, fumes, acids, alkalis, chemicals and waste. Waste includes material to be recycled, reconditioned or reclaimed.

Effect of Definitions. Words and phrases defined within a policy have a special meaning when they are used within that particular insurance contract. Undefined words and phrases are interpreted according to the following rules of contract interpretation.

- Everyday language is given its ordinary meaning.
- Technical words are given their technical meaning.
- Words with an established legal meaning are given their legal meaning.
- Where applicable, consideration is also given to local, cultural, and trade usage meanings.

Insuring Agreements

An *insuring agreement* is any policy statement to the effect that, under some circumstances, the insurer will make a payment or provide a service. Following the declarations, and possibly preceded by a section containing definitions, the body of most insurance policies begins with an insuring agreement—often, but not always, labeled "Insuring Agreement."

A policy may have more than one insuring agreement. Some policies provide more than one "Coverage," each coverage based on an insuring agreement. Examples include (1) the personal auto policy, which typically provides "liability," "medical payments," "uninsured motorists," and "damage to your auto" coverages; and the homeowners policy, which typically provides coverages for (1) "dwelling," (2) "other structures," (3) "personal property," (4) "loss of use," (5) "personal liability," and (6) "medical payments to others."

The term "insuring agreement" most often is applied to statements that introduce a coverage section of the policy. However, "insuring agreement" also is an entirely appropriate label for statements that introduce coverage extensions, additional coverages, supplementary payments, and so forth. Moreover, even relatively obscure unlabeled statements within declarations, definitions, exclusions, or conditions can serve as insuring agreements.

Introductory Insuring Agreement. The insuring agreements that introduce a coverage section of a policy *broadly* state what the insurer agrees to do under the contract, subject to clarification elsewhere in the policy. Insuring agreements usually contain one or more defined terms. An insuring agreement cannot be fully understood without examining any defined terms it uses.

The following two insuring agreements are fairly concise.

Inland Marine Policy Provision:

We will pay for "loss" to Covered Property from any of the Covered Causes of Loss.

The brevity of this insuring agreement can be deceiving. Before it can be *fully* understood, one must examine not only the definition of "loss," but also lengthy policy sections describing Covered Property and Covered Causes of Loss.

Workers Compensation Insurance Policy Provision:

We will pay promptly when due the benefits required of you by the workers compensation law.

While this insuring agreement is short, the applicable state workers compensation law, which does not appear within the policy, must be referenced before the insurer's promise can be fully applied to a specific claim. However, a general understanding of the nature, purpose, content, and effect of workers compensation statutes is all that is necessary to understand most of the remaining provisions of the contract.

Some insuring agreements are rather long or involved. Consider the following two examples, both of which also require examination of defined terms.

Business Income Coverage Form (and Extra Expense) Provision:

We will pay for the actual loss of Business Income you sustain due to the necessary suspension of your "operations" during the "period of restoration." The suspension must be caused by direct physical loss of or damage to property at the premises described in the Declarations, including personal property in the open (or in a vehicle) within 100 feet, caused by or resulting from any Covered Cause of Loss.

1. Business Income

Business Income means. . . .

Notice, by the way, that some defined terms here are capitalized, and some are in quotation marks. This particular form contains a definitions section. However, the definition of Business Income appears, not in the "Definitions," but within the insuring agreement section titled "Coverage." The special meaning of "Business Income" is highlighted by the use of capital letters. The last two lines of the above policy excerpt are not, strictly speaking, part of an insuring agreement, but the beginning of a definition.

Whether long or short, introductory insuring agreements merely state the basic thrust of the insurer's obligations in relatively broad terms. The full scope of coverage cannot be determined without examining the rest of the policy, since the insurer's obligations are invariably clarified or modified by other policy provisions.

Comprehensive Versus Limited in Scope. Insuring agreements can be divided into two broad categories.

- Comprehensive, all-purpose insuring agreements describe extremely broad, unrestricted coverage that applies to virtually all causes of loss, or to virtually all situations. This broad coverage is both clarified and narrowed by exclusions, definitions, and other policy provisions.
- Limited or single-purpose insuring agreements themselves confine coverage to certain causes of loss, or to certain situations. Exclusions, definitions, and other policy provisions serve to clarify, to narrow, and sometimes to broaden the coverage provided by this simple statement.

"Comprehensive" and similar terms are avoided in modern insurance policies. Terms like these can build up false expectations among insurance buyers. Such labels seem to imply that a policy, as a whole, provides unconfined, all-encompassing coverage. These connotations can make it difficult for an insurer to convince a court that a "comprehensive" or "all-risks" policy does not cover a particular loss.

Like other verbal shorthand used among insurance practitioners, these labels are misleading unless accompanied by further explanation when used with members of the general public. Even comprehensive policies are subject to exclusions and limitations, and this fact should be clearly communicated to avoid problems. One way of improving communications on this point is to avoid the use of misleadingly broad terminology when addressing members of the general public. Most policy forms themselves no longer use terms such as "all-risk" or "comprehensive."

Property Insurance. Property insurance insuring agreements fall into two broad categories which, in turn, relate to the ways in which covered causes of loss are described.

The more limited property insuring agreements restrict coverage to those perils, or causes of loss, listed in the policy. This approach is referred to by various labels, such as "named peril," "specified peril," or "specified causes of loss."

The insuring agreement of the federal Standard Flood Insurance Policy illustrates a single-purpose insuring agreement. Unfortunately, perhaps, this particular policy, created by an agency of the federal government, does not earn high scores for either readability or consistency with conventional insurance contract language, although it does resemble the 1943 Standard Fire Policy. (Some of the phrases in this insuring agreement are normally presented as conditions or exclusions in other property policies.)

IN CONSIDERATION OF THE PAYMENT OF THE PREMIUM, IN RELIANCE UPON THE STATEMENTS IN THE APPLICATION AND DECLARATIONS FORM MADE A PART HEREOF AND SUBJECT TO ALL THE TERMS OF THIS POLICY, THE IN- SURER DOES INSURE the Insured and legal representatives, to the extent of actual cash value, not exceeding the amount which it would cost to repair and replace the property with material of like kind and quality within a reasonable time after such loss, without allowance for any increased cost of repair or reconstruction by reason of any ordinance or law regulating construction or repair, and without compensation for loss resulting from interruption of business or manufacture, nor in any event for more than the interest of the insured, against all **"DIRECT PHYSICAL LOSS BY OR FROM FLOOD"** as defined herein, to the property described while located or contained as described in the application and declarations form attached hereto, or pro rata for 45 days at each proper place to which any of the property shall necessarily be removed for preservation from the peril of "Flood", [*sic*] but not elsewhere.

(As the "sic" indicates, insurance policies sometimes fail to follow standard English punctuation rules, especially, it seems, when it comes to placing quotation marks.) After literally wading through this long sentence while analyzing coverage for a possible claim, the reader should conclude that coverage applies only to losses caused by a flood, as defined in a separate, rather lengthy, definition.

The following insuring agreement appears in that portion of an inland marine policy covering contractors equipment.

We cover direct physical loss to covered property caused by: . . . .

A list of covered perils follows this provision. Coverage applies for loss to covered property *only if a listed peril caused the loss.* The first among the many listed (named, specified) perils is "fire," and the second is "lightning."

In the past, property insurance policies containing comprehensive insuring agreements often were referred to as "all-risk policies," and the insuring agreement invariably included a phrase such as *"all risks of direct loss or damage"* (italics added). This wording made it easy to identify the comprehensive nature of the policy, especially since "all-risks" policies usually followed a somewhat standard pattern of using exclusions to limit coverage. Experienced practitioners knew enough to examine the exclusions to determine the coverage of an "all-risks" policy or coverage.

To illustrate, the following insuring agreement appeared in a standard ISO homeowners policy (Form HO-3) with a 1970 edition date.

This policy insures under:
COVERAGE A—DWELLING AND COVERAGE B—APPUR-TENANT STRUCTURES against all risks of physical loss to the property covered . . . except as otherwise excluded or limited.

In 1983 insurers began refining their policy language to eliminate the word "all." For example, the equivalent provision from the 1984 edition of the ISO homeowners policy (Form HO-3) reads as follows:

COVERAGE A—DWELLING and

COVERAGE B—OTHER STRUCTURES

We insure against risks of direct loss to property described in Coverages A and B only if that loss is a physical loss to property; however, we do not insure loss: . . . .

(The 1990 edition uses "risk" rather than "risks.")

Omission of the word "all" is intended to reduce the chance of an unreasonably broad interpretation. Even though the "all" has been removed from the policy language, many authors and practitioners continue to use the convenient phrase "all-risks" to refer to policies of this type. "All-risks" is a simple two-syllable phrase with a long tradition in the language of insurance, and no universally acceptable substitute has emerged. The phrase "open perils" has sometimes been used; while this phrase eliminates the troublesome word "all," it does not clearly communicate the concept to either consumers or practitioners. Other suggestions have included phrases such as "risks-not-excluded," "perils-not-excluded," "causes-of-loss-not-excluded," "unscheduled perils," or "unnamed perils." While each has its advantages, none is widely used and all are more clumsy than the simple phrase, "all-risks." Even though this text will continue to use this convenient term to communicate with its readership of insurance professionals, it is best to avoid saying "all-risks" when describing this insurance coverage to members of the public.

Another typical agreement of the "all-risks" type appears in another inland marine policy covering contractors equipment. The policy quoted below was drafted by AAIS. This policy eliminates not only the "all," but also the "risks." However, the effect remains.

> We cover direct physical loss to covered property unless the loss is caused by a peril that is excluded. The loss must be due to an external cause.

Even though the identifying phrase "all risks" is absent, the coverage approach should readily be recognized by insurance students and practitioners. Like the "all-risks" insuring agreement quoted earlier, this one is followed by a long list of "perils excluded." Coverage applies for direct loss to covered property "by an external cause" (inherent vice and other self-destructive perils are not covered) *unless an exclusion applies.*

Liability Insurance. The business auto coverage form provides one example of a limited insuring agreement.

> We will pay all sums an "insured" legally must pay as damages because of "bodily injury" or "property damage" to which this insurance applies, caused by an "accident" and resulting from the ownership, maintenance or use of a covered "auto."

In a general sense, this liability coverage applies to one type of losses—those resulting from auto accidents. Coverage clearly applies only to accidents (as defined) involving autos (as defined), and coverage does not apply to non-auto-related incidents. However, the policy does not cover *all* losses arising from all auto accidents; a number of conditions and exclusions narrow the coverage.

The most popular standard policy that provided general liability coverage for businesses used to bear the name "*Comprehensive* General Liability" policy, and it was generally referred to as the "CGL." When this form was revised during the 1980s its name was subtly changed to "*Commercial* General Liability form," but its initials did not change and it is still known as the "CGL." Although "comprehensive" is not in the title, the insuring agreement is of the comprehensive type.

The insuring agreement of the current CGL (occurrence form) reads as follows:

> We will pay those sums that the insured becomes legally obligated to pay as damages because of "bodily injury" or "property damage" to

which this insurance applies. . . . This insurance applies only to "bodily injury" and "property damage" which occurs during the policy period. The "bodily injury" or "property damage" must be caused by an "occurrence." The "occurrence" must take place in the "coverage territory". . . .

(Some clarifying phrases, which appear along with the above wording under the heading "insuring agreement," have been deleted from this quotation for brevity.) The next section of the policy is labeled "exclusions," and it begins, "This insurance does not apply to. . . ."

This insuring agreement provides a very broad statement of coverage. It is broad enough, for example, to cover losses resulting from auto accidents. However, coverage is restricted by the exclusions—including exclusions that preclude coverage for most auto accidents.

The single-purpose insuring agreement defines the relatively narrow category of incidents to which it applies (auto accidents, in this case). The comprehensive insuring agreement, by contrast, broadly states that it provides coverage for an insured's liability for damages arising out of bodily injury and property damage—the insuring agreement does not limit coverage to a particular premises, to some specified operation, or to any particular activity. Additional policy provisions, such as an auto exclusion, chip away at this broad coverage. When all is said and done, whatever is within the scope of the insuring agreement and has not been chipped away by another policy provision, is covered.

Insuring Agreements for Extended, Additional, Supplemental Coverages.   Many insurance policies include some supplemental, more-or-less secondary, coverages, along with the main coverage. These may variously be labeled by such headings as "coverage extensions," "additional coverages," or "supplementary payments," or a supplemental coverage may simply have a descriptive heading or no heading whatsoever.

Strictly speaking, a "coverage extension" extends a portion of a basic policy coverage to apply to a type of property or loss that would not otherwise be covered, an "additional coverage" adds a type of coverage not otherwise provided, and "supplementary payments" involve liability insurance provisions clarifying the extent of coverage for certain expenses. However, specific policies may use the terms in different ways. A few examples will clarify these general statements.

The primary insuring agreements of the building and personal property coverage form provide coverage against direct loss to commercial buildings and/or personal property and/or personal property of others by a covered peril. This policy also includes secondary insuring agreements in the form of additional coverages and coverage extensions.

Briefly described, the *additional coverages* are as follows, and each has its own insuring agreement:

- Debris removal—pays the expenses to remove debris following a covered loss
- Preservation of property—provides off-premises coverage for covered property when it is removed to protect it against a covered loss at the premises
- Fire department service charge—pays fire department fees
- Pollutant clean up and removal—pays the expenses of cleaning up and/or removing pollutants following a covered loss

Each of these additional coverages applies for only a limited dollar amount and/or a limited amount of time, and each covers loss consequences that might not otherwise be within the scope of other insuring agreements.

The building and personal property coverage form also contains five *coverage extensions*, which generally extend coverage to encompass the following:

- Newly acquired or constructed property
- Personal effects and property of others
- Valuable papers and records—cost of research
- Property off-premises
- Outdoor property

Each of these extensions has its own insuring agreement.

Three popular "optional coverages" also are preprinted in the building and personal property coverage form, and each applies only when it is activated by an entry on the declarations page. Although they are labeled as optional coverages, the options in this particular form are not insuring agreements, but modifications of some of the miscellaneous provisions in the policy.

Policies providing liability insurance coverage commonly include "supplementary payments provisions" similar to the following provision in the personal auto policy.

SUPPLEMENTARY PAYMENTS

In addition to our limit of liability, we will pay on behalf on an "insured:"
1. Up to $250 for the cost of bail bonds required because of an accident, including related traffic law violations. . . .
2. Premiums on appeal bonds and bonds to release attachments in any suit we defend.
3. Interest accruing after a judgment is entered in any suit we defend. . . .
4. Up to $50 a day for loss of earnings, but not other income, because of attendance at hearings or trials at our request.
5. Other reasonable expenses incurred at our request.

The physical damage section of the personal auto policy contains a secondary insuring agreement that simply carries a descriptive heading as a label.

TRANSPORTATION EXPENSES

In addition, we will pay, without application of a deductible, up to $15 per day, to a maximum of $450, for ... transportation expenses incurred by you in the event of the total theft of "your covered auto.". ...

Other Provisions Functioning as Insuring Agreements. Policy provisions that grant or state coverage or restore coverage otherwise excluded, and therefore serve as insuring agreements, may appear within a definition, as an exception to an exclusion, or elsewhere in the policy, as shown in the following examples from the CGL policy.

Definition. As mentioned earlier, the insuring agreement of the CGL provides broad liability coverage, but this broad coverage is restricted by an auto exclusion, which reads in part as follows:

[This insurance does not apply to] "bodily injury" or "property damage" arising out of the ownership, maintenance, use or entrustment to others of any ... "auto" ... owned or operated by or rented or loaned to any insured. Use includes operation and "loading or unloading."

The definition of "auto" reads as follows:

"Auto" means a land motor vehicle, trailer or semitrailer designed for travel on public roads, including any attached machinery or equipment. But "auto" does not include "mobile equipment."

The CGL insuring agreement is broad enough to include claims involving liability arising out of motor vehicle accidents. The exclusion removes coverage for autos, but the definition of "auto" states that mobile equipment is not an auto. The *effect* of the last sentence in the definition, therefore, is to grant coverage (actually, to restore coverage otherwise excluded) for liability arising out of mobile equipment (subject to other policy provisions). ("Mobile equipment" has its own long definition, which includes such things as bulldozers and farm tractors.) An insurance practitioner might refer to the "mobile equipment coverage" of the CGL, even though the most specific grant of coverage appears within a definition. For these reasons, the final sentence of the above definition technically qualifies as an insuring agreement, although it is not often referred to that way in practice.

Exception to an Exclusion. The CGL also grants coverage for most businesses (more precisely, affirmatively states that it is not taken away) through an exception to the liquor liability exclusion. The entire exclusion, which concludes with the exception, reads as follows:

[This insurance does not apply to:] "Bodily injury" or "property damage" for which any insured may be held liable by reason of:

(1) Causing or contributing to the intoxication of any person;

(2) The furnishing of alcoholic beverages to a person under the legal drinking age or under the influence of alcohol; or

(3) Any statute, ordinance or regulation relating to the sale, gift, distribution or use of alcoholic beverages.

This exclusion applies only if you are in the business of manufacturing, distributing, selling, serving or furnishing alcoholic beverages.

Because of the exception in the final sentence of this exclusion, coverage applies to office parties and other liquor-related situations for businesses that are not *in the alcoholic beverage business*. This provision is frequently referred to as "host liquor liability coverage," and it is, in effect, an insuring agreement.

A semi-apologetic comment may be in order here. It might seem somewhat strained to refer to an exception to an exclusion as a "coverage." We are not entirely comfortable with this approach, but it is consistent with the language of insurance practitioners, and it is based in part on the development of some insurance forms. Many of today's standard basic insurance policies include some coverages that were excluded in earlier forms. Many of these excluded coverages could be purchased ("bought back") for an additional premium, and the "coverage" was then provided by a separate form or by an endorsement attached to the policy. Today some of these very same coverages exist in standard basic policies simply because they are not excluded, or because they are provided as exceptions to an exclusion. Often practitioners refer to them as "coverages"—even when there is no specific insuring agreement that serves as a grant of coverage. The best example is the so-called "products liability coverage" of the commercial general liability coverage form. Earlier liability policies added products liability coverage by endorsement; the present policy covers it simply by not excluding it.

Exclusions

Although the term "exclusion" often is reserved for policy provisions clearly identified as exclusions (for example, following an "Exclusions" heading), the term can accurately be applied to *any* policy provision whose function is to eliminate coverage for specified loss exposures—whether or not the provision is labeled as an exclusion.

Exclusions have been defined as "policy provisions that state what the insurer does not *intend* to cover." The word "intend" is important: The primary function of exclusions is to *clarify* the coverages granted by the insurer, not to *take away* coverage from the insured. Specifying what aspects of something an insurer does *not* intend to cover is a proven way of clarifying what aspects the insurer *does* intend to cover.

It can be difficult for policy drafters to express "what the insurer intends to cover" in language that will be interpreted as intended by the courts. The 1973 edition of the comprehensive general liability (CGL) insurance policy had a pollution exclusion that concluded with the seemingly straightforward words,

> . . . this exclusion does not apply if such discharge, dispersal, release or escape is sudden and accidental.

Combined with the insuring agreement, insurers have held that their intention was to exclude (carve out) coverage for most pollution losses (as described within the exclusion), but to provide coverage for losses resulting from sudden and accidental pollution. Gymnasiums have been filled with documents debating the meaning of these phrases and the insurability of pollution losses, and we will not attempt to summarize them in this brief paragraph.[5] In broad generalities, insurers' intentions were based on the premise that nonaccidental losses could be prevented or minimized, and that any coverage effectively encouraging pollution, by reimbursing polluters, should be against public policy. A seemingly sound pipe that burst without warning, or some other fortuitous event of that nature, was deemed a proper subject for insurance. Over the years, the courts interpreted the "sudden and accidental" exclusion so as to "find" coverage for many occurrences that insurers considered neither sudden nor accidental. After failing in many attempts to come up with a clearly worded pollution exclusion expressing their intent in words that the courts would uphold, many insurers simply gave up and excluded coverage for virtually all pollution losses. It was apparently possible to find policy language to state that *all* pollution losses were excluded, but it was not possible to find sustainable policy language that said "only sudden and accidental pollution losses are covered."

(We mentioned earlier that insurance policy language means whatever the courts say it means. In many cases, the interpretations of the courts have not been consistent with the alleged intentions of insurers. When mentioning disputes over the meaning of policy phrases, we try to avoid taking sides because *neither viewpoint is necessarily "right" or "wrong."* In theory, the burden lies on insurers' policy drafters to express their intent so clearly that courts can interpret the policy in no other way. In practice, it is not so easy as it may sound to develop policy language that clearly expresses an insurer's intentions as they might apply to a wide range of insureds and their future loss situations that have not yet occurred. Also, the claimant with many thousands of dollars at stake in a given fact situation has far more financial incentive after a loss to pursue a possible policy loophole than do the parties who must draft an entire policy to fit a limitless range of unknown exposures, using only experience and imagination to guess what kinds of losses might generate claims.)

Collectively, exclusions are said to serve at least six legitimate purposes:

1. Eliminate coverage for uninsurable loss exposures
2. Assist in the management of moral and morale hazards
3. Reduce the likelihood of coverage duplications
4. Eliminate coverages that are not needed by the typical purchaser
5. Eliminate coverages requiring special treatment
6. Assist in keeping premiums at a reasonable level

It can be difficult to relate a given exclusion to only *one* of the above purposes, because *any exclusion may serve more than one purpose.* This point is especially relevant in connection with the sixth purpose, "keeping premiums reasonable." All exclusions serve this purpose to some extent—it logically requires a higher premium to pay for the additional losses that might be covered whenever a policy is broadened by eliminating an exclusion.

Eliminating Coverage for Uninsurable Loss Exposures. One purpose of exclusions is to eliminate coverage for exposures that are considered uninsurable by private insurers. Nearly all property and liability insurance policies exclude losses arising out of war. (The main exception is the "war risks coverage" often available in ocean marine insurance policies covering vessels or cargo, even those that might pass through war zones, but at appropriately higher rates.)

Other common exclusions of uninsurable exposures involve losses due to intentional acts of the insured or other nonaccidental events, nuclear radiation, earthquake, flood damage to fixed-location property, normal wear and tear, and "inherent vice." (*Inherent vice* is a quality inherent in an object that tends to destroy it, as when iron rusts, wood rots, or rubber deteriorates.)

Each of these excluded exposures fails to sufficiently possess at least one of the characteristics of an ideally insurable loss exposure. War and nuclear losses involve an incalculable catastrophe potential. Inherent vice and similar perils are not accidental or fortuitous in nature but are predictable, expected, and, in varying degrees, controllable by the insured.

Assist in Managing Moral Hazards. *Moral hazards,* as the phrase is used by insurance practitioners, are defects or weaknesses in human character that lead some people to exaggerate losses or intentionally cause them, in order to collect insurance proceeds. Exclusions can help manage moral hazards to the extent that they eliminate coverage for intentional acts of the insured which are essentially uninsurable.

One such example is found in the liability section of the ISO homeowners policy:

> **Coverage E-Personal Liability and Coverage F-Medical Payments to Others** do not apply to "bodily injury" or "property damage" . . . which is expected or intended by the "insured"; . . . .

While this exclusion eliminates coverage for blatantly intentional harmful results, other conditions and miscellaneous provisions, discussed elsewhere in this text, make it difficult to successfully exaggerate losses.

Assist in Managing Morale Hazards. The term *morale hazards* refers generally to the tendency of people to be less careful about preventing losses when they are insured. Some exclusions assist in managing morale hazards by making insureds themselves bear the losses that result from their own carelessness. A good example is the following exclusion, which appears, not under the "Exclusions" heading, but within the "freezing" peril of the homeowners policy:

> This peril [freezing] does not include loss on the "residence premises" while the dwelling is unoccupied, unless you have used reasonable care to:
> a. Maintain heat in the building; or
> b. Shut off the water supply and drain the system and appliances of water.

As another example, many "all-risks" property insurance policies contain a so-called (but unlabeled) "voluntary parting exclusion" like the following:

> [We will not pay for loss or damage caused by or resulting from] voluntary parting with any property by you or anyone else to whom you have entrusted the property if induced to do so by any fraudulent scheme, trick, device or false pretense.

This exclusion comes into play when, for example, a customer presents a falsified voucher at a warehouse loading dock and claims merchandise to which the customer is not entitled. Sound verification procedures could presumably prevent some, but not all, losses of this type. Excluding coverage for "false pretense" losses encourages businesses to set up sound verification procedures; covering such losses would encourage sloppy verification procedures because of a belief that "our insurance will pay for any loss."

Reduce Likelihood of Coverage Duplications. It usually is unnecessary and wasteful if two insurance policies provide coverage for the same loss. It is unnecessary because coverage under one policy is all that is needed to indemnify the insured (unless policy restrictions or limits of insurance prevent full recovery). It is wasteful because, at least in theory, each policy providing coverage for a certain type of losses includes a related premium charge (which is admittedly negligible in some cases).

For example:

- Personal liability policies usually exclude losses arising from business activities.
- "Commercial property" insurance policies typically exclude autos from the description of covered property because auto physical damage insurance is readily available and widely purchased.

Generally speaking, standard insurance policies are carefully designed to dovetail with other standard policies—one policy picks up right where the other leaves off. This is especially true when the related policies are written by the same insurance company or insurance advisory organization.

For example, the business auto coverage form is intended to cover liability arising out of the loading and unloading of an auto, while the commercial general liability coverage form is intended to exclude loading and unloading coverage. This is accomplished by the policy provisions quoted below. Interestingly, the commercial general liability provisions address not only auto-related matters, but also those relating to aircraft and watercraft; yet, the auto-related provisions dovetail perfectly with those in the business auto coverage form.

Exclusion in the liability coverage section of the business auto coverage form:

[This insurance does not apply to] "bodily injury" or "property damage" resulting from the handling of property:
a. Before it is moved from the place where it is accepted by the "insured" for movement into or onto the covered "auto;" or
b. After it is moved from the covered "auto" to the place where it is finally delivered to the "insured."

Exclusion in the commercial general liability coverage form:

[This insurance does not apply to:] "Bodily injury" or "property damage" arising out of the ownership, maintenance, use or entrustment to others of any aircraft, "auto" or watercraft owned or operated by or rented or loaned to any insured. Use includes operation and "loading or unloading."

Definition in the commercial general liability coverage form:

"Loading or unloading" means the handling of property:
a. After it is moved from the place where it is accepted for movement into or onto an aircraft, watercraft or "auto;"
b. While it is in or on an aircraft, watercraft or "auto;" or
c. While it is being moved from an aircraft, watercraft or "auto" to the place where it is finally delivered. . . .

Nearly the same words are used in both forms to assure that one policy picks up precisely where the other leaves off. That is, when it comes to auto loading and unloading, one form excludes what the other covers, and vice versa.

Notice also the complementary relationship between exclusions and the definition. In the auto form, the exclusion describes the exposure that is not covered. In the general liability form, "loading and unloading" is mentioned in the exclusion, but the wording to describe "loading and unloading" is found in a definition.

Coverage does not always dovetail this neatly. However, it is reasonable to look for complementary exclusions and other dovetailing provisions when examining related policies, and it often is important to make sure they do dovetail without leaving unmanageable coverage gaps or expensive overlaps.

Eliminate Coverages Not Needed by the Typical Purchaser. A fourth purpose of exclusions is to eliminate coverages that are not needed by the typical purchaser of that type of insurance. For example, the operations of most businesses do not involve loading and unloading aircraft or watercraft, so the aircraft and watercraft loading and unloading exclusions quoted above do not affect most insureds. Likewise, the typical individual does not own or operate private aircraft, use the family automobile as a taxicab for hire, or rent portions of the family home for storage of others' business property—and coverage for such exposures is excluded by typical auto and homeowners policies.

People who do have these exposures may be able to obtain coverage separately, usually by paying additional premiums. It would be inequitable to require all insureds to share the costs of covering the substantial exposures of relatively few insureds. However, that is exactly what would happen if, for example, the personal auto policy were to automatically provide coverage whenever a covered auto is used as a taxicab.

(Insurers are not always permitted to exclude coverage for exposures not faced by the typical purchaser. For example, insurers might like to exclude auto liability coverage for drivers who have accidents while driving under the influence of alcohol or narcotics, but state insurance regulators would be very unlikely to approve such a policy exclusion because it would tend to eliminate a source of recovery for the innocent victims of drunken drivers. The effect is that auto policyholders who never drink and drive are required, in effect, to share the costs of accidents caused by those who do.)

Eliminate Coverages Requiring Special Treatment. A fifth purpose of exclusions is to eliminate coverages requiring special treatment. As used here, the term "special" means rating, underwriting, loss control, or reinsurance treatment substantially different from what is normally applied to the contract containing the exclusion. For example:

- Many standard policies covering valuable personal property exclude coverage for losses occurring while the property is on exhibition at a convention or trade fair. Paintings, stamps, coins, and other collectors' items sometimes are displayed in exhibits open to the public, and property on exhibit is especially vulnerable to loss by theft and other perils. Where the exposure exists, an underwriter may agree to provide coverage for an additional premium.
- Commercial liability insurance covering products liability typically excludes coverage for the expense of recalling products that are or may be defective. So-called "products recall" insurance is sometimes available from excess and surplus lines insurers that have carefully analyzed and priced the specific exposure.
- General liability policies usually exclude the so-called professional liability exposure. Physicians, attorneys, and other professionals may purchase professional liability insurance to cover losses arising out of errors or omissions in their professional activities.
- Commercial property insurance policies exclude coverage for steam boiler explosions. Steam boilers require trained inspectors not available to every insurance company.
- Liquor law liability of insureds engaged in the liquor business often is excluded in an insurance company's reinsurance treaty.

As mentioned earlier, exclusions may serve more than one purpose. Some of the exclusions mentioned above eliminate coverages not needed by the typical purchaser, who may not have the exposure. They also reduce coverage duplications for insureds who do obtain special insurance. Despite the apparent overlap, "requiring special treatment" can be considered a distinct purpose of exclusions. In some cases it is the only reason an insurer uses a particular exclusion. For example, boiler and machinery insurance relies heavily on the loss control expertise of boiler inspectors. Many insurers who write "commercial property" insurance do not have the facilities to handle boiler and machinery insurance but issue boiler and machinery policies reinsured by other insurers who possess the necessary expertise. To the insurance buyer, it may appear that the insurer is using two policies to do a job that might be done by one. From the insurer's standpoint, however, it is necessary to separate boiler and machinery losses from commercial property insurance losses when the boiler and machinery losses are borne by the reinsurer, who also underwrites and prices the boiler and machinery portion of the coverage.

Keeping Premiums Reasonable. A sixth purpose of exclusions is to assist in keeping premiums at a level that a sufficiently large number of insurance buyers will consider reasonable. This goal is shared by insurers, rate regulators, and consumers alike.

All exclusions serve this purpose to some extent. However, it is the primary reason for some exclusions, and it is the only reason for others. For example, consider the following exclusion from the "damage to your auto" section of the personal auto policy:

> [We will not pay for damage due and confined to]: . . .
> c. mechanical or electrical breakdown or failure; or
> d. road damage to tires.

The excluded losses are not exactly uninsurable. Auto dealers, tire shops, and various other organizations offer insurance-like service warranties covering just such losses. However, few people would be willing to pay the premiums necessary to include in their auto insurance policies coverage for such predictable losses. An insurance policy could probably be priced to reflect the expected costs of mechanical breakdowns or tire losses, but the insured would end up paying the projected costs of maintenance plus the insurer's expenses in administering insurance to cover the maintenance costs. Any insurer that included coverage for ordinary maintenance expenses under its normal auto policy would literally price itself out of the market.

Departing from property-liability insurance for a moment, one might expect that periodic tooth-cleaning and other routine dental expenses would not be covered by insurance for essentially the same reasons: The insured would ultimately pay the cost of the dentist's services plus the insurer's cost of administering the insurance. In fact, however, such routine dental maintenance expenses are routinely covered. The difference is that most dental insurance is written on a group basis and is paid for by employers (as a tax-deductible expense), providing employees with an untaxed benefit. The tax advantages may create savings for the consumer that offset the costly inefficiencies of using insurance to finance routine, predictable expenses. Additionally, this serves as a loss control device in that it prevents more costly claims.

As mentioned before, an exclusion is any policy provision that functions as an exclusion, whether or not it is labeled as an exclusion. Insurance policies contain many exclusionary features, and every one of them helps to keep premiums reasonable. All else being equal, when a comprehensive type of insuring agreement is used, the fewer the exclusions, the higher the expected loss costs—and vice versa.

Conditions

A policy condition is any provision that has the effect of qualifying an otherwise enforceable promise of the insurer, regardless of how it is labeled or where in the policy it is located. Some policy conditions are found in a section of the policy titled "Conditions." Many of these are discussed in Chapter 3. Others may be found almost anywhere in the forms, endorsements, or other documents that together constitute the entire contract.

In a policy's insuring agreement, the insurer promises to pay to the insured, to pay on behalf of the insured, to defend the insured, and/or to provide various additional services. However, these are not absolute, unconditional, "no-strings-attached" promises. A policy condition "attaches some strings." The insurer makes promises to pay, furnish a defense, or provide other services that are enforceable *only if* an insured event occurs *and* the insured has fulfilled its contractual duties as specified in the conditions of the policy.

Examples of common policy conditions include the insured's obligation to pay premiums, report losses promptly, provide appropriate documentation for losses, cooperate with the insurer in any legal proceedings, and refrain from jeopardizing an insurer's rights to recover from responsible third parties (under "subrogation" actions). If the insured does not do these things, the insurer may be released from any obligation to perform some or all of its otherwise enforceable promises.

Contract conditions in general are sometimes subdivided into two categories:

- A *condition precedent* precedes the existence of the obligation. For example, a grandfather tells his grandson, "This car is yours when you graduate." The condition of graduating must be satisfied before any transfer of title takes place.
- A *condition subsequent* qualifies an existing obligation by terminating it when a particular event occurs or fails to occur. Suppose the grandfather says, "This car will be yours unless you drop out of school." Dropping out of school is a condition that serves to void the gift.[6]

In a 1987 Iowa case, two insurance policies provided auto liability coverage.[7] The insurers did not receive notice that their insured had been involved in a hit-and-run accident until twenty-eight months after it occurred. During most of this period, the insured's involvement also was concealed from the police. Both insurers sought to avoid payment based on breach of their policy condition requiring prompt notice of a claim.

The first of these insurance policies contained the following provisions:

> What You Must Do For Us
>
> Here are a few things you'll have to do for us. Not only you, but anyone who's insured under this policy.
>
> If there's an accident or incident that may be covered by this policy, notify us in writing as soon as possible. You can give this notice to any of our authorized agents. . . .
>
> *We're not obligated to pay for your loss until you do all this.* [italics added]

The second policy's provisions read as follows:

> DUTIES AFTER ACCIDENT OR LOSS
>
> We must be notified promptly of how, when and where the accident or loss happened. Notice should also include the names and addresses of any injured persons and of any witnesses. A person seeking any coverage must. . . .

A list of duties followed.

Presumably because of the sentence italicized above, the court determined that the notice provision in the first policy constituted a condition precedent to liability of the company under the policy. Therefore, *the persons claiming coverage* under that policy were required to prove that failure to give notice to the insurer either was excused or caused no prejudice to the insurer. However, the somewhat different wording of the second policy placed the burden on the insurer to show prejudice. (It is not necessary to show prejudice in case of late notice in all states.) The Iowa supreme court did not base its decision on *this* issue because it agreed that both insurers were prejudiced by the delay (that is, their ability to conduct a defense was impaired). However, this case made it clear that it may not be sufficient simply to state the insured's duty— the insurer might still be on the hook unless policy conditions clarify the penalty for breaching the duty. A number of policies that previously lacked such a provision are being revised to include not only a listing of duties, but also the *conditions precedent language* such as the following:

> We have no duty to provide coverage under this policy unless there has been full compliance with the following duties:

Similar language is included in many other insurance policies to clarify the operation of conditions precedent.

Conditions subsequent include, for example, subrogation provisions requiring the insured to turn over its rights of recovery to the insurer after the insurer pays a loss.

Miscellaneous Provisions

Insurance policies often contain various provisions that do not strictly qualify as declarations, definitions, insuring agreements, exclusions, or conditions. They may deal with the relationship between the insured and the insurer, or they may help to establish working procedures for carrying out the terms of the contract, but they do not have the force of conditions. Actions that depart from the procedures specified in the miscellaneous provisions normally do not affect the insurer's basic duty to perform.

One example of a miscellaneous provision is a valuation provision setting forth standards for measuring losses under the policy. Some miscellaneous provisions are unique to particular types of insurers. For example:

- A policy issued by a mutual insurance company is likely to describe the right of each insured to vote in the election of the board of directors.
- A policy issued by a reciprocal insurer is likely to specify the authority of the attorney-in-fact to carry out its powers on behalf of the insured.

HOW TO READ AN INSURANCE POLICY

People read insurance policies for a variety of reasons. Two common reasons include determining the answers to these important questions:

- *After a loss:* Was the loss covered?
- *Before a loss:* What losses would be covered?

Ideally, every policyholder would read his or her policy as soon as it is received and have a basic understanding of what losses would be covered. Realistically, however, most insureds do not read their insurance policies until after a loss. At that time the policy often is carefully scrutinized in an attempt to find coverage for the loss. Insurers' claims representatives need to follow essentially the same process in applying coverage to a known loss. Insurance agents and brokers may follow the same approach in answering "What if?" questions raised by an insured (and underwriters may do so when dealing with producers' questions or evaluating an application).

The most effective after-loss policy analysis requires an understanding of how insurance policies are constructed and interpreted. The remainder of this chapter describes a basic approach to after-loss policy analysis.

After-Loss Policy Analysis[8]

This section of the chapter explains how to approach any property or liability insurance policy to determine whether, and to what extent, coverage applies for a known loss that has already occurred. This same system can be used in answering "What if?" questions about specific losses that might occur.

After a loss that may have been covered has occurred, a policy can be analyzed by answering the questions in the following outline:

1. Is this claim covered by the insurance policy?
   a. Is this claim within the scope of an insuring agreement?
   b. Does any exclusion eliminate or restrict coverage for this claim? (If so, are there any exceptions to exclusions that will restore coverage?)
   c. Have policy conditions been complied with?
2. If the answer to (1) is yes, then what dollar amount will be paid?

Note the outline format and sequence: There are two major questions—coverage and amount, and it is pointless to evaluate dollar amounts payable until it is determined whether the claim is covered at all. Questions 1a, 1b, and 1c must therefore be answered before proceeding to question 2.

This elementary point seems obvious; yet it is sometimes overlooked. In one such case, the insured's business tools were stolen from his auto, which was covered under an auto insurance policy. The insured presented the claim to a claims representative who agreed to pay $200 of the loss because the policy in question included $200 coverage for "personal effects." Only later did the claims representative realize that the business tools did not qualify as personal effects. The point bears repeating: *Before deciding how much should be paid, determine whether the claim is covered!*

Is This Claim Covered by the Insurance Policy? Barring extenuating circumstances (such as the insured's concealment of a material fact) or conditions outside the terms of the written contract, this question is answered in full by determining the answer to three other questions.

Is the Claim Within the Scope of an Insuring Agreement? An insuring agreement provides a broad statement of coverage that is then narrowed by exclusions and other policy provisions. If a claim is within the scope of an insuring agreement, it *may* be covered; if it is not, there is no need to search further except to determine whether another insuring agreement—or another coverage of the same policy or a different policy—might apply.

Does Any Exclusion Eliminate or Restrict Coverage for This Claim?
As explained earlier, exclusions carve out some of the coverage that is
within the broad scope of the insuring agreement. The best way to
analyze the effect of exclusions is to read *each exclusion* together with
the insuring agreement, omitting the words and phrases that do not
apply to the situation at hand.

Some exclusions have "exceptions," which may be located immediately following the exclusion itself or at the end of the "exclusions"
section of the policy. Before concluding that an exclusion applies, the
analyst should look for any applicable exceptions.

As mentioned earlier, exceptions to exclusions are sometimes referred to as "coverages." An exception to the exclusion might be considered an insuring agreement; at least it has the effect of serving to restore
coverage that otherwise would be taken away.

Sometimes an endorsement to a policy removes or replaces an exclusion, so it is necessary also to examine the endorsements before concluding that an exclusion precludes coverage.

Once it is determined that an exclusion knocks out coverage and
that no exception or endorsement restores coverage, there is usually no
point in analyzing other exclusions (except, perhaps, to bolster one's
reasons for denying a claim in the event the seemingly applicable exclusion is not upheld). If a loss is excluded by only one exclusion, it is still
excluded from coverage under the related insuring agreement even if
other exclusions do not apply.

At least, that is how it usually works. This simple "fact" of policy
interpretation is not *always* valid. One principle of contract interpretation is that the contract is to be read in its entirety. At times, something
in one seemingly unrelated provision sheds light on another provision
and affects the outcome of a claim. A simple example illustrates this
point. Everett's fence was damaged by a windstorm, and he wondered
whether coverage applied under his homeowners policy. The description
of covered property did not include any specific reference to fences.
However, he noticed that the "vehicles" peril read as follows:

> We insure for direct physical loss . . . caused by a peril listed below
> unless the loss is excluded in Section I—Exclusions. . . .

> **6. Vehicles.**

> This peril does not include loss to a fence, driveway or walk caused by
> a vehicle owned or operated by a resident of the **residence premises.**

The final sentence above is clearly an exclusion—it says vehicle damage
is not covered under certain circumstances. However, it also *implies*
that vehicle damage to a fence *is* covered when the exclusion does not

apply. If that is the case, Everett argues, the fence must be covered property, and it must be covered against loss by other covered perils. These arguments are persuasive in the absence of other indications to the contrary.

The lesson is that coverage usually is precluded if any exclusion clearly applies. However, other insuring agreements (including unlabeled insuring agreements) will sometimes apply, and other statements in the policy might provide further clarifications of coverage. Of course, other applicable forms and endorsements should also be considered.

Do Any Policy Conditions Affect the Coverage for This Claim? As explained earlier, many policy conditions deal with duties of the insurer and of the insured. In the vast majority of cases, both parties comply with their respective duties—the insurer does not send out improper notice of policy cancelation, the insured does not conceal or misrepresent information, the insured does promptly report the loss or claim and cooperate with the insurer, and so forth. However, policy conditions should not be ignored, because violation of a policy condition might change the situation with respect to an otherwise-covered claim.

Especially important are policy conditions relating to the time and place where loss must occur for coverage to apply. Also important, in some cases, are conditions relating to the timely payment of premiums.

What Dollar Amount Will Be Paid? Assuming a claim is covered, the insurer will pay an amount determined as specified in the policy. Valuation provisions are examined in much more detail in Chapter 6. However, a few points can be made here.

- Property insurance policies invariably contain a *valuation provision* stating how the value of insured property is to be determined. Two common valuation provisions describe *replacement cost* or *actual cash value* as the basis of measuring value.
- Liability insurance policies generally contain a promise to provide a defense and pay the amount for which the insured is legally responsible as damages. This might be the amount of a court award following a lawsuit. In a majority of cases, however, the amount is arrived at through an out-of-court settlement—in which both parties consider, among other factors, the amount that probably would have been awarded if the case had gone to trial.

In both property and liability insurance policies, the insurer may agree to pay some additional expenses—such as expenses to protect property against further loss and court costs, attorneys' fees, and other expenses to defend against a liability suit.

In determining the amount to be paid by the insurer, it is necessary to consider any deductibles, coinsurance provisions, or other loss-sharing provisions that may apply. Also, the insurer is not obligated to pay more than the limits of insurance that apply to a particular loss—which may be the policy limits or some sublimit within the policy. A degree of skill and experience can be helpful when finding and interpreting these various provisions, especially when several such provisions apply at the same time. These subjects are explained in greater detail later in this text.

Before-Loss Policy Analysis

It is much more difficult to analyze a policy when no particular loss has occurred. Before-loss policy analysis requires a wide range of skills such as:

- An understanding of the alternative ways in which insurance policies customarily describe coverage in addressing loss exposures
- An ability to identify and evaluate insurance policy provisions that represent departures from the customary approach
- An understanding of the exposures—the insured(s), the property, and the operations to which the policy will apply

Subsequent chapters will address the first two points by exploring the approaches used in a wide range of property and liability insurance policies. The third point is treated in other CPCU texts, particularly those used for CPCU 2, 3, and 4.

An even higher level of skills is involved in drafting insurance policies. While this course does not specifically address the topic "How To Write an Insurance Policy," the ideas here must be understood by those who become policy drafters.

SUMMARY

Although insurance policies are "least read best sellers," insurance professionals need to know how to read and interpret them. This skill requires an understanding of the physical construction and general content of insurance policies, as well as an organized approach to reading them.

Physically, an insurance policy may be analyzed according to several basic characteristics.

- It may be a single, self-contained document, or it may be modular, utilizing a selected set of documents designed as matching building blocks.
- It may be a preprinted "off-the-shelf" document, or it may be manuscript—specifically crafted to fit a particular situation.

- Preprinted policies may be standard policies, developed by a service organization or prescribed by law and used by many different insurers, or they may be nonstandard policies developed by an individual insurer.

When the courts interpret insurance policies, they apply a doctrine of adhesion that tends to favor a party that had no role in drafting the insurance contract documents—usually the insured.

Collateral documents may be physically attached to an insurance policy, or they may be incorporated into the contract because they are referred to in the policy. Applications, endorsements, insurer bylaws and relevant statutes, rating manuals, and other miscellaneous documents may serve in this role.

The content of a property-liability policy consists of many provisions, each of which can be classified as declarations, definitions, insuring agreements, exclusions, conditions, and miscellaneous provisions. These classifications refer more to the function performed by each provision than to the policy heading under which it may be found, and some provisions serve more than one function.

Declarations basically involve the information that personalizes a policy by naming the persons, property, and activities that may be covered, as well as the insurer providing the coverage. Definitions explain the meaning of certain terms of art used within the policy; undefined terms are given their ordinary meaning. Insuring agreements are coverage grants, although some provisions that clarify, restate, or restore coverage might also be considered insuring agreements.

Exclusions narrow the broad coverage grants provided by insuring agreements. Exclusions generally serve one or more of the following purposes:

- Eliminating coverage for uninsurable loss exposures
- Assisting in managing moral and morale hazards
- Reducing likelihood of coverage duplications
- Eliminating coverages not needed by the typical purchaser
- Eliminating coverages requiring special treatment
- Keeping premiums reasonable

Conditions precedent and conditions subsequent, as explained in this chapter, relate to duties and circumstances surrounding the coverage. Miscellaneous provisions deal largely with administrative matters and do not fall under any of the other categories.

Insurance policies may be read after a loss to determine whether the loss was covered or before a loss to determine what losses would be covered. After the loss, the questions to ask are the following:

- Is this claim covered by the insurance policy?

- If the answer to the above question is "yes," what dollar amount will be paid?

The second question should not be answered until the first has been satisfied. Answering the first question requires a determination of whether the claim was within the scope of an insuring agreement, whether any exclusion eliminates or restricts coverage, and whether any condition affects coverage.

Before-the-loss policy analysis requires imagination, insight, and experience to determine what losses might occur and to compare the provisions of one particular policy with those one might expect to find in other similar policies. These skills will be further developed in this course and in other CPCU courses. An even higher-level skill, beyond the scope of this course, involves the ability to draft insurance policies. This course, however, does provide a foundation for such skills.

Chapter Notes

1. John H. Magee, *General Insurance,* 3rd ed. (Homewood, IL: Richard D. Irwin, 1952), p. 8.
2. According to the dictionary, "everyday" is a single word when used as an adjective. Likewise, "fewer" should properly be substituted for "less" in the earlier item marked *"sic."* These two word choices in the model regulation unfortunately illustrate the word contortions sometimes found in insurance policies attempting to conform to a readability index. For example, standard ISO policies once referred to motor vehicles with "less than four wheels," a phrase that has since been corrected.
3. Personal Lines Property and Casualty Insurance Policy Simplification Model Regulation, Copyright 1986 NAIC.
4. Policy limits often apply "per occurrence," and multiples of a policy limit may be available to cover a loss related to multiple occurrences. These matters are examined further in Chapters 5 and 6 in connection with insured events and policy limits.
5. One of the landmark cases on this issue involved so many parties that the trial was conducted in a large gymnasium rather than a courtroom.
6. Ronald A. Anderson and Walter A. Kumpf, *Business Law,* 10th ed., (Cincinnati: South-Western Publishing Co., 1976), p. 261.
7. Bruns v. Hartford, 407 N.W. 2d 576 (Iowa 1987).
8. The approach here is based on the presentation in Barry D. Smith, *How Insurance Works: An Introduction to Property and Liability Insurance* (Malvern, PA: Insurance Institute of America, 1984), pp. 99-101.

CHAPTER 3

Common Insurance Policy Provisions

This chapter deals with some of the boilerplate in insurance policies—the seemingly ubiquitous provisions that often are overlooked. Most of the provisions discussed here typically are found in a "Conditions" section near the end of a self-contained policy or in a "common conditions" type form within a modular policy.

Two common types of provisions will be examined only briefly at the start of this chapter, with more detailed treatment in later chapters. These deal with (1) insured parties and covered property and (2) the time and the place for which coverage applies. Many other common provisions, examined here in detail, relate to the usually routine logistics of paying for, maintaining, or terminating coverage. Timely payment of premium and not canceling the policy usually are more-or-less taken for granted. However, each policy must contain provisions detailing what happens if normal processes do not take place—clarifying, for example, whether, when, how, and by whom a policy can be canceled before its normal expiration and how any resulting premium adjustments will be handled.

Other such policy conditions relate to the processes that must take place following a loss. These policy provisions are seldom consulted until after a loss actually occurs. They are rarely evaluated when making a before-loss analysis of applicable coverages.

Like the sun and the moon, most of the policy provisions we will explore in this chapter usually are taken for granted, and this is not entirely inappropriate once one knows they are there. Yet, they serve important roles, and the insurance world would be a much different place without them. The policy provisions examined in this chapter establish some of the basic parameters within which other policy provisions operate. To the extent possible, this chapter approaches each type of provision by outlining the situation or need that is addressed, citing typical provisions, and examining their implications. Where possible, variations among similar conditions and exceptions to the usual approach are examined. These variations and exceptions draw attention to some of the reasons these conditions should not always be taken for granted.

A word of caution: Although most of the provisions cited in this chapter are typical of those commonly used, the reader is warned not to assume that any one policy contains all of the provisions discussed here or that any specific provision of a given type is identical to the one cited here.

PROVISIONS CLARIFYING INSURED PARTIES OR COVERED PROPERTY

The complex subject of "insured parties" is explored in detail in Chapter 4; covered property is examined in Chapter 5. However, some related, rather general provisions, which appear in many policies, will be mentioned here.

Assignment

Insurance policies are personal contracts. As a general rule, ownership (and protection) of a property or liability insurance policy cannot be transferred to another party without the written consent of the insurer. Insurers preserve their rights to select their insureds by including an *assignment provision* in most insurance policies, such as the following one in the ISO homeowners policy.

Assignment

Assignment of this policy will not be valid unless we give our written consent.

If Francois sells his chateau to Michelle, he cannot include his homeowners insurance policy in the deal unless the insurance company agrees in writing.

Many modernized language insurance policies no longer use the "assignment" label. Consider, for example, the following provision in the common policy conditions, used with most ISO commercial insurance policies.

TRANSFER OF YOUR RIGHTS AND DUTIES UNDER THIS POLICY

Your rights and duties under this policy may not be transferred without our written consent except in the case of death of an individual named insured.

If you die, your rights and duties will be transferred to your legal
representative but only while acting within the scope of duties as
your legal representative. Until your legal representative is appointed,
anyone having proper temporary custody of your property will have
your rights and duties but only with respect to that property.

The first part of this "modern" provision is a traditional assignment
provision, whether or not it bears that label. This particular provision
goes on to extend protection to additional parties under certain circumstances.

The Effect. Policyholders usually do not request that a policy be
assigned when property or activities are transferred. Consequently, the
assignment provision usually is of little significance. But consider what
might happen in its absence: If assignment were not prohibited, a person
who normally would not qualify for insurance could become an insured
simply by arranging an assignment of someone else's insurance.

If assignment is attempted without the consent of the insurer, both
the new policyowner and the former policyowner can be left without
insurance protection. Because of the assignment provision, the insurer
would have no legal obligation to the would-be assignee. Moreover, the
insurer would have no obligation to the original named insured (assignor)
of the policy (assuming that party no longer has an insurable interest
at the time of the loss).

In practice, assignments are rare. Most people who acquire property
prefer to purchase new insurance policies from the insurer of their
choice. When assignments are requested, insurers typically are reluctant
to give their consent. Court decisions have held that the insurer waives
any defenses (such as misrepresentation in the application) that might
have been used against the former insured. There is little incentive for
an insurer to voluntarily weaken its position in this way.

Exceptions to the General Rule. Insurance on oceangoing
cargo usually is written so that the ocean marine insurance policy may
be assigned to other parties having an interest in the cargo as their
interests develop. In practice, the ownership of cargo might change
several times during the weeks when it is in transit from one port to
another. Yet, the physical characteristics and exposures of the insured
property do not change while the property is aboard a ship and completely outside the control of any owner. For similar reasons, other
property insurance policies occasionally are written to cover the interests of "for whom it may concern," or "the named insured or his assignees." Either approach is broad enough to include an assignee as an
insured.

This entire discussion relates only to an assignment of policy ownership and protection *before* any loss occurs. After a loss, any party with

a right to recover money under a property insurance policy may freely assign that right to another party. Such an assignment does not change the identity of the insured, diminish the insurer's defenses, or pose new hazards for the insurer.

No Benefit to Bailee

A *bailee* is a party having possession of the personal property of another and a duty either to return it to the owner or to deliver or dispose of it as agreed. When compensation is involved, the bailee is a *bailee for hire*. A dry cleaner, an auto service station, and a common carrier are examples. When no compensation is involved, the bailment is considered a *gratuitous bailment*, and the bailee owes a somewhat lesser degree of care.

Even when a high degree of care is required, a bailee is not legally responsible for all damage to property in its custody—only for damage caused by the bailee's negligence. If a tornado blows a car from a garagekeeper's hoist, it would hardly be appropriate to charge the garage owner for the damage. The tornado might as readily have damaged the vehicle in the owner's own garage.

What happens when Bill's covered property is damaged while in the custody of a bailee? Assuming Bill has applicable property insurance, Bill's insurance company will pay his claim. If possible, Bill's insurer will then attempt to recover its payment from the bailee through the process of subrogation. Bill, the property owner, is protected by his insurance, but the bailee is not. (The bailee may be protected by its own insurance, but that is not the issue here.)

The insurance company provides coverage for the property owner but not for the bailee, as stated in the *no benefit to bailee provision* of many property insurance policies. One example is the following provision in the personal auto policy:

NO BENEFIT TO BAILEE

This insurance shall not directly or indirectly benefit any carrier or other bailee for hire.

This provision relates specifically to bailees for hire; it does not preclude coverage for another driver to whom an insured lends the car.

A slightly different version appears in the ISO homeowners policy:

No Benefit to Bailee. We will not recognize any assignment or grant any coverage that benefits a person or organization holding, storing or moving property for a fee regardless of any other provision of this policy.

This provision relates primarily to household movers, though it would also apply to a public warehouse or to a furrier holding the insured's furs in cold storage.

The AAIS Inland Marine General Terms provision reads as follows:

No Benefit to Bailee. This Inland Marine coverage will not benefit those who are paid to assume custody of the covered property.

This provision encompasses all bailees for hire.

These provisions may describe somewhat different types of bailees for hire, depending on the exposures each policy addresses. But the effect is the same in all cases: Subject to other policy terms, an insured does have protection for loss to property in the custody of a bailee for hire. However, the bailee cannot benefit from this coverage. The property owner's insurance does not relieve the bailee of its legal responsibility.

A slightly different version appears in the commercial property conditions:

NO BENEFIT TO BAILEE

No person or organization, other than you, having custody of Covered Property will benefit from this insurance.

This provision encompasses all bailees, including both gratuitous bailees and bailees for hire.

More Than One Insured Person or Covered Location

Many insurance policies insure more than one person, and many cover property at more than one location. Questions then develop as to which insured the insurer should deal with, how actions by one insured might affect coverage for other insureds, or how conditions at one location might affect coverage at another location.

First Named Insured. In many insurance policies, more than one insured is named in the declarations and each is, by definition, a "named insured," referred to elsewhere in the policy as "you." For example, a commercial insurance policy might list as named insured "Jen Smith and Eric Jones doing business as the Jeneric Company, a partnership." Both the insurer and the insureds have a need to clarify whether either Smith, Jones, or both, need to be involved in any transaction with the insurer.

Many insurance policies do not specifically address this issue. However, when ISO commercial insurance policies were simplified in the mid-1980s, the wording of many provisions made it clear that the "first Named Insured" serves as the contact point for administrative matters. That is, the first named insured acts as an agent (not an "insurance agent") for all other named insureds in dealing with the insurance company. The "first Named Insured" is simply the one whose name appears first in the policy declarations (usually because it appeared first in the application for insurance). In this case, Jen Smith is the "first Named Insured."

The *coverage* applicable to the first named insured is no different from that of other named insureds, but the first named insured is the only one authorized to cancel the policy, receive notice of cancellation if the insurer cancels the policy, make changes with the insurer's consent, or receive any return premiums. The first named insured also is the person contractually responsible for the payment of premiums. The commercial general liability coverage form also specifies that the first named insured is the party who receives claim and occurrence data from the insurer, as well as advance notice of nonrenewal when applicable.

The crime general provisions form adds a special twist: "if the first named Insured ceases to be covered, then the next named Insured will become the first named Insured."

To the lay person, it might not seem to make any difference in what order the names appear in the declarations of a commercial insurance policy, but insurance professionals know it is important with some policies to list first the insured who should serve as a contact point—generally the named insured that handles insurance matters on behalf of all insureds.

Personal insurance policies covering an individual or husband and wife typically make no distinction between the first named insured and other named insureds who are members of the same economic unit. Many commercial policies also do not make this distinction. However, like other matters, this could change as insurance policy language evolves.

Separation of Interests. When several parties are insured in the same policy, conflicts can develop. For example, what happens with a property insurance policy if one insured intentionally causes property damage that results in a financial loss for all insureds—does the intentional damage exclusion preclude coverage for one insured or for all? Also, with property or liability insurance, if one insured breaches a policy condition—do other insureds still have coverage? Even more difficult, what happens under a liability policy if one insured sues another insured?

Many insurance policies contain a miscellaneous provision that addresses issues like those raised here. For example, the liability conditions of the homeowners policy include the following:

> **Severability of Insurance.** This insurance applies separately to each "insured." This condition will not increase our limit of liability for any one "occurrence."

This provision means coverage applies to one insured even if another insured has breached a policy condition. Likewise, coverage applies to each insured separately when a claim is brought against two or more insureds, but the insurer's total liability under the policy is not multiplied when a claim is made against more than one insured. This particular provision also means that coverage is not barred when one insured makes a liability claim against another insured—however, intrafamily suits are precluded in the homeowners policy by an exclusion.

Essentially the same situation is addressed in the commercial general liability policy provision titled "Separation of Insureds":

Separation Of Insureds

Except with respect to the Limits of Insurance, and any rights or duties specifically assigned to the first Named Insured, this insurance applies:

a. As if each Named Insured were the only Named Insured; and
b. Separately to each insured against whom claim is made or "suit" is brought.

The severability of interests (also called separation of insureds) provision in a liability insurance policy also means that each insured is entitled to a separate defense where the situation warrants.

Concealment, Misrepresentation, Fraud by One Insured. Concealment, material misrepresentation, or fraud by the insured may be sufficient legal grounds to render the insurance contract legally unenforceable under general contract law, even in the absence of any specific provisions in the contract. However, questions might be raised concerning whether or not the entire policy is voided, and whether one insured's fraud can result in no coverage for all insureds. Although many policies address these issues, the answers are by no means consistent, even among ISO forms.

Some policies contain a provision as strong as the following provision in the commercial property conditions:

CONCEALMENT, MISREPRESENTATION OR FRAUD

This Coverage Part is void in any case of fraud by you as it relates to this Coverage Part at any time. It is also void if you or any other insured, at any time, intentionally conceal or misrepresent a material fact concerning:

1. This Coverage Part;
2. The Covered Property;
3. Your interest in the Covered Property; or
4. A claim under this Coverage Part.

This particular provision voids coverage under that particular coverage part for concealment or misrepresentation by not only the named insured ("you"), but also by any other insured. It is applicable to fraud concerning this coverage part at any time, including intentional concealment or misrepresentation in connection with a claim. The ISO crime forms do not include any similar provision, partly because employee dishonesty insurance provides coverage for circumstances involving fraudulent acts.

The commercial general liability coverage form does not contain an explicit concealment, misrepresentation, or fraud condition but accomplishes somewhat the same effect with the following condition:

Representations

By accepting this policy, you agree:
a. The statements in the Declarations are accurate and complete;
b. Those statements are based upon representations you made to us; and
c. We have issued this policy in reliance upon your representations.

Note that this particular provision relates only to statements made by the named insured in applying for insurance. It has nothing whatsoever to do with statements made in connection with the claims process.

Other policies contain a variety of conditions relating to concealment, misrepresentation, or fraud. When the need arises, it can be necessary to carefully examine each applicable coverage form to determine the effect on the various parties to the transaction.

Actions of Parties Beyond Insured's Control. Depending on specific policy provisions, coverage may be voided if policy conditions are breached by actions of an insured. What happens if the actions of another party, not operating under the direction of an insured, lead to a breach of policy conditions?

The relevant provision in the ISO commercial property conditions form is typical:

CONTROL OF PROPERTY

Any act or neglect of any person other than you beyond your direction or control will not affect this insurance. . . .

The second half of this provision, not quoted above, addresses a somewhat separate issue related to breaches at separate locations and will be discussed shortly.

This provision addresses acts of persons other than the named insured ("you") and beyond the control of the named insured, persons who may or may not also be insureds. In short, the *named* insured's coverage is not affected by actions of people whom the named insured cannot direct or control.

Breach of Condition at One Location. The concept addressed here parallels the "separation of interests" issue, except that what is concerned here is separation of locations or properties rather than separation of insureds. The relevant question is this: If a policy condition is breached at one location, is coverage at other locations affected? For example, if a sprinkler system is not operational in a firm's warehouse, does the breach affect coverage for a fire in the firm's office building? (The conditions that may create these breaches are discussed later in this chapter.)

Because the insured has failed to meet all duties, one could argue that a policy should become voidable if a condition is breached at any location. However, it is not quite that simple. Often several exposures insured under the same policy could instead have been insured under different policies—with little or no difference in premium, but a single policy is more convenient. If different policies were used, a breach of one policy's condition would have no effect on the validity of a separate contract. It could be argued that insureds should not be penalized for covering separate exposures in the same policy. And that is how most insurance policies resolve the question.

A typical provision addressing this issue is found in the second half of the "Control of Property" provision of the ISO commercial property conditions form, which has already been quoted in part.

> The breach of any condition of this Coverage Part at any one or more locations will not affect coverage at any location where, at the time of loss or damage, the breach of condition does not exist.

This provision makes it clear that the breach of a policy condition at one location does not affect coverage for a loss at another location.

POLICY PERIOD AND TERRITORY

An insurance policy needs to specify when something must happen to trigger coverage, as well as what it is that must happen and where. The "when" is addressed in part by provisions relating to the policy period, the "where" by the policy territory. The discussion here centers on the ways in which policy periods and policy territories are defined; the nature of the triggering event is examined only briefly, with thorough treatment reserved for Chapter 5.

Policy Period

An insurance policy's coverage usually applies during a specified period of time. For example, a trip transit policy (covering property in transit during a single trip) may have a one-day policy period, personal auto policies tend to have a three- or six-month policy period, and some policies may be issued for a three-year period. Crop-hail insurance policies include an expiration date relating to the time when a particular crop normally is harvested. Some property and liability policies are even "continuous until canceled," which may mean that the same policy remains in force for a decade or longer.

Sometimes a policy is issued for an odd period of time, such as eight months, so that it will expire on the same date as other policies. This is not uncommon when a new coverage is added. For example, a firm might purchase crime coverage in May, with an expiration date in October when the rest of the firm's policies expire; all policies will probably be renewed in October for another year.

It is not enough to state the date when the policy period begins; the precise time must also be specified. In the past, it was common for liability insurance to take effect at midnight (or, more precisely, 12:01 A.M.). At the time, most property insurance took effect at noon. In part this anomaly resulted from the lack of coordination or cooperation between property insurance companies and casualty insurance companies. However, there also was some logic in this apparent inconsistency: It is much more likely that some liability-creating incident would happen in the middle of the day than at midnight when most people are asleep. If coverage were to begin at noon, it would occasionally be necessary to ask whether the incident happened in the morning (before the policy period began) or in the afternoon, and the answer would not always be clear. On the other hand, it is most likely that people will be around during the daylight hours to pinpoint the time of a fire or some other property-damaging peril, while a fire or other property-damaging peril beginning at any time after the business is closed for the day might not be detected until the next morning.

Today, many insurance policies are package policies providing both property and liability coverage, and it is desirable that the entire policy begin at the same time. Most property, liability, and other policies now begin and expire at 12:01 A.M. of the stated dates, one minute after midnight. That odd minute eliminates any uncertainty as to whether 12:00 A.M. might mean noon or midnight, or whether "midnight" means the midnight with which the specified date begins or the one with which it ends.

Sometimes a policy expiring at noon (which does not fall between dates) is replaced with one beginning at 12:01 A.M., or vice versa. When this seems likely, the replacing policy may contain a specific provision that either eliminates coverage for the twelve hours before the old coverage expires or else picks up the extra half-day's coverage. The 1983 businessowners amendatory endorsement, for example, included the following provision:

TIME OF INCEPTION

To the extent that coverage in this policy replaces coverage in other policies terminating noon standard time on the inception date of this policy, coverage under this policy shall not become effective until such other coverage has terminated.

Still, it is possible that a twelve-hour coverage gap could exist if the people involved in replacing one policy with another have not paid adequate attention to this seemingly minor detail.

What must happen during the policy period to trigger coverage? The answer varies between property and liability insurance and also among policies of each type.

Property Insurance Triggers. A property insurance policy necessarily contains one or more provisions clarifying the trigger of coverage. A typical example appears in the ISO commercial property conditions:

Under this Coverage Part:
1. We cover loss or damage commencing:
   a. During the policy period shown in the Declarations; and
   b. Within the coverage territory.

The General Rule. As a general rule, property insurance applies to losses commencing during the policy period. The single word "commencing" can be important when a loss occurs close to the time when the policy begins or expires. Suppose that a fire begins at 11 P.M. and continues to burn until 1 A.M., and that Policy A expires at 12:01 A.M. when Policy B becomes effective. Which policy applies? Or do both apply—one to the damage before 12:01 and the other to the rest of the damage (which would be very difficult to distinguish)? The entire loss is covered by Policy A, because it "commenced" during A's policy period.

The same would be true of a fire beginning at 11:59 P.M., just before the policy's expiration, and smoldering for a week—the policy in effect when the fire commences provides the coverage. This provision is especially significant for time element losses, which may continue for many months after they "commence." For example, an insurer may continue to pay business income losses for months after a business income policy expires, so long as the loss-producing event began during the policy period.

Exceptions to the General Rule. Some property insurance policies depart from this general rule for reasons relating to the type of coverage they provide. For example, a builders risk policy (covering a building under construction) terminates *before* the stated expiration date under certain circumstances that indicate construction is completed, such as when the building is occupied in whole or in part. Similarly, a crop-hail insurance policy expires when the crop is harvested.

Crime insurance presents a special situation that leads to an additional condition. Because employee dishonesty and some other crime losses often are not discovered immediately, some policies provide coverage for losses that occur during the policy period and are discovered within some specified period—often one year—after the end of the policy period. Losses discovered later are not necessarily without coverage—policies typically cover employee dishonesty losses occurring during prior policy periods but discovered during the current policy period (with appropriate provisions to prevent duplicate coverage).

Liability Insurance Triggers. Some liability insurance policies, such as the personal auto policy, deal with situations in which it is relatively easy to determine the time of the loss that triggers coverage. While occasionally it is unclear whether it took place before or after midnight, the time of an auto accident seldom becomes an issue. A condition in the personal auto policy states:

> This policy applies only to accidents and losses which occur . . . during the policy period.

With other types of liability insurance, especially those providing products liability coverage, it often is difficult to define the nature and time of the event that "triggers" coverage. Many liability policies have referred to bodily injury or property damage that occurs during the policy period, but countless hours have been spent in determining what that means. For example, when a person is exposed to a harmful substance over a period of time, does an occurrence take place at the time of the first exposure? At the time the harm is first manifest? During the entire period of time between the initial exposure and the manifestation?

Some insurance policies have addressed this problem by triggering coverage when a claim is first made, rather than by the occurrence of the loss-causing event. However, the claims-made approach can become even more complicated. The subject of liability triggers will be explored in more detail in Chapter 5 in the context of covered events.

Coverage Territory

The usual situation involves property located within the United States, in which case there is no particular reason to ponder the question of policy territories. However, the provision can take on special significance. It can be critical, for example, when covered property happens to be on a vehicle that has crossed the border into Mexico or Canada, or when covered property is in the possession of a person traveling abroad.

A typical policy provision is found in the commercial property common conditions form.

The coverage territory is:

a. The United States of America (including its territories and possessions);

b. Puerto Rico; and

c. Canada.

Only rarely would this provision become relevant, as the "commercial property" coverage applies almost entirely to property at fixed locations described in the declarations.

The commercial general liability coverage form, which often is a part of the same policy, includes a different provision within its definitions section.

"Coverage territory" means:

a. The United States of America (including its territories and possessions), Puerto Rico and Canada;

b. International waters or airspace, provided the injury or damage does not occur in the course of travel or transportation to or from any place not included in a. above; or

c. All parts of the world if:

(1) The injury or damage arises out of:

(a) Goods or products made or sold by you in the territory described in a. above; or

(b) The activities of a person whose home is in the territory described in a. above, but is away for a short time on your business; and

(2) The insured's responsibility to pay damages is determined in a "suit" on the merits, in the territory described in a. above or in a settlement we agree to.

Most of the implications of these provisions are beyond the scope of this course, but it is obvious that coverage, at least to some extent, can apply on a worldwide basis.

Some of the questions that might be relevant in connection with coverage territories include whether coverage applies to the following:

● Property in Hawaii or Alaska, away from the "continental United States"

● Property in transit between locations where coverage clearly applies

● Property in Puerto Rico or other U.S. territories or possessions (e.g., Guam, the Virgin Islands)

● Property or occurrences in or over Canada or Mexico, countries adjacent to the United States

Coverage territories describe broad geographical borders beyond which coverage does not apply. Other provisions within a given policy can be much more restrictive. Real property, for example, may be covered only at the address specified in the policy declarations; long-haul trucking exposures may be covered only within a described radius of operations.

It is important to consider *before* a loss whether coverage applies everywhere that there are exposures. And after a loss, it is relevant to consider whether the insured event involved a covered location.

Conformity With Statutes. An insurance policy provision is not enforceable if it conflicts with the applicable law of the state. Some policies contain an explicit provision addressing that point, such as the following provision from the AAIS inland marine general terms.

> **Conformity with Statutes** The terms of this Inland Marine coverage in conflict with statutes of the state where the policy is issued are changed to conform to those statutes.

While a conflict could occur with any policy, problems are more likely with some coverages—especially those dealing with exposures involving significant variations among state laws or foreseeable changes in state laws. Questions can arise as to whether such a conflict voids an entire policy or only that portion of the policy that is in conflict with the law. The following provision appears in a directors and officers liability policy.

> **Conformance to Statute**
>
> Terms of this policy which are in conflict with the statutes of those states wherein certain provisions and coverages included under this policy are not permitted are hereby amended to cover only those provisions and coverages as apply and conform to such statutes.

Extraterritorial Coverage. Some policies provide coverage for an insured located primarily in one state that may face covered exposures in other states. Where this is foreseen and the exposure may vary by state, the policy may contain a provision saying, in effect, that the policy provides the coverage required by that state's law. For example, the liability coverage of the personal auto policy contains the following provision:

> **OUT OF STATE COVERAGE**
>
> If an auto accident to which this policy applies occurs in any state or province other than the one in which "your covered auto" is principally garaged, we will interpret your policy for that accident as follows:
> A. If the state or province has:
>   1. A financial responsibility or similar law specifying limits of liability for "bodily injury" or "property damage" higher than the limit shown in the Declarations, your policy will provide the higher specified limit.
>   2. A compulsory insurance or similar law requiring a nonresident to maintain insurance whenever the nonresident uses a vehicle in that state or province, your policy will provide at least the required minimum amounts and types of coverage.

This relatively obscure provision can provide a significant amount of coverage under certain circumstances. Similar provisions are not found in all auto insurance policies, and their absence might be noteworthy for the insured who purchases minimum limits of liability coverage.

PROVISIONS MAINTAINING COVERAGE

A number of policy provisions relate, in a broad sense, to the continuation of coverage rather than to specific applications of coverage or to loss-adjusting matters.

Payment of Premium

A legally enforceable contract requires "consideration" by both parties, and the "consideration" of the insured is the payment of premium—or the promise to pay the premium. Reflecting this principle, many policies and endorsements contain wording to the effect that coverage is granted in consideration of the premium. This wording also implies that coverage does not exist if the premium is not paid. For example, the workers compensation and employers liability insurance policy begins with the following:

> In return for the payment of the premium and subject to all terms of this policy, we agree with you as follows.

Many policies have no further condition relating to premium payments. However, many also include additional provisions relating to the calculation of the premium. For example, policy provisions may clarify how premiums are determined and whether they may be changed while the policy is in force. Also, the initial premium for many insurance policies is based on an estimate of the exposures expected to develop during the policy period, and the final premium will be readjusted when the actual exposures are known after the policy period has ended. At that time an additional premium may be charged, or a refund may be made by the insurer, after examining (auditing) the insured's records.

Because the businessowners policy encompasses a variety of coverages, the *premiums provision* in the ISO businessowners common policy conditions illustrates many of the provisions sometimes found in other policies.

PREMIUMS

1. The first Named Insured shown in the Declarations:
   a. Is responsible for the payment of all premiums; and
   b. Will be the payee for any return premiums we pay.

2. The premium shown in the Declarations was computed based on rates in effect at the time the policy was issued. On each renewal, continuation or anniversary of the effective date of this policy, we will compute the premium in accordance with our rates and rules then in effect.

3. With our consent, you may continue this policy in force by paying a continuation premium for each successive one-year period. The premium must be:

   a. Paid to us prior to the anniversary date; and
   b. Determined in accordance with paragraph 2. above.

   Our forms then in effect will apply. If you do not pay the continuation premium, this policy will expire on the first anniversary date that we have not received the premium.

4. Undeclared exposures or change in your business operation, acquisition or use of locations may occur during the policy period that are not shown in the Declarations. If so, we may require an additional premium. If so, that premium will be determined in accordance with our rates and rules then in effect.

This particular provision not only requires that premiums be paid, but it also indicates who is responsible for handling premiums (the first named insured) and renewal options. Since insurers frequently revise their rates and periodically revise policy forms, the provision also deals with the premium changes that can occur when the insurer's premiums or forms change (rates and forms in effect at the time of the renewal or continuation apply). Since insureds often engage in new activities (such as adding a repair department to a store) or acquire additional property (such as adding an addition to a store), the provision also explains what happens when the insured's exposures change (an additional premium may be required, in accordance with the insurer's rules and rates in effect at the time of the change).

Provisions of this type obviously vary depending on the coverage involved, and they are examined in other CPCU courses, where applicable, in the context of specific policies.

Examination of Books and Records

Premiums for commercial insurance policies are often based on the dollar amount of annual payroll, annual sales, or goods in stock, which are recorded in the insured's financial records. Premium auditors, employed or retained by insurance companies, audit these records to determine the proper premium to charge. A policy provision is necessary to clarify the insured's duty to permit a premium auditor to perform.

For these reasons, insurance policies covering business operations often include a provision similar to the following provision in the ISO common policy conditions:

C. EXAMINATION OF YOUR BOOKS AND RECORDS

We may examine and audit your books and records as they relate to this policy at any time during the policy period and up to three years afterward.

Some policies include only a one-year time period.

Workers compensation insurance premiums are based on payroll figures, and the workers compensation and employers liability insurance policy includes two separate provisions.

F. Records

You will keep records of information needed to compute premium. You will provide us with copies of those records when we ask for them.

G. Audit

You will let us examine and audit all your records that relate to this policy. These records include ledgers, journals, registers, vouchers, contracts, tax reports, payroll and disbursement records, and programs for storing and retrieving data. We may conduct the audits during regular business hours during the policy period and within three years after the policy period ends. Information developed by audit will be used to determine final premium. Insurance rate service organizations have the same rights we have under this provision.

("Insurance rate service organizations" refers to organizations such as the National Council on Compensation Insurance, an advisory organization that compiles premium and loss data for use by insurers writing workers compensation insurance.)

An *insurance premium audit* is a methodical examination of an insured's operations, records, and books of account to determine the actual insurance exposure for the coverages provided, and it concludes with a precise report of the findings.[1] The primary reason for a premium audit is to verify the information necessary to compute the actual earned premium for the policy period. In addition, audits may be necessary to meet regulatory requirements. Premium audits also serve to encourage honesty on the part of some insureds who might be tempted to reduce their premiums by presenting false or misleading information to the insurer.

Audit provisions simply assure that the insurer has access to the information needed to fulfill its role under the insurance contract. However, insureds who are unaware of those provisions or the reason for them sometimes are puzzled when an insurance representative expects to scrutinize financial records—including sales or payroll information that can be highly confidential. Misunderstandings are reduced when producers prepare their insureds to expect audits and remind them of their insurers' contractual rights.

Audit provisions obviously relate only to policies for which the premium is based on an auditable exposure. Audit provisions are not necessary in personal auto policies, homeowners policies, or policies covering fixed-location property for a fixed amount.

The provisions discussed above deal primarily with access to the information necessary to compute a premium. Other provisions in many policies require the insured to maintain books and records adequate to establish the value of covered property at the time of a loss and to make these available to the insurer when necessary.

Cancellation

Cancellation is a specific action, taken by the insurer or the insured, to discontinue coverage that otherwise would continue until the end of the policy term. Cancellation must be distinguished from several closely related terms that are sometimes used interchangeably, but inaccurately, by lay persons:

- *Expiration*—the end of the policy term, at which time the policy *expires*, unless action has been taken to *renew* it (extend coverage for another term).
- *Nonrenewal*—a specific action by the insurance company to not make future coverage available when the current policy expires, rather than routinely renewing the policy for another period. Sometimes the term is also used to refer to an insured's decision not to continue coverage with the insurer for an additional policy period.
- *Termination*—bringing coverage to an end by cancellation, expiration, or nonrenewal.

A policy typically expires, is renewed, or is nonrenewed on its *anniversary* date, which is the specific day and month that it initially became effective. The anniversary date (which is yearless, e.g., "April 11") remains the same, while inception and expiration dates change with changes in the years (e.g., April 11, 1992). Policies with terms extending beyond one year may provide for termination or recalculation of premium at each anniversary.

It is the usual practice to keep a property-liability insurance policy in force until it expires and, when changing insurers, to change only on an expiration date, commonly known as an "x-date." In most cases, a policyholder can discontinue future coverage simply by not paying a premium to renew a policy when it expires. Generally, but not always, an insurer also can avoid future coverage by electing not to renew the policy, although some type of advance written nonrenewal notice to the insured may be required by law or by contract.

While it is *customary* to change insurers or to drop specific policies or coverages only at a policy's anniversary, it generally is *possible* to cancel a policy midterm. Therefore it is necessary for insurance policies to include provisions indicating whether, when, or under what circumstances the policy may be canceled, who has the right to initiate the cancellation, how much advance notice is required, what procedures must be followed, and how any necessary premium charges or refunds will be determined. These matters are generally addressed in a *cancellation provision*.

Cancellation by the Insured. Usually, the insured can cancel the policy at any time by following certain procedures. In many commercial policies, the cancellation must be handled by the first named insured. Normally, cancellation may be accomplished by returning the policy itself to the insurer or by providing the insurer with *advance, written* notice of the date when the policy is to be canceled.

Advance notice prevents a problem that might develop if retroactive notice of cancellation were permitted. An insured might otherwise request a backdated cancellation after surviving a period with no loss. Yet, if a loss had occurred during that period, the insurer would have been obligated to cover it. By having it both ways, the insured could have the equivalent of free insurance.

Advance notice is not always required, and retroactive cancellation requests sometimes are honored. If requested, an insurer might be willing to cancel coverage as of a specific past date if the insured had obtained other insurance effective on that date or if the exposure no longer existed as of that date. However, many policies provide *some* coverage even after the major exposure ceases to exist. Therefore, unless a specific policy provision addresses the issue, a judgment call is necessary when an insurer accepts or refuses a retroactive cancellation request. For example, an insurer might be requested to discontinue auto physical damage coverage on a particular car as of a certain recent date when the insured sold the vehicle. This request is logical, because the main exposure no longer exists. However, the insurer might have a sound basis for refusing to cancel retroactively. Even though the described vehicle was sold, the insured still had coverage for potential physical damage claims involving other vehicles. Auto physical damage insurance often provides coverage for physical damage to nonowned and newly acquired autos, as well as the one listed in the policy. Other policies also provide coverage for newly acquired or incidental exposures.

Once the insured has physically returned a policy to the insurer, it is not likely that the insured will attempt to make a claim for coverage under that discontinued policy, and it is highly unlikely that the claim could be enforced by the former policyholder. (This is not to say that an insurance policy operates like a "claim check." Failure to possess a policy does not normally make it impossible to enforce a claim, and in-force policies are not always in the possession of the insured.)

Written notice eliminates possible disputes over the terms of an oral agreement to cancel coverage. If faced with a loss that would otherwise have been covered, an insured might be all too willing to "forget" an undocumented oral cancellation request. The written notice requirement also makes it less likely that the insurer will make an error in canceling a policy, and its documentation of the insured's intent helps the insurer correct any errors.

Evidence of Insurance to Outside Parties. In some situations the policyholder has asked an insurance company to provide evidence of insurance to some outside party. In such cases, the insurance company often must notify the outside party of nonrenewal or midterm cancellation. If notice is not given, the insurance company might be obligated to pay a claim even though the policy has been terminated.

- The *standard mortgage clause* in insurance policies covering real property assures that the named mortgage holder will receive a specified number of days of advance notice before any cancellation or nonrenewal takes effect.
- *Certificates of insurance* may have been issued to third parties to assure customers that a given contractor has insurance. Until the insurance company notifies these customers that this insurance has been discontinued, these certificate holders may under some circumstances have a right to enforce coverage.
- *Financial responsibility filings* may be required of certain high-risk drivers; the insurer certifies with the state that the driver is insured. When a financial responsibility filing is in effect, the insurance cannot be canceled—even at the insured's request—until the state has been given adequate advance notice.

Cancellation by the Insurer. Many insurance policies can be canceled during the policy term by the insurer. However, the insurer usually cannot request immediate cancellation. Generally, the insurer is required to notify the necessary parties in writing no later than a specified number of days in advance of the cancellation date. (In many commercial policies, only the first named insured need be notified.) Advance notice is necessary to give the insured enough time to obtain replacement coverage or otherwise to deal with a previously insured exposure. A named mortgagee also is entitled to advance notice of the cancellation.

Many policies prohibit the insurer from canceling once a policy is in force, except for certain specified reasons, such as nonpayment of a premium. Some policies reduce the number of days' advance notice required when cancellation is for nonpayment.

Commercial property insurance forms in many states include a mandatory *cancellation changes endorsement* that grants the insurer permission to cancel coverage with only five days' notice to the first named insured for the following five reasons, as spelled out in more detail in the endorsement:

- Vacancy or unoccupancy beyond sixty days
- Damage for which permanent repairs have not been initiated within thirty days after initial payment of a covered loss
- Condemnation of the insured building
- Removal of fixtures and other salvageable building items
- Failure to furnish utilities for more than thirty days or pay property taxes for more than one year

A building with one or more of these characteristics may well have reached the end of its productive life. Any of these conditions indicates a potential moral hazard and a building that may soon succumb to arson. Upon becoming aware of such conditions, the insurer may reunderwrite the account. A decision might be made to continue coverage, but the insurer also has the right to cancel the policy with fewer days of advance notice than would normally be required.

Many state laws impose restrictions on cancellation or nonrenewal by the insurer—usually specifying the minimum number of days' advance notice or limiting the reasons for termination. When the statutory restriction is stricter than the provision in the basic contract, the additional restrictions often are reflected in a policy endorsement designed for use in a specific state. If not, the insurer still must comply with the law. However, explicit contract provisions help to ensure not only that the policyholder is aware of its rights but also that the insurer will not overlook its obligations.

When contract provisions specify advance notice longer than the minimum period required by law, the insurer is bound by the stricter terms of the contract. If the policy says the insurer must give at least forty-five days' advance notice and the state law requires at least thirty, the insurer must give at least forty-five days' advance notice of cancellation.

Insurers' cancellation and nonrenewal rights sometimes are restricted by legislators and regulators who think they are helping to assure the continued availability of insurance. However, when it becomes difficult for insurers to cancel their policies, the insurers inevitably become even more cautious in underwriting and accepting these policies in the first place. Thus, cancellation restrictions intended to improve insurance availability often have the opposite effect.

Premium Refunds on Canceled Policies. When a policy is canceled before its normal expiration date, the premium for the entire policy period usually has not been earned by the insurer. Only a portion, reflecting the time the policy was in force, has been earned. Assuming an advance premium was paid, the insured is entitled to a refund of any unearned premium. (In many commercial policies, the refund is made to the first named insured.) How the unearned premium is calculated may depend on who initiated the cancellation or the reason for the cancellation.

- If the policy is canceled by the *insurer*, the return premium is calculated on a *pro rata* basis. For example, if a one-year policy is canceled by the insurer and the cancellation is effective exactly six months after the policy's inception date, the insurer will return exactly 6/12, or 50 percent, of the premium to the insured.
- If the policy is canceled by the *insured*, the return premium in some policies is calculated on a *short-rate* basis, as stated in the policy's cancellation provision.

When a policy is canceled on a short-rate basis, the insurer keeps an extra portion of the premium, typically by returning only 90 percent of the unearned premium. The insured forfeits what is called a *short-rate penalty*. This cancellation penalty helps to reimburse the insurer's expenses. Remember, the insurer has incurred expenses in issuing a policy that it expected to be in force for the entire policy term; the insurer's initial expenses were to be covered with a portion of the premium that would be earned over the entire policy term. The short-rate penalty exists because the expenses of issuing the policy have still been incurred even when the premium for the entire term is not collected.

As noted earlier, policyholders typically do not change insurers while their current policies are in force; most such changes are made on an anniversary date.

It would not be fair to penalize the insured, by assessing a short-rate penalty, when *the insurance company* initiates the cancellation. That is why cancellation by the insurance company is almost always on a pro rata basis. There also has been a trend toward eliminating the short-rate penalty for cancellations initiated by the insured.

Cancellation Provisions. The cancellation provision in the ISO common policy conditions reflects the concepts described above.

CANCELLATION

1. The first Named Insured shown in the Declarations may cancel this policy by mailing or delivering to us advance written notice of cancellation.
2. We may cancel this policy by mailing or delivering to the first Named Insured written notice of cancellation at least:

  a. 10 days before the effective date of cancellation if we cancel for nonpayment of premium; or
  b. 30 days before the effective date of cancellation if we cancel for any other reason.
 3. We will mail or deliver our notice to the first Named Insured's last mailing address known to us.
 4. Notice of cancellation will state the effective date of cancellation. The policy period will end on that date.
 5. If this policy is canceled, we will send the first Named Insured any premium refund due. If we cancel, the refund will be pro rata. If the first Named Insured cancels, the refund may be less than pro rata. The cancellation will be effective even if we have not made or offered a refund.
 6. If notice is mailed, proof of mailing will be sufficient proof of notice.

Restrictions on Cancellation. Many insurance contracts limit insurers' cancellation rights to certain times or reasons. An example of such restrictions is found in the following portion of the "Termination" provision of the personal auto policy. This provision also imposes some constraints on any decision by the insurer not to renew the policy.

TERMINATION
A. Cancellation. . . .
 3. After this policy is in effect for 60 days, or if this is a renewal or continuation policy, we will cancel only:
  a. for nonpayment of premium; or
  b. if your driver's license or that of:
   (1) any driver who lives with you; or
   (2) any driver who customarily uses "your covered auto;"
   has been suspended or revoked. This must have occurred:
   (1) during the policy period; or
   (2) since the last anniversary of the original effective date if the policy period is other than 1 year; or
  c. if the policy was obtained through material misrepresentation.

B. Nonrenewal. If we decide not to renew or continue this policy, we will mail notice to the named insured shown in the Declarations at the address shown in this policy. Notice will be mailed at least 20 days before the end of the policy period. If the policy period is other than 1 year, we will have the right not to renew or continue it only at each anniversary of its original effective date.

According to these policy provisions, after sixty days the insurer can cancel a policy only for certain rather specific reasons. And the insurer is obligated to renew the policy unless notice of intent not to renew is made at least twenty days before the renewal date. However, an "Automatic Termination" provision not quoted above adds that the policy automatically terminates at the end of the current policy period if the insured does not, by paying the premium when due, accept the insurer's offer to renew or continue coverage.

These provisions in the standard personal auto policy are modified by an even more restrictive endorsement that is mandatory in some states; these restrictions make it more difficult for insurers to cancel coverage. On the other hand, some states may make it more difficult for policyholders to cancel coverage so as to make it easier to enforce compulsory insurance laws.

The personal auto policy has been used to illustrate restrictions on cancellation and nonrenewal. Other policies may contain somewhat different restrictions, possibly with different numbers of days' notice, depending on the nature of the coverage. For example, the ISO home-owners policy permits the insurer to cancel a policy that has been in effect for more than sixty days "if the risk has changed substantially."

Exceptions to the General Practice. Some policies cover expo-sures during a relatively limited time period; these policies may not lend themselves to a midterm cancellation with a premium refund. For example, the insured may cancel a standard flood insurance policy at any time, but a premium refund is available only if the policy is canceled because the insured sold the property or for certain other limited rea-sons. Otherwise, people might purchase a flood policy when a severe storm is forecast and cancel it when the major threat of loss has passed. Premiums are established on the assumption that people will pay an entire year's premium, even though some seasons are more threatening than others.

For similar reasons, midterm cancellation with a return of premium often is restricted on earthquake insurance, insurance covering growing crops, policies covering property during a specific trip, and other policies covering special events of a limited duration.

In some cases, the insurer who chooses to cancel a policy is obligated to make available some run-off coverage. For example, if an insurer cancels a claims-made liability insurance policy, which covers claims made during the policy period, the insurer may be obligated to make insurance available for claims made after the cancellation date because of events before the cancellation date. Also, the cancellation clauses of ocean marine insurance policies usually indicate that cancellation does not affect any exposure on which insurance has already attached prior to the effective date of the notice. This means that property already at sea or otherwise under the policy's protection is covered until it is deliv-ered to the point where insurance would otherwise terminate.

To enforce compulsory auto insurance laws, it has been suggested in some states that insurance companies issue a windshield sticker for the time period for which premiums have been paid. When and if such a law takes place, it probably will be accompanied with a stipulation that the car owner not be permitted to cancel his or her auto insurance while the sticker is in effect.

Policy Modifications

While a policy is in effect, either the insured or the insurance company may take some actions that modify the contract, a situation addressed by the changes provision. Insurer actions that modify coverage include not only endorsements to the existing contract issued to a policyholder, but also changes to other similar policies currently being sold to other policyholders, as explained in connection with the liberalization clause.

Changes. Many insurance policies contain a changes provision that specifically authorizes policy changes. Perhaps the most significant part of the provision is not that it permits changes, but that it limits them. The changes provision of the ISO common policy conditions reads as follows:

CHANGES

This policy contains all the agreements between you and us concerning the insurance afforded. The first Named Insured shown in the Declarations is authorized to make changes in the terms of this policy with our consent. This policy's terms can be amended or waived only by endorsement issued by us and made a part of this policy.

The insured (or, in this case, the first named insured) may request a policy change. If the insurer agrees, the change will be made. But no change is effective unless it is indicated in an endorsement to the policy. In other words, oral agreements to modify coverage are not permitted by the contract.

In practice, however, court decisions have held that the insurer can waive such "entire contract" provisions either orally or in writing, and it is accepted practice for an insurance representative to orally bind expansions of coverage just as the representative may orally bind coverage under an additional policy. In effect, the insurer may intentionally or unintentionally waive the contractual provision stating that policy terms may not be waived without an endorsement. Waivers are discussed more extensively in Chapter 9.

Liberalization. What happens when an insurer introduces a revised policy form that is somewhat broader than the insured's policy? This question is answered in the liberalization clause.

Some policies, such as the personal auto policy, include a liberalization clause within the changes provision. Others contain a separate liberalization clause, such as the following clause in the AAIS inland marine general terms.

Liberalization. If a revision of a form or endorsement which would broaden coverage without an additional premium is adopted during this policy period, or within 6 months before Inland Marine coverage is effective, the broadened coverage will apply.

The insured automatically receives the benefit of such broadened coverage.

This provision obviously is equitable because it gives existing insureds the same broadened coverage now offered to new insureds. However, the liberalization clause is not entirely for the benefit of the insured. If policies did not automatically provide the broadened coverage, insurers would be swamped with requests that policies be endorsed, or that they be canceled and reissued, whenever coverage is improved. Automatically providing this coverage is the more practical approach, and it eliminates considerable administrative hassle.

The building and personal property coverage form illustrates the effect of the liberalization clause. The specific wording of a vehicles exclusion in the first edition of that form inadvertently eliminated coverage that would otherwise apply to insureds' forklift trucks used to move stock in a warehouse. A revision to the form restored the coverage. As soon as an insurer adopted the revised form, insureds with an earlier version of the form also had forklift coverage because of the liberalization clause, even though they did not have coverage through other provisions of the contract.

Some liberalization clauses distinguish between policy revisions and revised policy editions, and they make it clear that the liberalization clause does not apply to new editions. Typically, a new edition of a policy contains some provisions that broaden coverage and others that restrict it. Insurers consider it unfair to give policyholders the best of both worlds—their choice of the broader provisions of either the existing policy or the replacement policy—at no additional premium.

Inspections and Surveys

Many insurance companies employ *loss control representatives* to inspect the premises and operations of businesses that apply for insurance. While the policy is in force, loss control representatives may make inspections and surveys, give reports to the insured, and recommend safety-related changes. Typical recommendations might be that warehouse fire extinguishers be of a proper type and capacity, or that construction workers wear hard hats.

The inspections and surveys provision makes it clear that the insurance company has the right to make such inspections and surveys. The condition also states that these are not safety inspections, that the insurance company does not take on the responsibility of protecting workers or the public from injury, and that the insurance company does not warrant that the business it inspected is safe or healthful or complies with applicable laws. This disclaimer is included because certain courts have held insurers liable for losses supposedly related to the inadequacy of such inspections.

The inspections and surveys condition in the ISO common policy conditions reads as follows:

D. INSPECTIONS AND SURVEYS

We have the right but are not obligated to:
1. Make inspections and surveys at any time;
2. Give you reports on the conditions we find; and
3. Recommend changes.

Any inspections, surveys, reports or recommendations relate only to insurability and the premiums to be charged. We do not make safety inspections. We do not undertake to perform the duty of any person or organization to provide for the health or safety of workers or the public. And we do not warrant that conditions:
1. Are safe or healthful; or
2. Comply with laws, regulations, codes or standards.

This condition applies not only to us, but also to any rating, advisory, rate service or similar organization which makes insurance inspections, surveys, reports or recommendations.

The final sentence gives not only the insurer, but also various rating and advisory organizations, the inspection right. An ISO subsidiary, Commercial Risk Services, Inc. (CRS), conducts property rating surveys on commercial and residential properties to help insurers evaluate expected loss costs for those buildings. This policy provision includes the CRS field rating representative under the protection of the disclaimer.

CRS and other organizations also provide loss control services to insurers for a fee. These organizations also must be permitted to make inspections and surveys, according to policy terms.

Even though they are performed primarily for the insurer's benefit, an insurer's inspections, along with any resulting recommendations, can be a valuable service to insureds. The insurer is not obligated to conduct inspections. However, many insureds value the assistance of the insurer in preventing losses, and they consider the quality of the insurer's loss control service and expertise an important factor in evaluating the insurer's performance. In fact, with respect to at least one line of commercial insurance—boiler and machinery—the insurer's inspection service may be the overriding reason for purchasing insurance.

While inspection and survey conditions are common in commercial insurance policies, they are uncommon in personal insurance policies. Even though the policy does not include a contractual right to conduct an inspection, in practice insurers may insist on a physical inspection of a dwelling or auto as a condition to approving an application for coverage or to renewing a policy. Of course these activities are not conducted under the terms of the policy but take place to determine whether an application for coverage will be accepted. Statements explicitly authorizing such inspections may appear on an application that the insured is requested to sign.

Suspending or Reducing Coverage

Some policy provisions indicate that coverage is suspended or reduced under certain circumstances.

Conditions Suspending Coverage. Some policy conditions "suspend" (temporarily interrupt) coverage *while* (but not after) a particular hazard exists. The 1943 Standard Fire Policy provided that, barring other provisions in the policy as a whole, the insurer would not be liable for loss occurring while the hazard was "increased by any means within the control or knowledge of the insured; or while a described building . . . is vacant or unoccupied beyond a period of sixty consecutive days." Today, conditions suspending coverage are increasingly rare in property and liability insurance, but they are not extinct. If specified in the policy, upon the existence of certain conditions or hazards, coverage under an otherwise enforceable policy is suspended.

Boiler and Machinery. A clear example is found in the boiler and machinery coverage form:

f. Suspension

Whenever an "object" is found to be in, or exposed to, a dangerous condition, any of our representatives may immediately suspend the insurance against loss from an "accident" to that "object." This can be done by delivering or mailing a written notice of suspension to:
(1) Your last known address; or
(2) The address where the "object" is located.

Once suspended in this way, your insurance can be reinstated only by an endorsement for that "object."

If we suspend your insurance, you will get a pro rata refund of premium for that "object." But the suspension will be effective even if we have not yet made or offered a refund.

Much of the success of boiler and machinery insurance is based, not on payment for losses, but on insurers' ability to prevent losses through boiler inspections. In the unusual case in which a boiler inspector discovers a very hazardous condition, the inspector will request that the boiler or machine be shut down until the condition is corrected. Normally, the insured willingly complies with this request, happy that the inspector has identified a hazardous condition before a serious loss occurs. In those rare situations where an insured is not willing to shut down a hazardous boiler or machine, perhaps because the hazard does not seem serious to the insured, the insurance company representative has the right to immediately suspend coverage. The threat of a suspension usually is enough to convince an insured that immediate action must be taken. If not, coverage can be suspended *immediately*—with no advance notice requirement or delay—so long as the suspension is in writing.

An insured would be hard pressed to force an insurer to pay a claim occurring while coverage was suspended because the insured has refused to correct a hazardous condition—it would be difficult to convince the courts that such a loss was not expected or intended by the insured.

Protective Safeguards. Often, an insurance policy is acceptable to the underwriter only because hazards are reduced by some loss control measure—such as a fire extinguishing system or an alarm system. Or the policy may receive a reduced rate to reflect the decreased hazards associated with some loss control measure. Under such circumstances, it is common to add a *protective safeguards endorsement* that suspends coverage when the protective device is not operative. Rather than relying on a separate endorsement, a protective safeguard provision is included within the preprinted language of some policies dealing with exposures that frequently involve protective safeguards. A typical example appears in the ISO camera and musical instrument dealers coverage form. The relevant part of this provision reads as follows:

PROTECTIVE SAFEGUARDS

You must maintain the protective safeguards stated by you to be in effect at a location when this coverage began.

If you fail to keep the protective safeguards:

a. In working condition at a location; and
b. In operation when you are closed for business;

coverage for which the protective safeguards apply is automatically suspended at that location. This suspension will last until equipment or services are back in operation.

This important provision often is not found in a basic coverage form but in an endorsement that may be added when protective safeguards are present. The experienced insurance professional will anticipate and search for this provision and will evaluate its effect whenever the situation warrants. Specifically, it might be important to determine which protective safeguards are relevant, whether coverage is suspended at one location or all of them when the safeguard is inoperative, and whether or not coverage is automatically reinstated when the safeguard is restored. Provision may also be made for temporary outages or maintenance of a protective system.

Conditions Reducing Coverage. Closely related to conditions that altogether suspend coverage are those reducing coverage in some manner (e.g., by limiting the amount payable) under certain conditions involving an increase in hazard. The vacancy condition of the building and personal property coverage form combines suspension of coverage for certain perils with reduction in coverage for others. The approach taken here is somewhat innovative: It *eliminates* coverage only for the perils most affected by vacancy, and it *reduces* coverage for damage by other perils.

Vacancy

If the building where loss or damage occurs has been vacant for more than 60 consecutive days before that loss or damage, we will:
   a. Not pay for any loss or damage caused by any of the following even if they are Covered Causes of Loss:
      (1) Vandalism;
      (2) Sprinkler leakage, unless you have protected the system from freezing
      (3) Building glass breakage;
      (4) Water damage;
      (5) Theft; or
      (6) Attempted theft.
   b. Reduce the amount we would otherwise pay for the loss or damage by 15%.

A building is vacant when it does not contain enough business personal property to conduct customary operations.

Buildings under construction are not considered vacant.

Vacant buildings present greater hazards for several reasons: They are attractive to vandals and thieves, and they are susceptible to undetected water damage or water damage relating to deterioration. Moreover, losses by any peril might not be detected and addressed in a building that is not in current use.

Conditions suspending or reducing coverage are closely related to some exclusions that exclude coverage while a certain hazard is present. One such exclusion, which has the same general effect as part of the above condition, is located within the freezing peril of the homeowners policy:

This peril does not include loss on the **residence premises** while the dwelling is unoccupied, unless you have used reasonable care to:
   a. maintain heat in the building; or
   b. shut off the water supply and drain the system and appliances of water.

"While" (during the time) the dwelling is unoccupied and preventive measures have not been taken, loss by freezing is not covered. As soon as the residence is occupied again, coverage for loss by freezing resumes.

INSURED'S DUTIES IN THE EVENT OF LOSS

Upon the occurrence of a covered loss—or one that *might* be covered or an incident that *might* lead to a claim, depending on the policy—

the insured incurs certain duties, as specified in the policy. The related contractual provisions are generally treated by the courts as dealing with procedural matters, rather than substantive matters. Substantive matters, such as cause of loss, time of loss, or insurable interest, go to the heart of the contract, and they are strictly enforced by the courts. The courts hesitate to interfere with the insured's basic substantive rights because of a technical error in procedure. Thus, the tendency of the courts is not to require literal compliance, but rather to avoid penalizing the insured if a good faith effort has been made to reasonably comply with a procedural requirement.[2]

Many insurance policies expressly state, in "conditions precedent language," that the insurer is not obligated to pay benefits unless the insured has complied with the policy's notice and claims provisions. Most policies state that the insured cannot sue the insurer to recover under the policy unless the insured has fully complied with the duties stated in the policy. It behooves the insured to avoid disputes over procedural matters by taking steps to fulfill policy conditions relating to the insured's duties in the event of a loss.

In general, the insured has a duty to expeditiously report the loss to the insurance company, to prevent further loss or damage, and to cooperate with the insurance company in evaluating and settling the claim. Specific details vary from one policy to the next, depending in part on the type of coverage. Because liability insurance involves a third-party claimant in addition to the insurer and the insured, policy provisions vary and property insurance and liability insurance will be treated separately here.

Property Insurance

When a loss occurs, the insured has several duties, typically spelled out in a separate set of policy provisions such as the following excerpt from the ISO building and personal property coverage form:

Duties In The Event Of Loss Or Damage

You must see that the following are done in the event of loss or damage to covered property:. . . .

This particular form then lists eight separate duties, some of which are combined under the following headings.

Notify the Police. Some property insurance policies cover events that might be the result of a crime. Obvious examples are crime insurance policies and "all-risks" policies that include coverage for loss by theft. Less obvious are those policies that cover fire damage (arson), vandalism, and pollution-related losses.

The building and personal property coverage form includes the following duty:

[You must]
a. Notify the police if a law may have been broken.

It is not the purpose of insurance to stand in the place of law enforcement. If a crime has been committed, the police should be given a chance to apprehend and prosecute the criminal and prevent future crimes. If the police are made aware of a crime, they may be able to apprehend the lawbreaker. Often, stolen property can be recovered or the lawbreaker can be held accountable to pay for the damage.

This notification provision also helps to prevent fraudulent claims. An insured who files a false theft claim would also be required to file a report with the police. Many people who are willing to file false insurance claims are somewhat more reluctant to file false reports with the police.

Although arson (fire) and vandalism are among the perils covered by most property insurance policies, the "notify the police" provision is absent from some property insurance policies that do not provide coverage against theft. It also is omitted in forms providing employee dishonesty coverage. Many employers prefer to handle fidelity claims quietly without the publicity that results when police are involved.

Notify the Insurer. According to the building and personal property coverage form, the insured must do the following:

[You must]
b. Give us prompt notice of the loss or damage. Include a description of the property involved.
c. As soon as possible, give us a description of how, when and where the loss or damage occurred.

The purpose of notifying the insurer is to allow the insurer to investigate and form an adequate estimate of its liabilities and to enable it to begin investigating the claim promptly. Delay can be prejudicial to the insurer if it prevents prompt investigation and handling. For example, it may become difficult to determine the cause of loss if a significant amount of time has elapsed before the insurer is notified. The specific conditions requiring notice of loss vary according to the type of coverage provided by each property insurance policy.

Most policies require "prompt" notice, or words to that general effect. This does not generally mean notice must be given immediately but rather that notice be given as soon as possible, depending on the circumstances. Whether notice has been given "promptly" enough, or whether it would have been "practicable" to give notice sooner, in any given case can be a question of fact for the courts to decide. Several factors may be relevant in any such case:

- The value of the property involved
- The length of the delay
- The reason for the delay
- Any change of condition during the delay[3]

Also relevant will be the extent, if any, to which the insurer's ability to safeguard its interests was impaired by the delay.

Mitigation of Loss. Common sense dictates that an insured should do what is reasonable to protect damaged property against further loss. In fact, there is a duty to do so. According to one author:

> Where a contract entitles a party to compensation for property loss or damage, such party has a duty *implied in the law* to take all reasonable steps to minimize the damages. If he fails to, the courts will cut down the damage award by the amount which could have been saved through appropriate action to protect and preserve the property at the time of the loss.[4]

Yet, people often are not sure whether they are authorized to tamper with property that will be the subject of an insurance claim or whether such tampering might jeopardize their ability to support the facts of the claim. Perhaps this attitude results from notions relating to "interfering with the scene of the crime," a concept more relevant to criminal investigations.

The mitigation of loss provisions make the insured's obligations fairly explicit. Again, quoting from the building and personal property coverage form:

> [You must]
> d. Take all reasonable steps to protect the Covered Property from further damage by a Covered Cause of Loss. If feasible, set the damaged property aside and in the best possible order for examination. Also keep a record of your expenses for emergency and temporary repairs, for consideration in the settlement of the claim. This will not increase the Limit of Insurance.

The last two sentences address, without completely answering it, the question of whether expenses to mitigate the loss, not authorized in advance, will be reimbursed by the insurer. The answer in this case is, to paraphrase the policy, "They will be considered." This suggests, but does not guarantee, that reasonable expenses will be paid. In practice, reimbursement for reasonable and necessary expenses is seldom an issue. Some nonstandard policy forms include a "loss adjustment" coverage, or some similarly named coverage extension, explicitly covering these expenses up to some stated limit such as $1,000 or $5,000.

The personal auto policy is somewhat more definitive.

> A person seeking coverage . . . must . . . Take reasonable steps after loss to protect "your covered auto" or any "non-owned auto" and their

[*sic*] equipment from further loss. We will pay reasonable expenses incurred to do this.

This provision affirmatively states that the insurer will pay mitigation of loss expenses limited only by the word "reasonable."

(By chance, the above policy excerpt illustrates also a few unrelated points relevant to policy interpretation, the general subject of this volume. The ungrammatical shift from third person ["a person"] to second person [" 'your covered auto' "] is awkward, but it occurs because "your covered auto" is a defined term. The plural pronoun "their," referring to a singular antecedent [" 'your covered auto' or any 'non-owned auto' "] apparently is a grammatical error introduced when the policy was revised. The previous policy edition, which handled non-owned autos differently, referred to " 'your covered auto' and *its* equipment" [italics added]. We certainly are not trying to be overly critical in pointing out mistakes made by those dedicated professionals who painstakingly draft and edit insurance policies; however, in a text dealing with policy interpretation, we do need to point out that insurance policies, like all published material, can be imperfect documents containing typesetting errors, misspellings, confusing or improper syntax, nonstandard punctuation, and other grammatical errors—all of which can present obstacles.)

In practice, mitigation expenses typically *reduce* the amount that would otherwise be payable by the insurer, rather than adding to the insurer's expenses. Suppose, for example, the insured's roof is partially damaged by an insured peril. By buying or renting a tarpaulin and tying it over the damaged roof, the insured is able to prevent rain from causing further covered damage to the building and its contents—damage that might be much more costly than the expense of the tarp. Obviously, the insurer would prefer to pay the lower cost of the tarp rather than paying the greater costs of a subsequent rain damage loss. Even if it does not rain before the tarp is removed and the roof is repaired, the cost of the tarp would normally be reimbursed by the insurer.

This policy provision requires the insured to take reasonable steps. While a tarp would be reasonable in these circumstances, some mitigation-of-loss expenses might not be reasonable under other circumstances. What is reasonable, and therefore covered, in any given case, is a question of fact.

As further examples, policies providing business income coverage typically state that they also cover extra expenses incurred to reduce the loss. Boiler and machinery policies cover "expediting expenses," sometimes to a specified dollar limit, to restore the boiler or machinery to operation. And many policies pay the expenses to recharge fire extinguishers or chemical fire extinguishing systems that discharged while attempting to contain a covered fire.

Cooperation With Insurer. Once the immediate crisis is over and the insurer has been notified of the loss, the insured cannot simply await payment. The insured has a duty to work with the insurer to assess the nature and extent of the loss. The building and personal property coverage form, which is typical of property insurance forms, imposes the following duties.

[You must]
e. At our request, give us complete inventories of the damaged and undamaged property. Include quantities, costs, values and amount of loss claimed.
f. Permit us to inspect the property and records proving the loss or damage. Also permit us to take samples of damaged property for inspection, testing and analysis.
g. If requested, permit us to question you under oath at such times as may be reasonably required about any matter relating to this insurance or your claim, including your books and records. In such event, your answers must be signed.
h. Send us a signed, sworn statement of loss containing the information we request to investigate the claim. You must do this within 60 days after our request. We will supply you with the necessary forms.
i. Cooperate with us in the investigation or settlement of the claim.

Most property insurance policies prescribe similar duties, with variations in the specific duties and their time frame, depending on the nature of the insured property. For example, the personal auto policy specifies that the insurer must be permitted to inspect and appraise the damaged property before its repair or disposal, while the homeowners policy details the information required in a proof of loss but does not include the generic "cooperate with us" requirement.

Examination Under Oath. The insurer has a right to request that any named insured ("you") be examined under oath. Although this right is not often invoked, its availability is very important to insurers, especially in cases of suspected arson, when fraud is suspected, or when the adjuster has otherwise been unable to obtain information about how a loss occurred. Examination under oath also provides an ideal way to support or refute information provided by written records supplied by the person being examined.

Examination under oath may be *demanded* (not "requested") of certain parties at any time by the insurer. In the provision quoted above, the insurer has the right to demand that the named insured ("you") be examined under oath; other policies may vary. The insurer may also *request* that parties other than those specified in this policy condition submit to examination under oath.

Examination under oath may be conducted by a claims adjuster, but it usually is conducted by an attorney chosen by the insurer. The person being examined is sworn in by a court reporter who then records every word said during the examination. The person being examined must answer any question material to the loss; the Fifth Amendment right against self-incrimination, which applies in criminal proceedings, cannot be invoked in this context. After completion of the examination, it is transcribed and sent to the examinee for his or her signature.

A demand for examination under oath usually is not made unless the insurer has reason to be suspicious about some aspect of the claim. If the demand is not complied with, the insurer has grounds for denying the claim.

Proof of Loss. Earlier property insurance policies spelled out in detail the information to be provided in the proof of loss simply referred to in the "duties" quoted above. When "commercial property" policies were simplified, the drafters recognized that, as a practical matter, it was not necessary to provide a detailed questionnaire until loss-adjustment time. Policies were therefore simplified with, "we will supply ... the necessary forms."

Proofs of loss (the "necessary forms") generally include the following types of information:

- The time and cause of loss
- The interest of the insured and others in the property
- The insurable cash value of the property and amount of loss claimed
- Encumbrances on the property
- Other insurance
- Nature of occupancy of the premises
- Any changes in the title, use, location, or possession of the property
- Attestation that the information is true[5]

The proof of loss must be sworn to, usually by having it notarized, and any material and knowingly false statement would therefore constitute fraud.

Abandonment Prohibited. One option available to the *insurance company* is to pay for damaged property and take over its ownership. However, the abandonment provision, also found in many property insurance policies, makes it clear that the *insured* has no right to elect this option.

Abandonment

There can be no abandonment of any property to us.

The concept of abandonment harks back to ocean marine insurance, one of the oldest forms of property insurance. Under the terms of a typical ocean marine insurance policy, the insured has the right to *offer* abandonment to the insurer. It is customary for marine insurers to accept an assignment of property when there is a hope that some salvage can be secured. However, the insurer does have the right to reject the abandonment offer. The insurer might reject abandonment in cases where the damaged vessel presents a liability—as with a ship that is blocking a shipping channel and must be removed immediately at considerable expense.

In some situations, abandonment would provide an attractive alternative for the policyholder. If they could, people often would like to "convert" a seriously damaged car to a total loss by turning it over to the insurance company in exchange for cash payment of the preloss value. However, most nonmarine property insurance policies make it clear that the insured cannot simply drop the property, take the money, and run. Insurance companies are in the insurance business, not the property-repair-and-resale business. Also, ownership of damaged property can present a considerable liability in some situations—especially if the property is toxic, radioactive, or otherwise contaminated.

Liability Insurance

As with property insurance, the insured must notify the insurer of a liability loss and cooperate with the insurer in its resolution. However, liability claims involve some differences because a third party is always involved.

The *notice* condition of liability insurance policies has produced quite a bit of litigation. Efficient and economical administration of liability insurance requires early knowledge of actual or potential claims so that proper investigation can be made.

The relevant section of the commercial general liability coverage form begins as follows:

Duties In The Event Of Occurrence, Claim Or Suit
a. You must see to it that we are notified as soon as practicable of an "occurrence" or an offense which may result in a claim.

Lack of prompt investigation may prejudice an insurer's ability to defend the insured. Therefore, the courts are more likely to enforce the notice requirement under liability contracts than under property insurance contracts. With the passage of time, evidence and witnesses become more difficult to obtain. What were originally minor injuries may become magnified and complicate settlement. Prompt notice also helps prevent and minimize future losses, thereby furthering the interests of the insured, the insurer, and the public in general. Furthermore, timely notice facilitates control of claims, promotes favorable settlements, and reduces litigation expenses and awards for damages. As a result, any delay that frustrates the purpose of the notice provision of the insurance contract is deemed to be prejudicial.

As noted above, the insured often is required to notify the insurer "as soon as practicable" of any occurrence that might result in a claim. Policy language may be even stronger in requiring "prompt" or "immediate" action when a claim actually is made or a suit actually is brought.

Who May Give Notice. It is obvious that an injured third party is vitally interested in preserving the insurer's obligation to pay claims on behalf of its insured. However, the third-party beneficiary's claim might be defeated if the insured failed to give the required notice. Therefore, the question sometimes arises concerning whether the injured claimant can report the accident information to the insurer, even if the insured fails to do so, and thereby legally satisfy the notice condition. In general, so long as reasonable and timely notice is given to the insurer, it does not matter how the notice gets to the insurer. The purpose of the notice is to give the insurer an opportunity to make an investigation.

This provision requires prompt notification of situations that *might*, at some future time, result in a liability claim against the insured. The insurer requires notification of such events even if they never do result in a claim or lawsuit. For example, suppose a man slips, falls, and sprains an ankle in the insured's store. The man might later decide to sue the store, and the store's insurer should be notified. Upon receiving notice of the occurrence, the insurer would have the opportunity to decide whether to contact the potential claimant, determine the cause of the slip, and arrive at a settlement if appropriate. Or the insurer might decide to wait and see whether a claim is presented. If he is not contacted by the insurer, the man might decide that the fall was caused by his own clumsiness, and he might not even consider a claim against the store. Regardless of the ultimate outcome, the *insurer* deserves the opportunity to determine how to proceed, as it is the insurer that will pay any resulting claim.

Liability insurance coverage is "triggered" by one of several possible things, depending on the policy involved. The trigger might be the time of an occurrence, the insureds' becoming aware of the occurrence, the insurer's receipt of notice of an occurrence, the bringing of a claim or suit, or something else. Liability triggers are discussed in more detail in Chapter 5.

Other liability policy provisions make it clear that the insured must keep dated records of claims-related transactions, keep the insurer fully informed, and cooperate in the insurer's defense or settlement of the claim or suit.

A final duty is intended to keep the insured from prejudicing the insurer's opportunity to manage the defense of the claim:

> No insureds will, except at their own cost, voluntarily make a payment, assume any obligation, or incur any expense, other than for first aid, without our consent.

If any insured agrees to assume responsibility for a loss, it might appear to be an admission of liability that could considerably weaken the insurer's ability to defend against the claim. However, insureds are, in effect, authorized to incur first aid expenses without jeopardizing their coverage. When life and limb are threatened, the highest priority must be placed on providing first aid. An insured may call an ambulance or hire a taxicab to take an injured person to a hospital. This provision does not say the insurer will pay first aid expenses; however, such coverage is found elsewhere in many liability insurance policies.

INSURER'S DUTIES IN THE EVENT OF A LOSS

Most of the wording in an insurance policy relates in some way to the insurer's duty to respond to the report of a loss. Some policies do not contain separate provisions dealing only with the post-loss *procedures* to be followed by the insurer. Others, however, do contain such procedural information.

Property Insurance

Most property insurance policies contain provisions relating to policy limits, deductibles, and the manner in which the value of lost or damaged property will be established. These provisions, which vary substantially among policies, will be examined in other chapters.

The building and personal property coverage form contains a long "loss payment" provision that includes most of the information common to property insurance forms. Other relevant information appears in other policy conditions.

Settlement Options. The loss payment provision begins by listing what might be considered the insurer's settlement options. This information might surprise many insureds, since there is a general perception that insurance companies are obligated only to pay money.

> **Loss Payment**
> a. In the event of loss or damage covered by this Coverage Form, at our option, we will either:
> (1) Pay the value of lost or damaged property;
> (2) Pay the cost of repairing or replacing the lost or damaged property;

    (3) Take all or part of the property at an agreed or appraised value; or

    (4) Repair, rebuild or replace the property with other property of like kind and quality.

  b. We will give notice of our intentions within 30 days after we receive the sworn statement of loss.

Most people realize that a property insurer will pay either the value of the lost or damaged property or the amount spent to repair or replace it, whichever is less. However, these are not the only options.

Under many policies, the insurer has the right to perform by providing the repair or replacement service rather than paying in cash. This option may be exercised when the insurer has some arrangement to purchase property or services at a discount. The insurer might have a priority repair arrangement with a retailer or a contractor providing repair services. Such arrangements are especially common with glass repair shops, and insurers often choose to provide the repair service on glass breakage claims. A disadvantage of this approach is that the insured is more likely to be dissatisfied with the outcome when the repair service provider is chosen by the insurer.

This option is sometimes exercised to address questionable claims situations. Suppose an insured has unsuccessfully been trying to sell a building, and that this well-insured building suddenly has a major fire of mysterious origin. There might be strong suspicions that the owner finally arranged a buyer for the building—the insurance company. Rather than playing this game and converting the unsellable building to cash, the insurance company could rightfully insist on repairing the building. This option would not be inappropriate, as it would restore the insured to the same position he or she was in before the loss.

Also available is the insurer's option to pay the agreed or appraised value of damaged property and then assume ownership of the damaged property, sometimes referred to as "salvage." Insurance company claims departments maintain active salvage operations, and money recovered through the sale of damaged property helps to offset insurers' expenses. Salvage is best known in connection with auto physical damage claims. A "totaled" auto has some residual value in used parts and recyclable materials that can be recovered by an auto junkyard. When an auto is declared a total loss, insurers typically pay the insured the preloss actual cash value and take title to the damaged vehicle. In turn, the insurer will sell it to an auto salvage yard, recovering some money in the process. Salvage is by no means limited to auto insurance; the salvage process is used with all kinds of property insurance—and also with liability insurance property damage claims, whenever residual value might be recovered from otherwise destroyed property.

The insurance company has thirty days after receiving the sworn statement of loss to announce whether it intends to pay the value of the property, pay the cost of repairs, pay the value of the property and take the property, or actually perform the repair or replacement service. Other policies may specify different time periods.

Extent of Insurable Interest. Another clause in the loss payment provision makes it clear that the insurer will not pay more than the insured's financial interest in the covered property. Insurable interests are discussed in detail in Chapter 4.

Other Owners of Covered Property. The coverage of many property insurance policies extends to cover property of others on the insured's premises or in the insured's care. In such cases, the insured could be placed into an uncomfortable position between the insurance company and the property owner, especially if there is any disagreement as to the value of the property. Yet, the insurance contract is between the insurance company and the insured, and the owner of other covered property has no contract with the insurance company.

This dilemma is addressed in the building and personal property coverage form by the following provision:

> d. We may adjust losses with the owners of lost or damaged property if other than you. If we pay the owners, such payments will satisfy your claims against us for the owners' property. We will not pay the owners more than their financial interest in the Covered Property.
>
> e. We may elect to defend you against suits arising from claims of owners of property. We will do this at our expense.

The insurance company has permission ("may") under the contract to settle claims directly with bailors (owners) other than with the insured. The insured is not obligated to meet other property owners' demands simply because a claim has been made. If the property owner is not satisfied and sues the insured, the insurance company may choose to defend the insured at the insurer's own expense.

When Loss Is Payable. Regardless of any explicit statement, the insurer is obliged to expeditiously pay covered claims. Some insurance policies state that the insurer is obligated to pay a claim within a specified period after receiving adequate information to handle it. The building and personal property coverage form, for example, contains the following provision:

> f. We will pay for covered loss or damage within 30 days after we receive the sworn statement of loss, if:
> (1) You have complied with all of the terms of this Coverage Part; and
> (2) (a) We have reached agreement with you on the amount of loss; or
> (b) An appraisal award has been made.

Claims for *covered* loss or damage should be paid promptly, and a realistic time limit certainly seems appropriate. But it is not that simple. On the one hand, it certainly makes sense for the insurance company to pay claims without delay. But on the other hand, there are times when time-consuming investigation is necessary to determine whether a claim is indeed covered. If arson-for-profit is suspected, it might, for example, take time to gather the evidence necessary to prove that the insured conspired to cause the loss. Such evidence might never be gathered—and the suspected arson may, in fact, have been a perfectly legitimate loss!

An insurer that delays the claim payment, waiting for proof that the claim was not covered, might rightfully be accused of breaching the contract (and, even worse, of acting in bad faith, which might lead to additional penalties under the law). In avoiding delays, on the other hand, an insurer might pay claims that are not covered—which is inequitable for other reasons. Claims adjusters often face ethical dilemmas in choosing a balance between timely claim payments—possibly paying uncovered claims—and exhaustive investigation—which may delay payments to deserving claimants.

Liability Insurance

Relatively few liability insurance policy *conditions* relate specifically to the *insurer's* post-loss duties. Two typical provisions, however, are relevant—the bankruptcy provision, discussed here, and the suit provision, discussed under a later heading.

Bankruptcy.   Liability claims are claims by a third party against an insured who may be legally responsible for the third party's injury or damage. Suppose the insured runs out of money, either because of the claim in question (the limit of insurance plus the insured's other assets might be inadequate to cover the entire loss) or for other reasons. If the insolvent insured has no liability insurance, the third-party claimant would be unable to recover damages from the insured. The resulting situation is sometimes compared with getting blood out of a turnip—turnips have no blood, and the insolvent insured/defendant in a liability case has no money. The purpose of liability insurance is to protect the insured who, in such a circumstance, is beyond protection. The question naturally might be asked, "Is the insurer still obligated to pay claims on behalf of an insolvent insured?"

Under most liability policies the insurer agrees to pay such claims *on behalf of the insured,* subject to applicable limits of insurance and other policy terms. Perhaps it might be said that the insurer cannot "pay on behalf of" someone who has no money and therefore could not be forced to pay. On the other hand, it might seem unfair to let the insurer, who was willing to accept the risk, escape payment simply because of the insured's misfortune. Moreover, if the insurer were to escape because of the insured's insolvency, the injured claimant would have no source of recovery. The bankruptcy provision makes it clear that the insurer is obligated to pay claims on behalf of an insured who is bankrupt. The condition in the commercial general liability form reads as follows:

Bankruptcy.
Bankruptcy or insolvency of the insured or of the insured's estate will not relieve us of our obligations under this Coverage Part.

Similar provisions are not generally necessary with property insurance, since claims are paid to the insured—whether or not the insured is bankrupt—not on behalf of the insured.

In a few policies, especially those drafted some years ago, the insurer may agree to indemnify the insured who has first paid the claim. In these policies the bankruptcy provision plays an important role, for obvious reasons.

RESOLVING DISPUTED CLAIMS

Despite other policy provisions, disputes arise regarding the amount to be paid or the existence of coverage. Two of the policy provisions that address similar issues—appraisal and arbitration—have names that often are confused, but the distinctions between these two provisions should be kept in mind.

Disagreement Regarding Values—Appraisal Clause

Sometimes both insurer and insured agree that the policy covers a given property loss, but they cannot come to an agreement regarding the value of the property or the amount of the loss. Disagreements of this type usually do not involve bad faith on the part of either insurer or insured. Many different factors affect the value or repair cost of any given property item, and reasonable parties can differ dramatically in their evaluations. Normally such disagreements can be resolved through negotiation (as discussed further in Chapter 9), but it occasionally becomes impossible to have a meeting of the minds. The *appraisal clause* makes it clear how an impasse can be resolved. (In fact, it also has the effect of encouraging the parties to negotiate between themselves to avoid the need to hire appraisers to accomplish the same goal.)

The appraisal clause in the building and personal property coverage form is typical:

Appraisal

If we and you disagree on the value of the property or the amount of loss, either may make written demand for an appraisal of the loss. In this event, each party will select a competent and impartial appraiser. The two appraisers will select an umpire. If they cannot agree, either may request that selection be made by a judge of a court having jurisdiction. The appraisers will state separately the value of the property and amount of loss. If they fail to agree, they will submit their differences to the umpire. A decision agreed to by any two will be binding. Each party will:

a. Pay its chosen appraiser; and

b. Bear the other expenses of the appraisal and umpire equally.

If there is an appraisal, we will still retain our right to deny the claim.

The appraisal provision does not say it comes into play "When the insurer thinks the property is worth less than the insured does . . .," but how else would they disagree on values?

The insured selects and pays for a "competent and impartial" appraiser, presumably one who is likely to believe the property values are on the high side, and the insurer selects and pays for one likely to support the insurer's viewpoint. The appraisers, not the insurer or the insured, select an umpire—presumably someone whose valuation expertise both respect. Since the appraisers presumably disagree regarding values, they also might disagree over the selection of an umpire, and the policy makes provision for that eventuality by permitting a judge to make the decision, upon the request of either appraiser. The expense of the umpire is shared by the parties. While the appraisers are selected by the interested parties, the umpire is the primary neutralizing influence in the appraisal process.

Once an umpire has been selected, each appraiser submits his or her opinion regarding the value of the property and the amount of the loss. Assuming that the opinions differ, the "differences" are submitted to the umpire. It may be that the appraisers agree on some items; the valuations of these items are not differences requiring input from the umpire.

Some people have explained appraisal by saying the umpire will agree with one of the two appraisers, and that will settle the matter. That is how it usually works, but that is not what the provision says. The provision says a decision agreed to by *any two* will be binding. It could happen that the two appraisers come to an agreement while the umpire is out in left field. Agreement by either (1) two appraisers or (2) one appraiser and one umpire finalizes the matter.

Also noteworthy is the statement that this agreement will be binding. Both the insurer and the insured agree in the contract that they will be bound by the outcome of an appraisal process, so far as the value of the property or the amount of the loss is concerned. However, valuation is only a part of the question. The other part is the basic question of whether the claim is covered at all. These two questions are unlinked by the final sentence in the appraisal provision. The insurer does not lose the right to deny a claim merely by agreeing to the value of the claim or the appraisal process.

Some policies specify a time frame during which the appraisal process must take place. The ISO homeowners policy, for example, states that each party must choose an appraiser within twenty days of the other party's request for an appraisal, and that the appraisers must agree on an umpire within fifteen days (or request a judge to make the choice). Such time limitations help to protect consumers by keeping the insurance company from putting pressure on the insured through delaying tactics. They also force the insured to expedite settlement so the insurer can have closure.

Suit

Any party to a contract can ask the courts to enforce the contract by bringing suit against the other party, subject to any constraints within the contract. Insurance contracts normally contain a provision specifying that the insured must comply with other policy provisions before bringing a lawsuit against the insurer.

Many policies also state a time limit within which suit must be brought. This enables the insurer to put some closure on the claim.

The suit provision in the ISO common property conditions reads as follows:

LEGAL ACTION AGAINST US

No one may bring a legal action against us under this Coverage Part unless:
1. There has been full compliance with all of the terms of this Coverage Part; and
2. The action is brought within 2 years after the date on which the direct physical loss or damage occurred.

Policies vary as to the time period during which suit must be brought. Homeowners policies specify a maximum period of one year; the physical damage coverage of the personal auto policy specifies no time limit, but in practice auto physical damage claims are almost always settled within a matter of months. ISO crime policies specify both a minimum and a maximum—legal action may not be brought against the insurer until at least ninety days after the proof of loss has been filed and within no more than two years after the loss is discovered.

Some insurance claims end up in court, especially when large amounts are at stake and the insurer and the insured disagree in their interpretation of policy provisions. The court system is the ultimate authority on the meaning and enforceability of the insurance contract.

As with property insurance, the insured can sue an insurance company to force it to perform under a liability insurance contract. One part of a typical liability contract's suit provision closely resembles the property insurance provisions. Quoting the commercial general liability coverage form:

> No person or organization has a right under this Coverage Part:
>
> . . . To sue us on this Coverage Part unless all of its terms have been fully complied with.

Some additional provisions, however, such as the following, are unique to liability insurance.

> [No person has a right] To join us as a party or otherwise bring us into a "suit" asking for damages from an insured. . .

Stated differently, this means that the third-party claimant does not have any right to bring suit against the insurance company. The claimant has no contract with the insurer to enforce.[6]

The suit provision, actually titled "Legal Action Against Us," of the CGL adds another paragraph:

> A person or organization may sue us to recover on an agreed settlement or on a final judgment against an insured obtained after an actual trial; but we will not be liable for damages that are not payable under the terms of this Coverage Part or that are in excess of the applicable limit of insurance. An agreed settlement means a settlement and release of liability signed by us, the insured, and the claimant or the claimant's legal representative.

When a liability claim is made, the claim might successfully be defended with the result that no damages are payable. The insurance company might instead arrive at an out-of-court settlement ("agreed settlement") without going through an actual trial. Or the case might go to court, and it might be appealed one or more times before a "final judgment" is reached. According to this provision, the claimant can sue the insurer to make the insurer pay a claim following a final judgment. The claimant can also sue the insurer to make the insurer pay if the insurer has agreed to an out-of-court settlement. But the claimant cannot sue the insurer while the case is still pending. Regardless of other circumstances, the provision restates the obvious: The insurer is not obligated to pay claims that are not covered or to the extent they exceed the limit of insurance.

Despite this final provision, the courts sometimes force insurers who have acted in bad faith to the detriment of the claimant to pay claims exceeding policy limits. This issue will be explored in Chapter 9.

Alternative Dispute Resolution

The suit provision is not necessarily limited to formal court actions. According to a definition in the farm liability coverage form (October 1988 edition):

> **"Suit"** means a civil proceeding in which damages because of "bodily injury," "property damage," "personal injury" or "advertising injury" to which this insurance applies are alleged. "Suit" includes:
> a. An arbitration proceeding in which such damages are claimed and to which you must submit or do submit with our consent; or
> b. Any other alternative dispute resolution proceeding in which such damages are claimed and to which you submit with out [sic] consent.

(The last line was intended to parallel the last line in subpart a. and the similar definition in other policy forms, "with our consent.")

Arbitration. Arbitration provisions are found primarily within the uninsured motorists coverage of an auto insurance policy. Uninsured motorists coverage resembles liability insurance in some ways, and it resembles property insurance in other ways. It resembles liability insurance because the insurer is obligated to pay only if an uninsured motorist, as defined, is legally obligated to pay damages to the insured. But uninsured motorists coverage is a first-party contract between the insurer and the insured; in that sense it resembles property insurance. A conflict of sorts is built into the coverage: The insured wants to prove that the uninsured motorist is liable for damages. The insurer, on the other hand, can escape payment by proving that the uninsured motorist was not liable. The insured and his or her own insurance company are set up to become adversaries.

The arbitration provision outlines a process for resolving disagreements as to whether the insured is legally entitled to recover damages. The same process also applies to the amount of damages. The concept closely resembles the process outlined in the appraisal clause of property insurance policies, but they can differ as to the issue being disputed. The following arbitration clause is taken from the personal auto policy.

> **ARBITRATION**
> A. If we and an "insured" do not agree:
>   1. Whether that person is legally entitled to recover damages under this Part; or
>   2. As to the amount of damages;
>   either party may make a written demand for arbitration. In this event, each party will select an arbitrator. The two arbitrators will select a third. If they cannot agree within 30 days, either may request that selection be made by a judge of a court having jurisdiction.

    B. Each party will:
1. Pay the expenses it incurs; and
2. Bear the expenses of the third arbitrator equally.

    C. Unless both parties agree otherwise, arbitration will take place in the county in which the "insured" lives. Local rules of law as to procedure and evidence will apply. A decision agreed to by two of the arbitrators will be binding as to:
1. Whether the "insured" is legally entitled to recover damages; and
2. The amount of damages. This applies only if the amount does not exceed the minimum limit for bodily injury liability specified by the financial responsibility law of the state in which "your covered auto" is principally garaged. If the amount exceeds that limit, either party may demand the right to a trial. This demand must be made within 60 days of the arbitrators' decision. If this demand is not made, the amount of damages agreed to by the arbitrators will be binding.

SUBROGATION AND SALVAGE

After an insurer has paid a loss to, or on behalf of, the insured, the insurer sometimes may recover all or part of its payment through subrogation and salvage. Subrogation, described in Chapter 1, is a means through which the insurer, after paying a claim, takes over any rights of recovery that the insured might have had against other parties. *Salvage*, mentioned earlier in this chapter, is the process of recovering, selling, or otherwise disposing of property on which a loss has been paid. The term "salvage" also is used to refer to the damaged property that may be sold for its "salvage value."

Both subrogation and salvage enable insurers to recover some of the money paid out in satisfying claims. An insurer's claims department generally is considered a "loss center"; for the most part the claims process generates expenses, not revenues. However, the subrogation and salvage operation within a claims department actually functions as a "profit center" that generates revenues for the insurer. Subrogation and salvage recoveries reduce an insurer's overall loss ratio and, because they serve as an additional source of revenue, reduce the premiums that would otherwise have to be charged.

Subrogation

In common law, two distinct types of subrogation are recognized.

- *Equitable subrogation*, also called legal subrogation, is effected by the operation of the law, and it arises out of a condition or a relationship. Equitable subrogation is permitted, solely as a matter of equity, to prevent unjust enrichment. It is denied only where its exercise would work an injustice. Since it rests on equitable principles, equitable subrogation does not depend on any contractual relationship between the parties.

- *Contractual subrogation*, also called conventional subrogation, exists where the right is created by contract. Since it rests on the law of contracts, its scope is measured both by terms of the contractual agreement and by the rights the insured has against a third party. A contractual subrogation agreement must be a binding contract.

Once the insurer's right of subrogation is established, the nature of the insurer's subrogation action will depend on the rights and remedies that the insured has against the tortfeasor. These rights could be based on any appropriate area of private law—negligence, strict liability, intentional interference, breach of contract, failure to discharge the legal duties of an agency relationship, and so forth.

When an insured's property sustains damage, the insured may or may not have a right to recover from another party. If a right of recovery exists, it usually is based on the negligence of the other party. Therefore, subrogation actions arising out of property insurance claims usually are based on negligence.

Subrogation Provisions. Insurance policies contain a variety of subrogation provisions reflecting the varying nature of the policies. Several will be quoted to illustrate the ways in which they vary.

Until recently, insurance policy subrogation provisions usually contained the title, "Subrogation," and many policies still use that caption—particularly those for large commercial insureds or seldom-used policies that generally are not revised simply to update the policy language. Most modernized policies use captions such as "Transfer of Your Rights of Recovery." These policies may not even mention the word "subrogation," which is not particularly meaningful to most insureds. However, insurance professionals will recognize that these "transfer of rights of recovery ..." provisions simply refer to subrogation.

Incidentally, subrogation provisions should not be confused with assignment provisions, which also may refer to transfer; the ISO common policy conditions' assignment provision, for example, is captioned, "Transfer of Your Rights and Duties Under This Policy."

The ISO homeowners policy includes the "subrogation" label in the following policy condition, which applies to both the property and liability coverages of the policy.

Subrogation. An "insured" may waive in writing before a loss all rights of recovery against any person. If not waived, we may require an assignment of rights of recovery for a loss to the extent that payment is made by us.

If an assignment is sought, an "insured" must sign and deliver all related papers and cooperate with us.

Subrogation does not apply under Section II to Medical Payments to Others or Damage to Property of Others.

Like many other subrogation provisions, this one states that the insured may waive its rights of recovery in writing before a loss occurs.

By implication, the insured may not waive its rights of recovery after a loss has occurred. The insurer takes over *the insured's* rights of recovery—*if any*. When its rights of recovery are waived in writing *before* a loss, the insured, of course, has no rights of recovery to transfer to the insurer. *After* a loss has occurred, the insured may not waive any rights of recovery. To do so would eliminate the insurer's rightful chance to recover through the process of subrogation. The "in writing" requirement addresses the possibility that the insured might conspire to make the insurer pay for a loss that should rightfully be borne by another party.

The homeowners policy specifically exempts two coverages from the subrogation provision. The exempted coverages are, in effect, no-fault coverages under which the insurer agrees to pay for medical expenses or property damage, up to a limited amount, even in situations in which the insured was not legally liable to pay damages to the claimant. It would be inappropriate to then subrogate on the basis of another party's fault.

The personal auto policy contains a subrogation provision with a different title and another coverage twist. (Although "subrogation" is not in the title of this simplified language policy, the word "subrogated" is used.)

OUR RIGHT TO RECOVER PAYMENT
A. If we make a payment under this policy and the person to or for whom payment was made has a right to recover damages from another we shall be subrogated to that right. That person shall do:
  1. Whatever is necessary to enable us to exercise our rights; and
  2. Nothing after loss to prejudice them.
  However, our rights in this paragraph (A.) do not apply under [physical damage coverage] against any person using "your covered auto" with a reasonable belief that that person is entitled to do so.

(There is a Paragraph B. to this provision, but it relates to salvage or "recoveries," discussed later.)

The "twist" in the above subrogation provision lies in the last sentence. The personal auto policy was designed so that physical damage coverage would "follow the car"; that is, coverage is intended to apply no matter who is driving the car. This intention would be violated if the insurance company were able to recover for collision damage from a borrower of the insured's car. However, the insurer logically should be permitted to attempt to recover any payments from a car thief.

The ISO businessowners common policy conditions include another subrogation provision that encompasses both property and liability coverages.

TRANSFER OF RIGHTS OF RECOVERY AGAINST OTHERS TO US

1. Applicable to Businessowners Property coverage:

   If any person or organization to or for whom we make payment under this policy has rights to recover damages from another, those rights are transferred to us to the extent of our payment. That person or organization must do everything necessary to secure our rights and must do nothing after loss to impair them. But you may waive your rights against another party in writing:
   a. Prior to a loss to your Covered Property.
   b. After a loss to your Covered Property only if, at time of loss, that party is one of the following:
   (1) Someone insured by this insurance;
   (2) A business firm:
     (a) Owned or controlled by you; or
     (b) That owns or controls you; or
   (3) Your tenant.
   You may also accept the usual bills of lading or shipping receipts limiting the liability of carriers.

   This will not restrict your insurance.

2. Applicable to Businessowners Liability coverage:

   If the insured has rights to recover all or part of any payment we have made under this policy, those rights are transferred to us. The insured must do nothing after loss to impair them. At our request, the insured will bring "suit" or transfer those rights to us and help us enforce them. This condition does not apply to Medical Expenses Coverage.

Without explicit policy provisions such as these, the insurer would still have a right to equitable subrogation. That being the case, one might logically wonder why nearly all property-liability policies contain subrogation provisions. Express subrogation provisions are considered necessary or desirable for the following reasons.

1. Since workers compensation, no-fault auto, and auto medical payments benefits are essentially health insurance coverages, most courts would not allow equitable subrogation. An express subrogation provision entitles the insurer to contractual subrogation (unless prohibited by statute or regulation).
2. As a general rule of common law, the insurer usually is not

entitled to exercise the right of subrogation until its insured has been paid in full. A strict interpretation of this rule would deny subrogation under contracts containing deductibles, coinsurance clauses, or "other insurance" provisions when the loss is not paid "in full." To circumvent the general rule and clarify the intent, the typical subrogation provision stipulates that the insurer will be subrogated *to the extent of its payment.* This is known in the law as subrogation *pro tanto*, which means "for as much as may be" or "as far as it goes." A *pro tanto* subrogation right may be exercised without the insurer's having first paid the loss in full.

For example, a collision insurer may pay its policyholder the portion of a loss in excess of the deductible and immediately attempt to recover its payment from a negligent party. Most insurers voluntarily follow the practice of assisting the policyholder in recovering the amount of the deductible, though the policyholder must sometimes bear a proportional share of the cost of recovery.

3. Many subrogation provisions contain wording to the effect that "the insured shall do nothing after the loss to prejudice [subrogation] rights." Such a phrase has the minimum objective of deterring the policyholder from signing any agreements or otherwise doing anything that might impair the insurer's right of recovery from another party. An insured's breach of this condition could even result in a denial of coverage.

4. Some insurers fear that failure to include an express subrogation provision, when revising a policy that formerly included a subrogation provision, might be construed as a voluntary waiver of the insurer's right of subrogation.

Recovered Property.   Suppose a camera was covered under an "all-risks" policy, the camera was stolen, the insurer has paid the claim after subtracting a deductible—and then the camera is recovered by the insurance company or by the insured. What happens next? Does the insurer automatically keep the recovered property? May the insured return the money and get back the camera, if desired? *Must* the insured return the money and take back the camera, even if a replacement camera has already been purchased? Similar situations occur when an insured reports that property has been stolen and, after settling the claim, finds that the property was merely misplaced.

In the absence of an explicit policy provision, honesty, good faith dealing, and common sense would take care of most situations. A *recovered property provision*, found in many property insurance policies, puts an official stamp of approval on the processes suggested by common sense. The provision in the ISO homeowners policy is typical:

Recovered Property. If you or we recover any property for which we have made payment under this policy, you or we will notify the other of the recovery. At your option, the property will be returned to or retained by you or it will become our property. If the recovered property is returned to or retained by you, the loss payment will be adjusted based on the amount you received for the recovered property.

It is up to the *insured* to determine whether or not to take back recovered property, but the insured does not keep both the property and the amount paid by the insurer. With this provision, the insured can consider a case to be closed once a property claim has been paid, and the insured can proceed to purchase replacement property without having to worry that the case will be reopened because property might be recovered. At the same time, the insured will be given the opportunity to take back recovered property, if desired.

SUMMARY

Many insurance policy provisions include background information that often is taken for granted but may have a profound effect on coverage for specific situations. This chapter deals with the background provisions often found in the "conditions" section of a typical property or liability insurance policy. Some of the provisions examined here are examined in more detail in other chapters.

Provisions in the first group, examined in more detail elsewhere, clarify the specific identity of persons insured or the specific property where coverage applies. The assignment provision generally forbids ownership of a property or liability insurance policy to be transferred to another person without the insurer's permission. The no benefit to bailee provision provides coverage to an insured for property in the custody of a bailee, but without protecting the bailee who might be responsible for the loss.

When more than one person is insured, the first named insured may be identified as the point of contact in all transactions between the insurer and the policyholders. A policy also may specify that each party's interests are treated separately and that one party's misdeeds may not affect the coverage of other insured parties. In a similar vein, it may be stated that conditions breached at one location do not affect coverage at other locations.

When coverage applies is determined in part by the policy period. Policy provisions make it clear what it is that must happen within the specified time period to trigger coverage. With property the trigger usually is that the loss must "commence" during the policy period. Liability triggers are somewhat more complicated and may include, for example, the happening of an occurrence or the making of a claim, as explored further in Chapter 5.

Where coverage applies is determined in part by the coverage territory described in the policy. Coverage may be modified to "conform to statute" or to provide "extraterritorial coverage" applicable in the jurisdiction where the loss occurs.

Provisions maintaining coverage typically specify that coverage is granted contingent on the insured's payment of premium. Audit provisions give the insurer the explicit right to examine the insured's books and records to determine appropriate premium charges. Cancellation provisions state the rights and procedures by which either party may cancel the insurance contract. A change provision may limit the methods by which policy changes may be effected, while a liberalization provision may automatically expand coverage whenever the insurer introduces a revised policy form with broader coverage but no additional premium. An inspections and surveys provision gives loss control representatives and others the right to inspect the insured's premises and operations for insurance purposes. And other important provisions may explain whether and how coverage is suspended. Under a typical boiler and machinery policy, the insurer's representative may immediately suspend coverage upon discovering a dangerous condition. Under other policies coverage may automatically be suspended while protective safeguards are not in use. Still other policy provisions, such as those dealing with vacancy, may limit coverage in the presence of a certain hazard.

Some insurance policy provisions have no practical effect until a loss occurs. Following an insured event, however, they specify the duties and obligations of both insured and insurer. Under a property insurance policy, the insured may be required to notify the police, to notify the insurer, to mitigate the loss, and to cooperate with the insurer. Abandonment of property to the insurer often is prohibited. Similar duties exist with respect to liability insurance, especially the duty to provide prompt notification of loss to the insurer.

The insurer also has duties following a loss. In connection with property insurance, the insurer has a choice whether to pay cash or exercise another settlement option. The loss may be adjusted to the extent of the insured's insurable interest, or it may be adjusted with other parties (such as guests) who own property that may be covered under the policy. The policy also may specify when the loss is payable. Liability insurance policies may include a bankruptcy provision stating that the insurer is not relieved of liability if the insured is bankrupt.

Claims disputes may occur. When a dispute over values occurs in settling a property insurance claim, the appraisal provision indicates how both parties may proceed to resolve it. The arbitration provision in uninsured motorists coverage similarly explains how an impasse between insurer and insured will be resolved when liability is the issue. When all else fails, the insured has the right to sue the insurer to enforce policy terms, but this right may be limited by certain time constraints within the suit provision. Alternative dispute resolution, as well as lawsuits, may be permitted as a means of resolving such disputes.

Finally, subrogation and salvage provisions provide the insurer with some rights of recovery. The subrogation provision transfers to the insurer who has paid a claim to, or on behalf of, the insured the right to recover damages from another party. This right, previously held by the insured, enables the insurer to recover damages to the extent of its payment. Salvage provisions permit the insurer to take ownership of damaged or recovered property, after paying the pre-loss value of the property, and to sell it to recover a portion of its loss.

Chapter Notes

1. Robert J. Gibbons, *Principles of Premium Auditing*, vol. I, 2nd ed. (Malvern, PA: Insurance Institute of America, 1986), p. 2.
2. Harold S. Daynard, *Between the Lines: A Guide to Property and Inland Marine Insurance Policy Interpretation* (Hartsdale, NY: BTL Publishing Co., 1986), pp. 432–433.
3. Daynard, pp. 438–439.
4. Daynard, p. 87.
5. Daynard, p. 444.
6. A few states have statutes permitting direct actions against insurers, some only for limited categories of cases.

CHAPTER 4

Insurable Interests and Insured Parties

The topics to be examined in this chapter relate to the "Who" question surrounding insurance policy analysis—specifically, the question as to which parties *may* and *do* have insurance protection in a given situation under a given policy. "Insurable interest" is a legal requirement of insurance contracts following from the principle of indemnity. As this chapter will explain, a person can enforce an insurance contract only if he or she possesses an "insurable interest." "Insured parties," in contrast, hinge on provisions within the insurance contract. While insurance coverage cannot be *enforced* in the absence of an insurable interest, coverage does not *exist* under any circumstances for any party whose interests are not insured under a valid contract of insurance.

The practical effects are these: Unless the circumstances clearly involve an insurable interest, an insurance policy *may* provide no enforceable coverage. Even in the presence of an insurable interest, an insurance policy *may* provide no protection to any party whose interest is not clearly insured under that policy.

The vast majority of insurance claims involve losses to insured parties clearly having an insurable interest. However, not every situation is crystal clear. Ideally, the more unusual situations are recognized and dealt with before a claim is made. In practice, borderline situations often are not recognized until after a loss has occurred, and they must be dealt with at that time.

INSURABLE INTERESTS IN GENERAL

Assuming the several other requirements for a legally enforceable contract are met, every insurance contract must also be supported by an insurable interest in order for it to be legally enforceable. Otherwise the contract is considered to be a gambling contract which is not legally enforceable.

Insurable interest is defined as the kind of exposure to financial loss a person must possess in order to have insurance coverage that is legally enforceable. Mary has an insurable interest in her house, auto, and personal property, since she would be hurt financially if a loss to them occurs.

When discussing insurable interests, "insurable" must be viewed in a *legal* sense. Having a legally insurable interest is not necessarily the same thing as having an insurable loss exposure, nor is it the same thing as being a policyholder. Even though an insurable interest exists, an applicant may not be able to obtain insurance because the exposure is "uninsurable" by underwriting standards. And even if an insurance policy has been issued, it cannot be enforced by a party who has no insurable interest in an insured event—even if that party is a named insured.

Whenever possible, questions of insurable interests should be resolved before the policy is issued. To avoid situations in which a claim must be denied based on a lack of insurable interest, both the insured and the underwriter generally avoid entering into an insurance contract unless they are certain that an insurable interest is involved.

Purposes of Insurable Interest Requirements

An insurable interest is necessary for the following three reasons:

- To prevent gambling
- To reduce intentional losses
- To enforce the principle of indemnity

Prevent Gambling.   Without an insurable interest, an insurance contract is a gambling contract, and gambling contracts cannot legally be enforced. For example, James could insure Mary's building, in which he has no insurable interest, betting (gambling) that the building will burn. If James could win this bet, he would receive a return that far exceeded the premium he otherwise would lose.

American courts have ruled that an insurance contract that is not supported by an insurable interest is unenforceable by either the insured or the insurer. This is consistent with the general refusal of the courts to enforce gambling contracts. Most private gambling contracts are illegal both by statute and by court decisions that view gambling as contrary to public policy.

Reduce Intentional Losses.   Insurance provides well-recognized opportunities for profit to an insured party who deliberately causes an insured event to occur. For example, after purchasing property insurance on Mary's house, James might deliberately start a fire to collect the insurance.

It is widely believed that the insurable interest requirement reduces intentional losses resulting from moral hazards. The temptation to cause a loss most likely is reduced in situations in which an insurable interest exists. For example, although James might destroy the property of an unrelated person like Mary for his own financial gain, he would presumably be somewhat less likely to set fire to his own house.

Enforce the Principle of Indemnity. The principle of indemnity holds that a person should not profit from an insured loss. Most property and liability insurance contracts are contracts of indemnity. In contrast to a valued contract, which provides for the payment of some preestablished dollar amount, a contract of indemnity provides for payment of a sum directly related to the amount lost, subject to some limitations.

One limit of recovery under an insurance contract of indemnity is the amount of the insured's insurable interest. The amount of the insured's insurable interest therefore places one upper limit on the amount that an insurer will pay for a covered loss. Other limits will be examined in Chapter 6. If the insurer paid more than the amount of the insured's insurable interest, the insured would be profiting from insurance and the principle of indemnity would be violated. By limiting the loss payment to the amount of one's insurable interest, the principle of indemnity is supported.

INSURABLE INTEREST IN PROPERTY AND LIABILITY INSURANCE

In property and liability insurance, the insurable interest—which must exist at the time of the loss—may be based on one or more of the following:

- Property rights
- Contract rights
- Potential legal liability
- Factual expectation
- Representative status

Time of an Insurable Interest

An insurable interest in life insurance must exist at the time of the application for insurance, while an insurable interest in property and liability insurance generally must exist at the time of the loss. If the insurable interest requirement is not met at the time of loss, the insured does not incur a financial loss. The principle of indemnity would be violated if a loss payment were made. For example, if Sam sells his car to Susan and transfers title to her, and the car is later totaled before Sam's collision coverage on it is canceled, Sam cannot collect from the insurer because he does not have an insurable interest in the vehicle at the time of loss.

Sometimes in property insurance, the insured does not have an insurable interest in the property when the insurance contract is first written but expects to have an insurable interest in the future when a loss could occur. As a simple example, Bob might purchase collision insurance on his new car several days before he actually picks up and takes title to the car. More complex situations regularly occur as property changes hands through a variety of commercial transactions.

Insurable Interest Based on Property Rights

The term "property" is commonly applied to buildings, autos, and other tangible objects having a physical existence. Indeed, that is the usage generally found within insurance policies. Although this usage is also found in the law, the legal concept of property is more accurately defined as a *bundle of rights*. These rights have an economic value because they are guaranteed and protected by law. Some rights pertain to physical objects of a tangible nature; others to intangible objects. The term "intangible" refers to property such as copyrights, patents, trademarks, and corporate stock certificates; although these represent valuable economic rights, they have no intrinsic value of their own.

In the legal sense, *real property* refers to rights in land, including rights to water, minerals, things permanently attached to land (such as buildings), and things growing on the land (such as trees). It also includes rights closely related to land, such as the right to have access to or use of the land of another. *Personal property* refers to all other property rights or, in other words, to all property that is not real property.

One party may possess the entire bundle of rights with respect to real or personal property, in which case the party is the sole owner. However, the bundle of rights may be divided among several parties, each with one or more rights, in which case there is incomplete ownership by any one party. The right or sum total of several rights a particular party possesses often is referred to as that party's "interest" in the property.

The term *estate* also has several meanings. In estate planning, "estate" ordinarily means all property owned by a person, including both real and personal property. However, "estate" is used also to describe a particular legal interest in property, and it often is combined with another word or phrase to describe a classification of property and to convey the nature and extent of the interest. For example, a *simple estate* is an estate owned by one party, whereas a *concurrent estate* is co-owned by two or more parties. Numerous additional classifications and subclassifications of estates exist in the complex field of property law.

For the purpose of identifying some common insurable interests based on property rights, it is not necessary to catalog all the various classifications of property estates. But it is important to acknowledge that full "ownership," in its ordinary sense, is not the only collection of rights that gives rise to an insurable interest. Something less than the full bundle can also be the basis of an insurable interest.

With respect to a specific item of property, the most comprehensive estate normally consists of the following two elements:

1. Outright and full ownership (extent of rights)
2. Unlimited time (duration of rights)

The total estate can be carved up to create lesser interests, either as to the extent of the interest or its duration. While these lesser interests are not always called estates, they all are property interests or rights, that is, some portion of the aggregate legal rights. Furthermore, just as an unqualified owner has an insurable interest in the owned property because of the possibility of financial loss, any party has an insurable interest in property when two conditions exist:

1. The party possesses a property right.
2. The value of the right would be diminished by the damage, destruction, loss of use, or theft of the property.

Specific examples of property rights that will meet the insurable interest requirement are discussed in the following section.

Ownership of Property. The ownership of property can support an insurable interest.

Full Value. *The owner of a fee simple estate has an insurable interest equal to the full value of the property.* The phrase *fee simple estate* refers to the full ownership of property; one party owns the estate, the estate can be passed to heirs by a will, and the owner has the right to sell, lease, give away, or use in any lawful way all or a portion of the estate. For example, Jane, who owns a commercial office building, has an insurable interest equal to the full value of the property. Total destruction of the property would result in a corresponding dollar loss to her, because the value of her rights would likewise be destroyed.

Although it generally is agreed that the fee simple owner's insurable interest is the full value of the property, the courts do not always define full value in a precise way. What is clear, however, is the intention of the courts to reinforce the principle of indemnity by limiting the amount of an insurable interest in property to the maximum dollar loss the owner could sustain from the property's total destruction. Thus, *for insurable interest purposes*, the full value of the property (the maximum dollar amount the owner could lose from its destruction) is generally equal to the sum of the loss of the property's *intrinsic value*, plus the loss of the property's *value in use*.

For example, assume that Jane's building is totally destroyed by a tornado. What total dollar amount would truly indemnify her for the destruction of the building? The total amount would equal her resulting maximum financial loss, which would also be the amount of her insurable interest. One element of the total loss consists of the cost of restoring the building with one of like kind and quality. This replacement cost amount would be sufficient to restore the building's intrinsic value. However, it may take six months to build a new structure. In the meantime, Jane will be deprived of the building's economic value in use. For example, assume that Jane operates a business in part of the building, rents another part to a tenant, and resides in the remaining part. During the period of time it takes to restore the building, she will lose money that she otherwise would have received in the form of business profits and rental income, and she probably will incur additional expenses to secure alternative living quarters. Thus, her total loss, which is the extent of her insurable interest, is the sum of (1) the replacement cost of the building (the direct loss of intrinsic value) plus (2) the lost profits, lost rental income, and extra living expenses for the period of restoration (loss consequences related to the loss of the building's economic value in use).

Effect of a Mortgage. The fee simple owner has an insurable interest equal to the full value of the property—even when the property is mortgaged or otherwise pledged as security for the payment of a debt. Since total destruction of the property does not relieve the owner of the obligation to repay the outstanding debt, the extent of the owner's insurable interest is not reduced by the amount of the debt. The owner, therefore, may insure the property for its full insurable value. *However, the lender also has an insurable interest in the property that has been pledged as collateral security for the debt, and the lender's interest normally is based on the amount of the debt.* The result is that the sum of the two insurable interests actually exceeds the full value of the property. To illustrate, suppose a building with a replacement cost of $5 million is mortgaged for $4 million. The owner's insurable interest of $5 million (in the building itself, ignoring its value in use) plus the lender's insurable interest of $4 million, equals $9 million, considerably more than the building's intrinsic value. Such situations are common when more than one party has an insurable interest in the same property.

The fact that more than one party may have an insurable interest, with the sum of these insurable interests exceeding the value of the property, creates an obvious potential for abuse. However, the presence of overlapping *insurable interests* does not necessarily mean that overlapping *coverage* will exist. Underwriters attempt to avoid issuing policies that would result in excessive amounts of duplicate coverage. Moreover, common insurance policy provisions such as subrogation provisions and "other insurance" provisions (all discussed elsewhere in this text) tend to reduce the chance of duplicate payments for the same elements of loss.

Property Owned by a Corporation. *With respect to property wholly owned by a corporation, the corporation—as a legal party distinct from its stockholders—has an insurable interest in the property equal to the extent of its full value.* American courts, with few exceptions, hold that a stockholder also has an insurable interest in the property of the corporation, even though the stockholder has no enforceable title to the corporation's property. A stockholder has the rights to receive (1) dividends declared by the corporation and (2) a proportionate share of the corporation's net assets after discharge of corporate debts if the corporation is dissolved. The courts reason that, because substantial damage to the corporation's assets could significantly lower the rights of a stockholder, a stockholder's potential loss is sufficient to prevent insurance on corporate property from becoming a mere wager. American courts, therefore, will enforce an insurance contract secured by a stockholder on corporate assets, but only to the extent of the actual loss that the stockholder would sustain if the insured corporate property were damaged or destroyed.

Multiple Ownership of Property. Multiple ownership of property can support an insurable interest. Buildings, land, autos, and bank accounts are examples of property frequently owned by two or more parties. Forms of multiple ownership include joint tenancy, tenancy by the entirety, and tenancy in common, as well as a tenancy in partnership, all of which are discussed under the following subheadings. Note that the following paragraphs discuss legally recognized interests, *not* how or whether to insure.

Joint Tenancy. A joint tenancy is an estate owned by two or more joint tenants. It is characterized by the fact that each tenant has an equal interest and each has the right of survivorship. Generally, joint tenants are related (for example, husband and wife and/or children). If Bob, Mary, and Bill are joint tenants and Bob dies, Bob's share goes equally to Mary and Bill (the survivors). If Bill then dies, Mary ends up owning the entire estate. A living joint tenant could sell his or her interest. But a joint tenant's share cannot be willed to another, because at the instant of death, the share of the deceased passes automatically to the surviving tenant(s). *Generally, each joint tenant has an insurable interest to the extent of the full value of the property.* Since any one of the joint tenants, as the only survivor, *could* quickly become the sole owner of the property, each tenant effectively stands to lose the full value of the property if it is destroyed.

Tenancy by Entirety. A tenancy by entirety is a special kind of joint tenancy that applies only to a husband and wife, and it cannot be terminated during their lifetimes unless both agree to the termination. Like joint tenants, tenants by the entirety have survivorship rights; unlike joint tenants, tenancies by the entirety cannot be severed by one party selling without the consent of the other. If the husband dies, his share of the property passes to the wife (or vice versa). *Each spouse has an insurable interest equal to the full value of the property.*

Tenancy in Common. A tenancy in common is an estate owned in either equal or unequal shares by two or more joint tenants who do not have survivorship rights. For example, if Bob and Bill own property as tenants in common and Bob dies, Bob's share does not automatically pass to Bill. Instead, Bob's share goes to the person(s) named in his will (or to Bob's heirs according to statute if Bob dies "intestate," that is, without a valid will). The surviving tenant might not get the deceased tenant's separate share through the will or the operation of the applicable intestate law. *In recognition of this possibility, the insurable interest of each tenant in common is limited in amount to the value of that tenant's share of the property.*

Tenancy in Partnership. A *partnership* is a type of business organization that involves the joint ownership of property. In a partnership arrangement, both the partnership as an entity and the individual partners may own property used in partnership activities. However, barring a contrary agreement among the partners, all property originally contributed by the partners when the partnership was formed, as well as property later acquired by the partnership in the course of a partnership business, becomes partnership property. Each partner holds an estate interest known as a *tenancy in partnership.*

Three characteristics of a tenancy in partnership are relevant to an analysis of insurable interests. First, no partner has the right to sell, bequeath, or otherwise dispose of partnership property for his or her personal interest. Second, when a partner dies, the deceased partner's heirs eventually acquire a share of the deceased's interest in partnership property. Third, when the partnership is dissolved, which may be either by agreement of the partners or by operation of the law, the partners share in the distribution of partnership assets, after satisfaction of creditors' claims, in the same proportion as they divided profits while the partnership was operating (in equal shares, unless the partners previously agreed to the contrary).

Several distinct insurable interests can arise out of partnerships. The extent of these insurable interests corresponds to the extent of the current value of the interest:

- *The partnership, as an entity, has an insurable interest in all property regularly used in the partnership.* This is true regardless of whether the property remains the sole property of one partner or becomes property held in tenancy in partnership.
- *With respect to property used in the partnership that remains the exclusive property of one partner, that partner also has an insurable interest for its full value.* Every other partner *also* has an insurable interest in such property to the extent that the value of that partner's interest in the partnership may be reduced by damage to that property.
- *With regard to property owned in tenancy in partnership, each partner has an insurable interest up to the same percentage of value in which that partner shares in partnership profits or in the distribution of jointly owned partnership assets.* If Bob and Bill are partners sharing profits equally, each has an insurable interest in property owned by the partnership to the extent of one-half of the value of such jointly owned property.

Community Property. A number of states have *community property laws* that distinguish between "separate property" and "community property." While these laws are not uniform, the following generalizations can be made.

Separate property generally consists of property that a husband or wife owns at the time of marriage, as well as property that each inherits or receives as a gift after marriage. Separate property remains the sole property of the respective spouse because it was not produced by their communal effort. *In general, each spouse has an insurable interest in his or her separate property to the extent of the full value of such property.*

Community property generally consists of all other property that either or both of the spouses acquire during marriage by their communal effort, and it represents a form of joint ownership. Under this concept, a husband and wife share equally in all community property, and the amount of their individual contributions to the joint effort does not change the equal interest. A gift to both spouses, of course, is community property.

Each spouse has an undivided one-half interest in the community property. At the death of one spouse, the community property is divided into halves. One half goes to the surviving spouse automatically. The other half goes to the heirs of the deceased spouse, who may or may not leave his or her half of the community property to the survivor by will. *Therefore, each spouse has an insurable interest in the community property, while both are still alive, equal to one-half the value of the community property.*

Condominium Ownership. Condominium ownership is an estate in real property that consists of the following two elements:

1. The ownership of a separately defined area, called a "unit." The "unit" looks similar to an apartment, though technically it may be nothing more than a "box of air" in a certain space.
2. A tenancy in common interest in the areas that serve the owners of all units. This element consists of the land, the building, hallways, storage rooms, parking lots, and other areas that serve more than one unit.

Each unit owner has a specified percentage interest in the common areas. The two elements combine to form an overall estate that may be sold, mortgaged, inherited, or otherwise treated like individually owned property.

State laws pertaining to condominiums vary, and the legal instruments that create the condominium and define the relationships among unit owners and the condominium association are not uniform. But despite these variations, *each unit owner normally has an insurable interest equal to the total value of the condominium estate, including not only the condominium unit but also the unit owner's specified percentage interest in the building, as well as any alterations and additions to a building by the unit owner.*

Life Estate. A life estate can support an insurable interest. It is an estate that lasts for the lifetime of a specific person. The holder of a life estate is known as a *life tenant.* The life tenant may possess, use, and enjoy the property during his or her lifetime. However, the life estate terminates at the death of the holder (the life tenant) or, less frequently, at the death of someone other than the holder. In either case, at the termination of the life estate, the property passes to another party known as the *remainderman* (or it reverts to the grantor of the interest, if no remainderman has been named or if the specified remainderman is not legally qualified to take the property).

To illustrate, suppose a husband who owns a house in fee simple stipulates in his will that his wife is to have a life estate in the house for as long as she lives; thereafter, his son is to have a fee simple estate in the house. The husband then dies. In this situation, the son is the remainderman, and he becomes the holder of a *future interest* known as a *remainder* at the time his father dies. The wife is the life tenant or the holder of the life estate. The life tenant (the wife, in this case) is entitled to possess and use the property during her lifetime, but she cannot pass it along to others in her will, since her interest terminates at her death. Similarly, though the wife theoretically could sell her life estate while she is still alive, it might be difficult to find a buyer, because the buyer's interest likewise would terminate at the instant of the wife's death. This is consistent with the general rule that the holder of a particular type of estate cannot transfer any greater estate to another person.

A life estate can be created other than through a will. For example, a son may make a gift to his mother of a life estate in property that the son holds in fee simple. If the son does not name a remainderman, the property reverts back to him at the mother's death. During the mother's life tenancy, the son's interest in the property is a future interest, known as a *reversion* or *reversionary interest*, and he is referred to as the *reversioner* or holder of such an interest. If the mother dies before the son, the son would again have a fee simple estate in property—the same interest he held before he created the life estate for his mother. If the son dies before the mother, the value of the reversionary interest becomes part of the son's estate.

Insurable Interests in Life Estates. To understand the insurable interests that may exist in a life estate, it is necessary to remember the various parties who may hold the property rights.

- The *life tenant* is the holder of the life estate.
- The *remainderman* is the holder of a remainder interest.
- The *reversioner* is the holder of a reversion or reversionary interest.

The life tenant has a *present interest* that gives the tenant the right to possess and use the property currently. The remainderman and the reversioner in the earlier examples both have a *future interest*, because their rights to possess or use the property do not become operative until some future point in time. Each of these three parties has valuable property rights, which may provide the basis of an insurable interest.

The *remainderman*, though holding only a future interest, could easily take over the rights of possession and use tomorrow if the life tenant dies then. Likewise, the life tenant could die when no remainderman has been named or when the specified remainderman has died before the life tenant. In both cases, the *reversioner* would immediately take over the rights to possess and use the property. In recognition of such realistic possibilities, *the remainderman who holds a future interest generally has an insurable interest equal to the full value of the property. The same is true of the reversioner.* Each of these two parties stands to lose the entire value of his or her rights, it is reasoned, if the property were destroyed by fire or some other peril. Accordingly, both a remainderman and a reversioner may enforce a contract that insures the property for its full insurable value.

The *life tenant* also has an insurable interest in the property in which he or she holds a life estate. The amount of the life tenant's insurable interest usually is determined in one of two ways, depending on the legal jurisdiction. First, *in some jurisdictions the life tenant's insurable interest is equal to the full value of the property in question.* Second, *in others, the life tenant's insurable interest is limited to the present value of the life estate, given the age of the life tenant (or other person whose life governs the duration of the estate).* The present value of the tenant's life estate would serve as an upper limit on the amount of the life tenant's insurable interest in jurisdictions that have adopted the present value approach. Courts rejecting this approach have insisted that the life tenant has an insurable interest equal to the full value of the property. This is based on the theory that the life tenant is indemnified only by an insurance payment large enough to restore the property to its pre-loss condition and permit it to be used in the same way as before the loss.

Regardless of how the amount of the life tenant's insurable interest is determined, the life tenant generally is under no legal obligation to repair or rebuild the property after it has been damaged or destroyed, unless (1) the damage or destruction is caused by a negligent or intentional act of the life tenant, or (2) the documents creating the life estate specifically obligate the life tenant to repair or replace the property. Nor is the life tenant legally obligated to insure the property for the benefit of the remainderman or reversioner, in the absence of an enforceable agreement to the contrary.

Tenancy for Years. A tenancy for years (also called an estate for years) can support an insurable interest. A tenancy for years is an estate that lasts for a definite period of time, such as six months, one year, five years, ten years, or even ninety-nine years. The holder of this type of estate, the *tenant,* has temporary possession and use of property owned by another party. A tenancy for years is most often created and governed by the specific terms of a lease, which is usually in writing. The property involved may be personal property—such as an auto, or real property—such as a parcel of land, a building, or a part of a building. In either case, the tenant normally rents the property from the owner-landlord at an agreed price. At the end of the specified period, the tenancy for years terminates (unless it is renewed).

Insurable Interest in Tenancy for Years. The insurable interest of the owner-landlord was discussed earlier. The insurable interest of the owner is the full intrinsic value of the property owned, as well as the owner's valid interest in insuring against the loss of rental income, the loss of business income, and the extra costs to replace the property. In addition, the tenant for years often makes "improvements and betterments," which become a permanent part of the real property. If so, the building owner has an insurable interest in the improvements, though actual responsibility for insuring them may be stipulated in the lease.

The holder of a tenancy for years may have several types of insurable interest in the property subject to tenancy. *Some courts hold that the tenant for years has an insurable interest in the full value of the property the tenant is renting from its owner.* As a practical matter, many owners insure the property themselves, since a typical tenant has no particular desire to insure the landlord's property. However, the tenant would have good reason to consider purchasing additional insurance in the tenant's own name under some circumstances, for example (1) if the tenant has an option to buy the property, (2) if the owner carries inadequate coverage, or (3) if the tenant is legally obligated by the lease to insure the property or return it in good condition at the end of the lease.

Unless an explicit agreement imposes additional duties on the tenant, the tenant generally is not responsible for damage to the property. Exceptions might include damage caused by a negligent or intentional act of the tenant or by someone for whom the tenant is responsible. Furthermore, in short-term leases the tenant usually is not responsible for the payment of rents if the property is severely damaged during the time it takes to restore the property to its pre-loss condition. However, in ninety-nine-year leases, the tenant often is required to continue rent payments throughout the entire duration of the lease, including the period during which the damaged property is being repaired or replaced. In either a long- or short-term lease, there may be specific provisions that treat the following:

- Who bears the consequences of loss to improvements and betterments made by the tenant
- Who is responsible for paying the utilities, cleaning, and providing maintenance services
- Whether rent paid in advance is refundable if the property is severely damaged
- Whether the tenant must pay a penalty for breaking the lease

- Whether the rent paid is subject to renegotiation after the property has been severely damaged or destroyed

All this suggests that when the relevant property is damaged or destroyed, the tenant for years may suffer the kinds of indirect losses associated with the temporary inability of the tenant to *use* the property.

It is extremely difficult to formulate accurate generalizations about insurable interests of tenants for years as they relate to various loss consequences. Loss exposures vary from tenant to tenant, and they are governed by a number of factors, especially the specific terms of the applicable lease agreement. For example, suppose a business tenant leases an entire building for ten years, and the building is destroyed by a fire at the end of the fifth year. The loss of the building's intrinsic value is borne directly by the owner, assuming that outcome is consistent with the lease. But what kind of insurable interest does the tenant have? *The insurable interest of the tenant depends on the loss exposures actually faced by the tenant.* The tenant's own personal property within the building, which could be insured for its full insurable value, is not germane to this discussion. As to improvements and betterments made by the tenant, the tenant clearly has a *use interest.* That is, the tenant expects to use the improvements and betterments as long as the tenant occupies the building, and this expected use of the property has financial value, even though the improvements and betterments themselves become part of the real estate belonging to the building owner. In addition, the tenant may have valid interests arising out of the substantial loss consequences involving the potential inability to use damaged or destroyed property for the period it takes to repair or replace the property and otherwise return to a normal level of business activity. Such consequences, as well as loss of business income and extra expenses to operate, could coincide with the reduction in value of the damaged building or contents.

Each of the loss exposures mentioned here is analyzed in detail in other CPCU texts. In short, the tenant for years may have a variety of insurable interests arising out of the relationship to leased premises. These interests are equal in amount to the losses of rights to use leased property. These use rights may substantially exceed the intrinsic value of destroyed property, and they often are based largely on the provisions of the lease agreement.

Future Interest. A future interest can give rise to an insurable interest. A future interest in property is a present right to take possession of the property at some specified future time. That time may be linked to a specified number of years—such as at the end of an estate for years, or to the occurrence of a specified event—such as the death of a life tenant. Examples of future interests include the previously discussed remainder interest held by a remainderman and the reversionary interest held by a reversioner. The precise nature of a future interest depends largely on the exact wording of the will or deed that creates the interest. In every case, however, the holder of the interest has a *present right*—not a contingent or possible right—to *future possession* of the property. Upon the occurrence of the specified event, or at the otherwise specified future point in time, what was once a future interest instantly "matures" and becomes a present interest in property. The holder takes possession of whatever kind of estate has been granted to him or her, whether a simple estate, a tenancy in common, or some other kind of estate.

The holder of a future interest has an insurable interest in the property the instant the future interest is created. The extent of the holder's insurable interest is the same as it would be if the future interested matured into a present interest immediately. For example, suppose Dick stipulates in his will that upon his death his wife Jane is to receive a life estate in the family mansion in which Dick has fee simple ownership. Then, when Jane dies, their daughter Sally is to have a fee simple estate in the mansion. Dick dies a few years after signing the will. At the instant of Dick's death, Sally acquires a future interest in the mansion. If Jane dies immediately thereafter, Sally will take possession of a fee simple estate, and as the holder of such an estate, has an insurable interest to the extent of the full value of the property. Accordingly, Sally may insure the mansion for its full insurable value any time after Dick's death, even if Jane is still alive and healthy. It does not matter whether Jane is thirty or ninety years old at the time. Sally acquires her insurable interest at the instant the future interest is created for her—at the time of Dick's death, in this case. The *amount* of Sally's insurable interest is not affected by the life expectancy of her mother, Jane.

It should be emphasized that in the above example the daughter, Sally, does not have any insurable interest in the mansion before her father dies, even though the possibility of her eventual inheritance is clearly spelled out in her father's will. Since the person making the will (in this case, Dick) can always change the will as long as he is alive, anyone named in the will is merely an *heir expectant* as long as the testator (will-maker) is still alive. An heir expectant generally does not have an insurable interest in the property covered by the will, because a mere expectancy does not in itself create a future interest. As soon as the testator dies, an heir does acquire a legally insurable interest in the property to be inherited, even before the estate is settled and the property distributed to the heirs.

Equitable Title. An equitable title can support an insurable interest. Generally speaking, there are two broad types of "title" in property law. *Legal title* to property is basically an enforceable right of its ownership and possession. The phrase is also commonly used to describe a deed, bill of sale, certificate of ownership, or other document that may serve as evidence of title. An *equitable title* to property is the enforceable right of a person who is the real owner, as a matter of equity, to obtain the legal title from another party, who is the owner of record without right of ownership. Through errors, misdeeds, or routine delays in processing property transactions, the rightful owners of property often are temporarily deprived of legal title or custody and possession of the property. For example, the purchaser of an auto normally encounters some delay between the time of purchase and the time the title document is received from the state. If an error occurs in processing, the owner may not receive the title document. The holder of an equitable title may establish the fact in court, if necessary, and obtain the legal title and the property.

It is well established that the holder of an equitable title to property has an insurable interest in the property, regardless of whether the holder has the legal title or has the property in his or her actual custody or possession. This rule has numerous applications in practice, especially in real estate sales transactions. In all situations involving holders of equitable title, the extent of the holder's insurable interest is the same as if the holder also had legal title. The amount of the insurable interest, then, depends on the particular kind of estate that is held.

Insurable Interest Based on Contract Rights

An insurable interest can be based on a contract right. A contract is an agreement between two or more parties who make a set of promises enforceable by law. A contract right is a legal right that one contracting party has against the other party or that party's property. In general, contract rights can be classified into two major categories:

- *Contract rights with respect to persons.* Under this type of contract right, the first party to a contract does not have a claim against any *specific property* of the second party. For example, under an unsecured loan, the debtor does not pledge any property as collateral for the loan. If the debtor fails to repay an unsecured loan, the creditor is only a *general creditor* and has no greater claim on any of the debtor's property than does any other general creditor.

- *Contract rights with respect to property.* Under this type of right, the first party has a claim on specific property held by the second party. For example, under a secured loan, the debtor pledges specific property as collateral to guarantee repayment of the loan. The creditor is a *secured creditor* who has the right to take the property and sell it if the loan is not repaid. This claim has precedence over the claims of general creditors.

In summary, a contract right with respect to a person gives the holder of that right a general claim against a person but no claim against any particular property. In contrast, a contract right with respect to property gives the holder a specific claim against particular property. With this distinction kept clearly in mind, let us next consider the insurable interest requirement with respect to each of these two types of contract rights.

Contract Rights With Respect to Persons. *In property and liability insurance, contract rights with respect to persons usually do not create an insurable interest because this type of right does not create any claim on specific property.* Thus, as stated earlier, an unsecured creditor does not have an insurable interest in any property of a debtor as long as the debtor is alive. However, if an unsecured creditor obtains a court judgment against a debtor and is legally entitled to make a claim against specified property to satisfy the debt, the creditor acquires a property right in the specified property and an insurable interest in it to the extent of the unpaid debt. Similarly, once a debtor dies, the rights of an unsecured creditor against the deceased become a property right against the property in the deceased's estate. The property right gives the unsecured creditor an insurable interest in at least some of the property in the estate (real property only in some jurisdictions), to the extent of outstanding debt at the time of death.

However, there have been some significant *exceptions* to the general rule that a contract right with respect to a person does not create an insurable interest in that person's property. The exceptions involved unusual situations in which the continued existence of certain property is considered by the court to be essential to that right. In these cases, the holder of a contract right with respect to a person was ruled to have an insurable interest in the essential property. This was the basis for the rulings in the following cases, all of which resulted in a decision that an insurable interest existed:

- A person hired under a long-term contract as superintendent in a factory was held to have a valid insurable interest in fire damage to that factory. Without that factory, the value of the insured's right to be paid for working as superintendent would be lessened substantially.
- A house mover was held to have an insurable interest in damage to a house that the mover had contracted to move, but that burned before the move was completed. The amount of the insur-

able interest was based on the compensation the mover would have received.

- An insured had invented and patented a process to be used in drilling for oil and had contracted with a drilling firm to use the patented process in return for paying the inventor part of the profits from particular oil wells. The inventor was held to have an insurable interest in damage to the machinery used to pump oil from the particular wells.

In each of these cases, it was held that the holder of the contract right had an enforceable insurable interest equal to the revenues that would have been received had the insured event not occurred.

Contract Rights With Respect to Property. *A contract right with respect to property generally creates an insurable interest in that property.* The holder of the right may experience a financial loss if the property is damaged or destroyed. Two types of contracts are particularly important in the creation of an insurable interest: (1) contracts in which payment of a debt is secured, and (2) contracts for the sale of property, including both real property and personal property.

Payment of a Debt. *A secured creditor has an insurable interest in property that secures the debt equal to the remaining balance of the debt.* This general rule is the source of the insurable interest every mortgagee and pledgee has in property that secures the payment of a debt.

The economic basis for this insurable interest is that damage to the mortgaged or pledged property can reduce the likelihood that the mortgagee or pledgee will be made whole. Although the debtor must still pay the debt even if the property is destroyed, the motivation and ability to do so may be lessened significantly. Also, if the borrower defaults, the creditor may not be able to sell the damaged property for as much as it could otherwise have been sold for, in order to satisfy the debt. This threat to the status of the creditor, though short of constituting a *certain* financial loss, is sufficient to support an insurable interest on the part of the creditor. The creditor's potential loss from the destruction of the property—the outstanding balance owed at the time of the damage to the property—is also the extent of the creditor's insurable interest.

A *lien* is a claim on property growing out of any contract on which money is owed. One party may become a lienholder because it is owed money for services performed for another party. When those services involve work on the debtor's property, the party performing the services may acquire a lien on that property. The lien may simply be based on the equitable principle that a party that performs services under contract should be compensated for those services. In some cases, however, it is based on a specific contract provision. In any case, *a lienholder has an insurable interest in property to the extent of the debt.*

The insurable interest of a lienholder can be illustrated by the following examples:

- A hotel has a lien on a guest's luggage for payment of unpaid room charges; the insurable interest is limited to the extent of the unpaid charges.
- A landlord has a lien on a boarder's personal property for non-payment of rent; the insurable interest is limited to the extent of overdue rent.
- A supplier of building materials to a construction site has a lien on the structure being built until the supplier is paid for the material; the insurable interest is limited to the extent of the unpaid bill for those materials.
- A moving and storage company has a lien on the property being moved or stored; the insurable interest is limited to the extent of the customer's bill.
- An attorney representing a third-party insurance claimant has a lien on settlement moneys to the extent of the agreed on charge for the attorney's services.

Sale of Property in General. The process of selling property involves transferring from the seller to the buyer the title, exposure to loss, and insurable interest in the property being sold. Before the selling process begins, the seller has title and insurable interest in the property. The seller's insurable interest is then based on the seller's property rights. When the selling process is completed, the buyer has legal title to the property. The buyer's insurable interest is then based on the buyer's property rights. *During the selling process, both the seller and the buyer may have simultaneous insurable interests in the property.* These interests are based on legal title, on equitable title, or on a security interest in the property, but the principles governing ownership transfer and related insurable interests differ significantly between the sales of real property and personal property. Therefore, these two types of property must be discussed separately.

Sales of Real Property. The buyer of real property has an insurable interest in the property at several possible points in the selling process *before* obtaining legal title. *For example, the buyer holding an agreement of sale for real property has been held to have equitable title to that property and an insurable interest in it.* By paying the agreed price and complying with the other terms of the agreement, the buyer may compel the owner to surrender legal title to the property. Under common law, a buyer of real property does not take legal title until the seller actually or constructively delivers the deed to the buyer. But the buyer has an equitable title to the property once the buyer and seller have agreed on the price and other terms of sale of the property. *The buyer's equitable title supports an insurable interest equal to the full value of the property, which is the measure of the potential loss to the holder of the equitable title as a result of damage to the property.*

During the time the buyer holds an equitable title to the property, the seller retains legal title until the deed is delivered to the buyer. *This legal title is the basis of an insurable interest for the seller equal to the full value of the property.* After delivering the deed to the buyer, the seller retains an insurable interest in the property if the seller has a security interest in the property as a mortgagee. (The same rule applies if payments are still due to the seller under a conditional sales contract.) *The insurable interest based on such a security interest is the unpaid balance of the mortgage (or purchase price in the case of a conditional sales contract).*

Sales of Personal Property. Sales of personal property are governed by the Uniform Commercial Code (UCC) that has been adopted in almost all jurisdictions. One part of the UCC deals with the sale of goods. The UCC permits the buyer and seller of such property to agree as to when title will pass between them. If they make no stipulation, the UCC provides that title passes to the buyer at the time and place at which the seller completes physical delivery of the goods as required by the terms of the contract, even though the seller may retain a security interest in the goods. Precisely where and when the physical delivery required by the contract becomes complete depends on the wording of the contract.

Based on the rules regarding title, the UCC sets forth three basic rules on insurable interests:

- The *seller* has an insurable interest in damage to the goods as long as the seller has title to the goods in accordance with either an agreement between the buyer and the seller or the UCC provisions dealing with title.
- The *seller* retains an insurable interest in the goods while the seller has a security interest in them, even after title to the goods has been transferred to the buyer.
- The *buyer* has an insurable interest in the goods as soon as the goods have been "identified," that is, as soon as the specified goods the buyer is to take can be distinguished from other similar goods the seller may have. Identification may occur when the buyer and seller reach a mutual agreement that is the basis for their contract, when the goods are segregated in a package, or when they are delivered to the buyer. Identification can create

an insurable interest for the buyer long before the transfer of title to the buyer or the satisfaction of the seller's security interest extinguishes the seller's insurable interest. Therefore, it is quite common for *both the buyer and the seller* to have simultaneous insurable interests in the property.

The preceding rules regarding the time that a buyer and a seller have an insurable interest in goods also affect the extent of each party's insurable interest in those goods:

- A *buyer* has no insurable interest in goods until they have been identified; thereafter, the buyer's insurable interest is equal to the full value of the goods, regardless of whether the buyer actually holds legal or equitable title to them.
- The extent of the *seller's* insurable interest in the goods depends on the point in the transaction at which the goods are damaged.

If goods are damaged at a time when title remains with the seller and the buyer need not pay for the property, the seller's potential loss and insurable interest both equal the full value of the property. If the property is destroyed after title has passed to the buyer and the buyer has paid for them, the seller faces no potential loss from damage to the goods and has no insurable interest in them. If the goods are destroyed at any time when the seller has a valid security interest, the seller's potential loss and insurable interest are limited to the unpaid balance of the debt.

Because a buyer and a seller may both have simultaneous insurable interests in the same goods, and because the buyer's insurable interest is never less than their full value, the sum of a buyer's and a seller's insurable interests in the same goods may exceed their full value.

Insurable Interest Based on Potential Legal Liability

Potential legal liability can support an insurable interest. In general, a person has an insurable interest in any event that may cause financial harm to that person. An insurable interest based on potential legal liability does not depend on whether the person has any legal or equitable title, but only on whether he or she can be held legally responsible for something that might occur. *The very fact that a person incurs a claim under a liability insurance policy is sufficient proof that the person has an insurable interest in the event that resulted in the claim.* In the absence of a claim, it is essentially a moot question as to whether an insurable interest exists; there would be little reason to raise the issue. Even when a claim is groundless, an individual may still incur a loss because of legal defense costs that arise out of the claim.

The ownership and operation of an auto provide several illustrations of an insurable interest based on potential legal liability. The owner and the operator of an auto unquestionably have an insurable interest in protection against any liability claim arising out of the use of that auto. In addition, a parent has an insurable interest in protecting against claims arising from a minor child's use of an auto owned by and licensed to the minor child in a jurisdiction with a statute that makes a parent legally responsible for such use. Similarly, an employer has an insurable interest in protection against claims arising out of an employee's use of the employee's own auto on business, since it has been established that an employer can be held liable for injuries and damages that result from the negligence of an employee while acting within the scope of employment. Insurable interest arising out of potential legal liability does not require an insurable interest in the property (such as an auto or building) involved in the situation giving rise to liability.

Bodily Injury and Property Damage in General. The typical liability insurance policy applies to claims for bodily injury and property damage under some range of circumstances. Before a loss, there is no precise basis for determining how large these claims might be, and there is no reason for the courts to impose any dollar limit on the amount of a party's insurable interest in the events covered by liability insurance. Either a natural person or a corporation theoretically could purchase an unlimited amount of enforceable liability insurance, if the buyer were able to find a willing insurer and were also willing and able to pay the premium.

Damage to Specific Property. A party's insurable interest based solely on potential legal liability does have an upper limit when legal liability may arise out of damage to *specific items of property*. An example occurs when one party is responsible for specific property that belongs to another. *In such a case, the maximum limit of the responsible party's liability, and of its insurable interest based on that liability, is the full value of the property, including the use value to the owner.* With the exception of possible liability for damage to the property, the insuring party typically has no other insurable interest in damage to the property for which it is responsible.

There are many examples of insurance being issued to a party that has an insurable interest based only on potential legal liability for damage to specific property of others.

- A bailee who takes temporary custody of property of others for a specific purpose, such as storage or repair, may insure his or her liability for damage to the property of others left in his or her custody. If the property is damaged under conditions that make the bailee liable, the bailee may collect the proceeds of insurance up to the full value of the property. However, after deducting any charges due the bailee for storing, repairing, or performing other services, the bailee must pay the remainder of the loss payment to the customer.

- A common carrier has an insurable interest in its liability for damage to the goods of others that the carrier has agreed to transport.
- The executor of an estate has an insurable interest in liability for damage to property included within the estate.
- A hotelkeeper has an insurable interest in liability for damage to guests' property.
- A tenant has an insurable interest in liability for damage to portions of the premises the tenant occupies.
- A contractor has an insurable interest in legal liability for damage to a building under construction. Most construction contracts stipulate that the contractor bears the exposure to loss during construction even though the partially completed building is the property of the party for whom it is being built. Even after the building is completed, the contractor may have an insurable interest in liability for damage to the building. This would occur if the contractor is liable under the construction contract to repair or replace the building if it is damaged within a specified period after completion.
- A person or business who has custody of property whose true ownership is unknown may insure against potential liability to the true owner if the property is damaged before the true owner becomes known.

Insurable Interest Based on Factual Expectation

A factual expectation exists when a party anticipates an economic advantage if the insured event does not occur, or, conversely, economic harm if the event does occur. The notion of factual expectation theoretically could serve as the basis for all insurable interests. Each type of insurable interest recognized earlier involves the expectation of financial harm from the occurrence of the insured event or of financial benefit from its nonoccurrence.

A factual expectation alone generally is not a valid basis for an insurable interest in property in the majority of United States jurisdictions. However, in those cases in which the courts have accepted a factual expectation as a valid basis for an insurable interest, the insured did not have to have any property right, contract right, or potential legal liability in order to establish an insurable interest. The insured person only had to show potential financial harm resulting from the event to be insured, examples of which follow:

- Wisconsin courts held that a husband living on real estate owned solely by his wife had an insurable interest in that property. The insurable interest was based on the factual expectation that the wife will continue to let him live on the land and farm it.
- An Illinois court ruled that a son had an insurable interest in buildings owned by his father when the father orally expressed the intention to will the building to his son. This ruling is an exception to the general rule that an heir expectant has no insurable interest in his or her legacy until the testator dies.

The focus on the insured's *economic position,* rather than legal interest, is the distinguishing mark of factual expectation as a basis for an insurable interest. The Insurance Law of New York State, for example, defines an insurable interest as including "any lawful and substantial economic interest in the safety or preservation of property from loss, destruction, or pecuniary damage."[1] In contrast, the California Insurance Code specifies that "a mere contingent or expectant interest in anything, not founded on an actual right to the thing, nor upon any valid contract for it, is not insurable."[2]

A factual expectation alone generally is not a valid basis for an insurable interest in most American jurisdictions. Some legal interest also is considered essential. This legal interest may be based on any of several foundations, such as a property right, a contract right, or potential legal liability. In those jurisdictions that do require some legal interest, any legal interest is sufficient to support an insurable interest, even when it is unlikely that the legal interest will materialize into actual ownership or possession of the property involved. For example, in such states, an eighty-five-year-old mother with a remainder interest in a home would have an insurable interest in that home even though it is currently occupied by a robust and healthy thirty-year-old life tenant. Though it is unlikely that her future interest will ever materialize into actual possession and use, the mother would be held to have an insurable interest.

To justify denying an insurable interest based solely on factual expectation, some courts have simply held fast to the doctrine that a legal interest is essential to an insurable interest in all situations. Giving some logical basis for this conclusion is the assertion that recognizing insurable interests based solely on factual expectation would permit the purchase of insurance by strangers who would suffer no real loss from the property's destruction. Some of them might possibly wish to damage the property or to use their insurable interest to mask a wager.

In jurisdictions that deny insurable interests based solely on factual expectations, a party with only a factual expectation who wishes to insure the particular property often can contractually arrange to have a legal interest in the property as well. For example, an heir expectant could enter into a contract with the present occupant under which the heir expectant assumes some responsibility for maintaining the property covered by a will under which the heir expectant stands to receive property. Such a liability for maintenance could create a clear legal interest for the heir expectant in the preservation of the property covered by the will. This legal interest would support an insurable interest recognized in any American jurisdiction.

Insurable Interest Based on Representative Status

A representative of someone else may have an insurable interest by virtue of the representative status. As noted earlier, agents, bailees, and trustees may have an insurable interest in property on the basis of contract rights or potential legal liability. Beyond these interests, the legal representative of a party may obtain insurance in its own name for the benefit of that party. For example:

- An agent may insure property in his or her name for the benefit of the principal.
- A trustee may insure property in his or her name for the benefit of the trust.
- A bailee may insure property in his or her name for the benefit of a bailor.

In these situations, the party obtaining the insurance is not required to have an independent insurable interest in damage to the property. The party derives the interest from its relationship with the person or parties whom it represents. Although the insurance is issued in the name of the party that obtains it, the "representative status" of the insured is sometimes shown by inserting, after the name of the insured, phrases such as the following:

- "For the benefit of _____" (if the interest of a specific party is being protected)
- "For whom it may concern" (if the interests of a class of entities are being protected)

Such phrases are not essential. If it can be shown that the insurance is obtained for the protection of others, the validity of the policy is not jeopardized by the fact that the party obtaining the insurance does not have an insurable interest in the covered property.

When legal capacity to insure the property is derived from status as the legal agent of a party who has an insurable interest, the party obtaining the insurance must fulfill the duties of a legal agent. This means that the person obtaining the insurance must act in the best interests of the party who has the insurable interest and must pay to that party all insurance proceeds. When the person obtaining the insurance (such as a warehouseman) represents a group of entities (such as the warehouse customers), it is not necessary that each party be identified or even be specifically known to the person obtaining the insurance. However, to be covered by insurance obtained in this way, the protected entity must meet the following two criteria:

- It must be within the group the purchaser intended to benefit by insurance.
- It must not have rejected the coverage.

INSURED PARTIES IN AN INSURANCE CONTRACT

The policy provisions that specify *who* is entitled to insurance protection are among the most important parts of an insurance contract. This section of the chapter will examine the important question, "Who is insured?"

Definition of Insured Parties

Insured parties are the various persons, corporations, partnerships, or other entities who are contractually entitled to receive a loss payment, specified services, or other benefits according to the terms of the insurance contract. An insured party may be specifically identified by name in the declarations page of the policy. However, other parties who are not named also may qualify as "insureds" under the policy. Although these insureds do not have to be named specifically, they must be clearly designated in some way in the policy if coverage is to apply. Insurance policies differ substantially in terms of the parties who are insured.

Rights of Insured Parties

Insured parties in an insurance contract possess a wide variety of valuable contractual rights. However, the number and types of rights vary depending on the policy and whether the insured is a "named insured" or simply "an insured."

For example, assume that Mary Jones owns a dress shop and is the only person listed as a named insured in the declarations page of her businessowners policy. She has the following contractual rights under the policy:

- *Enforcement of the contract.* Mary is protected under the policy and is entitled to loss payment according to the terms of the policy.
- *Legal defense.* If she is sued because of a business incident that qualifies as an insured event, based on the allegations of the claimant, she is entitled to a legal defense provided by the insurer.
- *Return of premium.* If the insurance is canceled, she is entitled to a refund of the unearned premium.
- *Initiate policy changes.* Subject to the insurer's underwriting rules and practices, Mary can initiate a policy change request. The insurer may respond by adding an appropriate endorsement that modifies the coverage in the policy.
- *Notice of cancellation.* Mary is entitled to advance notice if the insurer decides to cancel coverage.
- *Other rights.* Mary has the right to demand an appraisal if there is disagreement on the amount to be paid. If stolen property is recovered after a loss payment is made, she also has the right either to keep the loss payment and give the property to the insurer or to retain the property but refund the loss payment.

It should be stressed that all insured parties have rights in an insurance contract. Insured parties can include the named insured(s), assignees, secured creditors, family and household members, employees, officers, legal agents in an agency relationship, legal representatives of the named insured, and numerous other individuals or groups. Also, an *additional insureds endorsement* can be added to a policy to increase the number of insureds under the contract. This is not to say that members of each category are insured under every insurance policy; the extent of interests insured depends on the specific provisions of the contract in question.

The various types of insured parties can broadly be classified as insured parties specifically identified by name, insured parties identified by a relationship to another insured, and additional insureds.

Insured Parties Specifically Identified by Name

An insured party can be specifically identified by name in the declarations page of the policy. Parties specifically identified by name may include named insureds, assignees, and secured creditors.

Named Insured. The term named insured refers to the person, corporation, partnership, or other party or parties named in the declarations page of the policy. In a preamble to many simplified language policies, the pronouns "you" and "your" are defined as referring to the named insured shown in the declarations. Subsequently, throughout the policy, every time "you" is used, it refers to the named insured.

As noted in Chapter 3, some policies distinguish between the first named insured and other named insureds. Where this is the case, the first named insured is responsible for the payment of premiums and is the only named insured who is authorized to cancel the policy, receive notice of cancellation if the insurer cancels, make policy changes with the insurer's consent, receive claims and occurrence data from the insurer, and receive return premiums.

Other named insureds, who also are listed in the declarations page, can include individuals, corporations, partnerships, or any other entities with either an insurable interest in property or an exposure to potential legal liability.

Assignees. An assignment is the transfer of a property right from one party to another. The party that assigns the property right is called an *assignor*. The party to whom the right is transferred is called the *assignee*. An insurance contract provides valuable property rights, but an insurance contract cannot be validly transferred to another party without the insurer's consent. However, rights of recovery may be assigned after a loss.

Assignment After a Loss. The general rule is that *the right to receive a loss payment can be freely assigned to another party after a loss occurs, without the insurer's consent.* The right to receive loss payment is merely a claim for money. The assignee does not become a new insured after the assignment is made, nor does the assignee normally acquire any greater rights than those possessed by the assignor at the time the assignment is made. Likewise, the assignment usually does not diminish the insurer's legal defenses against the insured. Thus, the insurer could deny payment to the assignee on the grounds of fraud by the insured, breach of a policy condition, or lack of an insurable interest by the insured. Since assignment of the loss payment after the loss has occurred does not represent any increase in hazard, the assignment can freely be made without the insurer's consent.

Assignment Before a Loss. The most important pre-loss right in property and liability insurance is the right of the policyowner to receive protection against future losses. This right cannot be assigned. As explained in earlier chapters, a pre-loss assignment of a property and liability insurance policy has the effect of changing the insured. The insurer wants to decide for itself whether to insure an assignee. Therefore, the general rule is that property or liability policies cannot be assigned validly without the insurer's written consent. Most policies contain an assignment provision that makes this position explicit.

If an attempted assignment should take place without the insurer's consent, the lack of consent would not invalidate the entire policy. However, the effect may be equally serious, because the insurer has no legal obligation to the assignee; the named insured, to whom the insurer does have an obligation, usually would not have a valid insurable interest at the time of the loss. To avoid this disastrous situation, policy assignments should not be attempted without first securing the insurer's explicit approval.

Based on the strong statements here, this subject might seem to be a topic of frequent dispute. In practice, assignments of property and liability policies are not common, and most people prefer to obtain their own insurance rather than to attempt an assignment of insurance coverage arranged by someone else.

Secured Creditors. A creditor is a secured creditor when the debtor has pledged *specific* property as collateral for repayment of the loan. As noted earlier, a secured creditor has an insurable interest in such property. Property insurance to cover the creditor's insurable interest may be obtained (1) by the creditor's direct purchase of its own policy or (2) by making the creditor an insured under the debtor's policy. The latter may be accomplished by means of an assignment, a loss payable clause, or a standard mortgage clause.

Creditor's Own Insurance. Creditors can purchase their own insurance to cover their insurable interests. The managers of commercial lending institutions might justifiably feel that they can obtain broader coverage and will exercise greater care than many of their borrowers would exercise in selecting insurers and producers who are financially strong and reputable. Also, some creditors may desire to purchase the insurance from local firms that have deposits in their institutions. Additionally, the direct purchase of insurance assures the creditor that its own insurance will not be invalidated by acts or omissions of its debtors. Special coverages are available to meet the unique needs of lending institutions. Some of these special policies relieve the creditor of the administrative burden of filing debtors' insurance policies or otherwise checking to make certain the policies are kept in force.

From the viewpoint of the creditor, the chief disadvantage of purchasing its own insurance is that the creditor must pay the premiums. While the creditor may be able to pass along the insurance costs to borrowers in the form of higher loan charges, the creditor must be aware of any constraints imposed by regulations, statutes, or competitive considerations. It is common practice to require the *debtor* to insure the property pledged as collateral security for a loan, whether or not the creditor carries its own insurance as well.

Creditor Insured by Debtor's Policy. One way of insuring the secured creditor's interest in property would be to require the debtor to *assign* his or her insurance policy to the creditor before any loss occurs and to stipulate that the debtor must continue paying the premiums. However, assuming that the insurer consented to the assignment, the assignment of a property insurance policy would not by itself provide adequate protection for both parties. The creditor would be insured to the extent of the unpaid balance of the debt, but the debtor would no longer be an insured under the policy for which the debtor would be obligated to pay the premiums. In addition, the courts generally have held that a pre-loss assignment of a property insurance policy, if not accompanied by a related transfer of the property it insures, gives the assignee no greater rights than the assignor had in the policy at the time of the assignment. This means that the creditor (assignee) is subject to all the defenses the insurer may have had against the debtor (the former insured); consequently, the creditor may find its coverage jeopardized by the debtor's fraud or breach of a policy condition before the assignment became effective. Rather than accept an assignment of the debtor's policy, either creditors generally prefer to buy their own insurance or they insist that every debtor buy and maintain a policy containing an appropriate loss payable clause or mortgage clause.

A *loss payable clause* is commonly used to protect the creditor's interest in *personal property*, such as an auto that has been pledged as collateral for a loan. The typical loss payable clause names the creditor as the payee in a clause stating, for example, that "any covered loss is payable to the named insured and Porcine Bank, as their interests may appear." If a covered loss occurs, the insurer usually issues a claim check payable jointly to the creditor and debtor. If the insurance payment is less than the amount of the outstanding debt, the creditor is entitled to keep the entire payment and reduce the debt accordingly. If the payment is more than the amount of the outstanding debt, the excess is payable to the debtor. In practice, however, the creditor often wants to keep the loan intact and have the property repaired or replaced, in which case the creditor merely withholds its signature on the check until the repair or replacement is completed. (The creditor may also refuse to sign until the check is endorsed over to the repair shop, to assure that payment will be made.) In any case, the loss payable clause protects both the debtor and creditor, to the extent that the coverage is both valid and adequate in amount and scope, while at the same time giving the creditor first priority to any amounts payable by the insurer.

As a device for protecting the creditor, the loss payable clause may not be reliable in all legal jurisdictions. Many courts have held that the loss payable clause does little more than make the creditor an appointee or representative of the debtor and, as such, the creditor is entitled to no greater rights than the debtor has under the policy. The creditor would not be entitled to collect any benefits otherwise payable under the policy, according to this interpretation, if any act or omission of the debtor has served to invalidate the coverage. However, a few courts do interpret the loss payable clause as though it were a separate contract between the creditor and the insurer. The latter interpretation gives the creditor assurance that the creditor's rights under the policy cannot be jeopardized by an act or omission of the debtor.

The *mortgage clause* is commonly used to protect the creditor's (mortgagee's) interest in *real property* that has been pledged as collateral for a real estate loan. The mortgage clause is uniformly viewed as a separate contract between the insurer and the mortgagee. *The mortgagee's rights under the policy cannot be impaired by an act or omission of the debtor (mortgagor).* Thus, if Sam intentionally "torches" his mortgaged home, the mortgagee is fully protected up to its insurable interest under Sam's policy, even if Sam is not.

The typical loss payable clause is sometimes no more than a single sentence in the declarations or a simple endorsement. The standard mortgage clause is not really a clause at all; instead, it consists of several lengthy paragraphs that supplement other policy provisions and set forth in detail the many rights and few duties of the mortgagee. For creditors who wish to rely to some degree on insurance purchased and paid for by the debtor, both the loss payable clause and the mortgage clause provide much better protection for the creditor than an assignment of the debtor's insurance policy.

The mortgage clause of the ISO homeowners policy reads as follows:

Mortgage Clause.
The word "mortgagee" includes trustee.
If a mortgagee is named in this policy, any loss payable under Coverage A or B will be paid to the mortgagee and you, as interests appear. If more than one mortgagee is named, the order of payment will be the same as the order of precedence of the mortgages.
If we deny your claim, that denial will not apply to a valid claim of the mortgagee, if the mortgagee:
a. Notifies us of any change in ownership, occupancy or substantial change in risk of which the mortgagee is aware;
b. Pays any premium due under this policy on demand if you have neglected to pay the premium; and
c. Submits a signed, sworn statement of loss within 60 days after receiving notice from us of your failure to do so. Policy conditions relating to Appraisal, Suit Against Us and Loss Payment apply to the mortgagee.

If we decide to cancel or not to renew this policy, the mortgagee will be notified at least 10 days before the date cancellation or nonrenewal takes effect.
If we pay the mortgagee for any loss and deny payment to you:
a. We are subrogated to all the rights of the mortgagee granted under the mortgage on the property; or

b. At our option, we may pay to the mortgagee the whole principal on the mortgage plus any accrued interest. In this event, we will receive a full assignment and transfer of the mortgage and all securities held as collateral to the mortgage debt.

Subrogation will not impair the right of the mortgagee to recover the full amount of the mortgagee's claim.

Insured Parties Identified by Relationship to Another Insured

Most property and liability insurance contracts cover as an "insured" one or more parties that can be identified by their relationship to the named insured (or by their relationship to another insured, such as an assignee or creditor).

Generic Classifications. Many parties that have or acquire an insured status are not identified by name but become insureds if they are part of a generic class as cited in the policy. The most obvious example is the spouse of the named insured in a homeowners policy or personal auto policy. The definition of "you" in these policies refers to the named insured and the spouse if a resident of the same household. Throughout the remainder the policy, the pronouns "you" and "your" are used to refer collectively to the "named insured" and his or her spouse, and the spouse therefore possesses the same rights and privileges as the named insured who is named as such. For example, when Jane marries her boyfriend, her new husband automatically becomes a named insured under both her auto policy and her homeowners policy, even though he may not be specifically named in either.

The definition of "insured" also may confer an insured status automatically if the individual falls into a generic classification cited in the policy. Some parties who may be covered as insureds in a generic classification include the following:

- Family members
- Household residents
- Employees
- Legal agents
- Officers and directors
- Other classifications stated in the policy based on personal or business relationships with the named insured

Different types of policies may contain different definitions of "insured." Even different portions of the same policy may define "insured" differently, especially when the same policy provides more than one coverage. The same policy may also have slightly different definitions in different states to comply with state law.

For example, the following generic groups are among those whose members are covered as an "insured" under the liability section of the personal auto policy:

- Family members who are household residents
- An employer who is legally responsible for acts of an employee whose car is insured under the policy

The medical payments coverage and uninsured motorists coverage sections include different definitions of "insured."

Generic classifications appear also in commercial forms. For example, in addition to the named insured listed in the declarations, the following generic groups are among those covered under the page-long "Who is an Insured" section of the commercial general liability coverage forms:

- Members, partners, and their spouses of a partnership designated in the declarations, in connection with the conduct of the business
- Employees of the named insured acting within the scope of their employment
- Any real estate manager of the named insured
- Anyone who has temporary custody of the named insured's property if the named insured dies
- A legal representative if the named insured dies
- A person driving the named insured's mobile equipment on a public highway with the named insured's permission

Additional examples from these forms could be given, but the above should be enough to make the point. The important points are that a wide variety of groups can automatically qualify as insureds under the policy based on some relationship to the named insured, and policy language must be carefully scrutinized to determine whether a particular individual or organization is protected under the terms of a specific policy.

Legal Substitutes for the Named Insured. A legal substitute for the named insured can become an insured under the named insured's policy. A number of property and liability insurance contracts define an insured to include one or more of the following parties:

- *Legal representatives*—such as an executor, administrator, or a receiver in a bankruptcy proceeding
- *Personal representatives*—such as a holder of a power of attorney
- *Heirs and assigns*—a phrase that refers to parties who will inherit the named insured's property either by a will or by appli-

cable state law, as well as an assignee to whom an insurance contract has been assigned (with the insurer's consent)

Such parties are not separate insureds in a literal sense. These parties are instead acceptable legal substitutes for the named insured and are empowered to act on behalf of the named insured or, in the case of executors and administrators, on behalf of a deceased named insured. Since legal substitutes have only the legal rights possessed by the named insured, they can collect only for the named insured's covered losses, not for their own.

Additional Insureds[3]

A final way to acquire insured status is to be added as a so-called *additional insured* to the named insured's policy. This usually is accomplished by an appropriate endorsement. Insurance Services Office (ISO) has drafted numerous endorsements that can be used to add a person or organization to the named insured's general liability insurance policy. Three of them are summarized here:

- *Additional Insured—Owners, Lessees, or Contractors (Form B)*. This endorsement can be used to add a project owner or another contractor to the general liability policy of a contractor who is the named insured.
- *Additional Insured—Club Members*. Members of a golf club can be added to the golf club's general liability policy, but only for liability arising out of club activities or activities performed on behalf of the club.
- *Additional Insured—Vendors*. This endorsement allows a manufacturer or distributor to add a retailer or other seller of its products to its own commercial general liability policy or products liability policy.

Several important problems may be faced when an additional insured is added to a general liability policy.[4] These problems are summarized as follows:

- *Dilution of insurance limits*. When other parties are added to the named insured's policy, they share the limits that apply to any occurrence that results in a claim against both of them. The result is a dilution of the policy limits for the named insured.
- *Legal defense conflicts*. When a suit is brought against both the named insured and an additional insured, often the best defense for one party is to condemn the actions of the other party. The result is a severe conflict of interest for the insurer who has the

responsibility of defending both parties. Most states resolve this conflict by requesting separate counsel at the insurer's expense.

- *Providing unintended coverage.* Because the endorsement may not be clearly worded, an additional insured may be granted coverage for loss exposures the named insured does not intend to cover. Also, since an additional insured usually does not receive a copy of the named insured's policy, the courts could rule that the policy limitations do not apply to the coverage provided an additional insured.

- *Other insurance conflicts.* Another problem for both the named insured and an additional insured involves "other insurance" provisions that appear in both policies. An additional insured is covered by both its policy and the named insured's policy. General liability policies typically have identical other insurance provisions. However, the other insurance provisions in each policy could be different. The result may be costly litigation to determine the amounts paid by each policy.

- *Administrative problems.* In most cases, a specific endorsement must be added to the named insured's policy. This increases the administrative burden for the named insured, producer and insurer.

EXAMPLES

The preceding discussion has focused, at times in the abstract, on the insurable interest requirements and definitions of "insured." It is worthwhile to see how these concepts are applied in practice by examining some actual case situations.

Situations Involving Insurable Interest

Numerous legal decisions in property and liability insurance deal with the issue of *whether or not there is an insurable interest.*[5] In one case, a couple separated. As part of the separation agreement, the wife (named insured) transferred her interest in the home to her husband by a quitclaim deed. The husband subsequently purchased insurance on the home. However, the building was destroyed in a fire before the wife's policy was canceled. The husband's insurer paid the policy limits. The former couple then attempted to collect under the wife's policy. The court ruled that the wife did not have any insurable interest in the property after title passed. Nor was the husband an insured party under the wife's policy, because he was not a spouse or relative residing in her household as required by applicable policy language.[6]

As previously noted, an option held by a lessee to buy the leased property from the lessor can support an insurable interest. In one case, the insured made improvements to property he was leasing, since he expected to exercise a purchase option, and the rent he paid was being applied toward the purchase price. A fire occurred before the lessee actually purchased the property. The insurer denied payment to the lessee based on lack of insurable interest. Despite the fire, the lessee proceeded with the acquisition of the property and submitted the question of insurable interest to the court. The court ruled that an insurable interest existed equal to the full extent of the loss (subject to the policy limits), and that he had a pecuniary interest in the property because of the option to buy.[7]

Other legal decisions deal with the *extent of the insurable interest.* Each partner in a partnership has an insurable interest in the partnership property up to its full value. However, if partnership property is insured in the name of only one partner without any stipulation that the insurance is to benefit the other partners or the business partnership, it is presumed that the insurance covers only the interest of the insured. However, if it can be shown that the insurance is for the partnership's benefit, then it is possible to recover the full value of a loss even though all partners are not named in the policy. In one case, one partner applied for insurance on a tractor owned by the partnership and paid the premiums with partnership funds. The policy, however, was issued only in the name of one partner. A loss occurred. During the trial, the other partner confirmed that the insurance was purchased for the benefit of the business partnership. A court of appeals ruled that the policyowner could recover the full value of the loss since the insurance was purchased for the firm's benefit.[8] This problem could have been avoided by naming the business partnership initially as the named insured.

Situations Involving Insured Parties

Depending on the specific policy provisions involved, numerous individuals and groups may acquire insured status under any given policy, even though only one person or entity may be the named insured. We will use the liability coverage of the personal auto policy to illustrate this point. Despite its presumably "simplified" language, the personal auto policy is a complex document with many interrelated provisions. The discussion here relates only to the issue of which parties may qualify as "insureds." Further analysis, beyond the scope of this discussion, might examine questions of legal liability and other relevant policy provisions such as exclusions or "other insurance" clauses, before concluding that a given claim would be covered.

The definition of "insured" under the liability section of the personal auto policy reads as follows:

B. "Insured" as used in this Part means:
   1. You or any "family member" for the ownership, maintenance or use of any auto or "trailer."
   2. Any person using "your covered auto."
   3. For "your covered auto," any person or organization but only with respect to legal responsibility for acts or omissions of a person for whom coverage is afforded under this Part.
   4. For any auto or "trailer," other than "your covered auto," any other person or organization but only with respect to legal responsibility for acts or omissions of you or any "family member" for whom coverage is afforded under this Part. This provision (B.4.) applies only if the person or organization does not own or hire the auto or "trailer."

"You," "your," and "family member" are among the relevant terms within the above definition that are defined in the separate "definitions" section of the policy.

Throughout this policy, "you" and "your" refer to:
1. The "named insured" shown in the Declarations; and
2. The spouse if a resident of the same household.

"Family member" means a person related to you by blood, marriage or adoption who is a resident of your household. This includes a ward or foster child.

Mike is the named insured under a personal auto policy containing the above provisions. Although she is not named in the policy declarations, his wife, Lucy, also is a named insured (see the definition of "you").

Mike's daughter, Patti, lives in a dormitory during the school year while she attends college away from home. It is a question of fact whether she remains a resident of Mike's household. Although she does not live in the family home at the moment, she generally would qualify as a "family member" because her stay at college is temporary and she regards her parents' home as her permanent residence address. The facts of this situation are not unquestionably clear, and they might gradually or abruptly change as Patti completes her schooling and obtains permanent quarters away from home.

Patti drives a Ford titled in Mike's name and described in his personal auto policy (which brings it within the policy definition of "your covered auto"). Whether or not Patti is a "family member," she is an insured while driving this Ford because of the second provision under the policy definition of "insured."

What happens if Patti allows her boyfriend to drive the Ford? The boyfriend clearly is not a "family member," but he nevertheless qualifies as "any person using 'your covered auto.' " The boyfriend is an insured.

What if Patti is driving her roommate's car? Assuming she is a "family member" under her father's policy, Patti is an insured for the use of any auto, including her roommate's.

Suppose Patti is involved in an auto accident while using her car on a field trip to do research as part of her college studies. The injured party makes a claim against the college. Is the college an insured under Patti's policy? The definition of "insured" under the PAP extends coverage to any person or organization with respect to legal responsibility for acts or omissions of any family member. Therefore, the college is an insured. Note that we did not ask the *legal* question of whether the college was liable for the injuries, only the *coverage* question concerning whether the college was an insured. Patti's insurance company would be obligated to defend the college against this claim and, if the college were found liable, to pay damages awarded against the college. The college probably would also have other insurance in its own name and protecting its own interest.

Suppose instead of driving her own car to do research, Patti was driving a vehicle owned by her boyfriend. Both she and the college still qualify as "insureds." What if the vehicle she was driving was owned by the college? In this case, the college is not an "insured" because of the last sentence of the definition of "insured." Assuming she is a "family member," Patti, however, is an "insured" in this situation, under Mike's policy.

Although the question does not come up often, it is possible for a person who is responsible for an auto-related injury to be an "insured" even though he or she is not actually operating the auto. Suppose Patti carelessly slams a taxicab door on her boyfriend's hand, breaking some bones in the process. As a "family member," she is an "insured" under her father's policy for the "use of any auto." Use of an auto is not limited to driving it.

The purpose of these various scenarios is not to provide detailed analysis of the coverage of the personal auto policy. That topic is reserved for CPCU 2. Rather, the goal here has been to illustrate the variety of ways in which "insured" status may be granted or obtained.

SUMMARY

Among other things, in order to have a legally enforceable insurance contract one must have an insurable interest in the loss, and one must also qualify as a party whose interest is insured under an insurance policy. This chapter deals with insurable interests and interests insured as they apply to property and liability insurance.

Insurable interest requirements serve three purposes. They prevent gambling, reduce intentional losses, and enforce the principle of indemnity.

In property and liability insurance, the insurable interest must exist at the time of the loss. The insurable interest may be based on property ownership, on contract rights, on potential legal liability, on factual expectation, or on representative status.

Property ownership may take many forms, and the nature of ownership has a bearing on the extent of the insurable interest. This chapter explored these various ownership forms in detail, along with the ways in which each affects the insurable interest of the various parties. Among the avenues explored here were full fee simple ownership, the effect of a mortgage, and the insurable interests of corporate stockholders. Several forms of multiple ownership were examined, including joint tenancy, tenancy by entirety, tenancy in common, tenancy in partnership, community property, and condominium ownership. Other interests examined were those of a life estate, tenancy for years, future interest, and equitable title.

Insurable interests based on contract rights may involve contract rights with respect to either persons or property. Contract rights with respect to property may be acquired in connection with the payment of a debt, as well as the sale of either real or personal property.

The question of insurable interest is rarely raised in connection with liability insurance. There is little reason to raise the question in the absence of any claim, and the existence of a claim against an insured serves by itself as persuasive proof that the insured faced a loss exposure and, therefore, had an insurable interest.

Factual expectation usually is not an acceptable basis for an insurable interest. Representative status, on the other hand, often does provide such a basis.

Insurance contracts carefully specify the parties whose interests are insured and to whom coverage, therefore, applies. Those specified by name may include not only the named insured (who may be called "you" throughout most of the policy), but also assignees and secured creditors. Other insureds, who may have somewhat lesser rights, may be identified not by name but by describing their relationship to the named insured. Some parties whose interests are insured may, in fact, serve as legal substitutes for the insured. An insurance policy may also be endorsed to name or describe additional insureds.

Chapter Notes

1. Robert E. Keeton and Alan I. Widiss, *Insurance Law, A Guide to Fundamental Principles, Legal Doctrines, and Commercial Practices* (St. Paul, MN: West Publishing Company, 1988), p. 169.
2. California Insurance Code, section 283 (1955), cited in Keeton and Widiss, p. 170.
3. For exhaustive treatment of this topic, see Donald S. Malecki and Jack P. Gibson, *The Additional Insured Book* (Dallas, TX: International Risk Management Institute, 1991).
4. "Additional Insureds in Liability Insurance," *The Risk Report*, vol. 12, no. 6 (February 1990), pp. 3-4.
5. The legal cases cited in this section are based on "Interest Feature Property Policies," *FC&S Bulletins*, Fire and Marine volume, Misc. Property section, February 1990, pp. Ci 1-Ci 5.
6. Morgan v. American Security Insurance Co., 1988-89, C.C.H. (Fire & Casualty) 1078.
7. Georgia Farm Bureau Mutual Insurance Co. v. Mikell, 191 S.E. 2nd 557 (1972).
8. Aetna v. King, 265 So. 2d 716 (1972).

CHAPTER 5

Insured Events

An insurance policy is a conditional contract. When a certain type of event takes place, an insurer *may* be obligated to make a payment to, or on behalf of, one or more parties who both have an insurable interest and qualify as an insured under an insurance policy. However, the insurer will not be obligated to pay unless an *insured event* has taken place. An insured event must entail all of the following six elements, which are called the *elements of an insured event:*

1. Covered property or activity
2. Covered cause
3. Covered consequence
4. Covered (nonexcluded) circumstances
5. Covered location
6. Covered time period

The first four elements concern *what* things are covered, while the last two deal, respectively, with *where* and *when* they are covered.

A particular incident has been, is, or will be an insured event *only* if all six elements are involved. If even one element is missing, it is not an insured event—even if an insured party has suffered a fortuitous financial loss as the result of some mishap. For example, a loss that is not the result of a covered cause does not involve an insured event even if it involves covered property, a covered circumstance, a covered consequence, a covered location, and a covered time period.

When an insured event occurs, the insurer does not necessarily have an obligation to pay for a claim. The event is still an insured event, even if a policy condition is breached—if, for example, the insured has made material misrepresentations in the application for insurance. The insurer may not pay the entire amount of the loss—or any amount at all—because of policy limits, deductibles, or other limitations on the *amount* of recovery; these do not negate the existence of an insured *event*. (Conditions, limits, and deductibles are examined closely in other chapters of this text.)

In short, the six elements of an insured event may be thought of as necessary but not sufficient determinants of an insurer's contractual obligation to pay for a given loss or claim. That is, for a claim to be paid these six elements must be present *and* other requirements also must be met.

INSURED EVENTS UNDER PROPERTY INSURANCE POLICIES

Six elements of an insured event must be present for both property and liability coverages. The six elements of insured events under property insurance policies will be discussed first. Their application in a liability insurance context will be discussed later in this chapter.

Covered Property

According to the discussion of insurable interests in Chapter 4, the *legal concept* of "property" refers to a bundle of rights that have economic value because they are guaranteed and protected by law. While this legal concept of property is critical to the notion of insurable interests, it does not offer a practical way of identifying the *physical objects* of real and personal property that most often are covered under property insurance policies. The discussion here examines specific ways in which covered property is identified in various property insurance policies.

Property insurance policies come from a number of different sources. While standard property forms are developed as advisory products by the American Association of Insurance Services (AAIS) and Insurance Services Office (ISO), a wide variety of other policies also are in use:

- The forms of the Factory Mutual System and Industrial Risk Insurers are widely used among industrial and institutional organizations.
- The excess and surplus lines markets develop property forms for situations where the exposures of a given entity are difficult to insure in the standard market.
- Manuscript policies occasionally are drafted to meet special needs.
- Independently filed forms and policies of individual insurers may

contain many standard provisions combined with others that are unique.

Also, while many current property forms incorporate so-called "plain-English" or "easy-to-read" characteristics, others use more traditional insurance language. Given this diversity, it is understandable that specific approaches to insuring real and personal property vary. Yet, most property policies follow a similar pattern. The discussion here describes the general pattern, as well as some specific variations.

The General Pattern. All property insurance policies have a section of some sort describing *covered property*. In some cases, such as a jewelry floater or contractors equipment floater, the property subject to coverage may be specifically scheduled (listed) on an item-by-item basis. Most policies, however, do not list each specific item subject to coverage but describe covered property items in some generic manner.

Following the section of a property insurance policy that describes broad classes of *covered property*, a typical policy contains another section describing narrower subclasses of *property that is not covered*. Together, these two sections still do not usually contain *all* of the policy provisions relating to covered property. Policy provisions that appear elsewhere in the policy forms, or even endorsements, may add or exclude specific types of property for coverage against a particular peril.

For example, the broad homeowners policy form does the following, among other things:

- Includes as covered property "personal property owned or used by an 'insured' while it is anywhere in the world"
- Lists "aircraft and parts" among the "property not covered"
- Excludes coverage for "watercraft and their trailers, furnishings, equipment, and outboard engines or motors" that are outside a fully-enclosed building with respect to the perils of windstorm or hail damage

Aircraft and watercraft are personal property, encompassed by the broad generic description of covered property. Aircraft and parts, however, are one type of personal property that is not covered for any peril. Watercraft and related equipment located outdoors are covered for most perils, but they are not covered against windstorm or hail damage.

A similar pattern may be discerned in nearly all property insurance policies. The principal differences among commercial, residential, and auto physical damage forms lie in the types of property each seeks to cover. Both the common pattern and the differing definitions are illustrated in the following examples. Actual policy language is quoted here to illustrate specific principles without focusing on the full scope of the entire policy. For this reason, many of the quotations are not identified with specific policies or trade names.

"Commercial Property."[1] One form widely used to insure commercial fixed-location property stipulates that the policy applies to "direct physical loss of or damage to Covered Property at the premises described in the Declarations. . . ." The form then goes on to describe in rather precise terms what the covered property includes. The form divides the covered property into three categories, and insurance may be purchased on property in any or all categories.

Real Property as Covered Property. The first category of covered property generally encompasses real property. However, land is not included in the list, and some items that legally would be defined as personal property are. The form reads as follows:

> Covered Property, as used in this Coverage Part, means the following types of property for which a Limit of Insurance is shown in the Declarations:
> a. Building, meaning the building or structure described in the Declarations, including:
>   (1) Completed additions;
>   (2) Permanently installed:
>   (a) Fixtures;
>   (b) Machinery; and
>   (c) Equipment;
>   (3) Outdoor fixtures;
>   (4) Personal property owned by you that is used to maintain or service the building or structure or its premises, including:
>   (a) Fire extinguishing equipment;
>   (b) Outdoor furniture;
>   (c) Floor coverings; and
>   (d) Appliances used for refrigerating, ventilating, cooking, dishwashing or laundering;
>   (5) If not covered by other insurance:
>   (a) Additions under construction, alterations and repairs to the building or structure;
>   (b) Materials, equipment, supplies and temporary structures, on or within 100 feet of the described premises, used for making additions, alterations or repairs to the building or structure.

The above provision attempts to separate what is covered here, generally real property, from personal property which may be covered under another policy category. The distinctions made here do not track precisely with the legal distinctions between real and personal property. As is typical of commercial property forms, certain kinds of personal property are by stipulation within the category of buildings. Included within the policy description of "building" is personal property owned by the insured that is used to maintain or service the realty. Fire extinguishing equipment and outdoor furniture are examples.

The provision mentions both "buildings" and "structures." A building is a structure, but not all structures are buildings. Examples of nonbuilding structures are underground tanks, tunnels, television antennas, and billboards. The fact that this property insurance form specifically refers to "buildings" makes it necessary to also mention "structures" if they are to be covered. This very specific use of terms must then be taken into consideration throughout the form wherever the word "building" or "structure" is used.[2]

This covered property provision applies to those buildings and structures identified in the policy's declarations. While coverage also applies to additions under construction, alterations, and repairs—provided no other insurance is applicable—this form is not a complete substitute for a builders risk policy that is more specifically designed to protect parties with insurable interests in property during construction. However, any insured who fails to purchase a builders risk policy will still have coverage for this exposure.

Personal Property as Covered Property. The two categories of personal property covered in this same policy are (1) business property of the insured and (2) personal property of others. The related sections of this "commercial property" insurance form read as follows:

b. Your Business Personal Property located in or on the building described in the Declarations or in the open (or in a vehicle) within 100 feet of the described premises, consisting of the following unless otherwise specified in the Declarations or on the Your Business Personal Property—Separation of Coverage form:

 (1) Furniture and fixtures;
 (2) Machinery and equipment;
 (3) "Stock";
 (4) All other personal property owned by you and used in your business;
 (5) Labor, materials or services furnished or arranged by you on personal property of others; and
 (6) Your use interest as tenant in improvements and betterments. Improvements and betterments are fixtures, alterations, installations or additions:

  (a) Made a part of the building or structure you occupy but do not own; and
  (b) You acquired or made at your expense but cannot legally remove.

c. Personal Property of Others that is:

 (1) In your care, custody or control; and
 (2) Located in or on the building described in the Declarations or in the open (or in a vehicle) with 100 feet of the described premises.

 However, our payment for loss or damage to personal property of others will only be for the account of the owner of the property.

In light of the locational restriction on this business personal property to the described premises or within 100 feet of it, additional insurance of some type would be needed to cover the loss exposures presented by such property while in transit or at other locations.

The fact that this coverage provision refers to property "in or on the *building* described" (emphasis added) leaves open the question of whether business personal property within a structure likewise is covered. It also leaves open the question as to what is or are "premises" as opposed to building(s) or other structures. Some insurance policies use "premises" to refer to a building that has physical substance, while others use it simply to refer to a place. In this case, if the "place" meaning is applied, it would seem that "premises" probably is intended to include the surrounding land.

Although tenants' improvements and betterments form an integral part of the realty, they are treated as business personal property to protect the tenants' use interest in such real property for the duration of the lease. Tenants normally do not purchase coverage on the building they occupy. If this provision were not incorporated within the business personal property provisions of the form, it would be necessary for tenants to purchase separate coverage against loss to those improvements and betterments. Those who did not recognize and specifically insure this exposure would lack coverage.[3]

Both Real and Personal Property as Covered Property. While the most common practice is to cover real and personal property as separate categories of covered property, some policies combine them into a single category. A manuscript policy that combines real and personal property coverages for a large commercial firm might include a provision such as the one which follows:

Covered Property
This policy insures:
A. real and personal property (including that which is hereafter constructed, installed or acquired, including while in course of construction, erection, installation or assembly), which is
   1. owned by the insured, or
   2. owned by others, and
      a. which is in the insured's care, custody, or control (whether actual or constructive), including that which is leased, occupied or used by the insured; or
      b. which is intended for ownership, lease, occupancy or other use by the insured; or
      c. for which the insured,
         (1) shall have agreed to insure, or otherwise assume liability or responsibility for by contract (written or oral); or
         (2) may otherwise be liable by law.

B. shipments of property sold by the insured under F.O.B. point of origin, or other terms usually regarded as terminating shipper's responsibility short of point of delivery.

C. at the sole option of the insured:
1. the interest of others (except common carriers) in real and personal property;
2. the interest of consignees or purchasers in shipments of property sold by the insured under the terms of F.O.B. point of origin;
3. the interest of the insured's executives and employees in personal property owned by them (or by others for which they may be liable by law) while at locations or premises owned, leased, occupied or used by the insured; and
4. the interest of the insured in real and personal property of others (including improvement and betterments made thereto); and as respects improvements and betterments made by, or at the direction of, and/or at the expense of the insured, the insured shall be considered to be the sole and unconditional owner, notwithstanding any contract or leases to the contrary.

While some kinds of property are outside the scope of this particular policy, note that this coverage provision is designed to encompass virtually all of the entity's insurable interests in real and personal property, whether owned or nonowned, including real property in the course of construction and personal property in transit wherever it might be located within the territorial restrictions of the policy.

Property Not Covered. Except when insured property items are specifically listed or scheduled, property insurance policies invariably contain a section that describes certain types of property that is not covered. The typical "property not covered" provision reduces the likelihood of coverage duplications, and it eliminates coverage that is not needed by the typical purchaser or that requires special treatment. Even manuscript policies exclude certain kinds of property that generally require specialized coverage, such as money and securities, or property subject to ocean marine or aviation exposures.

A "property not covered" policy section is not an exhaustive list describing all otherwise-covered property for which coverage is not provided. Usually, some types of otherwise-covered property are not covered against damage by certain perils. Take, for example, vandalism damage to glass on a building covered under a "commercial property" policy written subject to the building and personal property coverage form and the causes of loss—basic form. This policy provides coverage on the building and does not exclude glass as "property not covered." However, the following exception appears under the vandalism peril:

We will not pay for loss or damage . . . to glass (other than glass building blocks) that is part of a building, structure, or an outside sign; but we will pay for loss or damage to other property caused by or resulting from breakage of glass by vandals.

Building glass is covered property for losses caused by fire, windstorm, and all other named perils except vandalism.

Residential Property. Despite other differences, the format for indicating and describing covered property under most residential insurance policies, including homeowners packages, corresponds closely to that of commercial property policies.

For the owner of a dwelling, residential property insurance offers the following three major categories of covered property:

A. The dwelling, including any structures attached to it
B. Any other structure(s), on the residence premises, which is set apart from the dwelling by a clear space, such as a detached garage
C. Personal property owned or used by the insured

The owner-occupant of a dwelling usually has an insurable interest in all three categories of property. An owner-landlord of unfurnished property may have an interest in only the first two. If the occupant of a residence is not the owner, then the tenant usually needs to cover only personal property.

All residential policies—like commercial property forms—not only contain a section describing "property not covered" but also exclude certain kinds of property against loss by some particular perils. For example, fences are not covered against loss caused by a vehicle owned or operated by a resident of the residence premises.

Motor Vehicles. Although motor vehicles are items of personal property, some types of motor vehicles commonly are excluded under the commercial and residential categories previously discussed. Autos usually are excluded; they typically are covered under auto insurance policies. Other motor vehicles (such as lawn mowers, forklift trucks, tractors, earthmoving equipment), often collectively referred to as "mobile equipment," may be covered or excluded depending on the nature of the property and the provisions of the specific policy. Autos and other motor vehicles may be owned, nonowned, or hired[4] and may be used for commercial or personal purposes—or both. The discussion here refers only to physical damage to motor vehicles and not to vehicle-related liability exposures, which will be discussed later.

Autos as Covered Property. One widely used personal auto policy includes the following provisions under the *coverage for damage to your auto* section of the policy:

> We will pay for direct and accidental loss to "your covered auto" or any "non-owned auto" including their equipment, minus any applicable deductible shown in the Declarations. We will pay for loss to "your covered auto" caused by. . . .

The nature of the covered auto in this policy hinges on the definitions of "your covered auto" and "non-owned auto." "Your covered auto" includes the auto described in the policy declarations. It also can include a newly acquired auto, provided the owner notifies the insurer in accordance with policy requirements.

Other exposures develop when, as is common today, people rent, lease, or borrow autos from others. On occasion, individuals also use a garage-furnished auto in place of their own auto, which may be undergoing repair or servicing because of breakdown, loss, or destruction. The physical damage coverage of the personal auto policy mentioned above encompasses physical loss or damage to autos of others. Not all personal auto policies necessarily extend coverage in this way. Some auto policies provide coverage for physical loss or damage to owned autos only.

The definitions of covered vehicles can be more complicated in policies providing physical damage insurance on commercial autos.

Automotive Property Not Covered. Generally, a policy written to cover a motor vehicle against loss or damage also covers the vehicle's equipment. However, audio equipment commonly is covered only if it is permanently installed in the covered auto, and some items of property are not covered at all. Items that may be entirely excluded are, for example, tapes, compact discs, two-way radios, and cellular telephones.

Mobile Equipment. Mobile equipment often is covered under a contractors equipment floater where each item of covered property is "scheduled" or listed with information such as a description of the property item, the name of the manufacturer, and the serial number. For a policy containing a schedule of covered property, including a complete description and coverage amount for each item, a typical policy description of covered property reads as follows:

Covered Property
We cover only those described items for which a coverage amount is shown.

Even though covered property is specifically listed, the same policy contains a section describing property not covered. This list may, for example, preclude coverage for property rented to others. Such items are not covered property even if they are listed in the schedule. A similar approach is taken in many other inland marine policies.

Property of Others. While property insurance deals most directly with property owned by the named insured, most policies also extend coverage to some property of others. A widely used commercial property form offers the following two methods for covering personal property of others:

- A "coverage extension" provides some automatic coverage. At the option of the named insured, coverage may be extended to cover personal property of others in the named insured's care, custody, or control. The insurance provided here commonly is subject to a dollar limit, and coverage applies only when the named insured elects to have the insurer pay for the covered loss. The election need not be made until after the loss occurs. This modest coverage extension may be adequate for businesses with only an incidental exposure involving property of others.
- A separate insuring agreement permits those who need it to purchase a specific dollar limit of coverage on property of others. This insuring agreement was quoted in the earlier discussion of personal property.

Bailees may prefer, instead, to forgo coverage under this form and instead obtain protection against loss to property of others in their care through a bailees customers floater or some form of inland marine insurance more specifically tailored to a particular situation.

Residential policies, in addition to covering personal property owned by the usual group of insureds who are both relatives and household residents, provide extensions of coverage to property of others—commonly subject to a special dollar limitation or contingent on the named insured's request that the insurer pay for the loss of property of others.

Specific details of coverage on property of others is examined in other CPCU courses in the context of these specific policies. The point here is that not only the named insured's property, but also property owned by others, may be described as covered property under a property insurance policy. This coverage may be subject to specific dollar limits, and it may not be automatic, requiring that the named insured elect to have this coverage apply to someone else's property. (In some cases the named insured will not choose to provide coverage for the benefit of someone else. The named insured, for example, might be angry with the other property owner for some reason—perhaps a guest's careless smoking destroyed not only the guest's property but property of the named insured as well. Or the named insured might need to apply the full limits of available coverage to cover his or her own loss.)

Newly Acquired Property. "Commercial property" insurance policies generally cover specified property at a described location. In addition, most policies include an extension whereby newly acquired or constructed real property, as well as newly acquired personal property, is covered automatically, subject to certain stipulations. (Although the phrase "newly acquired" seems wordy and redundant, we use it because it commonly is used in the language of insurance, and it does accurately connote an exposure that previously was not present.)

For either newly acquired or newly constructed real property, the typical policy restricts automatic coverage to a certain maximum dollar limit and a specified maximum period. Business personal property acquired during the policy period for use at these new locations also is commonly covered, again subject to dollar and time limits.

When personal property is not specifically described—as is generally the case with household contents, for example, newly acquired property is naturally covered, subject only to the usual restrictions on covered property. Some property forms written on specifically described personal property automatically cover additionally acquired property of the same general type.

Personal automobile policies typically provide automatic physical damage protection for most types of newly acquired autos; business auto policies are somewhat more variable, depending on the way the individual policy is configured. However, if those vehicles are to be covered against their physical loss or damage, the insurer generally requires notice of such intent from the insured within thirty days of the vehicle's acquisition.

Covered Causes

An insured event, under a property insurance policy, must involve a covered cause. Analyzing this second element of an insured event requires a basic understanding of the specified perils approach, the "all-risks" approach, the difference in conditions (DIC) approach, and a number of related concepts.

Specified Perils Approach. A "peril" is a cause of loss. When a policy specifically lists or names the perils against which it insures, it is said to be using the "specified perils approach." For example, a specified perils policy might name the perils of fire, lightning, explosion, windstorm or hail, smoke, aircraft or vehicles, and other perils that are specifically identified by name or are described.

A mere listing of perils does not mean that the policy is intended to cover every loss associated with one or more of them. On the contrary, policy definitions, exclusions, or both invariably restrict coverage by narrowing the meaning of some or all perils. For example, most specified perils forms that include the peril of "smoke" exclude smoke from agricultural smudging or industrial operations.

Some perils are given very precise definitions. Others are simply named without comment, in which case their interpretation is ultimately in the hands of the courts. For example, one popular policy defines the peril of "sinkhole collapse" as follows:

Sinkhole Collapse, meaning loss or damage caused by the sudden sinking or collapse of land into underground empty spaces created by the action of water on limestone or dolomite.

This very precise definition narrows the range of possible meanings of "sinkhole collapse."

In stark contrast, "fire" usually is named but not defined. Most courts have given "fire" a much narrower meaning in insurance policies than it has in ordinary conversation. Courts have said that fire is "oxidation rapid enough to produce flame or glow," but they also have held that policy coverage for "fire" does not extend to "friendly fires"—those deliberately set and remaining in their normal confines. Although logs burning in a fireplace constitute a fire in everyday language, destruction by fire of those logs is not an insured event because the friendly fire is not a covered peril.

Court interpretations do not always have the effect of confining coverage. In fact, courts often require insurers to pay losses that some people do not consider "caused by" a named peril.

The specified perils approach has the practical effect of placing the *burden of proof* on the insured. To obtain coverage, the *insured* must be able to prove that covered loss consequences were the proximate result of a covered peril. If such proof cannot be provided by the insured, the insurer is not legally obligated to pay the loss. In most cases this is a moot point because the cause of loss is obvious. In others, however, it is so difficult to prove the cause of a loss that the party who bears the burden of proof will not prevail.

Basic Perils Approach.   At one time, most buildings and their contents were covered against only the perils of fire and lightning. Coverage for these two perils was combined because lightning strikes often led to fire damage and it was not practical to attempt to distinguish the damage attributable to each peril. Coverage against other property perils also became available, and it eventually became common to provide *extended coverage* against a package of perils known as the *extended coverage (EC) perils*—windstorm, hail, aircraft, vehicles, riot and civil commotion, explosion, and smoke. Many property insurance policies included an *extended coverage endorsement,* which added all these perils for a single premium rate; in other policies these perils were written directly into the policy language. Often the peril of *vandalism and malicious mischief* (VMM) was added for a modest additional premium. For many years, a large number of businesses and residences were insured for the perils of *"Fire, EC, and VMM."* Some policies may still follow this pattern, but the basic perils package of most contemporary insurance policies includes some added perils, and the traditional "extended coverage" or "EC" package of perils has become dated. Even so, the terms or abbreviations still appear in many leases and other legal documents used or drafted by people who have not kept pace with insurance developments. "Extended coverage" is described here so that the term will not be unfamiliar to the reader who encounters it in practice.

When "commercial property" insurance is written, the basic perils approach commonly is provided by the "causes of loss—basic form." This form offers coverage against the following eleven named perils in a single package:

- Fire
- Lightning
- Explosion
- Windstorm or hail
- Smoke
- Aircraft or vehicles
- Riot or civil commotion
- Vandalism
- Sprinkler leakage
- Sinkhole collapse
- Volcanic action

(The last three are in addition to the old "Fire, EC, and VMM" combination.) Windstorm or hail, vandalism, or sprinkler leakage can be excluded by endorsement.

Where it still is available, the residential insurance forms that offer a limited number of perils sometimes are referred to as the basic dwelling form or the basic homeowners form. While the precise number of covered perils varies from one form to another, the typical basic residential insurance policy includes essentially the same perils as the causes of loss—basic form of commercial policies. The basic homeowners form also includes the peril of theft and volcanic eruption but omits the perils of sprinkler leakage and volcanic action. (Volcanic eruption is broader than volcanic action, and automatic sprinkler systems are not yet common in single family residences.)

Whatever the covered peril, restrictions generally apply under both residential and commercial policies. For example, the following exception typically applies to windstorm damage to property inside buildings:

Windstorm or Hail.
This peril does not include loss to the inside of a building or the property contained in a building caused by rain, snow, sleet, sand or dust unless the direct force of wind or hail damages the building causing an opening in a roof or wall and the rain, snow, sleet, sand or dust enters through this opening.

The basic perils approach also may be used in policies providing auto physical damage coverage. This approach often is used with commercial vehicles—particularly trailers and other vehicles with no substantial glass breakage exposure. It offers protection against physical loss or damage by the following "specified causes of loss":

1. Fire, lightning, or explosion
2. Theft
3. Windstorm, hail, or earthquake
4. Flood
5. Mischief or vandalism
6. The sinking, burning, collision, or derailment of any conveyance transporting the covered auto

Absent from this list is the most serious peril threatening most autos—collision. This is a basic peril of both personal and commercial auto policies that can be included, subject to a deductible, if collision coverage is specifically designated and the additional premium paid for it. Or collision coverage can be omitted, along with the commensurate premium charge.

Broad Perils Approach. The broad form approach offers coverage against a longer list of named perils than the basic form approach. The broad form homeowners policy begins with the perils of the basic form, but adds several more. A similar approach is taken in the causes of loss—broad form used to provide "commercial property" coverage.

Both residential and commercial broad forms use a similar approach in their coverage against loss or damage caused by breakage of glass; falling objects; weight of snow, ice, or sleet; and water damage, including freezing. The broad form peril of "falling objects" illustrates this point. "Falling objects" is not defined in either residential or commercial property forms. "Object" therefore could include anything—a tree, rock, meteorite, spilled paint, or even a fallen angel from a Christmas tree. To avoid carrying coverage to a ridiculous extreme, this peril is limited— not by defining the peril, but by excluding certain types of property from the coverage of commercial and residential policies: personal property in the open is not covered, nor is the interior of a building or its contents, unless the roof or outside wall is first damaged by a falling object. Likewise property policies generally cover loss by freezing, provided the insured takes reasonable measures to maintain heat in the building or dwelling or, if heat is not maintained, the insured turns off the water supply and drains the system or appliance.

Additional Specified Perils Approach. Certain causes of loss do not lend themselves to being automatically included in property insurance policies. They may, however, be covered through separate forms or endorsements. One such peril, which is catastrophic in nature, is earthquake. Virtually all forms of property insurance, barring automobile physical damage, many inland marine forms, and some manuscript property forms, specifically exclude loss caused by "earth movement" (which commonly is defined to encompass earthquake, landslide, or earth sinking, rising, or shifting). But generally excepted from the exclusion (and therefore covered) is loss or damage by fire or explosion (other than boiler explosions) that results from such earth movement. For example, gas escaping from mains broken by the earthquake may ignite, causing major fires. If a property owner wants to insure against the possibility of loss by earth movement, a residential policy usually can be endorsed to provide a certain amount of insurance. When it is a commercial entity's property that is exposed to loss, a causes of loss—earthquake form can be purchased.

Another peril in this category is flood. Like earthquakes, floods are catastrophic in nature. However, they are more predictable than earthquakes. For property in some low-lying areas, the question is not whether floods will occur, but when and how often. A loss that is certain is not something that the private insurance mechanism is well-equipped to handle. However, flood insurance on buildings and their contents is available through the National Flood Insurance Program sponsored by the federal government.

Auto insurance policies and policies covering personal property of a mobile nature generally include coverage against flood. Such property typically is not exposed to flood because it is fixed in a particular location, and mobile property often can be removed from an area endangered by flood.

As mentioned earlier, coverage for money and securities is excluded or severely limited under most property insurance policies. Also, most named perils property forms do not provide coverage against burglary, robbery, or any other form of theft. Crime insurance can cover money and securities and other property against a variety of crime perils that can be categorized into the following six classes:

1. Destruction or disappearance of money and securities
2. Burglary, which occurs when someone forcibly enters the place where the property is kept
3. Robbery, which involves the use of force or the threat of force against the person or persons from whom the property is taken
4. Theft, which encompasses any act of stealing
5. Employee dishonesty which, in a general sense, is theft of an employer's property by an employee
6. Forgery or alteration, which involves the signing of someone else's name to, or alteration of, a document

All of these are very general definitions of the perils.

Most residential policies include coverage against theft, subject to a specified dollar limitation on certain kinds of property. For example, theft, though the term itself is not defined under one standard homeowners policy, specifically "includes" coverage against "attempted theft and loss of property from a known location where it is likely that the property has been stolen." Covered causes include such obvious events as burglary, robbery, or larceny. Less obvious events also are covered when the circumstances at least show the likelihood or presumption that property was stolen and not merely misplaced—a situation sometimes referred to as "mysterious disappearance." The burden of proof is on the insured. However, homeowners policies generally limit theft coverage to exclude the following:

1. *Theft caused by the insured.* It would be against public policy to cover someone's own criminal acts.
2. *Loss by theft to a dwelling under construction, as well as materials and supplies for use in the construction.* These exposures are highly susceptible to loss in the absence of proper safeguards.
3. *Loss by theft to property contained in that part of the residence premises rented to other than an insured.* This exposure is difficult to control.

Item (1) above actually limits the theft peril, while (2) and (3) limit the types of property covered against this peril.

Even though theft is a covered cause of loss, certain kinds of property often are subject to sublimits applicable only to loss by theft. Common to residential policies, for example, is a $1,000 theft sublimit on jewelry, watches, furs, and precious and semi-precious stones, and a $2,000 theft limit on firearms of any type.

"All-Risks" Approach. The broadest approach in terms of covered perils is referred to by a number of different terms including "all-risks," "special coverage," "causes of loss—special form," and "open perils."

"All Risks of. . . ." "All-risks" insurance often is simply described as coverage against all perils except as otherwise specifically excluded; that characterization is simplistic and inaccurate. Whether coverage ultimately applies hinges not only on the exact insurance policy wording but also on certain conditions inherent in this coverage concept.

Various property policies cover "all risks of direct physical loss," "all risks of physical loss," or "all risks of loss." It is not easy to say whether these phrases are different, even after reading the entire policy. Some insurers undoubtedly believe the phrase "direct loss" within the "all-risks" insuring clause equates it with proximate cause. This rationale does not necessarily hold up in court. Other insurers may select the term "direct physical loss" as their choice to eliminate coverage for other loss consequences. Even if an "all-risks" insuring agreement is completely devoid of such references as "direct physical loss," it still may not necessarily mean that loss of use or other loss consequences are covered, since these consequences may be the subject of a specific exclusion elsewhere in the policy. In fact, it is common to see "loss of use" exclusions within policies that condition coverage on "all risks of direct physical loss."

Reference to "physical" loss, moreover, suggests that the covered property must first sustain some kind of tangible damage before the loss is covered. If that was the intent of the policy drafters, some courts have not been convinced. In one case, for example, an "all-risks" insurance policy that covered personal property against "loss or damage . . . resulting from all risk of direct physical loss" was held to cover loss sustained by the insured who was forced to vacate its building because of its imminent collapse, even though there was no direct physical loss to the covered property.[5] Another case involved the question of whether the accumulation of gasoline vapors within a church building constituted direct physical loss within the meaning of the property policy. The structure could not be used while that condition persisted. A court held that this was direct physical loss, thus opening the door for loss of use coverage to apply.[6]

"Risks of Loss." Even though the phrase "all risks" has been held not to be synonymous with "all losses,"[7] a growing number of insurers have dropped reference to "all risks" in their policies. The phrase "all risks" has sometimes given the mistaken impression that coverage applied to *all* risks of loss. The insuring clauses of some modern policies therefore refer to this coverage approach as "risks of loss." One such standard "commercial property" reads as follows:

> We will cover risks of direct physical loss, except as excluded or limited.

It remains to be seen whether this approach will alleviate all the problems experienced by insurers against whom judgments were rendered because of their policies' reference to "all risks." A problem still may exist because the word "risk" has been said to be somewhat difficult to define and "is an abstract term with no physical counterpart."[8]

In any event, the phrase "all risks" is so deeply seated in the jargon of insurance that it is still commonly used by practitioners to describe the broadest form of protection against loss or damage to property. Also, various commercial property forms have not been converted to use the presumably less troublesome wording. For our purposes, the phrase "all risks," hyphenated when used as an adjective, still serves to concisely label this approach to perils.

Difference in Conditions Approach. The term "difference in conditions" refers to the approach used in some policies that cover only those perils that are not covered by another policy. The most common application of this approach appears in the type of policy known as a "difference in conditions" (DIC) policy. Although there is no standard DIC policy, coverage commonly is written on an "all-risks" basis, subject to certain exclusions.

A DIC policy may list as being excluded all of those perils commonly found in a causes of loss—basic form, such as fire, windstorm, aircraft, vehicles, explosion, vandalism, and sprinkler leakage. What remains is coverage for the *difference* between an "all-risks" policy and one covering the perils that are specifically excluded. Among other things, this difference could include coverage against loss or damage by earthquake, flood (unless coverage is required through the governmental insurance program), contamination, collapse, extremes of temperature, and boiler damage because of earth movement.

The electronic data processing (EDP) policy's coverage on equipment leased to the insured is another form of protection that follows the DIC concept. Under a typical rental agreement the lessor is responsible for loss or damage to the property by certain perils. If it used the DIC approach, the lessee's EDP policy would then provide coverage only against losses for which the lessor is not contractually responsible.

Related Concepts. Among the concepts that can affect coverage under a property policy written on an "all-risks" basis are the concepts of *fortuity, external cause, ensuing loss, proximate cause,* and *concurrent causation.*

Fortuity. Fortuity means that the event—if it is to be subject to insurance—must take place by accident and be unexpected and unintended. So, while an insurance policy written on an "all-risks" basis may not specifically exclude, for example, damage to property because of its *ordinary* wear and tear or because of the insured's intentional misconduct, that does not mean that such forseeable losses are covered.[9] The preceding emphasis on *ordinary* wear and tear is intended to make clear that extraordinary or unusual wear and tear loss is fortuitous and not necessarily precluded from coverage. It depends on how the policy is worded. Generally, it is necessary that the policy be clarified by exempting *abnormal* wear and tear; otherwise, it is probably safe to say that all wear and tear loss is excluded. Note, however, that what normally is excluded is loss *due to* the wear and tear and not loss or damage that *ensues* from such wear and tear. Damage by an electrical fire caused by a worn extension cord would not be excluded on account of the cord's ordinary wear and tear.

The concept of fortuity also would preclude coverage against loss resulting from inherent vice or defect, whether or not an explicit exclusion applies. Inherent vice is a condition within a particular type of property that tends to make the property damage or destroy itself. The souring of wine, the rotting of fruit, and the deterioration of natural rubber over a prolonged period when it is not in use are all examples of inherent vice.

External Cause. When an "all-risks" policy limits its coverage to "all risks of direct physical loss from any *external cause,*" the question arises as to whether the additional reference to external cause adds yet another limiting condition. It appears the reason for mentioning external causes is to reinforce the intent that the policy apply only to fortuitous events. Thus, for example, if a loss were due to *normal* shrinking, cracking, bulging, or settling, it would not be fortuitous and, hence, not the result of an external cause; conversely, if the loss were due to *abnormal* shrinking, cracking, bulging, or settling, or if it were extraneous in nature, it would be fortuitous and externally caused.[10] This is not to say that such loss would necessarily be covered, since coverage would hinge on how the policy exclusion is worded.

Ensuing Loss. Most property policies written on an "all-risks" basis make exceptions to certain exclusions and grant coverage for *ensuing losses.* For example, a policy provision may exclude loss or damage from an earthquake or other earth movement but make an exception for, say, any fire or explosion that otherwise ensues.[11] So, even if damage directly attributable to nuclear reaction is excluded, other damage caused by an otherwise ensuing fire may be covered. The extent to which ensuing loss is covered hinges on the property policy in question.

Proximate Cause. An insured event must involve, among other elements, covered property, a covered cause, and a covered consequence. A peril can be considered to have led to a particular consequence only when a sufficiently close causal connection exists between the peril and the consequence. This "causal link" requirement is known as the *doctrine of proximate cause.*

Molded by court decisions, the doctrine generally holds that coverage for a loss is provided under a property insurance policy only if a covered peril is the proximate cause of a covered consequence. A peril is a *covered peril* if it is either (1) specified and not excluded in a specified perils policy or (2) not excluded in an "all-risks" policy. A covered peril is the *proximate cause* if it is the cause that initiates an unbroken chain of events leading to a covered consequence. Or, as stated in one court decision:

> Proximate cause is a cause which in a natural and continuous sequence, unbroken by any new and independent cause, produces an event, and without which the event would not have happened.[12]

An illustration may clarify the concept of proximate cause. A fire ignited an electrical tower on the insured's premises some distance from the building in which covered machinery was located. As a result of the fire, there was an electrical short circuit which, in turn, caused a sudden increase in the pressure on a belt driving a flywheel. The flywheel disintegrated, and its flying fragments damaged the covered machinery. The court ruled that the damage to the machinery was proximately caused by fire. Since the insurance policy covered direct damage (the covered consequences) by fire (a covered peril), the insurer had to pay for the damaged machinery, even though "collision with flywheel fragments" (or anything comparable) was not a covered peril. The fire unleashed an unbroken chain of events that resulted in the machinery damage. Fire was the proximate cause of the loss, and fire was indeed a covered peril.[13]

By applying the proximate cause doctrine to specific sets of facts, the courts have broadened significantly the coverage scope of many property insurance policies. For example, an insurer of property had to pay for spoilage of the insured's meat that resulted when the electrical power supply to the insured's cold storage facilities was interrupted because a windstorm had damaged power lines. The wind itself did not, however, blow on the meat. Applying the test of proximate cause, the interruption of the power supply by the windstorm set into motion a chain of events that culminated in the meat spoilage. Such spoilage therefore was within the contemplation of the policy provision that covered direct loss by windstorm.[14]

Another case involved a policy under which vandalism was a covered peril and water damage was not. Vandals threw electric switches, which caused a lack of heat and, in turn, caused pipes to freeze, burst, and release water, causing damage that was held to be covered under the vandalism peril. The reasoning was that, while water damage was in and of itself an excluded peril, the damage was the result of an unbroken chain of events originating in the peril of vandalism.[15]

There have been many court cases along the lines of those just cited, and in some cases the court has ruled in favor of the insurer that took the position that the loss in question was not proximately caused by a covered peril. The outcome in any specific situation depends on whether the courts judge an actual loss to be (1) the proximate result of a covered peril, or (2) too remotely connected to a covered peril to be considered its proximate result.

While the judicial trend may be toward liberalizing the doctrine of proximate cause, this is a developing, intricate area involving many varied sets of facts. Problems develop when a noncovered peril precedes a covered peril or when a noncovered peril follows one that is covered.

Although oversimplified, the following statements generally summarize the situation:

- It usually is not required that the covered peril itself physically inflict the property damage.
- The insured peril generally must be immediate, rather than remote, in terms of linkage, time, and distance.

Although it can be difficult to forecast how a court might interpret the proximate cause doctrine in light of a given set of facts, an understanding of the requirement of proximate cause is important to insurance policy analysis. For property insurance coverage to apply, a covered cause must not only be somehow involved, but it also must be the proximate cause of a covered consequence.

Concurrent Causation. The emergence of the troublesome doctrine known as *concurrent causation* caused many insurers to make noteworthy changes in their "all-risks" property policies. To oversimplify somewhat, this doctrine holds that if loss to covered property can be attributed to two or more causes—one or more excluded by the policy but one or more covered—then the policy covers the loss. In short, the doctrine seems to say that none of the exclusions of an "all-risks" policy has any effect if it is possible to identify another, nonexcluded, peril that is somehow involved in the loss event.[16]

The doctrine of concurrent causation evolved, in part, from a case in which record rains broke through flood-control facilities and inundated parts of a western city. As far as the insurers were concerned, this "flood" was clearly excluded. However, the holders of "all-risks" homeowners policies alleged that the proximate cause of the loss was "negligence of the water district"—a cause of loss that was not excluded. The court supported the policyholders' position on the basis that (1) the flood and (2) the negligent act of constructing flood control structures were independent, concurrent causes that interacted with one another to produce the loss. Although similar decisions were reached elsewhere, most concentrated in California. In a case involving earth movement—actually, a landslide—the policyholder successfully argued that a "faulty installation of a drain by a third party" was the cause of the landslide, and such negligent actions by third parties were not excluded.

The effect of the emerging concurrent causation doctrine was that the insurer with an "all-risks" property policy must pay unless *all* of the causes of loss were specifically excluded. In response to these court decisions, many "all-risks" policies were revised late in 1983. While most residential and commercial property policies now incorporate wording to combat the kind of decisions that gave coverage where it apparently was not intended, some manuscript and independently-filed policies do not incorporate this more restrictive wording.

Generally, the wording of concurrent causation exclusions is similar among all kinds of property policies that incorporate it. This exclusion commonly reads as follows:

> We will not pay for loss or damage caused by or resulting from any of the following. But if loss or damage by a Covered Cause of Loss results, we will pay for that resulting loss or damage.
> a. Weather conditions. But this exclusion only applies if weather conditions contribute in any way with a cause or event excluded in paragraph 1. above to produce the loss or damage.
> b. Acts or decisions, including the failure to act or decide, of any person, group, organization or governmental body.
> c. Faulty, inadequate or defective:
>   (1) Planning, zoning, development, surveying or siting;
>   (2) Design, specifications, workmanship, repair, construction, renovation, remodeling, grading, compaction;
>   (3) Materials used in repair, construction, renovation or remodeling; or
>   (4) Maintenance of part or all of any property on or off the described premises.

The reference to "paragraph 1. above" refers to that part of the policy where the earthquake, flood, war, nuclear, governmental action, power failure, and building ordinance exclusions appear. Other weather-related losses—such as windstorm—would be covered.

Paragraphs b. and c. address the "concurrent causes" of third-party negligence with respect to planning, maintenance, quality of construction materials, or poor decisions of governmental planning bodies. If, for example, a building code permits the construction of buildings that cannot withstand an earthquake—and an earthquake damages such a building—the insurer with this form will not pay the loss because a poorly planned building code was a concurrent cause of the loss. In the absence of this exclusion, coverage might apply even though earthquake is specifically excluded. Two independent causes of loss have converged on the covered property to cause the loss, neither one of which, alone, would have caused the loss. And, while earthquake is specifically excluded, negligence of the public body in enacting that building code—as the concurrent cause—is not otherwise excluded. The entire loss therefore would be covered. In light of the concurrent causation exclusion, independent causes of loss, where some are covered and others are excluded by the same policy, are not likely to result in coverage. Thus, coverage will not apply to flood losses, even if faulty design of a flood dike is a concurrent cause.

Covered Consequences

Discussion to this point has concentrated primarily on the types of property that may be lost or damaged and on the perils that might cause loss or damage. It is also necessary to recognize the types of consequences that may result when covered property is damaged by some peril. Property loss consequences include (1) reduction in value, (2) extra cost to replace, (3) loss of income, (4) extra expenses to operate, and many others not examined here.

Reduction of value in tangible property because of damage by a peril is a straightforward concept often referred to as *direct loss.* As mentioned, this term also is used in some insurance policies with results that are not completely clear. Another problem with this term is that it naturally leads to the less clearly definable antonym, *indirect loss.* A wide range of opinions exists among insurance authors and practitioners as to which loss consequences are direct and which are indirect. For example: Does the presence of debris increase the amount of the direct loss because expenses must be incurred to remove the debris before repairs can commence? Or is debris removal a separate "indirect" loss, somehow distinct from the direct loss? For the sake of clarity, this text generally refers to specific categories of loss consequences rather than using the imprecise labels "direct" and "indirect."

In terms of identifying a covered event, it is necessary only to determine *whether* a covered consequence is involved. The amount of the loss, the way in which that amount will be determined, and the amount payable by the insurer under the terms of the policy are separate questions addressed in other chapters.

Reduction in Value. When a peril damages covered property, there is an immediate reduction (sometimes to zero) in the value of the affected property. Such damage or destruction to tangible property is easy to recognize, although the exposure is not always easy to evaluate in advance of a loss.

A typical insuring agreement providing such coverage appears in the building and personal property coverage form:

> We will pay for direct physical loss of or damage to Covered Property
> at the premises described in the Declarations caused by or resulting
> from any Covered Causes of Loss.

Valuation provisions elsewhere in the form indicate that coverage applies on the basis of the property's actual cash value at the time of the loss. Actual cash value, as explained more fully in the next chapter, includes an allowance for depreciation.

It also is possible for a peril to cause reduction in the value of intangible property. The theft of trade secrets or valuable corporate information, for example, diminishes the value of such intangible property.

Extra Cost To Replace. The "extra cost to replace" is a loss consequence experienced whenever the damaged or destroyed property costs more to replace than its "actual cash value." "Extra cost to re-place" is a *covered* consequence when insurance is written on a replace-ment cost basis rather than an actual cash value basis.

Replacement cost coverage is an option under most "commercial property" policies. It is the standard approach in some policies, such as a typical businessowners policy. With respect to residential property, the most common approach is to cover the dwelling building for its replacement cost value and personal property for its actual cash value. Replacement cost coverage on personal property often is available as an option.

Autos and other property of a type normally subject to rapid depreci-ation are not commonly insured on a replacement cost basis.

Loss of Income. A firm may produce income by selling products, rendering services, or charging rent for use of property. When a firm is partially or totally shut down following damage to covered property, the stream of income that normally pays for operating expenses and pro-vides net profits may be slowed or come to a halt. In other words, an organization may lose income during a period for which operations are reduced or suspended because of property damage.

These consequences of damage or destruction to property can be insured by various policies that address these specific needs. Commonly used is the so-called *Business Income Coverage Form (And Extra Expense)* developed by ISO as one of its "commercial property" forms.

The insuring agreement of this policy reads as follows:

A. COVERAGE

Coverage is provided as described below for one or more of the follow-ing options for which a Limit of Insurance is shown in the Declarations:

(i) Business Income including "Rental Value."
(ii) Business Income other than "Rental Value."
(iii) "Rental Value."

... We will pay for the actual loss of Business Income you sustain due to the necessary suspension of your "operations" during the "period of restoration." The suspension must be caused by direct physical loss of or damage to property at the premises described in the Declarations, including personal property in the open (or in a vehicle within 100 feet), caused by or resulting from any Covered Cause of Loss.

1. **Business Income**
Business Income means the:
a. Net Income (Net Profit or Loss before income taxes) that would have been earned or incurred; and
b. Continuing normal operating expenses incurred, including payroll.
2. **Covered Causes of Loss**
See applicable Causes of Loss Form as shown in the Declarations.

"Rental value" is defined later in the policy to include the "total anticipated rental income from tenant occupancy" plus the "fair rental value
of any portion of the described premises which is occupied by you."

Detailed discussion of business income insurance is beyond the
scope of this text. However, the following two points must be emphasized:

- *Necessary elements must be present.* An insured event has not
  occurred unless the incurred loss of income, however described,
  is a covered consequence resulting because a covered peril has
  damaged or destroyed covered property.
- *What "covered property" must sustain direct damage.* To
  qualify as "covered property" within the framework of the elements of an insured event, there is no requirement that insurance apply to the cost of repairing or replacing the property
  itself. Only the loss of income needs to be a covered consequence;
  reduction in value or other consequences of damage to this property need not be covered.

In the form quoted above, the requirement is that there be "direct
physical loss of or damage to *property at the premises described in the
Declarations, including personal property in the open (or in a vehicle) within 100 feet*" (emphasis added). Note that the damaged property
may be either real or personal property, unless it is in the open. Note
also the absence of any requirement that the damaged property be
owned by the insured. Damage to a landlord's building, or to personal
property of another business on the same premises, as well as damage
to the insured's own property, might trigger business income coverage.

Extra Expenses To Operate. Extra expenses may be incurred
by a business or family during a period when the business or family is
unable to use property that has been damaged or destroyed and has not
yet been repaired or replaced. A business may incur extra expenses in
order to limit the duration of an interruption or to continue operations
despite the property damage (perhaps by renting alternate facilities). A
family may need to rent a hotel room or make other temporary living
arrangements during a period while the residence is uninhabitable because of property damage. In some cases, it may be possible to live in the
house but temporary water, electrical, heating, or cooking arrangements
may need to be made at some extra cost.

Both the extra expense incurred by a business and the additional
living expense incurred by a family are loss consequences that can be
covered by insurance.

The ISO homeowners policy, in its property insurance section, includes the following provisions:

If a loss covered under this Section makes that part of the "residence premises" where you reside not fit to live in, we cover, at your choice, either of the following . . .

a. **Additional Living Expense,** meaning any necessary increase in living expenses incurred by you so that your household can maintain its normal standard of living; or

b. **Fair Rental Value,** meaning the fair rental value of that part of the "residence premises" where you reside less any expenses that do not continue while the premises is not fit to live in.

The fair rental value provision here requires some explanation. Most often, a temporarily displaced family incurs additional expenses that go beyond the fair rental value of the untenantable premises. Sometimes, however, an individual or family whose home is being repaired will temporarily move in with friends or parents, incurring little or no actual expense in the process. The fair rental value coverage ensures that those who do so are not denied a fair right to insurance recovery because they elected—to the insurer's benefit—*not* to incur large additional expenses.

Covered Locations

An insured event must involve not only *covered property,* a *covered cause,* and a *covered consequence;* it also must involve a *covered location.* That is to say, the incident must happen within the geographical or territorial scope of the coverage provided under the particular policy in question. The coverage territory ranges from one narrowly defined place to anywhere, varying considerably among different types of property insurance policies and different types of property.

Residential and commercial buildings are by nature situated at fixed locations (except for some mobilehomes). Property coverage on them is restricted to the place specified in the policy declarations. However, the typical "commercial property" form automatically provides limited and temporary coverage on newly acquired real property that is situated within the fifty states of the United States of America and the District of Columbia. Homeowners and dwelling forms do not provide automatic real property coverage at newly acquired locations.

Except for the types of personal property that are not covered at all, the personal property coverage of homeowners policies extends to anywhere in the world. The same is true of separately purchased personal articles floaters. Worldwide coverage of (business) personal property also is available to business firms through the purchase of specialized inland marine floaters. Otherwise the basic property insuring agreement of most standard commercial property forms covers business personal property only while it is in the described building(s) or within 100 feet of the described premises. An "additional coverage" often provides a limited dollar amount of coverage for property temporarily off premises.

The coverage under many crime insurance forms is likewise restricted to the described premises, though some of the broader theft and crime coverages extend to off-premises locations and while the money, securities, or other covered property is being transported within the United States of America, the District of Columbia, Puerto Rico, and Canada.

Both the business auto and truckers policies are subject to a territorial limitation: the United States of America, its territories, possessions, or Canada.

Under the "commercial property" coverage part in the commercial *package* policy prescribed for use by many insurers, the coverage territory is defined in the *commercial property conditions* to encompass (a) the United States of America (including its territories and possessions), (b) Puerto Rico, and (c) Canada. The coverage territory of the commercial general *liability* forms which are part of this package policy is defined the same way, with some broadening provisions relating to international waters or airspace or products liability.

It sometimes is important to know what qualifies as a territory or possession of the United States. Finding a clear answer to a territorial question may not be easy. In one case, the insured entered into a contract with the U.S. Navy to perform services at an airbase in the Portuguese Azores Islands. A fire at the construction site caused extensive damage for which the contractor was held responsible. After repairing the damage, the contractor submitted a claim to the insurer, which denied coverage for two reasons: (1) the military facility in the Azores was not a "territory or possession" of the United States, and (2) the insurance agent did not have the authority to extend territorial coverage by a certificate of insurance. At the trial, the insured maintained that the term "possession" was ambiguous and should be used in its *juridical* sense as meaning "the detention and control . . . of anything which may be the subject of property, for one's use or enjoyment, either as the owner or as the proprietor of a qualified right in it. . . ." The insurance agent contended that because the terms "territory" and "possession," as used in the insurance policy, are ambiguous and susceptible to diverse meanings, they should be interpreted in their broadest sense to include military bases. The insurer, in turn, argued that the policy phrase "within the United States of America, its territories or possessions" should be construed in the insurance contract according to its plain, normally accepted meaning without expounding what that meaning actually is. The court agreed with the insurer.[17]

A growing number of businesses have exposures outside the continental United States. Wherever this is the case—even on a temporary basis—every insurance policy must be given individual attention to assure that otherwise insured events also involve an insured location.

Covered (Nonexcluded) Circumstances

An insured event must entail *covered circumstances.* Loss-related circumstances normally *are* covered unless there is some policy provision to the contrary. The question of covered circumstances, therefore, requires one to examine a policy, in light of the facts of the case, to determine whether the circumstances surrounding a particular claim might *not* be covered.

Although property insurance policies provide coverage for losses under most ordinary circumstances, they generally do not cover conditions or circumstances that are considered unusually hazardous for most insureds covered by the type of policy in question. Circumstances that are not covered may take either of two forms:

- Automatic suspensions of coverage during periods involving an increase in hazards
- Discretionary suspensions of coverage activated when dangerous conditions are discovered by the insurer

Automatic Suspensions of Coverage During Increase in Hazard. One coverage suspension, based on *use* of property, is found in the physical damage section of the personal auto policy and reads as follows:

> We will not pay for ... loss to "your covered auto" or any "non-owned auto" which occurs while it is being used as a public or livery conveyance. This exclusion ... does not apply to a share-the-expense car pool.

The use of an auto as a taxi or livery vehicle involves an intensity of use that greatly increases the probability of physical damage. Because such usage would require much higher premium rates, if the insurer were even willing to provide the insurance, coverage is suspended under the personal auto policy *while* the vehicle is exposed to public or livery use.

On the other hand, not only are ordinary car pools consistent with public policy in an age of concerns over energy, air pollution, and highway congestion, but also the addition of passengers to a commuter's car poses no unusual increase in physical damage hazards. Therefore, car pooling explicitly is recognized as a covered circumstance (although other circumstances might operate to preclude coverage for damage in a car-pool-related accident).

One of the common homeowners forms available today offers an example of an automatic coverage suspension based on hazardous circumstances. The relevant provision, which applies to the covered peril of vandalism or malicious mischief, reads as follows:

> This peril does not include loss to property on the residence premises if the dwelling has been vacant for more than 30 consecutive days immediately before the loss. A dwelling being constructed is not considered vacant.

This provision suspends coverage when the dwelling has been vacant beyond thirty days, but coverage is suspended only for loss by vandalism or malicious mischief. Generally, a dwelling is considered to be "unoccupied" when it is not being used as a residence. A dwelling is "vacant" when it is both unoccupied and devoid of furniture and contents. Some policies define these terms, but many do not.

Insurance students sometimes remember the difference between "vacancy" and "unoccupancy" by observing that the ubiquitous flashing neon "VACANCY" sign outside motels is wrong; it should read "UNOCCUPANCY."

Yet another example of an automatic coverage suspension can be found in an endorsement to the "commercial property" coverage part of some commercial package policies. The provision reads as follows:

> This insurance will be automatically suspended at the involved location if you fail to notify us immediately when you:
>
> 1. Know of any suspension or impairment in the protective safeguards; or
> 2. Fail to maintain the protective safeguards over which you have control in complete working order.
>
> If part of an Automatic Sprinkler System is shut off due to breakage, leakage, freezing conditions or opening of sprinkler heads, notification to us will not be necessary if you can restore full protection within 48 hours.

The protective safeguards referred to in this particular endorsement include any fire or alarm systems, automatic sprinklers, security service, service contract, or other such devices that are described in the policy. They must be maintained or kept in good working condition if they are truly to serve as safeguards. A similar endorsement may be used with burglary and robbery protective systems. For a business property that is particularly vulnerable to fire, burglary, or robbery, such safeguards may be deemed essential in order to keep the insurer's exposure commensurate with the premium charge.

Discretionary Coverage Suspensions. Unlike the previous examples in which coverage is suspended *automatically* while a certain condition prevails, the second broad type of circumstantial restriction involves a suspension of coverage that *may* be invoked *at the insurer's* *discretion* when a hazard is discovered. Such a provision, part of the typical boiler and machinery policy, reads as follows:

> Whenever an "object" is found to be in, or exposed to, a dangerous condition, any of our representatives may immediately suspend the insurance against loss from an "accident" to that "object." This can be done by delivering or mailing a written notice of suspension to:
>
> (1) Your last known address; or
> (2) The address where the "object" is located.
>
> Once suspended in this way, your insurance can be reinstated only by an endorsement for that "object."
>
> If we suspend your insurance, you get a pro rata refund of premium for that "object." But the suspension will be effective even if we have not yet made or offered a refund.

Unlike the provisions noted previously, this boiler and machinery clause does not result in an automatic suspension of coverage. Nor does it automatically restore coverage once the dangerous condition is rectified. The coverage suspension, if any, is discretionary on the part of the insurer's representative (generally a qualified boiler inspector), and it may be made effective by written notice to the insured. If suspended, the coverage can be reinstated only by endorsement—that is, with the written consent of the insurer.

Covered Time Periods

An insured event occurs only if a covered cause of loss falls within a time period covered by a legally enforceable insurance agreement. In property insurance, the so-called "policy period" is usually one year. However, the policy period is merely the *intended initial duration of the written contract*, not necessarily the *covered time period* of the enforceable agreement between parties.

- Coverage actually may become effective before a policy is issued, by means of an oral or written "binder"—that is, a legally binding agreement that serves as a temporary contract until the policy is issued.
- After the policy is issued, the coverage may be terminated by cancellation before it would otherwise expire, or it may be terminated by not renewing the policy beyond the time of its expiration—to the extent such terminations are permitted by policy provisions and state laws.
- Alternatively, as long as both parties are willing and have the legal capacity to keep on renewing the policy for successive time periods, the coverage could be continued for many years.

For all of the foregoing reasons, it is most accurate to think of the *covered time period* as the precise interval in time during which coverage legally applies. This interval lies between the moment of coverage inception and the moment of coverage termination. It is this time interval within which a covered cause must damage or destroy covered property under covered circumstances producing covered consequences, to qualify as an insured event.

Inception and Termination. Under an oral or written binder, coverage can become effective the very moment the applicant's offer is accepted by a person who has the legal capacity and authority to enter into such contracts on behalf of the insurer. For example, coverage becomes effective when an authorized agent says, "You are covered as of this minute for a period of thirty days." During those thirty days a complete written policy normally would be issued, but delays sometimes require a longer period. A binder could be renewed thirty days later or it could expire, unless the law of the given jurisdiction requires a cancellation for a binder. Normally it would be extended for additional periods by the insurer's representative until the policy itself is issued.

Once the policy is issued, the inception of coverage is governed by an explicit provision in the policy declarations, generally dated to coincide with the date of the original binder. The termination of coverage, however, is a bit more complicated.

- *The usual policy provision gives the* insured *the nearly unrestricted right to cancel the policy instantly by notifying the insurer (or agent).* Exceptions may apply in cases in which the insurer has been requested to go on record with some third party, certifying that coverage is in force. This might be the case when a driver has been required to provide the state with evidence of financial responsibility or when a subcontractor has requested that a certificate of insurance be furnished to the general contractor.

- *The usual policy provision also gives the* insurer *the right to cancel, a right that is restricted only by the requirement that the insurer provide the insured with written notice of its intention to cancel the policy on some date consistent with the minimum period of advance notice stipulated in the policy.* Any permitted cancellation would usually take effect as of the date and time specified in the written notice issued by the insurer.

A number of state statutes now severely restrict insurers from refusing to write, refusing to renew, or canceling auto or homeowners policies, except for a limited number of reasons (such as nonpayment of premium or revocation of a driver's license). Cancellation of commercial policies is restricted in a smaller number of states. The relevant statutes sometimes are reflected in an endorsement to the policy, but they apply even in the absence of an endorsement. The specifics of such statutes are beyond the scope of this chapter.

Most property insurance policies stipulate that the policy period is from one specified date to another at 12:01 A.M. standard time at some location, as in the following example:

> Policy Period: From 11-1-9x to 11-1-9y 12:01 A.M. Standard Time at your mailing address shown above.

The coverage inception is on November 1, 199x, 12:01 A.M. standard time at the mailing address shown. Other policies may designate that the standard time applies at the residence premises covered by this policy at the following address unless otherwise stated, or at the address where the covered auto is principally garaged.

Onset of Covered Causes. Once the covered period or interval is determined, when does a covered cause "fall within" that interval to make the loss an insured event? Generally a covered cause falls within the prescribed interval of time if the onset or beginning of the loss causation lies within the interval. As long as the loss from a covered cause *commences* during the policy period, it is not essential that the covered consequences lie entirely within the policy period. For example, suppose the policy period of a property form is from December 15, 199x, to December 15, 199y, 12:01 A.M. standard time at the location of the covered property. A fire destroys the property. The onset or the beginning of the loss occurs at the first moment the fire begins to damage the property.

- If the fire started to damage the property ten minutes before policy inception, the loss would *not* be an insured event, even if the fire continues to burn well into the policy period.
- If a fire starts to damage the covered property one hour before the policy's expiration date, the loss *is* an insured event, even if most of the damage occurs after the time of coverage expiration.

The same general principles apply to covered causes of loss other than fire. As a general rule, most losses involving property insurance policies deal with short-tail events—where the cause and result occur almost simultaneously.

When it comes to property insurance, most questions relating to policy periods are fairly straightforward. The time of some losses is somewhat more difficult to pinpoint, such as those involving off-season vandalism to a seasonal home, theft of property that is not immediately missed, or gradual water damage. The most noteworthy problems involve perils that take place over a prolonged time spanning more than one policy period. An example, which also is relevant to issues of concurrent causation, is the dwelling that is constructed on poorly prepared land and gradually is damaged as the dwelling moves, sinks, and cracks over a period of years. Suppose that, between the time of the initial construction and the dwelling's ultimate demise, two different insurers have provided property insurance on the house. The question could arise as to which of the insurers is accountable for payment of resulting damage, assuming such damage is indeed covered by insurance. What policy is triggered and therefore required to contribute toward paying for the damage? Is it the policy that was in force at the time damage commenced; is it the policy in force at the time of manifestation when damage became evident; or is it all policies that were in force from the initial damage to the time damage became evident? Unfortunately, there is no definitive answer to the foregoing questions in terms of *property* insurance losses (and it is an issue that has stirred considerable debate with respect to liability insurance, as mentioned later). In one of the few cases that dealt with this issue of progressive property damage, the court stated that when loss occurs over periods of successive policy periods and is not discovered until several years after loss commences, the "manifestation rule applies." Under this rule, the insurer whose policy period coincided with the time of manifestation is solely responsible for such loss once coverage is found to exist.[18]

Whether the above rule will be the majority opinion will be known only after many more court decisions in other jurisdictions. This whole subject does reveal, however, that some exposures of property insurance can present the same kind of "long-tail" coverage problems as confront insurers of liability insurance.

INSURED EVENTS UNDER LIABILITY INSURANCE POLICIES

For property insurance, the first element of an insured event is "covered property." In contrast, the first element of a liability insured event is the "covered activity." Otherwise, while the *titles* of the elements of an insured event are similar under both property and liability policies, there are some distinct differences between the two types of policies. These distinctions are the subject of the pages that follow.

Covered Activities

A liability insured event must involve a covered activity. Many different activities are covered by various forms of liability insurance. Some liability policies essentially cover only one type of activity, such as the services offered by a medical professional. Other policies combine coverage for many different activities. Examples of covered activities are those associated with the following:

- The ownership, maintenance, and use of autos, aircraft, and watercraft
- The ownership, maintenance, and use of premises, which can include a building, tunnel, mine, stadium, or other structure; driveways and walks; adjoining grounds; and vacant land
- The operations or activities that are conducted on, or emanate from, the covered premises
- The acquisition or formation of new business enterprises, operations, and activities, whether or not related to the current and existing activities of a given business venture
- The manufacture or sale of either finished products or components for use by other manufacturers
- The construction of dwellings, buildings, and structures not only during such operations, but also after they have been completed
- The manufacture, sale, distribution, or serving of alcoholic beverages
- The legal obligations assumed under a contract or agreement
- The services rendered as a professional
- The services rendered as an officer or director of a corporation or organization
- The custodial services rendered as a common carrier, private carrier, or other bailee for hire
- The employment of workers subject to workers compensation statutes

The above examples illustrate the general kinds of activities for which liability insurance is available.

It is difficult to generalize about liability insurance policies. The broadest, most comprehensive liability policies combine protection for a number of varying activities into a single package of coverage. Other policies are designed as specialized coverage for only one or a few such activities. Even standard policies can be substantially different because of endorsements that tailor the coverage to meet the coverage needs of the policyholder or the underwriting needs of the insurer.

The activities covered under a particular policy cannot be understood merely by referring to the declarations, insuring agreement, and policy definitions. It is necessary to read the entire policy contract including endorsements, taking into consideration the policy's exclusions or restrictions.

The business auto policy illustrates these points. The auto policy may designate coverage for accidents arising out of the ownership, maintenance, or use of a "covered 'auto.'" In the first place, covered activities must involve an "auto." As defined in the policy, an "auto," among other things, must be a vehicle designed for travel on public roads.

Depending on the way the policy is configured, "covered 'autos' " may include "any 'auto,' " or they may include "owned private passenger 'autos' " only, "owned 'autos' other than private passenger 'autos' only," "specifically described 'autos,' " "autos" that are "nonowned" or "hired" as those terms are defined, or any combination of these.

Coverage for "any 'auto' " means that activities involving any auto acquired during the policy period automatically are covered for the policy's duration without notice to the insurer. It also means that any auto rented or leased by, or used on behalf of, the policyholder also will be considered a covered auto.

Not all business auto policies define "covered autos" as "any 'auto.' " Because of underwriting requirements or policyholder preference, "covered auto" may be limited to the auto(s) described in the policy declarations. When that is done, no coverage applies for any auto that is rented, leased, or otherwise used on the policyholder's behalf.

The liability insuring agreement of the business auto policy reads as follows:

> We will pay all sums an "insured" legally must pay as damages because of "bodily injury" or "property damage" to which this insurance applies, caused by an "accident" and resulting from the ownership, maintenance or use of a covered "auto."

The fact that an activity involves a "covered auto" does not mean that business auto policy coverage will apply in all circumstances. An insured event also must involve a covered activity, which requires examining the relevant event in the light of all applicable policy provisions.

Assume for the moment that an insured, while operating a covered auto for business purposes, is involved in an accident in which he or she is legally responsible for the resulting bodily injury and property damage sustained by a third party. Based only on this information, it would be premature to conclude that the policy involves a covered activity. The phrase in the above insuring agreement, "to which this insurance applies," is a subtle way of saying that protection applies *unless there is an exclusion in the policy that specifically precludes it.* Before determining that a covered activity has taken place, it is therefore necessary to read all of the exclusions. If any exclusion applies, the insurer does not have an obligation to pay damages as stated in the insuring agreement.

The business auto policy, used to illustrate these points, uses a limited insuring agreement intended for one type of losses—those resulting from auto accidents. Other liability insuring agreements are of

the comprehensive type, essentially covering liability for damages arising out of all activities not otherwise excluded. Examples include the
commercial general liability coverage form and the personal liability
coverage of the homeowners policies.

Covered Causes

To be a covered event, for purposes of liability insurance, an incident
must entail not only a covered activity but also a covered cause. *Covered
cause* might be defined as a claim alleging legal obligation or responsibility, arising out of a particular type of injury or damage, to pay damages
to some third party. The damages themselves are not a component of
the covered cause, but rather are covered consequences. The three key
elements of covered cause are as follows:

1. The claim or suit
2. The legal obligation or responsibility alleged in the claim or suit
3. The nature of the alleged injury or damage

In most liability insurance policies, the insurer promises to defend
the insured against covered liability claims. This obligation to provide a
defense precedes any judgment.

The "legal obligation or responsibility" requirement does not mean
that coverage applies only after a claimant obtains a court judgment
against the insured. Also, it often is not necessary that the courts be
involved. In many cases, the insured's liability can be clearly established
without litigation. But when it turns out that the alleged liability is not
obvious from the facts or there is a dispute over fault, a court of law
may need to settle the matter.

A claim may allege that the claimant suffered bodily injury, property
damage, personal injury, or advertising injury, or was the victim of an
error or omission or the rendering or failure to render professional
services. To be a covered cause, the claim must involve one or more of
these types or sources of injury as described in the policy under which
coverage might be invoked.

These components of covered cause, under a liability insurance policy, will be analyzed a bit later in the chapter. First, it may be helpful to
take a brief detour that emphasizes the importance of distinguishing
questions of liability from questions of coverage.

Liability Versus Coverage. *When dealing with liability insurance questions, it is essential to clearly distinguish questions of
liability from questions of coverage. Both liability and coverage must
exist before the insurer has a clear obligation to pay the claim.*

In some cases, a liability insurance policy provides coverage for the nature of injury or damage claimed, but the insured has no legal obligation to pay damages under the circumstances at hand. For example, the claimant may have sustained bodily injury in an auto accident, but the accident may not have been caused by the insured—leaving the insured with no legal obligation to pay damages. Still, the insurer has an obligation to defend the insured if the insured's liability is alleged, and the insurer probably will do so. If the defense is successful, no damages will be payable.

Often the situation is not entirely clear-cut, and there is some question of whether the insured is liable as alleged. Usually the insurer will then mount a defense and deny or resist payment of the damages. In some cases, however, the insurer will attempt to negotiate an out-of-court settlement rather than incur the expense and uncertain results of a court action.

A situation may develop in which the insured party may be liable to pay damages to the claimant, but no coverage under the policy provides coverage for the damages claimed. Such a situation may occur, for example, when a claim is not founded on allegations that the insured's activities resulted in the claimant's bodily injury or property damage, as defined. For example, the claimant may obtain a judgment for damages resulting from age discrimination, but liability resulting from age discrimination is not a covered cause under a policy providing coverage against liability arising out of bodily injury and property damage.

Legal Obligation or Responsibility. Most liability insurance policies provide payment for damages that it is the insured's *legal obligation* to pay. The insuring agreement of the commercial general liability coverage forms, for example, reads in part:

> We will pay those sums that the insured becomes legally obligated to pay as damages because of. . . .

The insuring agreement of the business auto and truckers coverage forms reads in part:

> We will pay all sums the insured legally must pay as damages because of. . . .

The legal liability referred to in these and other liability policies may stem from one of the following:

- *Negligence*—failure to fulfill a duty imposed by tort law.
- *Statutory liability*—failure to meet a duty imposed by statute.
- *Contractual liability*—an obligation assumed under contract. (Legal liability that is contractual in nature involves an individual's voluntary assumption of some liability he or whe would not otherwise have under the law.)

It is beyond the scope of this text to discuss at any length all of the

216—Insurance Contract Analysis

issues that commonly are considered in establishing legal liability. These issues are amply addressed elsewhere in the CPCU curriculum. However, at the very minimum, it should be understood that whoever is making a claim or filing a suit against the insured alleging *negligence* must demonstrate the following basic elements:

1. A duty was owed to the claimant.
2. There was a breach of that duty.
3. Injury or damage has been the proximate result of that breach of duty.

Duty Owed to Others. The duty owed to another party can vary, depending on the situation. For example, the owner of residential or commercial property is responsible at common law for maintaining the premises so that people who enter such property are not unduly exposed to injury. Other duties exist for one engaged in manufacturing, selling, or distributing products; performing work for others; driving vehicles; flying aircraft; managing property for others; performing professional services; and almost every other business and personal activity.

Breach of Duty. Whenever a duty is owed to another, care must be exercised that the duty is not breached. In determining whether a duty has been breached, it is necessary to measure the alleged act or omission of the tortfeasor against a certain standard. The standard required will vary according to the circumstances or legal grounds in question.

Injury or Damage as a Proximate Result. The fact that a duty was both owed and breached does not by itself mean that the tortfeasor is automatically accountable for the consequences of any resulting injury or damage. Also required is that the breach of duty be the proximate cause of the resulting harm. In other words, there must be a causal relationship between the breach of duty and the resulting injury or damage.

As an insurance-related concept, the principle of causal relationship is similar to the proximate causation requirements of property insurance. If there is no causal relationship, for example, between the insured's use of an auto and the claimant's injury or damage, the auto insurer may not be required to pay the claimant's damages as sought.

One of the common tests for determining proximate cause is the so-called "but for" rule. If the injury would have happened even in the absence of the insured's negligence, then the insured's act or omission arguably was not the proximate cause. Conversely, if the injury would not have occurred "but for" the insured's failure to exercise the proper degree of care required by the circumstances, then the insured's negligence was the proximate cause of damage.

Two actual cases may help to illustrate these points. The issues here obviously involved questions as to whether the policy in question provided coverage for the claim, not whether the insured was liable for the damages. In one case a liquor store owner's eye injury, caused when a robber fired a pistol from his car as he escaped, was not considered an injury that arose "out of the ownership, maintenance or use of owned auto" coverage of the felon's auto liability policy. The court held that there was no causal relationship between the auto's use and the injury; also, the injury and the accident did not arise from the inherent nature of the auto as such.[19]

In another case, a passenger in an automobile was shot by a policeman who was in pursuit of the driver. The injured person filed suit against the driver's no-fault auto insurer, seeking coverage for the injuries. The court held that the policy did not cover the passenger's injuries because the injuries did not arise out of the operation of the vehicle. The court held that there must be some causative link between the use or maintenance of the vehicle and the injuries sustained in order for one person to become a "victim" within the scope of no-fault insurance coverage. The "but for" rule, the court explained, was not met, because the injuries were not caused by the vehicle's operation. The cause of the passenger's injuries, the court said, was a gunshot and not his being a passenger in another person's auto.[20]

Nature of Injury or Damage. Crucial to the subject of covered causes is the nature of the allegedly resulting injury or damage. The fact that *some* injury or damage follows as a proximate result of a breach of a duty owed by the insured does not necessarily mean that the insurer must pay. It also is necessary that the nature of the injury or damage (bodily injury, property damage, and so forth) be of the kind that is covered by the policy in question. The specific type of injury or damage to which coverage applies varies among liability policies.

Bodily Injury. Liability policies providing coverage for it generally define "bodily injury" this way:

> "Bodily injury" means bodily injury, sickness or disease sustained by a person, including death resulting from any of these at any time.

In the usual sense of the word, bodily injury is intended to mean physical harm to the human body and any resulting pain, suffering, sickness, disease, or death. A common question is whether emotional distress or mental trauma can be considered bodily injury even in the absence of some physical harm to the human body. This question commonly arises in actions by former employees who maintain that their alleged wrongful termination of employment or some other discriminatory practice by their former employer is so harsh, outrageous, and traumatic that it causes emotional distress and mental anguish.[21] The answer to that question is uncertain. At best, it depends on the circumstances and the jurisdiction. Courts of some states have held that emotional distress is bodily injury even in the absence of physical bodily harm, whereas other states have refused to stretch the meaning of the term that far without a broader policy definition.

Personal Injury. The term "personal injury" is used in different ways, both outside and within an insurance context. Especially when used by attorneys, "personal injury" sometimes is synonymous with "bodily injury." We also should note that "personal injury protection," in the context of no-fault insurance, refers to first-party no-fault coverages; this usage has no direct connection to "personal injury" as discussed here.

Insurance practitioners usually use the phrase "personal injury" to refer to a loosely related group of offenses, including libel and slander. It might help to think of bodily injury as injury to one's body, and personal injury as injury to a person's character or personality. However, the term "personal injury" is used in several different ways.

As used in some insurance policies, it is a broader term than "bodily injury." In these policies, bodily injury is one type of personal injury, and so are other offenses including libel, slander, and invasion of privacy. As used in other policies, the term "personal injury" encompasses only a certain specified group of offenses that do not include bodily injury. Among the offenses typically covered are libel, slander, defamation, wrongful entry or eviction, false arrest, wrongful detention, and malicious prosecution.

Advertising Injury. While there is no universal definition of "advertising injury," it generally is defined to encompass liability stemming from libel or slander, publishing material that constitutes an invasion of privacy, the misappropriation of advertising ideas, and the infringement of copyright, title, or slogan.

Generally, there is some overlap between personal injury and advertising injury when both phrases are defined in the same policy. This overlap does not result in duplicate coverage because the policy definition of personal injury generally excludes liability from advertising activities, while advertising injury covers only liability committed in the course of the insured's advertising activities.

A considerable amount of litigation involves allegations purportedly covered by advertising injury coverage. These actions commonly seek the payment of damages because of alleged liability stemming from such offenses as misappropriation of trade secrets, unfair competition, and piracy. The problem here is that "advertising activities" is not a defined term and that advertising can include a business letter of solicitation, a newsletter, or even a prospectus. Thus, it can be difficult to determine whether or not a covered activity is involved in a claim alleging . liability arising out of advertising injury.

Property Damage. The term "property damage" is typically defined in insurance policies as follows:

Property damage means:
a. Physical injury to tangible property, including all resulting loss of use of that property; or
b. Loss of use of tangible property that is not physically injured.

According to this definition, property damage includes not only direct damage to tangible property, but also *resulting* loss of use, as well as loss of use of tangible property that has not been physically injured. Close study of this definition reveals that it fails to encompass loss of use of intangible property (goodwill, copyrights, and so forth) in the absence of direct damage to tangible property. The word "physical," furthermore, is designed to preclude payment of claims for economic damages in the absence of physical damage to property.

On the other hand, the primary aim for the second part of the above definition is to encompass (and therefore, to provide coverage for) certain claims or suits where liability can result from loss of use of tangible property in the absence of its physical loss or damage. Suppose, for example, a major fire in a high-rise building is caused by one tenant's negligence. The entire area is roped off for safety reasons, and would-be customers are denied access to a nearby store, even though the store itself is undamaged. The store owner makes a property damage liability claim against the high-rise tenant who caused the fire on the basis that the undamaged store's loss of income was the result of the tenant's negligence.

Professional Liability; Errors and Omissions. The primary role served by a professional liability policy is to cover damages that are *not* based on bodily injury, property damage, personal injury, or advertising injury. The exposure addressed involves claims for economic damages that are the result of the improper rendering of professional services, errors in judgment, or omissions. An example is the bank that makes a computer programming error that affects the payroll records of a client firm. The result of this error is the overpayment of funds—which is not a bodily injury, property damage, personal injury, or advertising injury.

The specific bases of coverage under various liability insurance policies are examined in detail in other CPCU texts.

Covered Consequences

Liability insurance policies typically cover consequences of the following two types:

- The damages for which the insured is legally liable
- The cost of defending the claim brought against the insured, including some miscellaneous expenses

Damages almost never are *paid* unless the wrong allegedly committed by the insured arises from a covered activity and involves a covered cause. However, most liability policies obligate the insurer to *defend* the insured even when the claim seems to have no legitimate basis, unless the claimed consequences clearly are outside the policy's scope. If the claimant ultimately is awarded damages from a claim that originally appeared to be without merit, the insurer must pay those damages covered by the policy. Even if it turns out that the insured is not legally held responsible for the damages alleged by the claimant, the legal expenses incurred to come to that conclusion will be borne by the insurer.

Damages. The term *damages* is distinct from the term *damage*. Whether or not "damages" is defined or somehow clarified depends on the policy. In the absence of a specific definition or clarification in the policy, however, the common or plain meaning of this term must be relied on in determining what is payable. Most liability policies do not define or attempt to clarify what the term damages is meant to encompass in a typical insuring agreement, which reads as follows:

> We will pay those sums that the insured becomes legally obligated to pay as damages because of "bodily injury" or "property damage" to which this insurance applies.

Since the term damages does not appear in quotation marks, it is not defined in the policy. The policy therefore could conceivably encompass the payment of compensatory and punitive damages.

Compensatory Damages. Compensatory damages are money payments that *compensate* claimants for injury or damage they sustain. These damages can include reasonable medical expenses, the cost to repair or replace damaged property, the loss of a property's use value, lost wages, the loss of future wages, the imputed economic value of services lost in the past or in the future, and an amount which, in the judgment of the court, will compensate for such intangibles as pain and suffering, bereavement, and the like, depending on the nature of the action.

Punitive Damages. Punitive damages are intended to *punish* a wrongdoer for having injured the claimant or damaged the claimant's property through some outrageous conduct. The amount of punitive damages awarded in a given case may have no direct relationship to the actual monetary damage suffered by the claimant.

Punitive damages are sometimes said to be *exemplary* in nature—

that is, to set an example. Some insurance policies specifically exclude punitive damages, while others do not.

Moreover, not all states permit insurers to pay punitive damages on behalf of an insured even if they are awarded by a court in connection with a case also involving compensatory damages. From a public policy viewpoint, the "punishment" aspect of punitive damages seems rather indirect and ineffective if some other party—the insurer—bears the cost. From a risk management viewpoint, on the other hand, there is room to argue that punitive damages are as much a source of unexpected financial loss as compensatory damages and that the insured should also be entitled to insure against a judgment awarding punitive damages.

Whenever there is a conflict between the policy language and the prevailing law of the jurisdiction where coverage is to apply, it is the law that controls. So, if the law of a given jurisdiction makes punitive damages uninsurable, the insurer is under no obligation to pay such damages even though the policy could be interpreted as including coverage against those kinds of damages. Instead, the insurer is only obligated to inform the insured that it is prohibited by law from paying such damages.

Other Damages. Compensatory and punitive damages are not the only forms of damages payable in a liability claim. Professional liability policies, directors and officers liability policies, and other contracts designed to cover the economic damages resulting from an insured's wrongful acts often are broad enough in scope to encompass the *treble* (triple) *damages* that can be assessed because of violations of certain federal laws. Two federal laws that permit the trebling of damages are the Sherman Anti-Trust Act of 1892 and the Racketeer Influenced and Corrupt Organizations Act (RICO), which was enacted as Title IX of the Organized Crime Control Act of 1970. RICO has been applied in a number of cases that do not involve "racketeering" as it usually is understood.

Since treble damages are not considered to be punitive or exemplary damages as such, a policy needs to be quite explicit if the intent is to exclude such damages. It therefore is not uncommon to see liability policies contain exclusionary wording like that in the following two examples:

Example 1:

> This policy does not apply:
> to criminal or civil fines or penalties imposed by law, or otherwise, including but not limited to punitive, treble or exemplary damages or costs, and other matters which are uninsurable under the law pursuant to which this policy shall be construed.

Example 2:

> This policy does not apply:
> to any claim or suit based on, arising out of, directly or indirectly
> resulting from or in consequence of, or in any way involving any state
> or federal antitrust law or by whatever name called.

It is not necessary that the above exclusions or similar ones form a part of commercial liability and umbrella liability policies. Treble damage exposures of the above laws, as a general rule, do not involve actions dealing with bodily injury, personal injury, advertising injury, or property damage. And it would be difficult to say that the events underlying these actions could be considered an "occurrence," as that term is defined in the primary and umbrella liability policies. However, some insurers add provisions that specifically exclude such exposures purely as a matter of clarification.

Actions in Equity. One normally thinks of damages as the payment of money in compensation for a wrong. A persistent question concerns whether the undefined term "damages" in liability policies can include the costs and expenses incurred in litigating an action in equity. One such type of action is an injunctive relief proceeding in which a court is asked to order some act to be performed or, in other cases, to prohibit the performance of some act. For example, a court may require a landowner to fence his property to prevent his cattle from wandering onto adjoining property. These types of actions do not involve the payment of monetary damages, but considerable costs can be incurred in litigating such actions.

Environmental cleanup costs, whether mandated by state and federal law or voluntarily undertaken by insureds, present another area where considerable litigation has been fostered by the undefined term "damages." Insureds have argued that cleanup costs are damages payable by the liability policy. Insurers, on the other hand, have maintained that the undefined term "damages" does not extend to encompass equitable damages. Thus far, court decisions on this issue have been mixed.

To maintain coverage flexibility while attempting to prevent problems of this type, some insurers do not define the term "damages" but instead insert special exclusions in their policies to clarify the intent that coverage is limited to legal damages. For example, it is not unusual for a municipal government to be sued over a zoning dispute where the remedy sought is to rescind the decision made by public officials. To avoid having to pay the costs incurred in litigating such actions, a public official liability policy (which is comparable to the directors and officers liability policy for a private corporation) may contain an exclusion making the policy inapplicable to any claim based on or arising out of demands or actions seeking relief or redress in any form other than money damages, including but not limited to claims for injunctive relief.

While the above exclusion may be sufficient to avoid the kinds of problems for which it is designed, it still may be insufficient in an action that seeks both compensatory damages and equitable relief. The insurer's duty to defend is broader than the duty to pay damages. Thus, if part of the allegations are covered and part are excluded, the insurer has the obligation to defend the entire action, but the insurer still is obligated to pay only those damages that are covered by the policy.

Defense Costs and Other Claim Expenses. Apart from the payment of damages on behalf of an insured, virtually all primary liability insurance policies also provide what are called "supplementary payments" or "additional coverages." First and foremost, the insurer is obligated to defend the insured against any claim or suit involving an insured event, with counsel of the insurer's choice (so long as there is no conflict of interest), and to pay all costs of the defense provided. For example, the pertinent language of the personal liability section of a homeowners policy reads as follows:

If a claim is made or a suit is brought against an "insured" for damages because of "bodily injury" or "property damage" caused by an "occurrence" to which this coverage applies, we will . . . provide a defense at our expense by counsel of our choice, even if the suit is groundless, false or fraudulent. We may investigate and settle any claim or suit that we decide is appropriate.

These statements are then clarified and embellished in the additional coverages section of the policy, which states:

We cover the following in addition to the limits of liability:

Claim Expenses. We pay

a. Expenses we incur and costs taxed against an "insured" in any suit we defend;
b. Premiums on bonds required in a suit we defend, but not for bond amounts more than the limit of liability for Coverage E. We need not apply for or furnish any bond.
c. Reasonable expenses incurred by an "insured" at our request, including actual loss of earnings (but not loss of other income) up to $50 per day, for assisting us in the investigation or defense of a claim or suit, and
d. Interest on the entire judgment which accrues after entry of the judgment and before we pay or tender, or deposit in court that part of the judgment which does not exceed the limit of liability that applies.

In addition to the bearing of defense costs, the additional coverages also obligate the insurer to pay premiums on litigation bonds, interest on the judgment, and other reasonable expenses incurred by the insured at the request of the insurer. These coverages are not insignificant. They can amount to large sums of money. Along with insurer payments for damages and defense costs, they are "covered consequences" of the events insured under all applicable liability insurance policies. Similar provisions are found in most other types of liability policies. The exceptions include some umbrella liability policies and most directors and officers liability (D&O) policies. In fact, most D&O policies require executives or corporations to take the initiative and retain legal counsel. They are silent about how legal costs are to be handled but nonetheless reserve the insurer's right to associate with insureds during the litigation process to protect their own interests.

Liability claims often involve long delays between the time of injury or damage and the time when a court awards a judgment. Further delays may result if the court finds in favor of the claimant but the insurer appeals the decision to a higher court. These delays may lead to claims for interest based on the time value of money.

Pre-Judgment Interest. When the first court award is made, the court may award the claimant damages and an additional sum of money representing the interest that could have been earned if the claimant had received compensation at the time of the *injury* or damage rather than at the time of the judgment. This latter sum is referred to as *pre-judgment interest.*

Post-Judgment Interest. When a judgment against the insured is *successfully* appealed to a higher court, the claimant ultimately receives no payment of damages. However, when a higher court upholds the initial judgment, the claimant may be entitled not only to the amount of the judgment, but also to *post-judgment interest* as compensation for the interest that could have been earned on the money if the insurer had paid it at the time of the first *judgment.*

Covered Locations

The subject of covered locations entails two important aspects. The first concerns the location of the incident (that is, bodily injury or property damage), and the second deals with the location of a suit brought by the claimant against the insured.

Location of Incident. With very few exceptions, liability insurance policies extend protection to any location within a broadly defined policy territory. In auto insurance, the policy territory is defined as the United States of America, its territories or possessions, Puerto Rico, or Canada; accidents involving a covered auto while being transported between their ports are also protected by these policies. Conspicuous by its absence is coverage that extends to the neighboring country of Mexico. Special insurance is required by Mexican law to be purchased from a licensed Mexican insurance company.

The broadest definitions of covered locations can be found in umbrella liability policies. While the covered territory of some umbrella policies follows the form of the primary liability policies, most apply "anywhere in the world." Others, including personal umbrellas, apply anywhere or are silent as to territorial scope, presumably encompassing the entire universe. Homeowners policies, on the other hand, are not explicit as to the covered territory for purposes of liability coverage. Though many claims are associated with the residence premises, one can infer from the policy language that the liability coverage applies anywhere in the world.

Location of Suit. When a policy provides the insured with a defense, there usually is a territorial restriction dealing with *suits*. The coverage for injury or damage under a commercial general liability policy, for example, applies anywhere in the world when the injury or damage arises out of (1) goods or products made or sold by the named insured within the U.S., territories, possessions, Puerto Rico, or Canada, or (2) the activities of a person temporarily outside this territory on the business of the named insured. But in the case of a formal lawsuit under either of these circumstances, coverage is contingent on the filing of such suit within the United States of America, its territories or possessions, or Canada. Note that this restriction applies to suits. A mere liability *claim* is considered to be within the scope of coverage, even though such claim is made in a foreign country. The insurer is obligated to investigate and to settle any such claim wherever it arises. But if a claim culminates in a lawsuit, the *suit* must then be made within the policy territory as defined in the policy.

The worldwide scope of employers liability coverage—as commonly offered in conjunction with workers compensation insurance or by endorsement to a commercial liability policy—still requires that the "original suit" for damages be brought within the United States of America, its territories or possessions, or Canada. The stipulation of "original suit" is important. For example, if an employee is injured while temporarily in a foreign jurisdiction, it is necessary for purposes of the employer's protection that such suit be filed within the United States, its territories or possessions, or in Canada. If the original suit is instituted by that employee in a foreign country and a second lawsuit is brought within the United States or Canada as a formality required by law in recognition of the foreign court's judgment, the employer could be without protection.

Covered (Nonexcluded) Circumstances

Liability policies are structured to provide protection for all covered activities except those occurring under circumstances that are specifically excluded. Consider a business auto policy providing liability coverage. The insurer basically agrees to protect against claims resulting from the ownership, maintenance, or use of a covered auto. This does not mean the coverage applies in all circumstances. The insurer, for example, does not cover "any obligation for which the insured or the insured's insurer may be held liable under any workers compensation, disability benefits, or unemployment compensation law, or any similar law." This is another way of saying that the insurer does not cover liability *to* an insured's injured employee under circumstances where an auto accident "arises out of and in the course of employment" even if the accident involved a covered auto. Most liability policies have exclusions relating to the workers compensation exposure (except for workers compensation and employers liability policies, of course).

Like the physical damage section discussed earlier, the liability section of the personal auto policy excludes coverage under circumstances where an otherwise covered auto is being used as a public or livery conveyance, other than for share-the-expense car pools. Moreover, this policy makes it clear that no liability coverage applies to any person using a vehicle without a reasonable belief that that person is entitled to do so.

Virtually all commercial general liability policies exclude coverage for damage *to* products manufactured, distributed, or sold by the insured, as well as *to* work performed by the insured. Liability policies cover the insured's *legal obligations to others* as the result of such products or work.

Covered Time Periods

A covered time period has been defined as the precise interval in time during which the coverage legally applies. This interval lies between the moment of coverage inception and the moment of coverage termination. It is the time interval during which a covered cause must arise out of a covered activity if the incident is to qualify as an insured event.

With some exceptions, most *property* insurance policies deal with losses of the "short-tail" type. (The term "tail" refers to the line on a graph with claims paid on the vertical axis and time on the horizontal axis. While most claims are paid during—or soon after—the policy period, a few stragglers are not paid until some time in the future, giving the line on the graph a long "tail" to the right.) By the end of the policy period, the insurer knows with a comfortable degree of certainty how many losses have taken place during the policy period and approximately how much money is involved. Many liability insurance claims also are of the short-tail type; that is, the event and the resulting injury or damage are simultaneous. For example, a customer slips on the floor of a department store and fractures a wrist, or a motorist sustains facial cuts during an auto accident.

The claims covered under liability insurance sometimes are of the long-tail type. It may take a long time before a claim is made or suit is filed following an occurrence or event which causes injury or damage. For example, it can be several years after an error is made by a physician before the result manifests itself and generates a claim.

Liability insurance traditionally has been provided on a so-called "occurrence basis." To deal with a growing number of long-tail situations, insurers have introduced various coverage innovations that are not always fully understood by either insurers or their insureds. One of these policy innovations is known as a claims-made form. Another is the discovery form. Still others, for want of a better name, might be referred to as modified occurrence forms. The significant distinction among all of these forms is the "trigger" or event that activates the coverage of the policy.

Occurrence Basis. When a liability policy is written on an occurrence basis, the event that triggers coverage is the actual happening of injury or damage during the policy period. That is, coverage is triggered by the happening of the *event*. In the occurrence version of the commercial general liability coverage form, the portion of the insuring agreement that expresses the trigger reads as follows:

> We will pay those sums that the insured becomes legally obligated to pay as damages because of "bodily injury" or "property damage" to which this insurance applies. . . . This insurance applies only to "bodily injury" and "property damage" which occurs during the policy period.

In most incidents covered by liability insurance, resulting injury or damage is apparent at the time of the accident and there is no question of when the injury or damage occurred. In some cases, however, insurers have found themselves paying claims under "occurrence" coverages many years after the end of the policy period for injuries that occurred during the policy period and had gone undetected or were undetectable at the time. Examples include latent injury cases in which no claim is made until the injury manifests itself many years after the initial exposure to the conditions that caused it.

The most important point about a true occurrence trigger is that it does not limit the time period during which a *claim* can be made; as long as the injury or damage itself took place during the policy period, coverage applies even to claims made years later.

Discovery Basis. The discovery basis has been proposed as a liability policy trigger, and at one time it was proposed that future standard commercial general liability policies should incorporate a discovery trigger. However, the idea has not caught on, so it remains a largely theoretical approach.

When a policy is written on a discovery basis, coverage is triggered as soon as there is a reasonable belief that a loss-causing event actually has happened. That is, coverage is triggered when the loss is first discovered during the coverage period. Coverage is triggered by the date of *discovery*.

The concept of a "discovery" trigger actually exists with employee dishonesty insurance. A characteristic of the employee dishonesty exposure is that losses often are undetected for long periods of time, often extending beyond the period of the policy in force at the time of the dishonest act. Nobody knows whether this discovery-type trigger could be effective with liability insurance. Proving the time of "discovery" might create problems best avoided by using the claims-made approach—which, however, introduces a different set of problems.

Claims-Made Basis. For liability insurance on a claims-made basis, the criterion for coverage is that the claim alleging injury or damage be made during the current policy period, even though the event that gave rise to the injury or damage happened sometime earlier. It is the date of the *claim*, if it is within the policy period, that triggers the coverage.

In theory, the claims-made approach is ideal. Each insured buys a series of claims-made policies, each policy taking over when the preceding one expires. Unless coverage lapses, the insured should never be without coverage; there is always a current policy to provide coverage when a claim is presented.

In practice, it is much more complicated because many claims-made policies are subject to a *retroactive date*. Claims due to injury or damage that occurs before that date are not covered. An insured who replaces a claims-made policy with an occurrence policy, or with a claims-made policy with a later retroactive date, may face a time gap in coverage. Ideally, a retroactive date should remain fixed even when a claims-made policy is renewed or replaced, and it should reflect the retroactive date first designated for the insured on a claims-made policy.

When no retroactive date applies, coverage is offered for prior events no matter how long ago they took place. However, as an underwriting safeguard, the application for insurance commonly forms a part of the policy and includes a warranty by the insureds that they are not aware of any past events that might give rise to future claims.

In the claims-made version of the commercial general liability coverage form, the portion of the insuring agreement that expresses the trigger reads as follows:

> This insurance does not apply to "bodily injury" or "property damage" which occurred before the Retroactive Date, if any, shown in the Declarations or which occurs after the policy period. . . .

> This insurance applies to "bodily injury" or "property damage" only if a claim for damages because of the "bodily injury" or "property damage" is first made against any insured during the policy period.

Many claims-made policies also offer one or more extended reporting periods, sometimes referred to as "tail coverage." Technically, no additional coverage is provided,[22] only more time in which to report a covered claim. While there are many variations, extended reporting periods or "tail coverage" extends coverage to claims (1) first made after the expiration of the policy (2) for bodily injury or property damage that occurred before termination of the policy but after its retroactive date. The effect is to extend the time within which a claim can be made and covered.

At times, "tail coverage," or an extended reporting period, is unavailable or overly expensive. In some cases the insurer who provides the replacement policy is willing to provide retroactive coverage for a period long enough to cover any reported claims that previously were incurred but unknown and unreported. In contrast to the so-called "tail coverage," which extends the period at the end of the policy, the prior acts coverage sometimes is referred to as "nose coverage" because it sticks out at the other end, so to speak.

Policy Period. The policy terms applicable to liability insurance do not differ substantially from property insurance. Liability policies usually have a term of one year, but three- or six-month personal auto policies are common, and three-year policies also exist. Even when a policy is written for a three-year term, rate changes often are permitted at each anniversary.

A one-year policy starts on the specified date at 12:01 A.M. standard time at the named insured's address stated in the declarations, and it expires at 12:01 A.M. standard time on the same date of the next year.

Cancellation. As with property insurance, liability coverage may be cut shorter than the policy term if either the insurer or the insured elects to cancel the contract. Procedures are the same as with property insurance.

SUMMARY

An insurer is not obligated to respond under the terms of an insurance policy unless, among other things, an insured event takes place. An incident is not an insured event unless it entails all six "elements of an insured event." The first element of an insured event for property insurance is "covered property"; the first element for liability insurance is "covered activity." The following second through sixth elements are common to both property and liability:

2. Covered cause
3. Covered consequence
4. Covered location

5. Covered (nonexcluded) circumstances
6. Covered time period

Except for those property insurance policies that specifically describe individual items of covered property, the general approach is to begin with a broad description of "covered property." The description may loosely track with the legal categories of real and personal property, but the property covered under the "buildings and structures" category of an insurance policy often includes some items legally considered personal property, and vice versa. Following the description of covered property is a listing of "property not covered," which carves out coverage for some categories of property that might otherwise be covered under the broad "covered property" description. Also, some types of covered property are not covered against certain perils to which they are especially susceptible; these exceptions generally are handled within the portion of the policy describing covered causes of loss. Thus, the complete scope of covered property cannot readily be determined without examining the entire policy.

Covered causes, in property insurance policies, may be handled through either the specified (named) perils approach or the "all-risks" approach. When the specified perils approach is used, coverage is provided against only loss by the causes-of-loss (perils) identified in the policy. A basic specified perils policy provides coverage against a dozen or so perils, while a broad specified perils policy expands that list. Additional perils, such as earthquake, may be added by endorsement. When the specified perils approach is used, the insured has the *burden of proof* to show that a covered peril was the *proximate* (through an unbroken chain of events) cause of the loss. The "all-risks" approach, despite its name, really does not cover against *all* potential sources of loss. Rather, coverage is provided against loss by all causes not excluded—and many causes are excluded. The emergence of the *concurrent causation doctrine* pointed out some possible loopholes in the "all-risks" approach, but additional policy exclusions are now used to plug them. The *difference in conditions* approach basically permits a second property policy to supplement a first, more basic one by picking up coverage only for perils not covered under the first.

Covered consequences, under a property insurance policy, include *reduction in value, extra cost to replace, loss of income,* and *extra expenses to operate,* among others. Of course, an insured event has not occurred unless it involves consequences covered under an applicable policy of insurance. The loss also must take place at a covered location, as described in the policy, during a covered time period. Generally place and time are straightforward components of a property loss, although questions sometimes arise over which of several policies applies to "progressive" property losses that occur over a time period spanning more than one policy period.

Most, but not all, circumstances surrounding a property loss are covered. However, a policy may automatically suspend coverage during some period of increased hazard, and some policies (notably boiler and machinery policies) also permit coverage to be suspended immediately at the discretion of the insurer, when a serious hazard is discovered.

Under liability insurance policies, covered activities are of many types. The broad scope of coverage is stated within a liability insuring agreement. A covered cause necessarily involves both (1) a legal obligation or responsibility and (2) injury or damage of a nature covered under the policy. The nature of injury or damage may involve bodily injury, personal injury, advertising injury, property damage, professional liability, errors and omissions, and so on. Again, policy definitions can be crucial.

For liability insurance purposes, covered consequences involve compensatory and sometimes punitive damages, defense costs, and other claim expenses—including, but not limited to, pre-judgment and post-judgment interest. Coverage may apply not only to actions seeking monetary damages, but also to actions in equity.

Covered locations may become an issue for claims involving places outside the confines of the continental United States. It is important to carefully examine policy conditions relating not only to the location of the incident giving rise to the loss, but also to the location of the suit.

Covered circumstances, in a liability insurance policy, generally are defined by exclusions intended to narrow the scope of coverage to those incidents of a type for which the insurer intends to provide coverage.

Covered time periods have been problematic in liability insurance. Questions involve not the policy period, but what it is that must take place during the policy period to trigger coverage. Traditional occurrence-basis policies have generated covered claims made many years after the end of the policy period. The idea of first-discovery-basis policies has not caught on as an alternative, but the claims-made approach has been used with some types of insurance. Basically, the claims-made approach narrows the time period within which covered claims might be presented by covering claims made during the coverage period as defined. This simple concept is complicated by retroactive dates and "tail" coverage, and gaps in covered time periods can all too readily occur to one switching between occurrence and claims-made policies.

Chapter Notes

---

1. In this text, quotation marks are used around "commercial property" to refer specifically to the ISO forms on fixed-location property, as opposed to other contexts in which we might refer to commercial property in general.
2. Donald S. Malecki, "New ISO Builders Risk Form Is Not for Everyone," *Rough Notes,* March 1989, p. 36.
3. Harry F. Brooks and Donald S. Malecki, *Insuring the Lease Exposure,* 2nd ed. (Cincinnati, Ohio: The National Underwriter Company, 1989), pp. 229-231.
4. As defined in some policies, "nonowned" and "hired" are separate categories, the former including employees' autos used in the business of an employer and the latter including rented or borrowed autos.
5. Hampton Foods Inc. v. Aetna Casualty & Surety Co. 787 f.2d 349 (1986).
6. Western Fire Insurance Co. v. First Presbyterian Church 165 Colo. 34, 37 P.2d 52 (1968).
7. Stephen A. Cozen and Richard C. Bennett, "Fortuity: The Unnamed Exclusion," *The Forum,* vol. XX, no. 2, Winter 1985, p. 225.
8. Cozen and Bennett, p. 224.
9. Cozen and Bennett, pp. 226-227.
10. Cozen and Bennett, p. 227.
11. Donald S. Malecki, "Careful Research Pays Off When Offering Earthquake Coverage to Commercial Clients," *Rough Notes,* November 1990, p. 60.
12. Paulson v. Fire Insurance Exchange, 381 S.W. 2d 199 (1965).
13. Lynn Gas & Electric Co. v. Meriden Fire Insurance Co. 158 Mass. 570, 33 N.E. 690 (1983).
14. Federal Insurance Co. v. Buck, et al., 382 S.W. 2d 305 (1964).
15. Fawcett House Inc. v. Great Central Insurance Co., 159 N.W. 2d 269 (1968).
16. Eric A. Wiening, "An End to All-Risks Insurance?" *The Risk Report,* vol. VI, no. 6, February 1984.
17. Seitlin & Company v. Doebler v. Hartford Ins. Co. 1986 C.C.H. (Fire & Casualty) 909.
18. Prudential-LMI Commercial Ins. v. The Superior Court of San Diego County 798 P.2d 1230 (1990).
19. Vanguard Ins. Co. v. Cantrell, 1973 C.C.H. (Fire & Casualty) Auto 7684.
20. Erie Insurance Exchange v. Eisenhutyh, et al., 451 A.2d 1024, (1982).
21. See, for example, "Confronting Employment-Related Claims for Emotional Distress," Paul K. Lees and Marlas Werkown, *Defense Counsel Journal,* October 1989, pp. 454-459.
22. While no additional sources of loss are covered, an aggregate limit sometimes is restored if it has been impaired by claims within the basic policy period.

CHAPTER 6

Policy Limits and Loss Valuation Provisions

In previous chapters the nature of a legally enforceable insurance contract was examined, and the *who, what, where,* and *when* questions of coverage were considered in discussions of insurable interests, insured parties, and insured events. When an insured event occurs to an insured party with an insurable interest who is covered under a legally enforceable contract and no policy conditions have been violated, the next question to be addressed is, "How much?" More specifically, "How much is payable to, or on behalf of, the insured party(ies)?" This question is addressed by the policy provisions and legal doctrines that determine the dollar amounts of coverage under property and liability insurance policies.

This chapter begins an analysis of the "How much?" question by examining policy limits (also known as "limits of insurance" or "limits of liability") and loss valuation provisions. Together, these provisions and their interpretation define the *maximum* amounts payable for covered losses under any given policy. The next two chapters explore other aspects of this "How much?" question by examining provisions that may reduce the amounts otherwise payable: Chapter 7 examines loss-sharing provisions (such as coinsurance and deductible provisions), and Chapter 8 deals with situations involving multiple sources of recovery, especially those addressed in provisions dealing with other insurance. External factors relevant to the "How much?" question are among the topics discussed in Chapter 9.

POLICY LIMITS

Most property and liability insurance policies contain one or more limits on the amount payable for claims covered by the policy. Policy limits usually are expressed in dollars, but nonmonetary limits—such as time (number of hours or days)—are occasionally found. And some notable policies or portions of policies, for various sound reasons, contain no explicit policy limit.

Policy limits often are referred to as *limits of liability*, and many policies use this phrase. As the phrase suggests, "limits of liability" refers to the limits, or the extent, of the insurer's *liability*, or responsibility, under the policy. The term can be a bit confusing, however, because it seems to relate to liability insurance, but it is used also with property insurance. Further confusing the point in connection with liability insurance, the *insurer's* contractual liability to its insured, arising out of obligations undertaken in the insurance contract, is predicated on the *insured's* liability to others under the law. Many modern insurance policies eliminate the troublesome word "liability" and refer instead to *limits of insurance*. However, others continue to use "limits of liability."

Policy limits represent the *maximum* amounts the insurer will pay for losses to which the limits apply. They serve as the *upper* limits on the amounts insurers are contractually obligated to pay *to insureds* under property insurance policies, or *on behalf of insureds* under most liability insurance policies. (Some liability policies promise to reimburse the insured after the insured has paid a liability claim.)

Reasons for Policy Limits

Policy limits are among the devices used by insurers to clarify the extent of their contractual obligations. Other devices, such as exclusions and conditions, usually limit the insurer's obligation in verbal terms. Policy limits, however, generally limit the insurer's maximum obligation in dollar terms.

Suppose that insurance policies contained no dollar limits but attempted to define the extent of coverage entirely in verbal terms. Property insurance policies might contain an agreement, for example, to pay "whatever it costs" to repair or replace lost or damaged property. Bodily injury liability insurance policies might promise to pay whatever damages an insured is legally obligated to pay because of bodily injury to another. These open-ended approaches, while generally not feasible, are not exactly impossible either. In fact, as discussed later, they are used with some types of insurance in cases where the insurer's maximum dollar obligation is generally constrained by external factors.

From the insured's standpoint, verbal limits without dollar limits would eliminate many problems associated with inadequate dollar amounts of coverage. However, policy limits are useful for most policies because they perform several valuable functions, including capping the insurer's obligations, accommodating consumer preferences, and reflecting insurer capacity.

Capping Insurer's Obligations. While it is obvious that policy limits cap the insurer's obligation toward each insured or for each claim, the reasons for such a cap are less obvious.

One rationale is that policy limits help make it possible for the law of large numbers to operate. Without upper limits, potential losses under some insurance policies could be infinitely large—at least in theory—making average loss prediction more difficult. Given a decrease in predictability, insurers and their reinsurers would have to charge higher premiums to allow for the greater uncertainty, or they would withdraw from the market.

Another reason for capping the insurer's dollar obligations applies in situations in which verbal limitations would not be feasible. Examples might include an irreplaceable "priceless" art object or a products liability loss affecting thousands of claimants.

Insurance policies occasionally use limits to accomplish much the same effect as an exclusion—capping the insurer's obligations at some nominal amount rather than eliminating it completely. It sometimes is difficult to word an exclusion that eliminates the undesired coverage but provides all the coverage that is desired. Despite careful efforts at such wording, the courts often fail to interpret exclusions as insurers intend them; as a result, insurers pay for losses they thought were excluded. Sometimes it is easier to state what is covered than it is to state what is excluded. This seems to be the reason that insurance policies occasionally provide specific coverages subject to rather nominal limits. An example lies in the pollutant cleanup and removal "additional coverage" of the building and personal property coverage form. After general liability policies were revised to exclude coverage for nearly all third-party pollution losses, first-party pollution claims began to appear as claims for debris removal under property insurance policies. Historically, it has been difficult for insurers to develop liability insurance policy language that clearly excludes pollution losses of a type that are not readily insured. Rather than attempting once again to develop a satisfactory policy exclusion, insurers instead provided specific coverage for cleanup costs—and then made that coverage subject to a fairly nominal $10,000 annual aggregate limit. The rationale seems to be that the courts are more likely to interpret consistently an explicit statement of coverage with a dollar limit than a statement that completely excludes coverage on a verbal basis.

Accommodating Consumer Preferences. Consumers can benefit in at least two ways when they are given a choice of policy limits:

- Consumers often can select a property or liability insurance policy limit that meets their coverage needs or desires.
- Since premiums are reduced for lower policy limits and vice versa, consumers can select an amount of insurance consistent with their ability to pay for it.

In practice, consumer choices usually are subject to some constraints. Underwriters are generally unwilling to provide property insurance in amounts too far below or above the value of the insured property. Underinsurance fails to serve the needs of a consumer, who faces an inadequately covered loss, and it also creates problems for insurers, as explained further in Chapter 7. Overinsurance does not serve the insured, who is paying for coverage that cannot be used. Moreover, a moral hazard exists when there is a possibility of collecting a property insurance claim substantially exceeding the value of the property.

Liability insurance presents different challenges in accommodating consumer preferences. Small dollar losses are far more likely than large losses. Reflecting this fact, liability insurance premium rates drop off substantially as limits of insurance increase. Many policyholders who purchase a minimum amount of liability insurance could purchase substantially larger amounts of coverage for little extra cost. While it is desirable to provide insurance buyers with coverage they can afford, it is undesirable to provide insurance limits that fail to cover a significant loss. Insurers often offer no less than a minimum limit, such as $100,000, on certain types of liability coverage. Auto liability coverage minimums are established by state financial responsibility statutes.

Another dimension is added in connection with the personal injury protection (PIP) coverage of many auto policies providing no-fault insurance coverage. First-party medical benefits under an auto insurance policy provide coverage that duplicates coverage already available to many policyholders who have group medical expense and disability income coverage. Consumers benefit when people without other coverage are able to purchase high limits of PIP coverage while those with duplicate coverage have the relatively inexpensive option of choosing low PIP limits.

Reflecting Insurer Capacity. An insurer sometimes imposes an upper policy limit to keep the extent of its obligations within its financial capacity to absorb losses. For example, a fire insurer might refuse to write more than $100,000 of coverage on an unprotected building with an insurable value of $600,000. Or a liability insurer might write a maximum of $1 million of products liability insurance for any one manufacturer. Either decision could reflect an underwriting decision that avoids "putting too many eggs in one basket" or a limitation imposed by reinsurance requirements.

In these cases policy limits confine the insurer's loss exposures to an amount that is considered safe in relation to the individual insurer's financial capacity to absorb losses, taking into account its surplus and reinsurance. Detailed discussions of insurer capacity and reinsurance are beyond the scope of this text.

Types of Policy Limits in Property Insurance

A variety of methods is used to express limits in property insurance policies, and these methods can be grouped into several different categories. Unfortunately, no uniform labels are consistently applied in practice to these different categories. Within insurance policies themselves, limits are not necessarily referred to as specific limits, blanket limits, sublimits, and the like. In order to analyze and compare different approaches to policy limits, it has been necessary for us to choose some descriptive labels that do not necessarily correspond with titles used in insurance policies, although most of them are within the working vocabularies of insurance practitioners.

Per Item Versus Per Occurrence Limits. Some property insurance policy limits are applied to each item, while others are applied per occurrence.[1] There seems to be little practical distinction between "per item" and "per occurrence" coverage, except in the treatment of limits after a loss. The question here is, "What happens to the limits applying to covered property after the insurer has paid a claim on that property?" Different approaches are possible.

Some policies providing "per item" coverage contain a *restoration of limits provision*—in some policies called a *loss clause*—that addresses this issue. At least two different approaches are possible:

- Some policies simply state that limits are restored after a loss or that payment of a loss shall not reduce the limits of the policy.
- Others state that limits are not reduced by a partial loss. After paying a total loss, however, the insurer refunds the unearned premium for insurance on that item.

Occurrence limits require no such terms. The focus is on the occurrence rather than on the property, and each occurrence is covered up to a certain limit. The dollar limits remain in effect for each new occurrence.

Specific Limits. A *specific limit* is a dollar amount that sets the upper limit on the amount the insurer will pay, per item or per occurrence, for each loss associated with a particular item or class of property.

Separate Limits. When a single policy contains several specific limits, these limits are considered *separate limits.* Separate limits might apply to each of several items or classes of property. Consider, for example, a building and personal property coverage form including the following limits:

- $120,000 on the building at 114 Main Street
- $80,000 on business personal property at 114 Main Street
- $140,000 on the building at 312 South Street
- $60,000 on business personal property at 312 South Street

Each of these specific limits is truly a separate limit. The limit on one building cannot be applied to the other building, and the limit on a building cannot be applied to cover personal property or vice versa.[2]

Homeowners policies provide another common example of separate limits. A typical homeowners policy providing $100,000 coverage on the dwelling building would also provide separate limits for:

- $10,000 on other structures
- $50,000 on personal property
- $20,000 on loss of use

Usually, each of these limits applies separately.[3] While this is commonly considered a "$100,000 policy," the insurer might be obligated to pay up to $180,000 for a serious loss.

Scheduled Versus Unscheduled Property Limits. Specific limits most commonly apply to a single item of property (such as a building) or to a class of property (such as personal property). Personal property items typically are not individually listed, or "scheduled," and policy limits apply to all "unscheduled" items of covered property collectively. For example, the personal property coverage of a homeowners policy applies a single limit of coverage to all the insured's personal property without listing any individual objects of property. Although the term "blanket" is better applied to circumstances described later, it would not be inaccurate to say that such unscheduled items are covered on a blanket basis.

Property is said to be "scheduled" when the policy covers a list, or "schedule," of particular property items, each of which is listed and precisely identified with descriptions, serial numbers, or other identifying marks or characteristics. Each item of scheduled property typically is subject to a limit that reflects the amount of insurance applying to that single property item alone. Specific items of property, such as jewelry, furs, or cameras, may be listed on a scheduled personal property endorsement attached to the homeowners policy. When this is done, a limit of insurance is stated for each scheduled property item.

Sometimes both scheduled and unscheduled property are covered within the same policy; each item of scheduled property is subject to its own limit, while the limit for a category of unscheduled property applies collectively to all items within that group of property. For example, the policy issued to a stamp collector might insure a number of prized stamps on a scheduled basis, with a separate amount of insurance listed for each stamp specifically described. The same policy might provide another limit of unscheduled coverage—sometimes referred to as "blanket" coverage in this context—on several books of less-valuable stamps. As another example, a small contractor might purchase a specific scheduled limit of insurance on a backhoe, another separate specific scheduled limit of insurance on a bulldozer, and a separate specific limit of unscheduled, or blanket, insurance on other tools and equipment.

Blanket Limits. A blanket limit is a policy limit that applies to two or more items or classes of property and/or to property at two or more locations. Suppose an insured owns buildings and personal property at two locations with the values shown below:

- $120,000 on the building at 114 Main Street
- $80,000 on business personal property at 114 Main Street
- $140,000 on the building at 312 South Street
- $60,000 on business personal property at 312 South Street

With specific insurance, one would purchase separate limits of coverage on each of these four items. With blanket insurance, one could instead purchase $400,000 coverage applying to loss to any or all of these items.[4]

A blanket limit is especially helpful where the aggregate value of a business firm's movable property is fairly constant but where the values may shift between insured locations. In the example above, *blanket* insurance would provide sound protection if, at the time of the loss, the insured had $90,000 of business personal property at 312 South Street and $40,000 at 114 Main Street. *Specific* insurance in the amounts shown above would not be adequate to cover a $90,000 loss at 312 South Street and would simultaneously represent overinsurance, and a waste of premium dollars, when only $40,000 of personal property is at 114 Main Street.

It is more difficult to support the use of blanket insurance to cover buildings, because their values generally do not shift or rapidly change. And for that matter, blanket insurance often is used even when personal property values are not subject to substantial shifts from one location to another. In practice, blanket insurance often is used as a hedge when several locations are covered. By using a blanket limit of coverage over all locations rather than a specific limit at each location, the insured reduces the likelihood that it will be penalized, following a loss, for underestimating (and therefore underinsuring) the value of property at any particular location. Also, the applicable limit will not be less than the value of the loss at any one location.

Although blanket insurance may appear to be simpler than specific insurance, it actually is more complex to handle and is no panacea for the ills of underinsurance. Blanket insurance adds complexity to the processes of underwriting, rating, and claims adjusting. Blanket insurance rates are, in effect, constructed by specifically rating coverage at each location and then dividing the sum of these separate premiums by the total insured values to come up with an average rate. Additional loadings may be applied when there is a large difference in the published fire insurance rates among insured locations. When claims are involved, it may be necessary to establish insurable values at all locations to determine whether a coinsurance penalty should be applied. (Coinsurance penalties are examined in Chapter 7.)

Sublimits. The limits discussed above, which usually are selected by the insured and entered in the policy declarations, are upper limits on the amount of recovery. In addition to these upper limits, many property insurance policies also contain one or more "sublimits" within the preprinted form. A *sublimit* is a limit within an upper limit that imposes a smaller limit for some particular kinds of property or types of losses.

The ISO homeowners policy, for example, contains the following sublimit for personal property usually located at an insured's secondary residence. Though expressed as a percent or dollar sublimit, the percentage would come into play only when the limit of liability for Coverage C (personal property) is less than $10,000.

> Our limit of liability for personal property usually located at an "insured's" residence, other than the "residence premises," is 10% of the limit of liability for Coverage C, or $1000, whichever is greater.

Insureds with significant exposures at a lakeside cottage or other seasonal dwelling should purchase coverage on that particular exposure.

The personal property coverage of the homeowners policy also includes a number of sublimits under the heading "special limits of liability" as shown in Exhibit 6-1. As mentioned, these sublimits do not increase the maximum overall limit applicable to personal property. Rather, they impose smaller limits on the listed types of personal property. Three of the sublimits apply only to loss by theft to specified types of property; loss by other perils is not restricted by the sublimit. The reasons for these particular sublimits are discussed in more detail in another CPCU text. In general, however, they eliminate coverage for exposures of an extent not found in the typical home. Nominal exposures are covered by the standard homeowners policy subject to these limitations; extensive exposures are better handled under a more specialized type of insurance.

To illustrate the application of the sublimits shown in Exhibit 6-1, suppose that a homeowners insured has a $50,000 upper limit on un-

Exhibit 6-1
Special Limits of Liability in the ISO Homeowners Policy

Special LImits of Liability. These limits do not increase the Coverage C limit of liability. The special limit for each numbered category below is the total limit for each loss for all property in that category.

1. $200 on money, bank notes, bullion, gold other than goldware, silver other than silverware, platinum, coins and medals.

2. $1000 on securities, accounts, deeds, evidences of debt, letters of credit, notes other than bank notes, manuscripts, personal records, passports, tickets and stamps. This dollar limit applies to these categories regardless of the medium (such as paper or computer software) on which the material exists.

   This limit includes the cost to research, replace or restore the information from the lost or damaged material.

3. $1000 on watercraft, including their trailers, furnishings, equipment and outboard engines or motors.

4. $1000 on trailers not used with watercraft.

5. $1000 for loss by theft of jewelry, watches, furs, precious and semi-precious stones.

6. $2000 for loss by theft of firearms.

7. $2500 for loss by theft of silverware, silver-plated ware, goldware, gold-plated ware and pewterware. This includes flatware, hollowware, tea sets, trays and trophies made of or including silver, gold or pewter.

8. $2500 on property, on the "residence premises," used at any time or in any manner for any "business" purpose.

9. $250 on property, away from the "residence premises," used at any time or in any manner for any "business" purpose. However, this limit does not apply to loss to adaptable electronic apparatus as described in Special Limits **10.** and **11.** below.

10. $1000 for loss to electronic apparatus, while in or upon a motor vehicle or other motorized land conveyance, if the electronic apparatus is equipped to be operated by power from the electrical system of the vehicle or conveyance while retaining its capability of being operated by other sources of power. Electronic apparatus includes:

    a. Accessories or antennas; or

    b. Tapes, wires, records, discs or other media;

    for use with any electronic apparatus.

11. $1000 for loss to electronic apparatus, while not in or upon a motor vehicle or other motorized land conveyance, if the electronic apparatus:

    a. Is equipped to be operated by power from the electrical system of the vehicle or conveyance while retaining its capability of being operated by other sources of power;

    b. Is away from the "residence premises"; and

    c. Is used at any time or in any manner for any "business" purpose.

    Electronic apparatus includes:

    a. Accessories and antennas; or

    b. Tapes, wires, records, discs, or other media;

    for use with any electronic apparatus.

Form HO 00 03 04 91, Copyright Insurance Services Office, Inc.,,1990.

scheduled personal property and that a fire totally destroys all the insured's personal property. Suppose the fire destroys $500 of money, $800 of securities, a $1,000 boat, a $600 outboard motor, and a $4,000 fur coat (subtotal: $6,900), plus additional clothing, furniture, and appliances. In determining the total amount of recovery (ignoring deductibles, for the sake of this discussion), the insured could count:

- $200 of money (see sublimit 1)
- $800 of securities (the actual value, less than sublimit 2)
- $1,000 for watercraft, including the motor (see sublimit 3)
- $4,000 for the coat (sublimit 5 applies to loss by theft, not fire)

This totals $6,000, leaving $900 uncovered. If the remaining loss amounts to no more than $44,000 (that is, the $50,000 limit minus $6,000 for covered property losses discussed above), the insured would be compensated in full for the remaining property. If the remaining loss amounts to more than $44,000, the insured would recover only a total of $50,000 (the policy limit). And even if the rest of the property amounts to less than $44,000, the insured will not be compensated for any of the $900 loss that exceeds the sublimits.

Three of the homeowners sublimits cited above apply only to loss by theft to specified types of property. A similar set of sublimits appears in the causes of loss—special form used to provide "all-risks" coverage on commercial buildings and personal property. (The "all-risks" coverage of this form includes theft, and these sublimits serve to limit theft coverage for certain target items not found in most business operations.)

> For loss or damage by theft, the following types of property are covered only up to the limits shown:
> **a.** $2,500 for furs, fur garments and garments trimmed with fur.
> **b.** $2,500 for jewelry, watches, watch movements, jewels, pearls, precious and semi-precious stones, bullion, gold, silver, platinum and other precious alloys or metals. This limit does not apply to jewelry and watches worth $100 or less per item.
> **c.** $2,500 for patterns, dies, molds and forms.
> **d.** $250 for stamps, tickets and letters of credit.

The building and personal property coverage form also includes a $1,000 per occurrence sublimit for signs attached to buildings. Physically located in the "commercial property" coverage form rather than a causes-of-loss form, this sublimit provision applies regardless of the peril causing the loss.

Additions and Extensions of Coverage. Some policies include sections with titles such as "additional coverages," or "extensions of coverage" that are included automatically in the policy for no identifiable premium charge. Unfortunately, terms such as "additional coverage," "coverage extensions," and so forth are not used consistently by policy drafters, and it is necessary to read beyond the heading to discover whether separate limits or sublimits are involved. Some additions or extensions provide coverages with separate limits that apply *in addition* to other policy limits. Others, however, provide coverages subject to sublimits that *do not increase* the overall dollar amount of coverage under the policy.

The building and personal property coverage form includes five "coverage extensions," each subject to a separate limit. The extensions are as follows:

- Newly acquired or constructed property
  - Buildings—25 percent of the building limit but not more than $250,000 per new building
  - Business personal property—10 percent of the limit of insurance for your business personal property but not more than $100,000 at each new building
- Personal effects and property of others
  - $2,500 limit at each described premises
- Valuable papers and records—cost of research
  - $1,000 limit at each described premises
- Property off premises
  - $5,000 limit
- Outdoor property
  - $1,000 limit but not more than $250 for any one tree, shrub, or plant

The same form also contains four "additional coverages":

- Debris removal
  - 25 percent of the amount paid for the direct physical loss or damage plus the deductible
- Preservation of property
  - No stated limit
- Fire department service charge
  - $1,000 limit—no deductible
- Pollutant clean up and removal
  - $10,000 limit

Are these sublimits or do these limits apply in addition to the policy limits? Some are of each type, as indicated by the following "limits of insurance" provision:

The limits applicable to the Coverage Extensions and the Fire Department Service Charge and Pollutant Clean Up and Removal Additional Coverages are in addition to the Limits of Insurance.

Payments under the following Additional Coverages will not increase the applicable Limit of Insurance:

1. Preservation of Property; or
2. Debris removal. . . .

The provision goes on to state that the policy will provide up to $5,000 additional debris removal coverage under some circumstances that are not particularly relevant to this discussion of limits.

The ISO homeowners policy provides the following nine additional coverages, some of which provide separate amounts of additional coverage:

- Debris removal: "This expense is included in the limit of liability that applies to the damaged property. If the amount to be paid for the actual damage to the property plus the debris removal expense is more than the limit of liability for the damaged property, an additional 5 percent of the limit of liability is available for debris removal expense."
- Reasonable repairs: "This coverage . . . does not increase the limit of liability that applies to the covered property."
- Trees, shrubs, and other plants: Coverage applies for up to 5 percent of the dwelling limit of liability with a maximum of $500 per tree. "This coverage is additional insurance."
- Fire department service charge: "This [$500] coverage is additional insurance."
- Property removed: "This coverage does not change the limit of liability that applies to the property being removed."
- Credit card, fund transfer card, forgery, and counterfeit money: "This [$500] coverage is additional insurance."
- Loss assessment: The policy includes no specific comment as to whether this $1,000 coverage provides additional insurance.
- Collapse: "This coverage does not increase the limit of liability applying to the damaged covered property."
- Glass or safety glazing material: "This coverage does not increase the limit of liability that applies to the damaged property."

Non-Dollar Limits. Not all property insurance limits are expressed in dollars, as shown in the following examples:

- The limit of liability for auto physical damage coverage usually is the actual cash value of the stolen or damaged property or the amount to repair or replace the property, whichever is less.
- Some homeowners policies provide *guaranteed replacement cost* coverage. Subject to no stated dollar limit, the insurer will pay the actual cost of repairing or replacing the damaged or destroyed dwelling building.
- Bailees customers coverage for dry cleaners sometimes provides

coverage on customers' clothing and other goods that is subject to no dollar limits.

● Businessowners policies include coverage for loss of business income that is actually incurred within twelve consecutive months after the date of direct physical loss or damage. This "additional coverage" is not subject to the limits of insurance.

Careful analysis of these examples reveals that the extent of the insurer's dollar obligations is not as open-ended as it seems. Autos are regularly bought and sold on the open market, and the actual cash value of an auto can readily be determined by examining the publications that track used auto selling prices. By knowing the make, model, year, and mileage of a covered auto, both the insurer and the insured can readily establish its current dollar value. Auto physical damage insurance rates are basically calculated on the basis of such information.

In practice, guaranteed replacement cost coverage is generally provided on a homeowners policy only after the insurer (or the insurer's representative) has formally estimated the replacement cost value of the home. To qualify for guaranteed replacement cost coverage, the insured must purchase a dollar amount of insurance equal to that estimated value. By guaranteeing to pay the full replacement cost of the home, even if it is more than the dollar limit in the policy, the insurer actually does little more than guarantee the accuracy of its estimate and assume the inflation risk.

A dry cleaner generally finds it difficult to determine the value of customers' goods being processed and stored. This problem would make it difficult to purchase appropriate dollar limits of insurance, so another approach is sometimes used. When bailees customers coverage is written with no policy limit, the insured is required to submit periodic reports of receipts derived from dry-cleaning operations. A fairly consistent relationship exists between the amounts collected and the value of the merchandise processed. In other words, receipts are directly proportionate to the values exposed to loss. Premiums are then based on receipts rather than on values, giving the insurer a premium consistent with the exposure and giving the insured coverage adequate to cover any loss.

The businessowners policy was developed with simplification in mind, providing a broad set of coverages needed by the typical small business, in a package whose premium could be computed based on a small number of rating factors. The premium for business income coverage is basically built into the premium charged for building and/or personal property coverages. In theory, there is a fairly consistent relationship between the amount of property exposed to direct loss and the potential amount of business income loss. Most small businesses' income losses do not last more than a few months. The twelve-month limit is intended to place a cap on the insurer's obligations, which would keep a claim from becoming totally unreasonable. Eligibility rules and underwriting guidelines are intended to screen out applicants whose business income exposure might be disproportionate to the property values. Thus, insurers generally consider their business income loss exposures under this policy to be proportionate to the direct property loss exposures. However, the possibility exists of a loss that is not consistent with these assumptions.

The point here is that property insurance policies do not always contain dollar limits. However, policies without dollar limits generally are based on the premise that some other information serves as a surrogate in establishing the maximum extent of the insurer's dollar obligations.

Variable Limits. During recent decades the inflation rate sometimes has been in the double-digit range. People are generally aware that the value of many property items tends to rise over time, increasing at rates that depend on a variety of external factors. These changing values raise serious questions about the adequacy of property insurance limits expressed in fixed dollar amounts. The insured who purchases limits barely adequate at the outset may have limits that are quite inadequate by the time the policy expires. On the other hand, the insured who purchases more-than-adequate limits at inception is paying for more insurance than necessary at the outset. Various practices address this problem, as detailed in the following paragraphs.

Annual Increases as Underwriting Practice. Some insurers address the inflation problem by automatically increasing property insurance limits and premiums at each annual renewal, unless the increases are rejected by the insured. The amount of the increase typically is based on an average annual inflation rate, as measured by one or more price level indices. While this is obviously a sound approach, it fails to guarantee adequate coverage limits for the policyholder, for several reasons:

- The policyholder who is underinsured at the beginning of the policy period will still be underinsured after renewal.
- Even if coverage is adequate at the beginning of each policy period, it is likely to be inadequate at the time of loss—especially if a total loss occurs just prior to renewal. This happens because coverage limits are not increased between renewal dates.

Property insurers have used several approaches to providing limits that increase automatically, according to a predetermined method, during the policy period.

Inflation Guard. The "inflation guard," so named because it is intended to guard against economic inflation, was originally developed for use with homeowners policies. It subsequently became available for insurance on commercial buildings, where it was formerly known as an "automatic increase in insurance endorsement." The endorsement was so often used that this approach is now available as an option preprinted in the standard building and personal property coverage form, where it is labeled "inflation guard."

In the homeowners policy, the optional inflation guard endorsement applies to all property coverages—dwelling building, other structures, personal property, and loss of use. In the building and personal property coverage form, it applies only to the coverages indicated in the declarations.

Earlier inflation guard endorsements increased coverage every three months (actually three times during a policy year since the final increase coincided with the policy anniversary) by a certain percentage. This approach reduced the problems associated with increases in values during the policy *year*, but did nothing about increases during each of the three-month periods. Current policies prorate a preestablished percentage increase over the entire policy year, with increases determined on a daily basis rather than every three months.

For example, assume the Clyde Building is insured on a policy with a $365,000 limit, and this policy includes the optional inflation guard coverage and specifies a 10 percent annual increase. This means that coverage will be increased by 10 percent of $365,000, which comes to $36,500, during the year of the policy. One hundred dollars, which is 1/365 of that increase (because $365,000/365 = $100), applies each day. If a loss occurs after the policy has been in force 100 days, the applicable policy limit is not $365,000, but $375,000 (because $365,000 limit + [$100 per day × 100 days] = $375,000).

The inflation guard approach clearly overcomes some of the deficiencies of fixed-dollar limits. Still, it is not a perfect solution for two reasons:

- If the policyholder is underinsured at the outset, the endorsement does not correct the basic coverage inadequacy.
- The selected percentage, which presumably is based on expected inflation rates, may bear little or no relationship to actual rates of inflation.

Indexed Limits. Insurers occasionally have offered indexed limits in an attempt to reflect actual rates of inflation. Generally, an indexed limit is a policy limit that is linked, in a predetermined manner, to a price level index such as the United States Department of Commerce Construction Cost Index or the Department of Labor's Consumer Price Index.

Indexed limits can be more accurate than the inflation guard approach in maintaining adequate limits. Yet, indexed limits are not without shortcomings. Government indexes are used primarily because they are readily available. However, price level indexes measure *aggregate* price level changes. They do not provide precise measures of increases in the labor and materials costs of repairing or replacing a particular insured's property at the time and location of the loss. At best, indexing can be a helpful supplement to an appraisal or other more individualized approaches to maintaining limits that reflect current values.

New Policy Editions. While the above approaches attempt to increase overall policy limits to reflect inflation, they have no effect on policy sublimits expressed in fixed dollars. A $1,000 jewelry sublimit, for example, may gradually become inadequate as the value of gems and gold increases over time. When new policy editions are introduced, such sublimits may be increased. These changes, however, are by no means automatic, nor are they within the control of the insured.

Types of Policy Limits in Liability Insurance Policies

Policy limits in liability insurance can be examined from many perspectives. While some aspects resemble property insurance limits, the distinctive nature of liability insurance lends itself to a number of differences.

Liability Coverage Limits. Many liability insurance policies include coverages—such as medical payments coverages and no-fault first-party auto coverages—that do not actually provide "liability" protection. The discussion under this heading deals only with the true liability coverages of a "liability policy." Liability coverage involves the insurer's agreement to pay, usually on behalf of the insured, sums that the insured will become legally obligated to pay as damages for bodily injury or property damage.

Per Event Limits. Chapter 5 discussed policy "triggers" in connection with events insured under liability policies. Depending on the event that triggers coverage, liability insurance policies typically contain limits that apply per accident, per occurrence, or per claim. A *single limit,* also known as a *combined single limit,* applies a dollar maximum to all incidents (accidents, occurrences, claims) subject to the limit, whether it involves liability arising out of one injured person, several injured persons, property damage, or any combination thereof. The following provision from the liability section of the personal auto policy presents an example.

A. The limit of liability shown in the Declarations for this coverage is
   our maximum limit of liability for all damages resulting from any

one auto accident. This is the most we will pay regardless of the number of:
1. "Insureds;"
2. Claims made;
3. Vehicles or premiums shown in the Declarations; or
4. Vehicles involved in the auto accident.

A personal auto policy with a combined single limit of $500,000 would provide coverage for any one auto accident for up to $500,000 for liability arising out of bodily injury, property damage, or any combination of the two.

Split limits, which are now less common than in the past, use separate limits for bodily injury and property damage liability claims. For example, a policy might provide $500,000 bodily injury liability coverage limits and $100,000 property damage liability coverage limits. These might sometimes be expressed as 500/100 limits.

Some split-limit policies actually contain three separate limits—a bodily injury limit applicable to each injured person, a larger bodily injury limit applicable to two or more injured persons, and a property damage limit.

Split limits truly are *separate* limits. Suppose Audrey is an insured under an auto insurance policy that has 25/50/10 limits (that is, $25,000 per person for bodily injury to one or more persons, $50,000 per accident for bodily injury to two or more persons, and $10,000 per accident for property damage). Audrey negligently causes a covered accident resulting in no injuries but $15,000 damage to another driver's car. The insurer would pay no more than $10,000 for this damage—Audrey could not apply any of the bodily injury limits to cover her property damage liability. Likewise, if Audrey negligently caused $27,000 in bodily injury to Mrs. Smith and $4,000 to Mr. Smith, the insurer would at most pay $25,000 to Mrs. Smith and $4,000 to Mr. Smith. Or if she were responsible for $134,000 in bodily injury to all five members of the Smith family as well as the $15,000 in property damage to the Smiths' car, the insurer would pay the claimants no more than $60,000—that is, $50,000 for bodily injury and $10,000 for property damage, the maximum amount payable for any one accident under the 25/50/10 policy limits.

Aggregate Limits. An aggregate limit is a specific upper limit on the amount an insurer will pay for the cumulative total of damages from all covered events during the covered period. An aggregate limit typically is two or three times the limit that applies per event (that is, the per accident, per occurrence, or per claim limit), and it usually is expressed as an annual (policy year) limit.

To illustrate, suppose a policy has a single limit of $100,000 per occurrence and an annual aggregate limit of $300,000. Three covered losses occur during the first six months of the policy term, the first for

$50,000, the second for $120,000, and the third for $200,000. The insurer would pay $50,000 for the first and $100,000 each for the second and third losses, for a cumulative total of $250,000 during the first six months. At this point the insured has accumulated $250,000 in insured losses and would have only $50,000 (that is, $300,000 − $250,000) of coverage available for the remaining six months of the policy period. If another separate occurrence results in damages of $60,000, the insurer's payment of $50,000 would exhaust the $300,000 annual aggregate limit; $300,000 was the most the insurer had agreed to pay for the cumulative total of all separate occurrences during the entire policy year. Once an aggregate limit has been used up in the payment of claims, the insured is without further protection under that coverage.

Aggregate limits seldom are found in the liability coverages of homeowners, personal auto, and other policies covering personal and family exposures. As a practical matter, individuals and families rarely have two or three separate substantial liability losses during a single policy term. However, aggregate limits are quite common in commercial liability coverages.

Up until the mid-1980s, general liability policy coverage for liability arising out of business premises and operations in progress often was not subject to an aggregate limit. In theory, an insurer could be required to pay up to the per occurrence policy limit many times because of events during a single policy period, with no true cap on the extent of the insurer's cumulative liabilities under the policy. In practice, multiple occurrences resulting in severe losses during a policy period were quite rare. Those that did take place were likely to be unpredictable, fortuitous events of the type insurance is designed to handle. However, there were cases in which the courts treated a series of related incidents as separate occurrences, with the entire policy limit available separately for each. And there was a growing realization that newly recognized exposures could create substantial liabilities for insurers under policies that had long since terminated.

Defense Costs and Supplementary Payments. A few specialized liability policies include defense costs within the policy limit. In other words, the policy limit is the maximum amount the insurer will pay for any combination of damages *and* defense costs together. However, under the vast majority of liability insurance policies, defense costs are paid *in addition to* the maximum amount payable for damages, and there theoretically is *no dollar limit* on the amount the insurer might be required to pay in defending the insured against a claim for covered damages. Strictly speaking, this statement is true only for defense costs and claims expenses incurred before the payment of the insurer's total limit of liability. A typical liability insuring agreement stipulates that the insurer's obligation to defend arising out of a given accident, occurrence, or claim terminates when the amount it pays for damages equals the specified limit of liability.

Suppose an insurer has issued an insurance policy providing professional liability coverage subject to a $100,000 policy limit. Further suppose that the insurer incurs investigation and defense costs of $470,000 in connection with a professional liability claim in which the trial court holds the insured liable for $90,000 in damages. This example might appear unrealistic because it might seem that the insurer would settle with a claimant long before incurring such substantial defense and claims costs. However, the example is not that far-fetched. Among other possibilities, the claimant might have refused an offer to settle for the policy limit, hoping to get more from a jury. In this example, the insurer would be required to pay all the defense costs of the initial trial. Suppose the plaintiff then appealed the case in a higher court. The insurer would probably end up paying all the costs of defending the appeal. But the insurer's defense obligation would end the moment its total payment for *damages* reached its limit of $100,000.

Insurers often are required to pay out, for defense costs and damages combined, amounts well in excess of the limit of insurance for damages. But the notion that the liability insurer's defense obligation is "unlimited" in amount is largely theoretical. Practical limitations constrain the theoretically unlimited nature of a liability insurer's obligation to pay defense costs:

● According to most policies, the insurer has the exclusive right to control the defense. Although the insurer obviously cannot control the claimant or the claimant's attorney, the insurer can select its own defense counsel and monitor the case. The insurer can keep tabs on the defense costs and attempt to negotiate a settlement if costs threaten to become disproportionately high.
● Premiums on litigation bonds and first-aid expenses, although they are covered, seldom amount to large sums of money.
● Reimbursement of the insured's loss of earnings, necessitated by the insured's involvement in the investigation or defense of a claim, is limited to a nominal sum, such as $50 or $100 per day, and the involvement giving rise to the loss of earnings must be at the request of the insurer. Although this cost typically is covered, it rarely becomes substantial.

Defense costs sometimes appear to be nonproductive transaction costs that drive up the cost of the insurance mechanism without providing monetary benefits. It would not be appropriate to conclude this discussion without underscoring the genuine *benefits* of a sound defense: Often a strong defense results in a finding of "no liability" on behalf of the insured and no payment for damages by the insurer. A legal decision in favor of the insured may establish good case law and discourage other similar claims. It may send a signal to plaintiffs' attorneys and other would-be claimants that the insurer will vigorously defend such claims rather than paying to get rid of them. Where damages are awarded, the award may be substantially reduced because of evidence introduced through a sound, if costly, defense. Of course, insurers do not always prevail in the cases they choose to defend, and defense costs sometimes are incurred on claims that could have been settled out of court by paying the amount originally claimed for damages. Conversely, insurers sometimes pay smaller questionable claims—even those they probably could win—to avoid defense costs or to preclude the possibility of a very large judgment.

Limits for Non-Fault-Based Coverages. The liability section of the homeowners policy automatically includes two coverages that are not, strictly speaking, "liability coverages" since they operate without the requirement that the insured be legally liable for damages. These two coverages are as follows:

- Damage to property of others (an "additional coverage" with a $500 limit)
- Medical payments to others (Coverage F, usually with a limit of $1,000, or higher if the insured so chooses)

These two coverages both respond for incidents that *might* give rise to a liability claim, and both provide relatively small limits of coverage that are available even when the insured is not at fault (liable). By providing non-fault-based coverage for small claims, the insurer can make a prompt claim payment without admitting the insured was negligent, therefore preserving its possible defenses against a larger claim. These coverages also make for some "good will" for the insured whose insurance pays for another party's injuries or property damage.

Coverage details appear in other CPCU texts. However, a brief example involving a covered medical payments claim will show how this non-fault-based coverage maintains goodwill and reduces litigation. Doris injured her knee and incurred medical expenses of $500 when she fell in her friend Jim's driveway. Doris asked Jim to pay her medical expenses because she felt they were caused by a hazard in his driveway. Jim notified his insurance company, which readily paid Doris's claim under the "medical payments to others" coverage of Jim's homeowners insurance policy. Consider what might have happened if Jim had liability coverage but did not also have medical payments coverage:

- The insurer might have attempted to defend Jim, at some expense, showing that Doris's fall was caused by her own clumsiness, and not by some negligence on Jim's part.

● Jim's insistence that he was not negligent in maintaining his driveway and that he was not responsible for Doris's clumsiness might have cost him their friendship.

● Jim might instead have agreed with Doris's side of the story to help her recover her expenses from his insurance company.

● Recognizing a situation in which a defense would be costly, the insurance company might pay Doris's expenses of $500. Doris might subsequently bring a larger claim for additional medical expenses or disability, and the insurer would be estopped (prevented) from denying this subsequent claim since it has already admitted Jim's liability by paying the first claim.

Paying the $500 medical payments claim preserves Jim's goodwill and eliminates the need for litigation. Should a subsequent liability claim be made, the insurer's payment under the medical expenses does not estop the insurer from denying payment under the liability coverage.

Damage to Property of Others in Homeowners Policies. In standard homeowners policies, the upper limit for damage to property of others is a specific limit of $500 per occurrence. This limit usually cannot be increased, even for an additional premium. Larger claims for which the insured is legally liable are covered by the liability coverage, which has minimum limits of $100,000.

Medical Payments in Homeowners Policies. Under homeowners forms, the usual base limit for medical payments to others is $1,000 per person. For a small additional premium, this limit may be increased to as high as $5,000. Subject to this limit, the insurer agrees to pay "necessary medical expenses that are incurred or medically ascertained within three years from the date of an accident causing bodily injury." Coverage does not apply to the named insured or residents of the household. Homeowners policies of twenty years ago included a $250 per person limit and a $25,000 per accident limit, presumably capping the insurer's obligations to apply to no more than 100 people injured in a single accident. Current homeowners policies contain no per accident limit, probably because of the low probability that such a limit would ever be invoked.

Medical Payments in Commercial General Liability Policies. Medical payments coverage is built into commercial general liability policies, usually with a limit of $5,000. The limit is the most the insurer will pay because of bodily injury sustained by any one person and caused by an accident on the insured's premises or because of the insured's operations. Covered expenses must be incurred and reported within one year of the date of the accident. Per occurrence and aggregate limits also apply, as described later under "hierarchies of limits."

Medical Payments in Auto Policies. Because medical expenses of both the named insured and passengers are covered, auto medical payments coverage differs sharply from homeowners or commercial general liability medical payments coverage. Where available, auto medical payments coverage limits are offered in modest amounts similar to those of homeowners policies.

Auto No-Fault Coverage Limits. Auto no-fault insurance is based on statutes passed in some states in response to a range of issues. It is difficult to generalize accurately about no-fault insurance because of the substantial variations among state laws.

Generally speaking, nearly all personal injury protection (PIP) endorsements used to provide auto no-fault coverage in accordance with statutory dictates provide specified amounts of what are essentially life and health insurance coverages restricted solely to losses arising out of motor vehicle accidents, regardless of who is negligent. The usual endorsement provides at least some coverage for medical expenses, funeral expenses, survivor benefits, loss of income, and the replacement of essential services.

Only two jurisdictions currently offer medical expense coverage with no dollar limits. Funeral and burial expenses usually are covered subject to a specific dollar limit, such as $1,000 per person. Survivors of an insured who dies in an auto accident are paid a continuing income of up to a certain amount per week for up to a specified number of weeks, or up to a stated dollar maximum. Loss of income and substitute services benefits are payable subject to daily, weekly, or overall maximums.

Workers Compensation and Employers Liability Limits. The standard workers compensation and employers liability insurance policy provides the insured employer with two broad kinds of coverage:

- Part One—Workers Compensation, pertaining to the employer's obligation to provide workers compensation benefits embodied in applicable statutes.
- Part Two—Employers Liability, pertaining to the employer's liability exposures under common law.

Workers Compensation Limits. The workers compensation insuring agreement is quite simple:

We will pay promptly when due the benefits required of you by the workers compensation law.

A policy definition clarifies what is meant by "workers compensation law."

Workers Compensation Law

Workers Compensation Law means the workers or workmen's compensation law and occupational disease law of each state or territory named in item 3.A. of the Information page. It includes any amendments to that law which are in effect during the policy period. It does not include the provisions of any law that provide nonoccupational disability benefits.

The state(s) or territory(ies) whose workers compensation laws are referenced here are listed in the policy's declarations ("information page"). It is not necessary for the policy to spell out dollar limits for this coverage; the workers compensation statutes state the limitations that apply.

Generally speaking, all workers compensation statutes require employers subject to the law to pay medical expenses and compensation for disability or death due to the employment-related injuries and diseases of employees, as defined by the statute. All states now require the payment of medical expenses without any upper dollar limit. However, the amounts payable as compensation for death, disability, dismemberment, and related benefits are invariably governed by specific limits set forth in the relevant statutes.

Employers Liability Limits. The employers liability insuring agreement says that the insurer "will pay all sums [the employer] must pay as damages because of [covered] bodily injury to your employees." This wording is typical of the wording in other liability insurance policies' insuring agreements. The declarations (information page) contains three limits of liability:

- Bodily injury by accident—limit applies per accident, regardless of the number of injured employees
- Bodily injury by disease (per employee)
- Bodily injury by disease ("policy limit," actually an aggregate limit)

The basic limits for these coverages are $100,000, $100,000, and $500,000, respectively. They may be increased as high as $1,000,000/$1,000,000/$10,000,000 according to manual rules. At least one state requires that this coverage be provided without limits for claims arising in that state.

Defense Costs and Supplementary Payments. Defense and supplementary benefits are payable *in addition to* the limits payable under Part One or the applicable limit of liability under Part Two. Unlike other liability policies, the insurer's obligation under the workers compensation coverage for defense and claims expenses is literally unlimited. The insurer's obligation to defend a workers compensation claim does not end when the insurer has paid the amounts required by statute. However, the

Exhibit 6-2
Hierarchical Liability Limits of the CGL

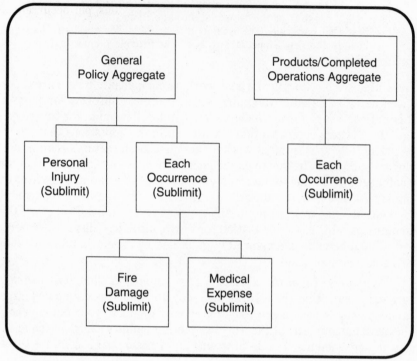

Adapted with permission from Jack P. Gibson, CPCU, CLU, ARM, *Contractors Guide to the 1986 Commercial General Liability Program,* Copyright 1985, RCI Communications, pp. 20-21.

INSURER'S

~~employer's~~ obligation to provide a defense for employers liability claims does end once the insurer has paid the applicable limit of liability.

Hierarchical Limits. The commercial general liability (CGL) coverage form includes a set of limits illustrated by Exhibit 6-2. A chart of these limits resembles the hierarchical structure of a typical organizational chart.

Restoration of Limits. Although the phrase "restoration of limits" generally is used only with property insurance, the concept also applies with liability insurance. Per person and per event limits are not reduced when a claim is paid. In contrast, aggregate limits are designed to be consumed by a series of claims.

Per Person Limits. A per person liability limit is not reduced for future losses, because such a limit is applied per accident, occurrence, or claim. Clearly, the intention is to make a per person limit available to *each* separate event covered during the policy term. However, if the policy also contains an annual aggregate limit, it may come into play and eliminate coverage for future claims.

Per Event Limits. A per event limit (per accident, per occurrence) is designed to put a lid on the insurer's total payment for a particular accident, regardless of the number of claimants. Once exhausted, the per event limit cannot be restored *for that particular event.* Yet, the full limit is automatically restored for future events, in effect, by its application to each separate event (assuming no problem because of an aggregate limit).

Aggregate Limits. An annual aggregate limit, found in some liability policies, limits the amount the insurer will pay for the cumulative total of all separate accidents, occurrences, or claims during the policy period. Once exhausted, an annual aggregate limit is not automatically replenished until the beginning of the next policy year, assuming the policy is renewed. In the meantime, a partially or fully exhausted aggregate limit can be restored to the original amount only by the payment of an additional premium subject to, and only with the consent of, the insurer.

Some claims-made policies, such as the claims-made version of the commercial general liability coverage form (CGL), give the insured the right to purchase optional "unlimited tail" coverage, under specified conditions, for claims that are made after the policy period and arise out of occurrences taking place before policy expiration. While the complex nuances of claims-made coverage are beyond the scope of this course, it is necessary to at least mention that aggregate limits are reinstated for claims covered under this "supplementary extended reporting period" coverage.

For coverages not subject to an upper dollar limit, such as the medical expense coverage mandated by workers compensation laws, there obviously is no need for restoration of policy limits. Nor is there a need to restore the already unlimited defense benefits under the standard workers compensation coverage. As to other liability policies, the insurer's duty to defend ceases as soon as it has paid its limit of liability for damages. Such policies are silent as to whether exhausted defense coverage can be restored, but it seems implicit that defense coverage is automatically restored whenever the limits of insurance are restored.

Increasing Policy Limits. No inflation guard type of endorsement is available for use with liability coverages. To the extent that any policies provide unlimited coverage, there is no need for variable policy limits. This is true of most liability policies' unlimited coverage for defense costs.

Workers compensation coverage pays the benefits required by statute. Workers compensation statutes do involve a form of indexing because they tie weekly income benefits to the state's average wage. Income benefits are based on the latest average wage figure available at the time the benefits *begin.* Unfortunately, benefits usually are not adjusted after payments begin, even though they may be payable over a period of many years. Changes increasing statutory benefits automatically increase benefits for *future* claimants—there is no need for a policy change because the policy provides benefits prescribed in the statute. However, increases in statutory benefits seldom are applied retroactively to persons already disabled.

The lack of variable policy limits is essentially moot when it comes to limits of insurance for bodily injury and property damage. The crucial question is, *"What limit will be large enough to cover damages that could arise out of a claim under the current policy?"* Unfortunately, asking that question is ultimately like asking, "How high is up?" If an insured had liability insurance limits of $100,000 ten years ago and carries limits of $200,000 today, the insured has a higher dollar limit of coverage. But is the insured better covered for tomorrow's loss? Is the insured adequately covered?

LOSS VALUATION PROVISIONS

A property insurance policy provides coverage only to the extent of an insured party's insurable interest. Recovery under both property and liability insurance policies is also restricted by policy limits—when an insured event occurs, an insurer will not pay more than the applicable limit of insurance. However, insurable interests and policy limits are not the only factors that determine the amount payable under an insurance policy. Also relevant is the method that will be used to place a value on the covered loss.

In property insurance, loss valuation depends heavily on the loss valuation provisions in the policy—and, in turn, the ways in which they are interpreted by courts and measured by external factors. Liability insurance loss valuation depends primarily on factors external to the policy that determine the amount of those damages which the insurer ultimately will pay on the insured's behalf.

Property Insurance

Lost or damaged property usually is not repaired or replaced directly by the insurance company. The insurer usually fulfills its obligations by paying money. The insurance policy states, in a very general manner, the approach both parties will use to determine how much the covered property is "worth" for loss settlement purposes.

Although "actual cash value" is still the fundamental measure of property values for this purpose, "replacement cost" valuation is becoming increasingly common. Replacement cost is discussed first, because it forms the most logical basis for comparison with other valuation methods.

Replacement Cost. Under property insurance coverages written on a replacement cost basis, there is no deduction for depreciation used in loss valuation. The insurer's payment is based on the current cost, at the time of loss, of repairing or replacing the damaged or stolen property with *new* property of like kind and quality.

The following excerpt from the AAIS general conditions part (property coverage) contains the information typically found in a replacement cost valuation provision.

> **Replacement Cost** When replacement cost coverage is indicated in the declarations for property coverage, the valuation shall be the replacement cost without any deduction for depreciation.
>
> This replacement cost provision does not apply to: objects of art, rarity or antiquity, or property of others.
>
> The replacement cost is limited to the cost of repair or replacement with similar materials on the same site and used for the same purpose. The payment shall not exceed the amount you spend to repair or replace the damaged or destroyed property.
>
> Replacement cost valuation does not apply until the damaged or destroyed property is repaired or replaced. You may make a claim for actual cash value and later for the replacement cost if you notify us of your intent within 180 days after the loss.

The key to this valuation provision appears in the first sentence, "without any deduction for depreciation." Other provisions merely clarify the nature of replacement cost—"replacement with what, where, and when?"—and exclude objects, such as antiques, for which replacement cost valuation is not suitable. The types of property excluded from replacement cost valuation vary among policies, depending on the nature of the insured property.

The insurer's payment is subject to the applicable policy limits, of course, as well as to other policy provisions (such as a deductible) that may affect the amount of recovery.

Replacement cost is the cost of replacing lost or damaged property with new property of like kind and quality, *at current prices.* When covered property is valued on a replacement cost basis, even if property is several years old or its replacement cost now exceeds the amount for which it was originally purchased, the insured is entitled to receive the current cost to buy the property new. Likewise, if the cost new has decreased, as has often been the case with items such as electronic equipment, replacement cost coverage will indemnify the insured by paying the current new cost even if it is less than the original purchase price.

Limitations on Replacement Cost Recovery. It sometimes is suggested that replacement cost provisions violate the principle of indemnity ("the insured should not profit from the loss") because they provide betterment by paying for replacing old property with new. On the other hand, it also is sometimes said that a property owner receives no direct financial benefit from replacement cost insurance, even when it applies to property subject to wear and tear. Suppose a homeowner's replacement cost insurance pays the full cost of replacing a ten-year-old roof damaged in a windstorm. Since residential roofs generally last fifteen to twenty years, the homeowner has perhaps received some betterment—the old roof was due for replacement in another five or ten years, while the new roof will not need to be replaced for another fifteen to twenty years. But looking at it another way, before the windstorm the homeowner had a house with a sound roof; after the repairs were completed, the homeowner once again had a house with a sound roof. Is that "profiting" from the loss? Another way of looking at it is that the insured without replacement cost coverage would have to come up with cash to cover a part of the roof replacement five or ten years earlier than was expected; replacement cost insurance eliminates this unexpected call for immediate cash. When the situation is considered from these perspectives, there seems to be little if any real profit for the insured.

The question of whether or not new-for-old property replacement violates the principle of indemnity is largely academic. However, the principle would be violated if an insured were able, in effect, to "sell" old property to the insurance company for the cost of new property. To avoid obvious moral hazards, most policies, like the one quoted earlier, provide replacement cost coverage only when the insured has actually replaced the damaged or destroyed property. Unless or until the property actually is replaced, the insured is entitled only to "actual cash value" settlement on a depreciated basis. What if the insured chooses not to repair or replace the property? Another paragraph of this replacement cost provision describes the alternative.

Variations exist among policies on some of the fine points relating to these provisions such as, for example, whether the insured must rebuild a building with one of identical construction, in the same location, or for the same purpose, to qualify for payment on a replacement cost basis.

Comparable Material and Quality. Often a particular model or style of an item is no longer made. In a strict sense, the item has become "irreplaceable." However, the replacement cost for property "of comparable material and quality" still can be determined. For example, if a particular style of an armchair or an appliance with certain features is discontinued, something comparable will exist, often from the same manufacturer. The replacement cost for the original armchair can be based on the cost of the existing model. Settlement on this basis generally causes no problem with the insured, so long as the replacement item is not inferior in any way.

Actual Cash Value. The phrase "actual cash value" (ACV) has appeared in U.S. property insurance policies for at least 150 years. Actual cash value remains the valuation approach in a majority of standard policies providing property insurance. The following policy provisions are typical of those specifying that property is valued on an actual cash value basis.

Personal Auto Policy Provision:

LIMIT OF LIABILITY

A. Our limit of liability for loss will be the lesser of the
  1. Actual cash value of the stolen or damaged property; or
  2. Amount necessary to repair or replace the property. . . .
B. An adjustment for depreciation and physical condition will be made in determining actual cash value at the time of loss.

Homeowners policy provision:

Loss Settlement. Covered property losses are settled as follows:
a. Property of the following types:
  (1) Personal property;
  (2) Awnings, carpeting, household appliances, outdoor antennas and outdoor equipment, whether or not attached to buildings; and
  (3) Structures that are not buildings;
  at actual cash value at the time of loss but not more than the amount required to repair or replace.

Although the term "actual cash value" is not defined in most policies, it is one of the most important terms in property insurance. The courts have had a major role in providing definitions that generally take one of the following approaches:

● Replacement cost minus depreciation
● Market value
● Broad evidence rule

Replacement Cost Minus Depreciation. Most property has its highest value when new. New property has not aged or deteriorated through use. With the passage of time, most property loses value—that is, it "depreciates"—in a fairly steady and predictable manner, largely because of age and use.

A common euphemism for depreciation is "betterment." The amount by which an aging object has depreciated equals the amount by which a brand new object of that kind is "better." When property is insured for its actual cash value, the amount of loss settlement is reduced by the "betterment" that would exist were replacement cost values used. Another way of looking at depreciation is that it is a deduction to reflect the value of the use the insured has already gotten from the property.

Even though the *concept* of depreciation is fairly simple, disagreements regularly arise after a loss regarding the *amount* of depreciation to be applied to a property item. Generally speaking, the insured has an interest in minimizing the amount of depreciation, thus maximizing the actual cash value of damaged or destroyed property. On the other hand, the insurer obviously has a financial incentive to maximize the amount of depreciation.

Because it has not depreciated, the actual cash value of brand new property usually is the same as its replacement cost. Depreciation represents any loss of value, which can result from physical wear and tear, age, obsolescence, and numerous other factors.

- *Physical wear and tear.* Physical wear and tear is the most obvious cause of loss of value. The useful life of many items is determined solely by the time it takes the object to become too worn to serve its purpose. Physical wear and tear often occurs at a steady rate throughout the life of an item, and it can be calculated as a fixed amount, or percentage, per year. For example, if a carpet is expected to last eight years, it would lose 1/8 (that is, 12.5 percent) of its value every year. At five years of age it will have lost 5/8 (that is, 12.5 percent × 5 = 62.5 percent) of its value. The amount of depreciation would be subtracted from the *current* replacement cost to determine actual cash value. If the current replacement cost of the five-year-old carpet is $1,000, then its actual cash value would be $375 (because $1,000 minus [62.5% × 1,000, or $625] = $375). The rate at which a particular item wears out or otherwise depreciates depends on the nature of the item and the circumstances of its use. Eight years may be an average life expectancy for a carpet. Other items depreciate faster or more slowly, on average. Clothing, for example, will depreciate faster and cannot usually be expected to last eight years. Furniture, on the other hand, will last more than eight years in normal use. Components of a building exhibit widely differing life expectancies. A roof might predictably wear out within twenty years, whereas an element of the frame carpentry might last indefinitely, remaining as good as the day it was installed.

Many insurance companies publish guides for use by their adjusters, setting forth the average expected life of various items. These are guidelines only. They represent an *average* life for the various items, and there can be considerable variation around the typical averages. One must take into account the circumstances under which the particular property has been used. These circumstances may indicate a much longer or shorter expected life than the average. Carpeting might last only a few years under heavy use or abuse, or it might last indefinitely if it is a treasured Oriental subject to little wear and excellent care.

The simple approach of depreciating by fixed percentage each year is called *straight line depreciation*. Although it usually is sound, straight line depreciation does not automatically fit every case. Some items do not depreciate in value at all, or they are so new at the time of loss that it would be unrealistic to deduct depreciation. Other items depreciate at a more rapid rate than is indicated by straight line depreciation.

- *Age.* The age of an object usually corresponds closely to the extent of physical wear and tear, but it may be considered a separate factor. All else being equal, a newer object usually is worth more than an older one. Exceptions obviously exist, as with a fine red wine that gains in value as it ages.

   Age alone should not cause an object to lose much of its value, so long as the object is functionally sound. However, older objects may lose value as the result of obsolescence.
- *Obsolescence.* Obsolescence is the loss of value because of changes in technology, shifts in fashion, or other external factors. An object may lose value through obsolescence even though it has incurred no wear and tear. In addition, obsolescence can occur suddenly, regardless of an object's age. Fashions change overnight. Advances in technology and reductions in the real costs of manufacturing have quickly rendered obsolete items only a year or two old.

   A classic case illustrating "other external factors" involved the value of a fairly new brewery building, built before Prohibition and destroyed by fire shortly after the passage of the Prohibition Act. This building was designed to be a brewery, and it was of limited value for any other purpose. The building had depreciated more because of its obsolescence than because of its age.

Market Value. Many courts have ruled that actual cash value means fair market value. The market value of an item is the amount at which a knowledgeable buyer, under no unusual pressure, would be willing to buy and at which a knowledgeable seller, under no unusual pressure, would be willing to sell. The ability to establish market value of an object depends on the existence of a sufficient number of buyers and sellers and a complete flow of information regarding products, prices, and buyers and sellers. Such a market exists for private passenger autos, which are regularly bought and sold on an open market; prices are compiled, recorded, and regularly available in various auto industry publications, which are used as a basis for adjusting total losses to insured autos. For many items, however, the market is very irregular or imperfect, or there is no market at all. These conditions occur when there are not enough potential buyers or sellers, or when the transaction information is too difficult to obtain. The courts that have criticized the market value approach have invariably done so in circumstances under which there was no properly functioning market. Under such circumstances, the market approach may be inappropriate.

Market valuation is particularly useful when there are no objects of like kind and quality for sale, as is the case with antiques, works of art, and other collectibles. In addition, market valuation can be the most accurate measure of the "worth" of some older buildings built with obsolete construction methods or using materials no longer available. In these cases a true replacement cost does not exist.

The market value of real property reflects the value of the land, as well as the value of any structures affixed to the land. Most property insurance policies cover only buildings and other structures; for insurance purposes, the value of the land is irrelevant. Generally, the value of the land is unaffected by damage or destruction of a building, and any change in the value of property following a loss must be due entirely to changes in the value of the building. However, this is not always the case. Sometimes the value of land increases following a loss to a building that, for example, failed to make the best use of the location. Conversely, land may lose value following a building loss if zoning codes require that a different type of building must now be constructed.

Broad Evidence Rule. Many states have adopted the broad evidence rule, which explicitly requires that *all* relevant factors must be considered in determining actual cash value. The factors typically applied vary somewhat between buildings and personal property.

The following elements have repeatedly appeared in the decisions of courts applying the broad evidence rule in determining the actual cash value of a building.

1. Reproduction cost less depreciation
2. Market value opinion based on (1) above and (3) and (4) below
3. Capitalization of income

4. Comparison sales of similar property
5. Opinion of qualified appraiser, where the opinion is based on factors other than (1), (3), and (4) above
6. Prior sales of the subject property, if a bona fide, arms-length bargain
7. Pre-loss contract to sell the subject property
8. Attempts to sell the subject property, including "listed" price with brokers, and bona fide offers received by the insured
9. Insured's purchase price plus cost of capital improvements
10. Assessed values for real estate tax purposes
11. Insured's statements as to value whether in official proceedings for tax relief, or in income tax returns, or in the assured's own books of account
12. Age and construction of building; prior unrepaired damages; depreciation
13. Obsolescence
14. Present use of building and its profitability
15. Alternate building uses
16. Present neighborhood characteristics; long-range community plans for the area where building is located; urban renewal prospects; new roadway plans
17. Insured's intention to abolish building
18. Vacancy, abandonment
19. Excessive tax arrears
20. Original cost of construction
21. Inflationary or deflationary trends[5]

Court decisions involving personal property vary, but they can generally be summarized as follows:

- *Residential personal property* is valued at its replacement cost new at the time of loss, less depreciation. Its value in the second-hand market (used furniture and clothing stores) is not the test of its value.
- *Personal property in use* (furniture, fixtures, and machinery) generally is to be valued at its replacement cost new at the time of loss, less depreciation. Unlike household personal property, this class of property has a *used market*. Where an owner has purchased such property second hand, the market value of similar property in the same condition has been held to be its actual cash value.
- *Personal property in the hands of merchants* (stocks of merchandise) is to be valued at replacement cost rather than the dealer's selling price. Freight and other transportation charges are to be added. However, active merchandise that cannot be

replaced within a reasonable time is worth, to the owner, what it would have been sold for. Depreciation in its broadest sense is generally recognized by the courts and must be deducted.

- *Personal property in the hands of a manufacturer* is held by the majority of courts to be valued at the manufacturer's selling price, provided this valuation standard is not inconsistent with policy provisions. Any unincurred charges—transportation expenses, for example—may be taken into consideration.[6]

Actual Loss Sustained. Business income coverage is provided on an "actual loss sustained" basis. Earlier business interruption insurance forms emphasized—and even capitalized—this phrase:

> . . . this Company shall be liable for the ACTUAL LOSS SUSTAINED by the Insured resulting directly from . . . interruption of business. . . .

The current business income coverage forms continue to use the words, but in a much less emphatic way. We have added the italics in the following policy excerpt to highlight the key words:

> We will pay for the *actual loss* of Business Income you *sustain* due to the necessary suspension of your "operations" during the "period of restoration."

However expressed, the effect is comparable to that of "actual cash value" coverage on direct property losses. As further expressed in much more detail in other policy provisions, the intent is to support the principle of indemnity by making the insured whole but not creating an opportunity for profit.

Other Loss Settlement Approaches. Settlement at replacement cost or actual cash value, with payment in cash, is the standard loss settlement practice. Other settlement provisions are used in special cases.

Repair or Replace Option. Most claims are settled for cash. However, most property insurance policies give the insurer the right to have repairs performed or to replace lost or destroyed property. The insured cannot insist that the insurer repair or replace the property, but the insurer, itself, can elect to do so.

Normally, insurers do not choose to invoke this option. Doing so opens the door for disagreement with the insured regarding the quality of the repairs or the adequacy of the replacement, and it puts an extra burden on the insurer to oversee the organization providing the repair or replacement service. Insurers sometimes exercise the repair or replace option when it provides a less expensive way to settle the claim or when the insured is suspected of trying to profit from the claim. Sometimes it is exercised because the insurer's buying power enables it to purchase products or services, such as replacement of broken glass, at a lower price than could be negotiated by the individual consumer.

Valued Coverage. Valued coverage may be provided by the terms of the policy or, in some cases, by a valued policy statute.

A number of states have so-called *valued policy statutes* that require a property insurer to pay the full face amount of the policy if insured property is totally destroyed by a peril specified in the statute and covered by the policy. Many valued policy statutes apply only to dwellings and other buildings and then only to the perils of fire and lightning. The purpose of valued policy statutes, most of which have been in existence for a long time, is to eliminate abuses and disputes in cases in which an insurer might otherwise collect a premium for a large limit of insurance but pay a claim for a much smaller amount after deducting depreciation. In theory at least, the insurer has the opportunity before issuing a policy to inspect every covered location and determine whether it is overinsured. In practice, valued policy laws have probably had little effect on the frequency of inspections or amounts of insurance sold.

When a valued policy law applies and a building is *totally* destroyed by fire, the insurer usually must pay the policy limit. The actual cash value, or replacement cost, matters not, and the insurer seldom has the option of rebuilding the destroyed property. Most valued policy laws, however, permit the insurer to settle *partial* losses on the basis of their actual cash value at the time of the loss or, if smaller, the costs of repairing or replacing the damaged property with like kind and quality. Some laws stipulate that payments for partial losses are to be a percentage of the amount of insurance, with the percentage corresponding to the degree of damage to the property.

Functional Valuation. In some cases it is not practical to replace either buildings or personal property with property of like kind and quality, and the actual cash value approach to valuation also does not match insurance needs. The functional valuation approach is available to restore the building so that it can be used, taking into account both total and partial losses.

"Functional valuation" of either buildings or personal property is available by endorsement to some ISO commercial policies. The property subject to that approach is scheduled in the endorsement along with a limit of insurance for each item or type of described property.

The *functional building valuation endorsement* provides that the insurer will pay the least of the following amounts if repair or replacement is contracted for within 180 days of the loss:

- If the building is a total loss, the cost of a new, less costly but functionally equivalent building

- If a building is a partial loss, the cost of restoring the building in the same architectural style, using less costly material if available
- The amount actually and necessarily spent on repair or replacement with less costly material if available
- The limit of insurance applicable to the damaged building

If the claim is not made on a repair/replacement basis, loss settlement will be based either on functional replacement cost minus depreciation or on market value exclusive of land value. *Market value* is defined in the endorsement as the price the property might be expected to realize if offered for sale in a fair market.

The owners of a stately older building currently used as an office but originally constructed as a residence have exposures that might, under some circumstances, be met by a functional or market value approach to valuation. This coverage would restore the stately appearance, as well as the function of the building, following a partial loss; provide a functionally equivalent but different-looking building in the event of a total loss; or provide the funds with which the insured might be able to purchase an equivalent building on the open market.

The *functional personal property valuation (other than stock) endorsement* provides that the insurer will pay the least of the following amounts if repair or replacement is contracted for within 180 days of the loss:

- The cost of replacement with the most closely equivalent property available
- The amount actually and necessarily spent on repair or replacement
- The limit of insurance applicable to the damaged items

If a claim is not made on a repair/replacement basis, loss settlement will be the least of market value, replacement cost less depreciation (in effect, actual cash value), or the limit of insurance.

A similar approach is provided for residential buildings by the homeowners modified coverage form, sometimes called Form HO-8. Most homeowners policies value the dwelling building on a replacement cost basis. However, replacement cost coverage is not a good match for older homes that once were luxurious but now have obsolete styling and materials and are located in economically depressed areas. It might cost $300,000 to replace, with materials of like kind and quality, a home with a market value of $75,000. Insureds are reluctant to purchase $300,000 of insurance under such circumstances, and insurers are reluctant to sell it because of the obvious moral hazard.

The modified homeowners policy form addresses this problem by providing coverage for the functional replacement cost of the damaged dwelling. The insurer will pay no more than the amount required to repair or replace the property using common construction materials and methods. An old home with obsolete or custom construction would be functionally restored, but the insurer would not pay the added cost of restoring it to its pre-loss condition. Wallboard, for example, might be used to replace a plaster wall. If the home is not repaired or restored at the same site, the insurer will pay the least of the following:

- The limit of liability (that is, the policy limit)
- The amount covered repairs would have cost if made
- The market value of the building, excluding land (in some states actual cash value is used instead)

Selling Price Clauses. As explained earlier, personal property usually is valued at its actual cash value, and the actual cash value of a merchant's stock is generally the same as its replacement cost.

A so-called *selling price clause* is automatically included in some forms covering business personal property. This clause provides that stock that has been sold, but has not yet been delivered, is valued at its selling price, less discounts and expenses. In short, this sometimes is referred to as "sold but not delivered."

The actual cash value of manufacturers' stock often is held to be the same as its selling price. An optional *manufacturer's selling price endorsement* makes it explicit that finished goods manufactured by the insured will indeed be valued at their selling price, even if not yet sold. In short, this sometimes is referred to as "manufactured but not sold." (Once the stock is sold, the "sold but not delivered" coverage of the selling price clause applies.)

Cost of Reproduction. The cost of researching, reproducing, or transcribing is a commonly used basis for insuring valuable papers and records. The value of these items lies not in the value of the paper and ink, but in the value of the information recorded on the paper with the ink. The cost of reproduction is, basically, the cost of restoring the information.

Papers and records that cannot be restored—such as the original artwork of a greeting card manufacturer—are sometimes insured on a valued basis. For papers and records that can be restored, the amount of recovery is limited to research and other expenses necessarily incurred to reproduce the valuable papers and records.

Pair or Set Clauses. In many policies covering personal property, pair or set clauses clarify the insurer's obligation in situations involving the loss of a part of a matched pair or set. Examples include a pair of earrings, a pair of candle holders, a set of fireplace tools, or a set of silverware. Suppose a single earring is lost or stolen. Ignoring the single-earring fad that may make the second item in the pair worthless for some wearers, the value of a single earring surely is less than one-half the value of the original pair. If the insurance policy did not address this issue, an insured might appropriately argue that the remaining earring-without-a-partner no longer has any value, as it cannot be worn.

Many policies do address this issue. The homeowners policy, for example, contains the following pair or set clause.

> **Loss to a Pair or Set.** In case of loss to a pair or set we may elect to:
> **a.** Repair or replace any part to restore the pair or set to its value before the loss; or
> **b.** Pay the difference between actual cash value of the property before and after the loss.

This language specifies the differential actual cash value *of the entire pair or set* as the basis for valuation, and it explicitly acknowledges the insurer's right to repair or replace any part of a pair or set to restore its pre-loss value. Indirectly, it also tells the insured that loss of half the pair does not constitute a total loss.

Use Value of Improvements and Betterments. Often, a tenant makes improvements to a landlord's building that become a permanent part of the building and will remain with the building when the tenant moves out. Since property that is part of the building belongs to the landlord, a tenant's insurable interest in this property is based not on ownership but on a "use interest"—the tenant has an enforceable legal right to use the property until the lease expires.

The building and personal property coverage form specifies three different approaches that may be used in determining the tenant's recovery when the tenant's improvements and betterments are damaged or destroyed by a covered cause of loss:

1. When the owner replaces the improvements without charge to the tenant, the tenant's insurance pays nothing.
2. When the tenant makes prompt repairs, the improvements and betterments coverage pays based on the actual cash value of the improvements just as though the tenant owned them.
3. When the improvements are not replaced, payment is based on unamortized original cost. For example, if the improvements were installed exactly nine years before the loss and exactly one year remains on the lease after the loss, the insured would recover one-tenth of the original cost of the improvements. The remaining nine-tenths would be amortized because the insured has gotten nine out of the expected ten years of use from the original investment.

Money and Securities. Some crime insurance policies provide coverage for money and securities, types of property that are excluded by most other property insurance policies. These crime policies include provisions stating how money and securities will be valued. The question is not so simple as it sounds, since securities values are subject to minute-by-minute change, and money values, in some currencies, fluctuate with the international market. The following provisions apply:

- When a loss involves money, as defined, the insurer will pay no more than its face value. As to foreign money, at the *insurer's* option, loss of money issued by any country other than the United States of America will be paid (a) at face value in the money issued by the country in question or (b) the USA dollar equivalent *determined by the rate of exchange on the day the loss was discovered.*
- When a loss involves securities, the insurer will pay no more than the value of such securities at the close of business on the day the loss was discovered. At the *insurer's* option, loss may be settled by paying the value of such securities or replacing them in kind.

Liability Insurance

In addition to defense costs, the maximum amount an insurer will pay, under most circumstances, under a typical liability insurance policy is *the lesser of* (1) the applicable policy limit or (2) the compensable amount of the loss.[7]

As noted in Chapter 4, the *insured* has an unlimited insurable interest in potential legal liability. The maximum amount a third-party claimant may recover in liability damages is not limited by any requirement that the *claimant* must have an insurable interest—the claimant is not a party to the insurance contract. Rather, the insurer is obligated, subject to the terms of the policy, to pay the claimant's damages on behalf of the insured, and the extent of the insured's liability to the claimant is founded on tort or contract law principles.

When a jury trial is involved, the compensable amount of the loss is *whatever amount the jurors decide to award to the plaintiff as damages.* Subject to policy limits, that is the amount the insurer will pay on behalf of the insured. Though the judge has the power to reduce, or to set aside, the award if it "shocks the conscience of the court," this is not done very often. Moreover, neither the judge nor the jury is bound by the applicable policy limit. If the jury awards a judgment in excess of the policy limit, the liability insurer is not obligated to pay the excess— it falls on the shoulders of the insured/defendant.

Most cases do not go to a formal trial, and the compensable amount of the loss is determined by informal negotiations between the liability insurer (or the insurer's attorney) and the claimant (or the claimant's attorney). Generally, both parties are guided by trying to anticipate what a court of law would do if presented with the same facts. The insurer naturally wishes to minimize the amount of the settlement, while the plaintiff wants to maximize it. Negotiation is encouraged because both parties are aware of the time and expense of a formal trial. In most types of liability insurance, the insured/defendant has no right to prohibit a settlement or to influence its amount when the settlement is within policy limits. For amounts beyond policy limits, the insured has a right to his or her own legal counsel to protect the insured's financial interests, usually at the insured's own expense.

The liability insurer usually has control over the defense costs and the amount it wishes to offer as a settlement. It may not have any appreciable "control" over the plaintiff, the plaintiff's attorney, or the court.

For the most part, the loss valuation methods in liability insurance are not governed by policy provisions. The policy limit normally serves as a lid on the maximum amount an insurer will or must pay for damages, of course. Otherwise, the liability insurer has much less to say about the maximum amount of recovery than the property insurer does for its insureds.

SUMMARY

Policy limits and loss valuation provisions are two important elements that lead to determination of the amount payable by an insurer for a covered loss.

Policy limits (limits of liability, limits of insurance) exist for three reasons—to cap the insurer's obligations, to accommodate consumer preferences, and to reflect the insurer's capacity. Although terminology is not used consistently among insurance policies, various characteristics of property and liability insurance policy limits can be identified. A given property insurance limit may possess more than one of the characteristics described in the chapter.

Some property limits apply a maximum amount of recovery for each item damaged or destroyed, while others apply a maximum for a single occurrence. Specific limits, applicable to only one item, type, or location, can be contrasted with blanket limits that apply a maximum amount of coverage to several items, types of property, or locations. Separate limits apply only to a specific item or group of items. When property items are individually listed or scheduled, a limit of insurance applies to each scheduled item. In contrast, unscheduled property items are covered as a group. Sublimits impose smaller limits on narrower categories of property that otherwise would be covered for a greater amount as part of a broader group of property. Some sublimits apply only to loss by certain perils, such as theft, while others apply to loss by any peril.

Further complicating the matter—depending on the specific policy language used, additions or extensions of coverage in property insurance policies may or may not add additional dollar amounts of coverage over and above otherwise applicable limits of insurance. Some property policies or coverages contain no explicit dollar limits but rely on external constraints to cap the insurer's obligation. Others provide variable limits of coverage in the amount of annual increases, inflation guards, or indexed limits. Periodic policy revisions provide an opportunity for insurers to upgrade preprinted sublimits to reflect changing exposures or inflation.

Liability limits of insurance may prescribe the insurer's maximum obligation per event or, in the aggregate, within a given policy year. Defense costs and supplementary payments usually, but not always, are available in addition to the stated dollar policy limits. While no maximum dollar amount may apply to these costs, they are constrained, to some extent, by external factors.

Liability insurance policies may contain some coverages that apply regardless of fault. In most cases, a nominal dollar limit of coverage is provided to help preserve the insured's good will toward injured parties and, not incidentally, to enable the insurer to pay minor claims without admitting any liability on the part of the insured. These coverages include damage to the property of others in homeowners policies; medical payments in homeowners, general liability, and auto policies; and auto no-fault coverages. The current commercial general liability policy includes a hierarchy of limits that has the general appearance of a chart showing the reporting relationships within the management structure of an organization.

Workers compensation limits are prescribed by each state's workers compensation statute rather than by amounts stated in the policy. Employers liability coverage, generally provided within the same policy, is subject to explicit limits.

Aggregate limits are designed to be eaten away through the payment of losses. Per person and per event limits, on the other hand, are not reduced for future losses when a loss is paid.

Because of the many external factors affecting liability losses and judgments, it is very difficult, if not impossible, to determine what amount of liability insurance is adequate. Likewise, there is no ready method for determining whether existing limits of insurance are adequate in coping with inflationary changes. Likewise, the value of a liability loss depends primarily on court awards and similar external factors rather than on explicit valuation provisions of the types found in property insurance policies.

Property is commonly valued, for insurance purposes, on the basis of its replacement cost or its actual cash value. The difference between the two is depreciation which, in turn, is a function of physical wear and tear, age, and obsolescence. Other factors affecting property valuation are market value and the broad evidence rule. Business income policies use the phrase "actual loss sustained," or its equivalent, to prescribe a valuation approach that roughly resembles actual cash value.

Other loss valuation options appearing in some property insurance policies include the repair or replacement option (giving the insurer the right to physically restore the property rather than paying dollars to the property owner), valuation on the basis of functional value, valuation based on selling price, pair or set clauses, and special valuation provisions applicable to money and securities.

Chapter Notes

1. Aggregate limits, described later, are common in liability insurance but rare with property insurance.
2. A minor exception to this statement involves some personal property items pertaining to the maintenance of the building, such as fire extinguishers, that could arguably be classified as either "building" or "personal property." Since these items are covered one place or the other, the distinction is moot unless the limits under "building" or "personal property" coverage are inadequate.
3. The policies of some insurers have permitted the "other structures" limit to be applied to the dwelling building in cases where no "other structure" is present. An example would be a home with an attached garage and no detached garage or outbuilding.
4. In practice, one would probably purchase a lower limit of coverage, say $360,000 of coverage subject to a 90 percent coinsurance clause. Coinsurance is discussed in Chapter 7.
5. National Committee on Property Insurance, *ACV Guidelines*, 1982, pp. 12–13.
6. *ACV Guidelines*, pp. 24–25.
7. Occasionally an insurer is held to payments in excess of the policy limit when the insurer is found guilty of bad faith or negligence in failing to settle the claim for less than the policy limit.

CHAPTER 7

Loss Sharing Provisions

Loss sharing provisions in property and liability insurance policies may require the insured to bear part of the dollar amount of covered losses. As suggested in the previous chapter, the insured may share in a loss because the applicable limit of insurance is inadequate to cover the loss in full. In that sense, inadequate policy limits may result in loss sharing. However, the focus of this chapter is not on limits that cap the insurer's obligation but on other provisions that tend to involve the insured, along with the insurer, in paying for losses that are within policy limits. Among such provisions are (1) deductibles (including self-insured retentions), and (2) coinsurance clauses and other policy provisions designed to encourage insurance to value.

DEDUCTIBLES

A *deductible* is a portion of a covered loss that is not paid by insurance. Deductible clauses or deductible provisions, referred to simply as "deductibles," are found in most property insurance policies. With liability insurance they are still the exception, rather than the rule, but their use is increasing.

Reasons for Deductibles

Deductibles serve several purposes:

1. They reduce morale hazards and encourage loss control.
2. They reduce insurers' loss costs and loss adjustment expenses by reducing the number of *insured* losses.
3. They reduce the premium cost to the insured.

Reduce Morale Hazards and Encourage Loss Control. *Morale hazard* is a condition that exists when a person is less careful than he or she otherwise would be, knowing that insurance will cover a loss. Some insureds are not inclined to expend *their* time, effort, and money to prevent losses that, if they occur, will be paid by *the insurance company*. Why install an expensive burglar alarm if burglary losses will be covered by crime insurance?

In reality, the situation is not quite so simple. An insured that fails to exercise proper loss control measures may find it difficult to obtain insurance or may pay a higher premium for the insurance. And it may be difficult or costly to continue insurance coverage after a preventable loss occurs. Still, the presence of insurance to pay for losses can reduce the incentives for loss control measures that might prevent those losses or reduce their severity.

Because deductibles may require the insured to participate financially in every loss, deductibles are said to reduce morale hazards and encourage loss control. The insured with some of its own funds at stake is likely to help prevent losses.

Reduced Losses and Loss Adjustment Expenses. When a covered property insurance loss occurs, the insurer must pay any amounts necessary under the contract to indemnify the insured. In addition to these direct loss costs, the insurer must expend time, effort, and money in investigating and settling the claim. Substantial administrative expenses are involved in recording and processing each reported claim and in accounting for all related expenses and loss reserves.

Often—especially with small claims—the insurer's administrative expenses in handling the claim can approach or exceed the amount payable to the insured as indemnity. Since loss adjustment expenses must be reflected in insurance premium rates, the cost of adjusting many small losses can have a substantial impact on the level of the insurance premium that must be paid by insureds as a group. This expensive process of passing money back and forth sometimes is referred to as "dollar trading" and generally is regarded as an inefficient use of resources. Property insurance deductibles help to eliminate "dollar trading" and permit the insured to handle small, often foreseeable, losses efficiently as normal out-of-pocket expenses, while preserving the role of insurance in protecting against major unpredictable losses.

When a covered liability claim is made, the insurer must, if necessary, provide a defense and pay any damages ultimately due the claimant. Most liability claims are not small, and it is important for insurers to be involved from the outset in the defense of liability claims. For these and other reasons mentioned later, deductibles often are not suitable for liability insurance.

Reduced Premium Cost. Because deductibles reduce insurers' overall loss costs and loss adjustment expenses, they also reduce the amount of premium that must be charged by insurers. The amount by which the premium is reduced is not directly proportional to the size of the deductible but is on a sliding scale that reflects the decreasing probability of larger losses. Exhibit 7-1 illustrates this principle by showing the deductible credits (premium reduction) typically applicable to a property insurance policy providing $1 million coverage for fire and related perils on a building with a fire insurance rate of $1.00 per hundred.

As the exhibit illustrates, the premium credit is not directly proportional to the size of the deductible but builds much more slowly than the size of the deductible increases. By shifting from a $1,000 deductible to a $2,500 deductible, one could reduce premiums by $300 while increasing retained exposures by $1,500. The premium reduction for shifting from a $50,000 deductible to a $75,000 deductible also is $300, but in this case retained losses are increased by $25,000.

A basic risk management adage states, "Don't risk a lot to save a little." Even though their firm could afford to retain a $75,000 loss, few if any risk managers would consciously choose to retain an extra $25,000 in property losses in order to save $300 in premium. The net effect is that deductible credits tend to encourage the purchase of medium-sized deductibles that eliminate dollar trading for small losses but provide a source of recovery for larger losses. The range in which "medium-sized" falls will vary considerably, depending on the situation.

Impact of Deductibles

Deductibles do not accomplish their three purposes equally well for all lines of insurance.

Encouraging Loss Control. Deductibles can be effective in encouraging loss control in virtually all lines of insurance. But they perform this function most effectively in lines for which losses are likely to be large, provided the deductible also is large enough to have a noticeable financial impact on the insured who suffers a loss that might have been prevented.

Reducing Expenses and Premiums. Deductibles are most effective in reducing expenses and premiums when applied to lines for which small, partial losses are common. Auto collision insurance is an example. Collision insurance is desirable for many auto owners who otherwise could not readily afford to replace their entire car or pay large repair bills. But many collision losses involve only a few hundred dollars. Collision insurance without any deductible clause would be prohibitively

Exhibit 7-1

Premium Credits for Various Deductibles

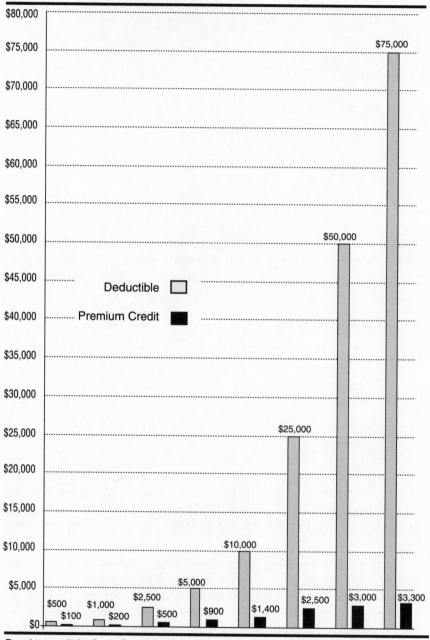

Premium credit for Basic Group I perils on a building with a premium rate of $1.00 per hundred and a limit of insurance of $1,000,000. Based on *Commercial Lines Manual,* copyright ISO Commercial Risk Services, Inc., 1983, 1989, 2nd ed., 10-90, p. CF-95-97.

expensive because of the costs incurred in adjusting and paying many small claims. Collision insurance with a deductible of $500, more or less, provides the necessary coverage; yet it helps control insurance costs by making the insured responsible for paying the entire cost of small losses or a portion of large losses.

A deductible would be far less effective in reducing the cost of other types of insurance. Take satellite launch property insurance, for example. Partial losses to satellites are rare; most losses will be total losses involving millions of dollars. Even a $50,000 deductible would not further encourage loss control, nor would it substantially reduce insurance costs. The expensive all-or-nothing nature of satellite exposures makes this example clear, though somewhat unusual. More common examples might be "all-risks" property insurance coverage on a stained glass window being shipped from the manufacturer to the end user, or similar coverage on an original painting at an exhibition. In addition to other characteristics, the owner generally has a strong emotional aversion to damage to items such as these, apart from any financial consideration.

Impact in Liability Insurance. Because they are much less effective in liability insurance, deductible clauses are far less common in these coverages than in property insurance. One problem with liability deductibles is that insureds may not report seemingly minor incidents until the situation has escalated. This runs counter to the need of the insurer to take control of claims from the outset to prevent or reduce their escalation.

The major reason for this disparity between property and liability insurance is the difference in their respective loss settlement processes. In settling a property insurance claim, the insurer is dealing directly with its own insured and can simply withhold the amount of the deductible when it pays the claim. Liability claim settlements, on the other hand, are negotiated with third-party claimants rather than with the insured. To get the claimant to settle and sign a release, the insurer usually must pay the agreed settlement amount in full, without reduction for any deductible in the policy. The insurer then has a right to recoup the amount of the deductible from the insured. The value of that right depends on the insured's ability and willingness to pay. Consequently, insurers are rather selective in choosing the insureds for whom they will write liability insurance with deductible clauses.

When liability coverage is written with a deductible, the insurer usually provides "first dollar" defense cost coverage just as it does for policies without deductibles. In most cases, the deductible does not apply to defense costs, but only to the amount paid to the claimant in settlement of the claim. However, some policies are written with a deductible applicable to both defense costs and the payment of damages.

Although deductibles are not in common use with most liability lines, they are used rather frequently with some specialty liability lines, such as professional liability and directors and officers liability. For those lines, the deductibles usually are large and are used primarily to encourage loss control. Deductibles also may be used with bailees customers policies, especially for laundries and dry cleaners. Small losses are common under such policies. Small losses can be settled directly by the insured with a minimum of expense, thus eliminating dollar trading, encouraging loss control, and reducing the cost of insurance.

Types of Deductibles

Deductibles can be placed in two broad categories.

- A *per event* deductible applies to each item, each location, each claim, or each occurrence. As explained below, per event deductibles can be variously expressed as dollar amounts, percentages of some value or amount, or time periods.
- An *aggregate* deductible is a dollar deductible applicable to a given time period, typically a one-year policy period. It is possible to combine an aggregate deductible with a per event deductible, in which case the per event deductible is eliminated or reduced for losses occurring after the aggregate deductible has been satisfied.

In any case, the insurer does not indemnify the claimant for *losses* that fall within the deductible, no matter how that deductible is expressed. Under the terms of some liability insurance policies, however, the insurer may pay defense costs, even though it has no ultimate responsibility to pay a third party.

There are many types of deductibles—some common, and others obscure or obsolete. Despite the variety of those discussed here, the list is not exhaustive. Many additional approaches to deductibles can be taken, depending on the nature of the exposure and the insured's willingness to retain losses.

Straight Deductibles. A straight deductible is expressed as a specified dollar amount. For personal lines of insurance, deductibles are likely to be relatively small, usually less than $1,000. Deductibles in commercial insurance policies may be very large, ranging upward to a million dollars or more.

While they may appear similar at a glance, not all $1,000 deductibles are alike. Variations exist in what this dollar amount is subtracted from or the number of times it may be applied.

Amount of Loss Versus Amount Otherwise Payable. Under a straight deductible clause, the insurer deducts a specified dollar amount from either of the following:

● The amount of loss
● The amount otherwise payable (that is, the amount it would otherwise have paid in the absence of the deductible)

In either case, nothing is paid by the insurer if the amount of loss is equal to or less than the deductible amount. (In some liability policies defense costs may be borne by the insurer.)

When the deductible is subtracted from the amount of the loss, the insured may be able to collect the policy limit if the loss is large enough. When subtracted from the amount otherwise payable, the insured can never collect the entire policy limit; the most the insured can collect is the policy limit *less* the amount of the deductible.

To illustrate, assume an insured suffers a $110,000 loss under a policy with a $100,000 limit of insurance and a $5,000 straight deductible.

● If the deductible applies to the *amount of loss*, the insured will be paid the policy limit—$100,000. The $110,000 loss, less the $5,000 deductible, equals $105,000, an amount exceeding the policy limit of $100,000.
● If the deductible applies to the *amount otherwise payable* in the absence of the deductible clause, the most the insured could collect for the loss would be $95,000. The amount the insurer would have paid in the absence of the deductible would be the $100,000 limit of insurance, and subtracting the $5,000 deductible leaves a recovery of $95,000.

The "amount otherwise payable" type of deductible sometimes is referred to as a deductible that "erodes limits" because, as illustrated, the insured can never collect the full limit shown in the policy.

Per Item Versus Per Location Versus Per Occurrence Deductibles. Under a policy providing property insurance coverage, the deductible may be applied separately to each item or location, or the deductible may apply only once for a single occurrence. Accordingly, the same dollar deductible can produce dramatically different results, depending on the circumstances. To illustrate this point with a simple example, assume a commercial bakery owns twenty trucks that are parked on two of its lots, several blocks apart, when a severe hailstorm causes at least $250 in damage to each truck. The trucks have physical damage (property insurance) coverage—including "hail" damage—subject to a $250 deductible.

● If the $250 deductible applies per occurrence, the bakery will retain only $250.

- If the $250 deductible applies per location, the bakery will retain $250 for each of the two locations, for a total of $500.
- If the $250 deductible applies per vehicle, the bakery will retain $250 for each of the twenty vehicles, for a total of $5,000.

A typical deductible provision reads as follows:

DEDUCTIBLE

We will not pay for loss or damage *in any one occurrence* until the amount of loss or damage exceeds the Deductible shown in the Declarations. *We will then pay* the amount of loss or damage in excess of the Deductible, *up to the applicable Limit of Insurance.* [italics added]

The quoted deductible applies on a *per occurrence* basis (not per item, location, or claim—per claim deductibles are discussed below) to the *amount of the loss* (not the amount otherwise payable).[1]

Per Claim Versus Per Occurrence Deductibles. Deductibles under *liability* policies may apply either per claim or per occurrence. The per occurrence deductible is more common. Per claim deductibles sometimes are used in connection with professional liability insurance.

- Under a *per claim* deductible, the deductible amount is applied separately to each claim under the policy, even if all claims arise from the same occurrence. Several persons might make claims, or claims might be made against more than one insured.
- Under a *per occurrence* deductible, the deductible amount is applied only once to all claims arising from a single occurrence, regardless of the actual number of claims involved.

To illustrate the difference, suppose Mr. Druggs, a hospital pharmacist, inadvertently uses a contaminated drug to mix a batch of prescriptions, and as a result ten patients become ill. Each of the ten patients makes a claim against Mr. Druggs, who subsequently is found liable; each of the ten is awarded $100,000 in damages, for a total of $1 million.

- With a $10,000 *per occurrence* deductible, Mr. Druggs would retain $10,000 of the loss resulting from this occurrence.
- With a $10,000 *per claim* deductible, Mr. Druggs would retain $10,000 for each patient's claim, for a total of $100,000.

Split Deductibles. Insurance policies occasionally use a split deductible in which the policy, for example, carries one theft deductible but a lower dollar deductible for other covered causes of loss. A higher deductible on theft gives the insured a greater incentive to guard against theft, spares the insurer the economic burden of investigating small theft claims, and eliminates some dollar trading.

Percentage Deductibles. The straight deductible clauses discussed above have specified the amount to be deducted in dollar amounts,
but deductible amounts sometimes are specified as a percentage of any
one of the following:

- The amount of insurance
- The value of the insured property
- The amount of the loss

Obviously, the dollar amount of a percentage deductible increases as
the amount of insurance, the amount of the loss, or the value of the
insured property increases.

Amount of Insurance Versus Value of Insured Property. Earthquake insurance usually is subject to a deductible stated as a percentage
of either the amount of insurance or the value of the insured property.
The percentage frequently is in the range of 5 percent to 10 percent of
the amount of insurance or the value of the property. Higher and lower
percentages are sometimes offered, depending on the nature of the covered property and perils.

To illustrate these two approaches, assume the Shaker Company
purchases $100,000 of earthquake coverage on a building valued at
$500,000. The earthquake coverage is subject to a 10 percent deductible.

- If the 10 percent deductible applies to the amount of insurance,
  Shaker would retain the first $10,000 of each insured loss.
- If the 10 percent deductible applies to the value of the insured
  property, Shaker would retain the first $50,000 of each insured
  loss.

The most common approach—and seemingly the most logical one—
is to base percentage deductibles on the amount of the insurance. However, when the deductible is based on the amount of insurance, an insured can get a lower dollar deductible by buying less insurance, a
situation that *discourages* the purchase of insurance to value (and that
tends to contradict other policy incentives discussed later in this chapter).
Where this is viewed as a serious problem, insurers sometimes base the
percentage on property values.

Amount of Loss. Deductibles may be stated as a percentage of
the loss. Such deductibles sometimes are used in medical professional
liability insurance for physicians and surgeons. The clause might provide
for a deductible equal to 10 percent of the amount of the claim settlement, possibly with a dollar cap. For example, the deductible might be
10 percent of the claim amount but not more than $25,000.

Because the insured participates in every loss, a percentage deductible sometimes is referred to as a *loss participation clause.*

The percentage of loss approach is quite common in major medical expense health insurance policies, where it usually is referred to as "coinsurance" or percentage participation. This type of "coinsurance," actually a form of deductible, is completely different from insurance-to-value "coinsurance" provisions in property insurance, discussed later in this chapter.

Franchise Deductibles. While deductibles applicable to large losses encourage loss control and reduce morale hazards, the other purposes of deductibles are best served by eliminating the layer of coverage applying to *small* losses. As to large losses it is difficult, for example, to come up with a compelling theoretical reason why an insurer should want to subtract a $250 (or so) homeowners policy deductible before paying a major fire claim for $300,000.

Under a straight deductible clause, the deductible amount applies to all claims, large or small. A franchise deductible eliminates the expense of settling small claims while providing full coverage for large claims. This approach saves the adjustment expenses associated with frequent small claims while providing full coverage for the larger claims.

Under a franchise deductible, the insurer does not pay any of the loss if the total amount of loss is equal to or less than the deductible amount. However, if the loss amount exceeds the deductible amount, the loss is paid in full without any deduction. For example, if the franchise deductible amount is $500 and the loss is $500, the insurer would pay nothing. However, if the loss is $501 or more, the insurer would pay it in full.

Franchise deductibles have been used for many years in ocean marine insurance, the nature of which often involves all-or-nothing losses. Their use in other lines of insurance has been largely unsatisfactory. While a franchise deductible approach is attractive in theory, it is apparent that some insureds might be tempted to exaggerate the amount of small losses in order to obtain reimbursement, especially if the actual loss is near the deductible amount. This temptation to exaggerate the loss is the reason that franchise deductible clauses are seldom used except in ocean marine insurance. Even many ocean marine policies now include straight deductibles instead of franchise deductibles.

Disappearing Deductibles. Disappearing deductibles were an attempt to incorporate the advantages of the franchise deductible while eliminating the disadvantages. In effect, they combined the franchise deductible concept with the percentage-of-loss deductible concept. Disappearing deductibles were used for many years in homeowners policies. True to their name, they have virtually disappeared, having been replaced in recent years with straight deductibles.

Although they are essentially extinct, disappearing deductibles presented an appealing approach to a practical problem. To avoid the temptation to loss exaggeration that arises from franchise deductibles, disappearing deductibles did not drop to zero as soon as the loss amount exceeded the deductible amount. Instead, they gradually diminished as the loss amount increased, reaching zero at some point.

A $50 disappearing deductible clause frequently applied to property losses under early homeowners policies. Under this clause, the insurer did not pay anything for losses of $50 or less. If a loss was greater than $500, it was paid in full up to the policy limits, with no deduction. For losses between $50 and $500, the amount deducted by the insurer gradually decreased from $50 to zero as the amount of the loss increased. At these intermediate levels, the amount paid by the insurer was calculated by the following formula:

$$(\text{Amount of loss} - \$50) \times 1.11 = \text{Amount Payable}$$

The $100 deductible clause included in some early homeowners policies worked exactly the same way except that the multiplier (1.11 in the above formula) was changed to 1.25 and the $50 was replaced by $100. Exhibit 7-2 illustrates the amount recoverable for losses of various sizes under a policy with a $50 disappearing deductible. As indicated, a full $50 deductible applies to losses of $50 or less, while no deductible is subtracted from losses over $500.

Similar disappearing deductibles have been available for auto physical damage at various times. However, they were optional and not widely used.

Disappearing deductibles avoided the weaknesses of both the straight deductible and the franchise deductible. They provided the insurance buyer with a full recovery for larger losses; yet they eliminated the costly coverage for nickel-and-dime losses. However, these advantages—appealing though they are to a student of insurance—were overcome by practical disadvantages. Disappearing deductibles were difficult for consumers to understand or appreciate. All they saw was a complicated formula that appeared to have no useful function other than to reduce the amount the insurer would pay. Straight deductibles may be less compelling in theory, but they are much easier to deal with in practice.

Time Deductibles. It is customary in some lines of insurance to state deductibles, not in dollars, but in terms of time. A time deductible often is referred to as a *waiting period*.[2]

The personal auto policy provides coverage up to a specified dollar amount (currently $15) per day for transportation expenses (such as renting a substitute auto) if the insured vehicle has been stolen. However, the payment does not begin until forty-eight hours after the theft,

Exhibit 7-2
$50 Disappearing Deductible

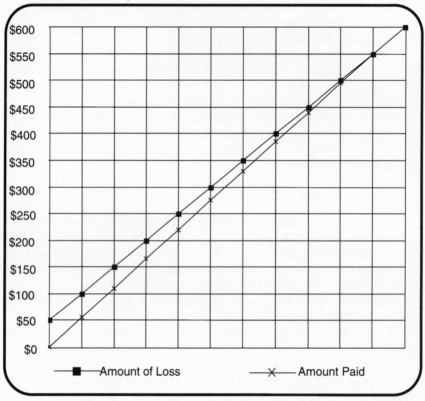

so there is a two-day waiting period deductible. Many stolen cars are recovered within that time period.

The time deductible in the transportation expenses provision of the personal auto policy reads as follows:

> We will pay only expenses incurred during the period:
> 1. Beginning 48 hours after the theft; and
> 2. Ending when "your covered auto" or the "nonowned auto" is returned to use or we pay for its loss.

Income loss coverages under standard boiler and machinery policies may be written with a time deductible, although a dollar deductible may also be used. As with disability insurance, the election of a longer waiting period results in a lower premium. Small claims are eliminated because damage from minor accidents to insured objects often can be repaired within the waiting period.

The deductible provision in a boiler and machinery coverage form reads as follows:

DEDUCTIBLE
1. **Time Deductible**
   If a time deductible is shown in the Business Interruption Schedule, we will not be liable for any loss under this endorsement occurring during that specified time period immediately following the commencement of liability.
2. **Dollar Deductible**
   If a dollar deductible is shown in the Business Interruption Schedule, we will first subtract the deductible amount we would otherwise pay under this endorsement. We will then pay the amount of loss or expense in excess of the deductible, up to the applicable Limit of Loss.

Split deductibles are possible with time deductibles as well as dollar deductibles. In the health insurance area, for example, some disability income policies provide for immediate payment of benefits for disability resulting from accidental injuries but do not pay benefits for disability resulting from sickness until the insured has been disabled for two weeks. Time frames other than "immediate" or "two weeks" are also possible.

Some insurance policies have provided "retroactive coverage" for the waiting period—an approach that resembles franchise dollar deductibles. With retroactive coverage, there is no payment when the duration of the loss is less than the waiting period. However, once the waiting period is satisfied, the loss is paid in full—retroactive to the beginning of the waiting period. For example, a disability policy with a two-week waiting period would pay nothing for a disability lasting less than two weeks. However, if a disability lasts more than two weeks, it is covered in full, including the two-week waiting period. Such provisions have been included in workers compensation coverage in some states, but they were written in the state statutes, not in the policy provisions. Retroactive coverage for a waiting period is not a common practice with other property or liability insurance.

Aggregate Deductibles. The deductibles discussed up to this point apply separately to each insured event, whether an event is characterized as loss to a covered item, loss at a covered location, a single claim, or a single occurrence. Such deductibles may leave the insured exposed to substantial monetary losses if several insured events occur within a short period and the insured must retain the deductible amount each time.

Some insureds seek greater confidence in their maximum retained loss potential by buying policies with aggregate deductibles. Under an aggregate deductible, all losses that occur during a specified period of time, usually a policy year, are accumulated to satisfy the deductible. When the sum of all the losses exceeds the deductible amount, the insurer begins to pay the amount in excess of the deductible.

Aggregate deductibles have been used most often for liability insurance, but commercial property insurance policies sometimes include such deductible clauses. An aggregate deductible sometimes is used along with a straight or percentage per event deductible. One approach has the insured retaining all claims under the per event deductible and the insurer paying the excess; however, once the insured's retained losses because of the per event deductible have reached the aggregate amount, subsequent claims are paid in full with no deductible—or, perhaps with a reduced deductible. (To illustrate the reduced deductible, a policy provision might state that 95 percent of the amount of each covered claim will be paid by the insurer after the aggregate deductible has been satisfied, with the insured retaining 5 percent.)

From a risk manager's perspective, the ideal deductible might be an aggregate deductible applicable to all insurance coverages. The risk manager is more likely to be concerned with the collective impact of deductibles during a fiscal year than with the specific policies in which the deductibles are contained. Broad aggregate deductibles of this nature are uncommon, but they may sometimes be arranged for very large insurance buyers.

Self-Insured Retentions (SIRs). Some liability insurance policies are written subject to a self-insured retention or SIR, which bears a strong resemblance to a large deductible.

Umbrella policies provide excess coverage with no deductible, corridor,[3] or coverage gap for liability claims covered by certain primary ("underlying") liability insurance policies. They also cover some claims not covered by other insurance; in these cases, coverage is subject to an SIR. The insurer is not involved in claims for less than the amount of the SIR, and the insurer is involved only to the extent claims exceed the SIR.

A personal umbrella policy contains the following provisions that apply this concept, which is referred to here as a "retained limit":

Coverage A—Personal Liability
We will pay that portion of the damages for personal injury or property damage a covered person is legally responsible for which exceeds the retained limit.

DEFINITIONS

"Retained limit" means the larger of:
(a) the total of the applicable limit(s) of all required underlying insurance described in Schedule A and any other insurance available to a covered person;
(b) $1,000.

Many personal umbrellas have a self-insured retention as low as $250, rather than the $1,000 retention cited above. Like deductibles, self-insured retentions may apply per claim, per occurrence, or on an aggregate basis.

Some policies with self-insured retention clauses specifically prohibit the insured from purchasing other insurance to cover the retention. Such a provision frequently is found in directors and officers liability policies. This practice is not common in other policies, however.

Policies With No Deductible

Certain types of policies typically are written with no deductible. Generally this is done because a deductible is not in keeping with the general characteristics of that particular line of insurance. As mentioned earlier, this is the case with most liability insurance coverages, although SIRs are common in umbrella liability policies, professional liability policies, and some other specialty coverages dealing with large loss exposures.

Deductibles usually are not found in personal articles floaters— inland marine policies that cover certain of an individual's scheduled personal property items subject to scheduled limits. The insured property (jewelry, for example) often is compact and valuable for its size; therefore, total theft losses, rather than partial damage losses, often are involved. In other cases, the amounts of insurance typically involved are such that a deductible would eliminate all or a substantial portion of the coverage for many items such as musical instruments or cameras.

Plate glass insurance is unusual in that partial losses are almost impossible. They are not quite impossible because repairable damage to a sign painted on the glass would be covered under a plate glass policy. But a pane of glass itself either is broken or it is unbroken. Therefore, a deductible that eliminated coverage for partial losses would have no practical effect other than to reduce the amounts recoverable by the insured.

Policies providing time element coverage may have a time deductible, but often they have no deductible at all. The business income coverage form and the loss of use coverage of the homeowners policy are two examples of common time element coverages with no deductible. There is a sound reason behind this approach, however. In both cases, time element coverage applies only when there has first been direct damage to property—damage that usually is insured under another coverage. So although the insured retains no deductible under the time element coverage, the insured usually does retain another deductible applicable to that event.

INSURANCE TO VALUE

One family of loss-sharing provisions is designed to promote the purchase of insurance to value. The most prominent member of this family is the coinsurance clause. It and other related provisions require those who have not insured to value to participate with the insurer in any loss. Before introducing the members of this family of insurance-to-value provisions, this chapter explores the reasons it is desirable— for both the insurer and the insured—to encourage the purchase of insurance to value. *Insurance to value*, in this context, refers to a limit of insurance that approximates the maximum potential loss. This chapter also examines other means of accomplishing similar objectives.

The Importance of Insurance to Value

The desirability of encouraging insurance to value became apparent early in the history of property insurance. The vast majority of losses in most property insurance lines involve a small portion of the value of the insured property, and total losses are rare. It is estimated that only 2 percent of all property losses are total losses.[4] Unless prohibited by some insurance policy provision or underwriting practice, a person who was willing to retain the very small chance of having a very large loss could buy insurance for a fraction of the value of the insured property and still have complete coverage for *nearly* all losses.

For example, assume that Buildings A and B are identical in construction, protection, occupancy, and exposure and are subject to the same fire insurance rate of $1.00 per $100 of insurance. Each building has an insurable value of $100,000. The owner of Building A buys full insurance to value ($100,000), while the owner of Building B buys only $25,000 of insurance. The insurance premium for Building A is $1,000 per year, while the owner of Building B pays only $250 in premium. If there were no insurance-to-value provision in their policies, both building owners would collect exactly the same amount on any loss up to $25,000, even though the owner of Building A paid four times as much insurance premium. Of course, the owner of Building B would not collect in full for losses over $25,000, but losses exceeding one-fourth of the value of a building are relatively unusual.

If these were the operative practices of two large groups of building owners over several years' time, the building owners following the Building B example would contribute 25 percent as much premium as those whose practice resembled that with Building A, and they would siphon off a disproportionately large share of paid loss dollars. This situation is inherently inequitable—people who took the underinsurance approach to buying insurance would in the aggregate collect a larger part of their premiums in losses, in comparison with those who purchased insurance equal to the full value of their property. Those who purchased insurance approximating the full value of their property would be bearing too large a share of the cost of the insurance mechanism, and those who are underinsured would pay less than their fair share.

All of this assumes all parties would pay the same rate per $100 of insurance. One solution to the inequity is to charge a higher rate to those who underinsure, and another is to limit their recovery at the time of the loss.

It might be appropriate to create a sliding scale rating system that would charge equitable insurance rates differentiated according to the extent of insurance to value. But there is a flaw in the process even when it charges an equitable rate to those who choose to underinsure, because underinsurance fails to meet the insurance needs of those who suffer the rare major loss. By many measures, the best solution is one that encourages insurance adequate to cover both large and small losses and does so at a fair and equitable rate level. These complementary goals are met through a combination of rating techniques, policy provisions, and underwriting practices.

Rating Techniques That Promote Insurance to Value

Rate structures that reflect the decreased probability of larger losses also serve to encourage insurance to value. For example, in crime insurance it has been common practice to charge a higher rate per $1,000 of insurance at lower levels of insurance. A typical rate schedule might appear as follows:

First $5,000 of insurance	$125 per thousand
$5,001 to $10,000	$100 per thousand
$10,001 to $20,000	$70 per thousand
Over $20,000	$40 per thousand

This decreasing scale of rates reflects the relative rarity of larger losses, but it also makes larger amounts of insurance attractive to the insured and, consequently, makes it more likely that insurance to value will be carried.

Insurance-to-Value Provisions

Insurance-to-value provisions are policy conditions that encourage the insured to carry insurance at least equal to some major portion of the maximum possible loss or the maximum probable loss. They encourage insurance to value by reducing benefits for those who are underinsured or by providing extra benefits to those who are insured to value.

For *property* insurance, the amount of insurance required usually is stated as a percentage of the value of the covered property at the time of loss. Many such insurance-to-value provisions are loss-sharing provisions because the insured who does not carry the required insurance to value will share a portion of any loss.

Insurance-to-value requirements are less common in *liability* insurance, primarily because it is difficult or impossible to determine the maximum possible liability loss in most situations. In a few instances, such as the exposure for liability for damage to or destruction of specific items of property, it is possible to determine the maximum loss. An example would be fire liability coverage, which protects a tenant against its potential legal liability to a landlord for fire damage to a building; the maximum possible covered loss is the value of that building. Insurance to value—reflecting the value of the damageable property—is sometimes required in such cases.

Coinsurance. The insurance-to-value-related concept of "coinsurance" in property insurance should not be confused with "coinsurance" in health insurance which, as mentioned earlier, really is a type of deductible.

A coinsurance clause is a property insurance policy provision that "requires" the insured to carry an amount of insurance equal to or greater than some stated percentage of the insurable value of the covered property. The coinsurance percentages most commonly used are 80, 90, and 100 percent. The insurable value usually is the actual cash value, the replacement cost value, or some other value as described in the valuation clause of the policy. Although it often is referred to as a "coinsurance *requirement*," it is not altogether mandatory—the policy does not cease to provide coverage if the insured fails to meet the "requirement." If the "requirement" is not met, the policy remains in effect, but the insured is penalized by receiving only a partial recovery when a covered loss occurs.

The 80 percent coinsurance clause is the most common. However, the insured can elect a higher percentage when purchasing insurance, and there may be an advantage in doing so. *The premium rate per $100 of insurance decreases as the coinsurance percentage increases.* Therefore, an insured who buys insurance equal to the *full* insurable value of the property can qualify for a lower premium for the same limit of insurance by electing to increase the coinsurance percentage, from 80 percent, to 90 or 100 percent. However, as the coinsurance percentage increases, the margin for error is reduced, and it becomes increasingly important for the insured to be certain that the limit of insurance remains adequate as insurable values change.

The Coinsurance Clause. In older fire insurance policies, the coinsurance clause was included in a rather complicated sentence that read as follows:

> In consideration of the rate and(or) form under which this policy is written, it is expressly stipulated and made a condition of this contract that the Insured shall at all times maintain contributing insurance on each item of property covered by this policy to the extent of at least the percentage specified on the first page of this policy or endorsed hereon of the actual cash value at the time of the loss, and that failing to do so, the Insured shall to the extent of such deficit bear his, her or their proportions of any loss.

In current commercial property policies, the following clause is used. This clause explains the coinsurance concept in considerably more detail and is followed by several examples.

> Coinsurance
>
> If a Coinsurance percentage is shown in the Declarations, the following condition applies.
>
> a. We will not pay the full amount of any loss if the value of Covered Property at the time of loss times the Coinsurance percentage shown for it in the Declarations is greater than the Limit of Insurance for the property.
>
> Instead, we will determine the most we will pay using the following steps:
> (1) Multiply the value of Covered Property at the time of loss by the Coinsurance percentage;
> (2) Divide the Limit of Insurance of the property by the figure determined in step (1);
> (3) Multiply the total amount of loss, before the application of any deductible, by the figure determined in step (2); and
> (4) Subtract the deductible from the figure determined in step (3).
>
> We will pay the amount determined in step (4) or the limit of insurance, whichever is less. For the remainder, you will either have to rely on other insurance or absorb the loss yourself.
>
> [Two examples follow.]
>
> b. If one Limit of Insurance applies to two or more separate items, this condition will apply to the total of all property to which the limit applies.
>
> [An example follows.]

The Coinsurance Formula. The penalty for failure to meet the coinsurance requirement is a reduction in the amount paid by the insurer to settle a claim. The amount paid by the insurer is calculated by the following formula:

$$\left(\frac{\text{Limit of insurance}}{\text{Value of covered property} \times \text{coinsurance percentage}} \times \frac{\text{Total amount of}}{\text{covered loss}} \right) - \text{Deductible} = \frac{\text{Most that}}{\text{will be paid by insurance}}$$

Insurance students often condense this formula to "Did over should times loss minus deductible" or, in formula form:

$$\left(\frac{\text{Did}}{\text{Should}} \times \text{Loss} \right) - \text{Deductible}$$

"Did" is the amount of insurance carried. "Should" is the minimum amount that should have been carried to meet the coinsurance requirement based on the insurable value of the property *at the time of the loss.* Deductibles were explained earlier, and the ways in which deductibles and coinsurance provisions are combined will be examined later in greater detail.

An example will illustrate the application of the formula. Assume that Susan Smith owns a store building with an insurable value of $300,000. She insures the building in the amount of $200,000 under a policy with a 100 percent coinsurance clause. The building sustains damage of $60,000 as a result of an insured peril. Making the necessary substitutions in the above formula yields the following results:

$$\text{Insurer payment} = \left(\frac{\$200,000}{100\% \times \$300,000} \times \$60,000 \right) - \text{deductible}$$

$$= \left(\frac{\$200,000}{\$300,000} \times \$60,000 \right) - \text{deductible}$$

$$= \left(\frac{2}{3} \times \$60,000 \right) - \text{deductible}$$

$$= \$40,000 - \text{deductible}$$

If the coinsurance percentage in the above example had been 80 percent, the percentage most frequently used, the calculation would have been as follows:

$$\text{Insurer payment} = \left(\frac{\$200,000}{80\% \times \$300,000} \times \$60,000 \right) - \text{deductible}$$

$$= \left(\frac{\$200,000}{\$240,000} \times \$60,000 \right) - \text{deductible}$$

$$= \left(\frac{5}{6} \times \$60,000 \right) - \text{deductible}$$

$$= \$50,000 - \text{deductible}$$

Points To Remember. Three important factors must be kept in mind when applying the coinsurance formula:

1. *The formula applies only when there is inadequate insurance to value—that is, when the limit of insurance is less than the insurable value times the coinsurance percentage,* when the "did" is less than the "should."
2. *The insurer never pays more than the applicable limit of insurance.* If the amount of the loss is greater than the minimum limit of insurance required by the coinsurance clause ("should"), the *formula* may indicate that the insurer will pay more than the amount of insurance carried. However, the *insurer's obligation* will not exceed the applicable limit of insurance.
3. *The insurer never pays more than the amount of the loss.* If the amount of insurance carried ("did") is greater than the minimum limit of insurance required ("should"), the coinsurance formula will indicate that the insurer will pay more than the actual loss sustained. However, the insurer's maximum obligation is limited to the actual loss sustained in virtually all policies.

Examples. Exhibit 7-3 illustrates the ways in which 80, 90, and 100 percent coinsurance clauses would apply in a variety of situations. The first three columns show the insurable value of the property, the applicable limit of insurance, and the amount of the loss. The last three show the amounts recoverable, before subtracting a deductible, under a policy with an 80, 90, or 100 percent coinsurance clause. Readers are urged to study the exhibit carefully and to make some computations of their own to verify their understanding. Pay special attention to those situations in which the amount of recovery is based on the applicable limit of insurance or on the amount of the loss rather than the amount developed through application of the coinsurance formula.

The first set of examples illustrates what happens if insurable values change while the limit of insurance is unchanged. This situation is all too common when insurance limits are not periodically reviewed. A $40,000 loss is used for each example in this set. Notice the extent of underinsurance that must be involved before each of the different coinsurance clauses reduces the amount of recovery to less than the $40,000 amount of the loss.

The second set of examples illustrates the effect of different amounts of loss when property with an insurable value of $100,000 is insured for $70,000—which is 70 percent of its insurable value. Notice that a coinsurance penalty applies for even a relatively small loss. Also note that, to a certain point, the dollar amount of the penalty is larger with 90 and 100 percent coinsurance than with the 80 percent clause. For the larger losses, however, the coinsurance clause loses its impact entirely, and the $70,000 limit of insurance is paid.

The third set of examples shows the effect of different limits of

Exhibit 7-3
Application of Coinsurance Clauses

Insurable Value	Limit of Insurance	Amount of Loss	Amount Recoverable Before Deductibles 80% Coinsurance	90% Coinsurance	100% Coinsurance
Insurable values change:					
$100,000	$100,000	$40,000	$40,000	$40,000	$40,000
110,000	100,000	40,000	40,000	40,000	36,364
120,000	100,000	40,000	40,000	37,037	33,333
130,000	100,000	40,000	38,462	34,188	30,769
140,000	100,000	40,000	35,714	31,746	28,571
150,000	100,000	40,000	33,333	29,630	26,667
160,000	100,000	40,000	31,250	27,778	25,000
170,000	100,000	40,000	29,412	26,144	23,529
180,000	100,000	40,000	27,778	24,691	22,222
190,000	100,000	40,000	26,316	23,392	21,053
200,000	100,000	40,000	25,000	22,222	20,000
Different amounts of loss:					
$100,000	$70,000	$ 10,000	$ 8,750	$ 7,778	$ 7,000
100,000	70,000	20,000	17,500	15,556	14,000
100,000	70,000	30,000	26,250	23,333	21,000
100,000	70,000	40,000	35,000	31,111	28,000
100,000	70,000	50,000	43,750	38,889	35,000
100,000	70,000	60,000	52,500	46,667	42,000
100,000	70,000	70,000	61,250	54,444	49,000
100,000	70,000	80,000	70,000	62,222	56,000
100,000	70,000	90,000	70,000	70,000	63,000
100,000	70,000	100,000	70,000	70,000	70,000
Different limits of insurance:					
$100,000	$ 10,000	$85,000	$10,000	$ 9,444	$ 8,500
100,000	20,000	85,000	20,000	18,889	17,000
100,000	30,000	85,000	30,000	28,333	25,500
100,000	40,000	85,000	40,000	37,778	34,000
100,000	50,000	85,000	50,000	47,222	42,500
100,000	60,000	85,000	60,000	56,667	51,000
100,000	70,000	85,000	70,000	66,111	59,500
100,000	80,000	85,000	80,000	75,556	68,000
100,000	90,000	85,000	85,000	85,000	76,500
100,000	100,000	85,000	85,000	85,000	85,000
100,000	110,000	85,000	85,000	85,000	85,000

insurance on property with a $100,000 value, using an $85,000 loss to illustrate the changing amounts of recovery. Take a look at the 80 percent coinsurance column, which shows what happens when the amount of loss ($85,000) exceeds the amount of insurance required by the coinsurance clause ($80,000). In such a situation, calculations resulting from the coinsurance formula would suggest an amount of recovery that exceeds either the limit of insurance or the amount of the loss. Because the insurer will never pay more than those amounts, the amount determined by the coinsurance formula in these cases is discarded. Up to a certain point, the amount of recovery is capped by the limit of insurance. Beyond that point, it is capped by the amount of the loss.

Coinsurance in Business Income Coverage. The examples to this point involve direct losses to buildings and personal property. Coinsurance clauses also are used in some forms of time element insurance. For example, the business income coverage form includes the following coinsurance clause. Notice how the amount of insurance required is specified in this form.

Coinsurance

If a Coinsurance percentage is shown in the Declarations, the following condition applies . . .

We will not pay the full amount of any loss if the Limit of Insurance for Business Income is less than:

    a. The Coinsurance percentage shown for Business Income in the Declarations times

    b. The sum of:

        (1) The Net Income (Net Profit or Loss before income taxes), and

        (2) All operating expenses, including payroll expenses,

        that would have been earned (had no loss occurred) by your "operations" at the described premises for the 12 months following the inception, or last previous anniversary date, of this policy (whichever is later).

Instead, we will determine the most we will pay using the following steps:

    1. Multiply the Net Income and operating expense for the 12 months following the inception, or last previous anniversary date, of this policy by the Coinsurance percentage;

    2. Divide the Limit of Insurance for the described premises by the figure determined in step 1; and

    3. Multiply the total amount of loss by the figure determined in Step 2.

We will pay the amount determined in step 3. or the limit of insurance, whichever is less. For the remainder, you will either have to rely on other insurance or absorb the loss yourself.

As mentioned earlier, insurance-to-value provisions require insurance to a certain percentage of the probable or possible maximum loss. In the case of tangible property, the probable or possible maximum loss refers to the insurable value of the covered property, and a coinsurance percentage of at least 80 percent is the norm. For business income coverage, the amount of insurance required by the coinsurance formula is *based on* net income and operating expenses during the twelve-month policy period. However, the probable duration of a business interruption may be shorter or longer than twelve months, depending on factors (size and type of building, for example) affecting the insured's length of recovery from a direct property loss. The longer the period of recovery, the greater the business income loss. Reflecting these variables, coinsurance clauses of 50, 60, 70, 80, 90, 100, and 125 percent are available.

Avoiding Coinsurance Penalties. The potential for substantial coinsurance penalties causes great concern among many buyers and sellers of insurance. Of course, coinsurance penalties can be avoided by purchasing an amount of insurance equal to or exceeding the coinsurance requirement, but that is not always feasible or practical. Some "informed guesswork" may be required. Further, the insurable values often cannot precisely be measured until the property actually is rebuilt or replaced.

The amount of insurance needed to meet the coinsurance requirement is based on the value of the insured property *at the time of the loss,* but the limit of insurance is determined *when the policy is purchased.* Obviously, a covered loss may occur a year after the policy purchase, or sometimes after an even longer period, and values may change during that period. Various steps can be taken to cope with this dilemma.

Revise Limits Periodically. During periods of rapid inflation, the insurable value of covered property may increase substantially during the period between policy inception and loss. The amount of such increase is difficult to predict. Of course, the insured can increase the policy limit during the policy term, but the need for such an increase may not be recognized in time.

Inflation Guard. The optional "inflation guard" clauses mentioned in Chapter 6 may be used to increase policy limits automatically in an attempt to reflect anticipated inflation. An annual percentage increase is selected in advance, and it may not accurately anticipate the actual effects of inflation. However, the endorsement does provide a way to cope with inflation, at least in part.

Since the inflation guard gradually increases applicable policy limits during the policy period, it also may make it easier for insurers to sell the idea of increasing insurance limits when the policy is renewed.

Property Appraisals. At any given time, there may be substantial room for disagreement between the insured and the insurer as to the insurable value of a building. The opportunity for disagreement is especially great when the building is insured for actual cash value, because the parties must agree on both the cost of reconstruction and the amount of depreciation applicable. Regular and frequent appraisals by a qualified appraiser will reduce such disagreements substantially but may not eliminate them entirely.

Peak Season Endorsement. Another way of avoiding coinsurance penalties involves the use of a peak season endorsement. Described more fully later in connection with the discussion of fluctuating stock values, a peak season endorsement adjusts policy limits according to a prescribed schedule, but it does not eliminate the coinsurance provision from the policy. The approach is most usable for businesses whose property values follow a cyclical pattern.

Alternatives to Coinsurance. Insurers have developed several forms and techniques for avoiding the coinsurance penalties that can arise from valuation problems.

Flat Policies. Some insurers are willing to write property insurance policies with no coinsurance clause or to remove the coinsurance clause from the policy. A property insurance policy without a coinsurance clause is sometimes called a flat policy. In most cases, there will be a very substantial additional charge (such as a 300 percent increase in the rate per $100 of insurance) for removing the coinsurance clause from a policy typically written with coinsurance. That charge makes this option prohibitively expensive under most circumstances—it usually is more attractive to spend the premium dollars on higher limits of insurance.

Some coverages are usually written on a flat basis. A prime example is personal property coverage on a homeowners policy issued to a tenant. One reason for using flat insurance lies in the difficulty of determining the actual cash value of a typical residential tenant's personal property, not to mention frequent changes as specific possessions are acquired, worn or used, and discarded.

Agreed Value Clause. By specifying in advance a value agreed to by the insurer as sufficient to meet the "should" requirement of the coinsurance clause, the agreed value clause can eliminate the possibility that the insurer will impose a coinsurance penalty at the time of the loss. All the insured need do is have a limit of insurance equal to or greater than that value. (In the past this coverage modification was provided by a so-called "agreed *amount* endorsement." However, it eventually was recognized that what really was agreed to was the value of the property, and the name of the clause was revised for greater accuracy.)

The specified "agreed" value is based on a "statement of values," submitted by the insured. Assuming the statement is acceptable to the insurer, the policy's coinsurance percentage is applied to it to produce what might be called the "agreed value amount." If that amount is equaled or exceeded by the limit of insurance applying to the property, the coinsurance clause is suspended. The issue of coinsurance compliance will not be raised after a loss. While an agreed value clause is in effect, the insured knows in advance what dollar limit of insurance must be carried in order to avoid a penalty. Except under unusual circumstances, the insured purchases an amount of insurance satisfying the agreed value and therefore can be assured that no coinsurance penalty will apply.

Note that an agreed value clause does not convert the policy to a valued policy. The loss valuation specified in the policy, actual cash value, for example, continues to apply. The insurer still is obligated to pay only the actual loss sustained or the face amount of insurance, whichever is less. The purpose of the agreed value clause is only to eliminate the risk of a coinsurance penalty. Also, the agreed value clause does not protect the insured against underinsurance. For example, if the limit of insurance equals an agreed amount based on 80 percent coinsurance, the coinsurance clause would be suspended, but the insured would still be vulnerable to that portion of a very large or total loss that exceeds the policy limit.

The agreed value clause is used most often on policies insuring buildings, but it is sometimes used on coverage for machinery and fixtures, on stocks of goods held for sale, or on other personal property. It also may be used on policies covering loss of business income. There is a premium increase, typically 5 percent, applied when the agreed amount clause is used.

Fluctuating Stock Values. Coinsurance problems may be equally great with stocks of raw materials and finished goods held for sale by wholesalers, retailers, and manufacturers. The value of such stocks at any given time usually is not difficult to determine, but the value may vary rather widely during the policy period, especially for seasonal businesses. Toy stores, for example, usually have much higher stock values in the fall in preparation for Christmas sales than they do at other times of the year. Other businesses may have peak values at other seasons.

If the insured sets the limit of personal property coverage equal to some average of stock values, there is an exposure to a coinsurance penalty and underinsurance when stocks are at their peak seasonal value. If stock coverage is set equal to peak values, a coinsurance penalty will be avoided, but at the cost of being overinsured and incurring excessive insurance costs during other parts of the year. Policy limits can be changed during the year to track stock values, but this approach may result in a coinsurance penalty if the person responsible fails to make the changes as required. Insurers have developed methods for coping with the insurance problems arising from fluctuating stock values.

Peak Season Endorsement. For firms that have clearly defined seasonal patterns, a peak season endorsement is a simple and possibly adequate solution. This endorsement varies the limits of stock coverage on a seasonal schedule. It provides higher limits for the seasons when the insured's stock values are high and lower limits during the seasons when values are low. Thus, the insured pays for high limits only when they are needed and not for the entire policy term.

For example, the endorsement might provide limits of insurance as follows—and as shown in Exhibit 7-4—on a policy with an effective date of February 1:

February 1 through April 30	$75,000
May 1 through August 31	$100,000
September 1 through December 31	$150,000
January 1 through January 31	$100,000

Insurance premiums are simply prorated depending on how long during the year each limit applies.

Reporting Form Policies. A reporting form policy tracks actual values rather than attempting to predict them. Therefore, although it is somewhat complex, it provides a good solution to insuring fluctuating stock values for many business firms.

Under a reporting form policy, the *limit of insurance* typically is set greater than the highest stock values expected during the year. An initial premium is paid, but it is adjusted at the end of the policy term based on the full values actually reported by the insured. If, for example, the limit of insurance is $1 million, and the average reported value is $800,000, only the $800,000 is considered in calculating the final premium payable. The premium also is based on the 100 percent coinsurance rate, which is lower than the 80 percent rate.

With a reporting form, the insured can be certain of adequate insurance without paying an excessive premium for coverage during periods of low stock values. The standard coinsurance clause does not apply to property insured under the reporting form, but that form includes a

Exhibit 7-4

Peak Season Endorsement Illustrated

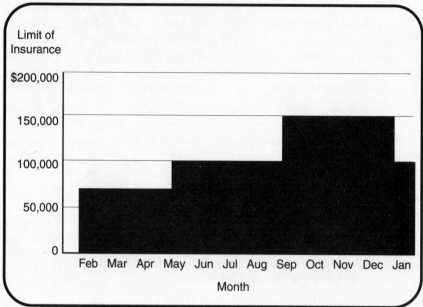

coinsurance provision of its own, titled *full reporting*. That clause is quoted below.

Full Reporting. The COINSURANCE Additional Condition is replaced by the following:

COINSURANCE

a. If your last report of values before loss or damage, for a location where loss or damage occurs, shows less than the full value of the Covered Property at that location on the report dates, we will not pay a greater proportion of loss, prior to the application of the deductible, than:

(1) The values you reported for the location where the loss or damage occurred, divided by

(2) The value of the Covered Property at that location on the report dates.

b. For locations you acquire after the last report of values, we will not pay a greater proportion of loss, prior to the application of the deductible, than:

(1) The values you reported for all locations, divided by

(2) The value of the Covered Property at all locations on the report dates.

The value reporting form requires the insured to report the value of the property insured thereunder on a daily, weekly, monthly, quar-

terly, or annual basis. If the insured files every report by the date when
it is due, as indicated in the form, and if the insured reports values
correctly, the insurer is obligated to pay all losses in full (subject, of
course, to the policy limits and any applicable deductible).

If the insured reports values lower than those that actually existed,
a loss sharing provision becomes applicable. If all required reports have
been filed but the values reported were less than the values on the
reporting date, the amount the insurer will pay is determined (subject
to the specified policy limit) by the formula:

$$\left(\frac{\text{Value reported}}{\substack{\text{Value that should} \\ \text{have been reported}}} \times \substack{\text{Total amount of} \\ \text{covered loss}} \right) - \text{Deductible} = \substack{\text{Most that will be} \\ \text{paid by insurance}}$$

The "value that should have been reported" is, in most cases, the full
value of the covered property.

If the policy covers more than one location, with a separate limit of
insurance for each location, values must be reported separately for each
location and the formula would be applied separately to each location.

Because the value that should be reported equals 100 percent of the
insurable value of the property, the full reporting clause is essentially
the same as a 100 percent coinsurance. (The difference is that coinsurance applies as of the date of the loss, while the full reporting clause
applies as of the date of the report.) That is why rates for 100 percent
coinsurance are used with reporting form policies.

If reports have not been submitted in a timely manner, a different
loss sharing provision, titled "Failure to Submit Reports," applies. That
clause is shown below:

4. Failure to Submit Reports
   If at the time of loss or damage you have failed to submit:
   a. The first required report of values:
      (1) We will not pay more than 75% of the amount we would
          otherwise have paid; and
      (2) We will only pay for loss or damage at locations shown in
          the Declarations.
   b. Any required report of values after the first required report:
      (1) We will not pay more for loss or damage at any location than
          the values you last reported for that location; and
      (2) We will only pay for loss or damage at locations reported in
          your last report filed before the loss.

Under this provision, if the insured fails to file the first report required
under the policy, the insurer will pay only 75 percent of what it would
have been required to pay if reports had been filed in a timely manner
with correct values.

If the first report was filed but loss occurs while a later report is past due, the insurer will not pay more than the values reported on the latest report it actually received before the loss. In either case, the automatic coverage for newly acquired locations does not apply. The insurer will pay only for losses at locations shown on the declarations page of the policy or on reports filed under the policy.

Of course, these penalties are avoidable by simply filing the required reports correctly and promptly. The reports are filed after the insured values are known, so no estimates of future values are involved. Thus the uncertainty of estimating insurable values is not a factor.

Despite their attractive features, reporting forms are not a panacea. Problems arise—all too frequently—when somebody fails to follow through in making a report when due or in ensuring its accuracy. Because values reported are directly reflected in premiums, there may be a tendency to understate reported values with the unfortunate possible result that losses will not be paid in full. Another problem can be failure to increase policy limits when reported values exceed the limits. The limits are *not* automatically increased when values in excess of the limits are reported, even though a premium will be charged based on the reported values.

Similar value reporting provisions are used in a variety of commercial insurance policies. Examples include parcel post policies, motor truck cargo policies, and ocean marine cargo policies. A reporting approach also may be used with other policies for which it is difficult to establish at the beginning of the policy term the values that will be exposed to loss under the policy.

Monthly Limit of Indemnity. Some business income policies include a clause, somewhat different from the coinsurance clause, that encourages insurance to value and impose a loss-sharing penalty in certain situations. The monthly limit of indemnity approach focuses less on the total dollar amount exposed to loss and more on the time element—that is, the period of time during which a loss of business income may occur. It does not require insurance to a specified percentage of insurable value, as the coinsurance clause does. But it places limits on the percentage of the total amount of insurance that can be collected for loss incurred during a specified period of time.

Monthly Limit of Indemnity
... The most we will pay for loss of Business Income in each period of 30 consecutive days after the direct physical loss or damage is:
(1) The Limit of Insurance, multiplied by
(2) The fraction shown in the Declarations for this Optional Coverage.

The ISO business income coverage form can be written either with coinsurance or with a monthly limit of indemnity clause applicable. The monthly limit of indemnity clause is activated by inserting a fraction in the appropriate space on the declarations page of the policy. If that fraction is "¼," then no more than one-fourth of the coverage limit can be collected for loss in any thirty-day period. The actual loss payment would be the lesser of (1) the actual loss sustained, or (2) one-fourth of the limit of coverage.

To illustrate the application of this clause, assume that the General Store carries business income coverage with a limit of insurance of $200,000 and a "¼" monthly limit of indemnity. It sustains a covered loss of business income as follows:

First 30 days after loss event	$60,000
Second 30 days after loss event	40,000
Third 30 days after loss event	30,000
Fourth 30 days after loss event	20,000
Total amount of loss	$150,000

The amount the insurer would be obligated to pay (ignoring any deductible that might be applicable) would be:

First 30 days	$50,000
Second 30 days	40,000
Third 30 days	30,000
Fourth 30 days	20,000
Total payment	$140,000

The remaining $10,000 for the first thirty-day period would not be paid even though the policy limit of $200,000 had not been exhausted. In order to avoid sharing the loss in this example, the insured would have needed a policy limit of $240,000 instead of the $200,000 carried (because $60,000 is one-fourth of $240,000). In this example, additional amounts would be payable if the interruption lasted for a longer period, but only for the losses incurred during that period.

In order to make a full recovery under a *coinsurance* clause, the insured must estimate future insurable values correctly, or possibly overestimate them. For income loss coverage, the insurable value is the future income of the firm. Under the monthly limit of indemnity clause, however, it is necessary only to estimate the maximum amount the firm will need to recover in any one thirty-day period to cover its lost profits and necessary continuing expenses. For some businesses, especially smaller start-up operations, this is an easier amount to estimate.

Homeowners Policy Provisions. Homeowners policies that include coverage on the dwelling building also have a provision to encourage insurance to value. This provision directly applies only to the building coverage. However, since the other property coverages of a homeowners policy are generally a fixed percentage of the coverage on the dwelling building, the effect is to encourage an adequate amount of insurance for all property coverages in the policy.

The insurance-to-value provision in homeowners policies bears a strong resemblance to a coinsurance clause, but it differs in two major respects. Instead of a penalty for failing to provide insurance to value, it offers a reward for insuring to value (that is, to 80 percent or more of the replacement cost value of the dwelling building or other structures). That reward is the payment of building losses at replacement cost, subject to policy limits, for those who insure to value.

Also under the homeowners insurance-to-value provision, the insured never collects less than the actual cash value of the building loss—even if the amount of insurance is less than 80 percent of the actual cash value—unless, of course, the applicable policy limits are inadequate to pay the actual cash value of the building loss. A coinsurance clause contains no such "floor" provision.

The amount payable by the insurer may be either the replacement cost value of the loss, the actual cash value of the loss, or something in between. Those who are slightly underinsured based on the 80 percent test will collect an amount somewhere between the actual cash value and the replacement cost value of the loss based on a coinsurance-like formula.

The applicable provision of the homeowners policy is found in the loss settlement condition of the homeowners form, which is quoted below:

[Losses to] Buildings under Coverage A or B [are settled] at replacement cost without deduction for depreciation, subject to the following:
(1) If, at the time of loss, the amount of insurance in this policy on the damaged building is 80% or more of the full replacement cost of the building immediately before the loss, we will pay the cost to repair or replace, after application of deductible and without deduction for depreciation, but not more than the least of the following amounts:
   (a) The limit of liability under this policy that applies to the building;
   (b) The replacement cost of that part of the building damaged for like construction and use on the same premises; or
   (c) The necessary amount actually spent to repair or replace the damaged building.
(2) If, at the time of loss, the amount of insurance in this policy on the damaged building is less than 80% of the full replacement cost of the building immediately before the loss, we will pay the greater of the following amounts, but not more than the limit of liability under this policy that applies to the building:
   (a) The actual cash value of that part of the building damaged; or
   (b) That proportion of the cost to repair or replace, after application of deductible and without deduction for depreciation, that part of the building damaged, which the total amount of insurance

in this policy on the damaged building bears to 80% of the replacement cost of the building.

(3) To determine the amount of insurance required to equal 80% of the full replacement cost of the building immediately before the loss, do not include the value of:

(a) Excavations, foundations, piers or any supports which are below the undersurface of the lowest basement floor;

(b) Those supports in (a) above which are below the surface of the ground inside the foundation walls, if there is no basement; and

(c) Underground flues, pipes, wiring and drains.

(4) We will pay no more than the actual cash value of the damage until actual repair or replacement is complete. Once actual repair or replacement is complete, we will settle the loss according to the provisions of b.(1) and b.(2) above.

However, if the cost to repair or replace the damage is both:

(a) Less than 5% of the amount of insurance in this policy on the building; and

(b) Less than $2500;

we will settle the loss according to the provisions of b.(1) and b.(2) above whether or not actual repair or replacement is complete.

(5) You may disregard the replacement cost loss settlement provisions and make claim under this policy for loss or damage to buildings on an actual cash value basis. You may then make claim within 180 days after loss for any additional liability according to the provisions of this Condition 3. Loss Settlement.

This provision works as follows:

1. If the policy limit applicable to the dwelling building is at least equal to 80 percent of the full replacement cost of the dwelling building immediately before loss, the insurer will pay the cost to repair the damage, subject to the policy limit and any applicable deductible, without any deduction for depreciation.

2. If the amount of insurance is less than 80 percent of the replacement cost of the building, the insurer will pay an amount determined by the formula:

$$\text{Payment} = \frac{\text{Insurance carried}}{(80\% \times \text{Replacement cost of building})}$$
$$\times (\text{Replacement cost of loss} - \text{Deductible})$$

3. If the amount calculated in (2) is less than the actual cash value of the loss, the insurer will pay the actual cash value of the loss—with no deductible—or the policy limit, whichever is less.

Exhibit 7-5 shows how the amount payable under a homeowners policy (ignoring deductibles) would be affected as the insurable value changes, using for this example a dwelling building loss with an actual cash value of $28,000 and a replacement cost value of $40,000 under a homeowners policy with a $100,000 applicable limit of insurance. Com-

Exhibit 7-5

Application of Homeowners Policy Loss Clause

Insurable RC	Limit of Insurance	Amount of Loss-RC	Amount of Loss-ACV	Amount Payable
$100,000	$100,000	$40,000	$28,000	$40,000
110,000	100,000	40,000	28,000	40,000
120,000	100,000	40,000	28,000	40,000
130,000	100,000	40,000	28,000	38,462
140,000	100,000	40,000	28,000	35,714
150,000	100,000	40,000	28,000	33,333
160,000	100,000	40,000	28,000	31,250
170,000	100,000	40,000	28,000	29,412
180,000	100,000	40,000	28,000	28,000
190,000	100,000	40,000	28,000	28,000
200,000	100,000	40,000	28,000	28,000

RC = Replacement Cost
ACV = Actual Cash Value

pare the amount payable under this form with the amount payable under a similar policy with an 80 percent coinsurance clause, as illustrated in the first group of figures in Exhibit 7-3. Notice that the homeowners policy loss settlement clause always provides minimum coverage for at least the actual cash value of the loss.

Businessowners Policy Provisions. The property coverage of businessowners policies might be viewed from two perspectives. On the one hand, businessowners policies contain no coinsurance clause or similar penalty for underinsurance. It generally is assumed that the insured will purchase insurance to value and that the underwriter will verify that an appropriate relationship exists between values and limits. On the other hand, although businessowners policies contain no penalties for underinsurance, they also include one provision that tends to maintain insurance to value on the building and another that rewards those who have insured their personal property to value.

Building Coverage. The ISO businessowners policies, and perhaps others as well, contain an *automatic* inflation guard provision that increases the stated limit for the building(s) by an annual percentage of 8 percent, or a different percentage if so indicated in the declarations. The annual percentage is applied on a pro rata basis throughout the policy year.

Personal Property Coverage. A *seasonal automatic increase* clause applies only if the limit of liability in the declarations equals 100 percent or more of the insured's *average* personal property values for the twelve months preceding the loss. When applicable, this clause acts somewhat like a peak season endorsement that automatically kicks in when needed by increasing the businessowners limit of liability for business personal property by 25 percent. This provision encourages policyholders to maintain a personal property limit of insurance at least equal to their *average* insurable value.

Underwriting Techniques for Achieving Insurance to Value. Some policies or coverages, such as the building coverage of the businessowners policy, do not include an insurance-to-value requirement. Even when policy provisions provide incentives for insurance to value rather than penalties for underinsurance, it usually is desirable for the insurer to encourage insurance to value. With insurance to value, the insurer receives a higher premium commensurate with the underlying loss exposures. Remember, most losses are small. Except with respect to moral or morale hazards, the underlying probability of loss is not affected by the amount of insurance. In addition, the insured who is encouraged to insure to value is better served by coverage adequate to cover a major loss.

While exceptions may be encountered, it generally is desirable for the underwriter to verify the value of the property and to require insurance to a substantial percentage of the insurable value as a condition of providing coverage. Several techniques are available to underwriters in determining or estimating property values.

Detailed Appraisal. One method of achieving insurance to value is for the insurer to require a detailed appraisal to determine the value of the covered property at the time the insurance is underwritten. An appraisal involves a detailed inspection of the building by a skilled appraiser who then calculates the cost of replacing the building based on analysis of all of the construction features and materials.

The appraisal may be made by an employee of the insurer or by an independent appraiser. The cost of the appraisal may or may not be borne by the insurer. Knowing the value of the property in question, the insurer then insists that the insured carry insurance equal to a stated percentage of the appraised value as a condition of obtaining coverage. Alternatively, the appraisal may provide the basis for coverage on an agreed value basis.

Appraisals are effective in achieving insurance to value, but they involve several problems. The most obvious problem is expense. A substantial amount of expense is incurred in a detailed appraisal. This technique is more often used in connection with properties with high values for which the appraisal expenses constitute only a small part of the premium. Another problem is that all appraisals involve some margin of error, and the true cost of replacing property is never known until a replacement has been done.

Rough Appraisals (Formal Estimates). The premiums for smaller properties, such as single-family residences, cannot support the cost of a detailed, on-site appraisal. Some insurers calculate an approximate value for such properties as the basis for establishing insurable values and limits of insurance.

Three approaches are used in calculating such approximate values:

- *Construction Cost Index.* If the original cost of constructing the property is known, it is adjusted upward (or possibly downward) by an index of construction costs to approximate the cost to replace the structure at current prices of labor and materials.
- *Square Foot Cost.* The floor area of the building is multiplied by a figure representing the square-foot cost of constructing a similar building at current price levels.
- *Cubic Foot Cost.* A slightly more elaborate version, this technique uses the cubic-foot volume of the building rather than the floor area.

The cost per square foot (or cubic foot) depends upon the type of construction, the features of the building, its geographic location, and other factors. Of course, if the property is to be insured for actual cash value, the insurable value may be less than the replacement cost calculated by the foregoing techniques, depending on the age of the building. Applicable physical depreciation, if any, must be reflected in the calculation of actual cash value.

Historically, insurers were reluctant to specify the value of property at the time of policy issuance. The feared that establishing a value initially might complicate settlement negotiations when losses occur. Most property insurers believed that the determination of insurable values at policy inception was the responsibility of the insured, and that the insurer was concerned with valuation only at the time of loss. This reluctance to establish value at policy inception has diminished greatly in recent years. This change in attitude resulted from three factors:

1. The necessity for increased premiums to cover losses, especially during periods of rapid inflation
2. Dissatisfaction among policyholders when their insurance proved inadequate to cover their losses
3. The availability of more accurate construction cost information from governmental and private sources

Guaranteed Replacement Cost. Some insurers now agree to cover the full replacement cost of any loss, even if it exceeds policy limits, if the insured buys the amount of insurance recommended by the insurer based on the insurer's appraisal. While this desirable policy feature appears to reflect generosity on the part of the insurer, it also reflects the reality that the insurer would likely end up paying the full loss anyway. As explained more fully in Chapter 9, the insurer could be held responsible for any loss resulting from the insured's "detrimental reliance" on information provided by the insurer. If the insured chose an inadequate limit of insurance based on the insurer's appraisal, the insurer's appraisal would probably be found faulty.

COMBINING COINSURANCE AND DEDUCTIBLES

As with the proverbial chicken and egg, questions often arise as to which loss-sharing computation clause—the coinsurance clause or the deductible clause—comes first. The order in which they are applied can make a substantial difference in the amount the insurer is required to pay. For example, assume the following facts:

Value of building	$5,000,000
Coinsurance percentage	80%
Amount of insurance	$3,000,000
Amount of loss	$2,500,000
Deductible amount	$100,000

If the deductible is applied before the coinsurance clause, the insurer would first calculate the loss net of the deductible and then apply the coinsurance formula. In this case, the insurer would pay $1,800,000, determined as follows:

$$\frac{\$3,000,000}{\$4,000,000} \times (\$2,500,000 - \$100,000) = \frac{3}{4} \times \$2,400,000$$

$$= \$1,800,000$$

If the coinsurance clause is applied first, the insurer would pay

$$\left(\frac{\$3,000,000}{\$4,000,000} \times \$2,500,000\right) - \$100,000 = \$1,775,000$$

The order of application of the clauses depends on the wording of the two clauses in the relevant policy form. Many policy forms provide for the coinsurance clause to be applied first, but others provide for the deductible to be subtracted from the amount of the loss, before coinsurance is applied, rather than from the amount otherwise payable based on coinsurance alone.

Some policies may not specify clearly which applies first. In case of such ambiguity, it is likely that a court would consider the doctrine of adhesion and use the order that provides the insured with the greatest recovery. This usually will mean that the deductible should be applied first.

COMBINING DEDUCTIBLES AND POLICY LIMITS

Usually, deductibles and limits of insurance present no conflicts. However, in some situations both may operate to reduce the insured's amount of recovery, and various ways of combining these provisions may create different results.

In some cases a property loss deductible can be "absorbed." To *absorb a deductible* is to apply the deductible to the loss the insured has actually suffered before applying any limits of insurance. If the applicable limit can be exhausted by the loss amount that exceeds the deductible, then the entire limit should be collected by the insured without further application of a deductible.

The following example illustrates this point. One evening burglars stole the following items from Roy's house:

Item	Value	Basis
Television	$320	ACV
Video cassette recorder	250	ACV
Cash	500	Face value
Total	$1,070	

Roy is insured under a homeowners policy with a $250 per loss deductible and a $200 sublimit applicable to money. The loss may be adjusted as follows:

Item	Recovery	Basis
Television	$320	ACV
Video cassette recorder	250	ACV
Cash	200	Money sublimit
Total	$770	

Roy has suffered a $300 uninsured loss of cash ($500 was stolen; $200 was recovered from his insurer) that cannot be paid under his insurance policy. Since he already has shared in the loss to the extent of $300, no further deductible will be subtracted. It could be said that his $250 deductible has been absorbed by the excess $300 cash loss.

A slightly different example illustrates how a deductible may be partially absorbed. Dale has a homeowners policy with a $500 deductible when the following items are stolen from her home:

Item	Value	Basis
Diamond necklace	$1,400	ACV
Camera	300	ACV
Rifle	500	ACV
Stereo set	1,200	ACV
Total	$3,400	

According to policy provisions, the following should be paid on each item:

Item	Recovery	Basis
Diamond necklace	$1,000	Jewelry theft sublimit
Camera	300	ACV
Rifle	500	ACV
Stereo set	1,200	ACV
Total	$3,000 − $100 = $2,900	

Dale has an excess loss of $400 because of the jewelry theft sublimit. $400 of her $500 deductible will be absorbed by this excess, and only $100 will be subtracted from the $3,000, leaving Dale with a total recovery of $2,900.

The principle of absorbing a deductible applies in commercial property coverage as well as in homeowners policies. Whenever a claim exceeds the limits set in the policy, there is potential for applying the excess loss to the application of the deductible in order to absorb part or all of the deductible. In order to absorb all of a deductible, the excess loss amount must equal or exceed the deductible amount.

Deductibles are commonly absorbed by insurers, but the practice is not specifically described in most insurance policies. Yet, many claims adjusters regard it as the correct approach. The only exception would be for policies that clearly state that the deductible is to be applied to the amount otherwise payable rather than to the full value of the loss. As noted earlier, such a policy never would pay the full amount of its stated coverage limits.

SUMMARY

Loss sharing provisions, the topic of this chapter, are policy provisions that may require the insured to bear part of the dollar amount of covered losses. Two broad categories of loss sharing provisions are

(1) deductibles and (2) policy provisions designed to encourage insurance to value.

Deductibles exist for three primary reasons—(1) to reduce morale hazards and encourage loss control, (2) to reduce loss costs and loss adjustment expenses, and (3) to reduce premiums. The extent to which they accomplish these objectives varies with the type of insurance. Deductibles are not well suited for many types of liability insurance where it is desirable that the insurer be involved at the "first dollar" level of any claim.

Deductibles may be characterized in many ways. *Straight (dollar) deductibles*, simple though they may appear, are not all alike. As explained, the deductible may apply per item, per location, per occurrence, or per claim. *Percentage deductibles*, in similar fashion, may subtract a percentage of the amount of insurance, the value of the insured property, or the amount of the loss. *Franchise deductibles* apply only to losses beneath a certain level. *Disappearing deductibles*, which have gone the way of the dinosaur, managed to combine the features of both straight and franchise deductibles, but they were doomed by their complexity. *Time deductibles*, usually applicable to losses involving a time element, are essentially waiting periods that must elapse before payment will be made. *Aggregate deductibles* add a somewhat different twist by setting a maximum amount that the insured must retain during a policy year or some other specified period. Finally, the term *self-insured retention* (SIR) is applied to the large deductible-like provisions found in umbrellas and some other forms of liability insurance policies.

Insurance to value is desirable for both insureds and insurers. Insureds who insure in an amount approximating the full extent of their loss exposures are in a position to recover in full for any foreseeable loss. Insurers whose policyholders purchase insurance to value receive premiums that fairly reflect the loss exposures, taking into account the decreasing probability of increasing loss amounts as reflected in the rating structure for some lines of insurance.

The most common insurance-to-value provision is the coinsurance clause, simply expressed as "did over should times the loss." The coinsurance formula penalizes the policyholder who does not insure to value. Examples were presented in the chapter that also made it clear that the insured will never recover more than the limit of insurance or the amount of the loss.

Coinsurance provisions raise the specter of a potential penalty following a loss if, for whatever reason, the amount of insurance did not satisfy the "should" in the formula based on values at the time of the loss. The methods for avoiding coinsurance penalties include periodic revision of policy limits, the use of an inflation guard provision, property appraisals to confidently establish insurable values, and the peak season endorsement. Alternatives to coinsurance include no-coinsurance (flat) policies and the use of an agreed value clause.

Fluctuating values increase the difficulty of providing insurance to value without overinsuring. A peak season endorsement may be used to automatically adjust policy *limits* to reflect predictable seasonal variations in values. Alternatively, a reporting form approach may be used to adjust *premiums* to reflect the actual amounts of property exposed to loss. These amounts are determined based on periodic reports that must be timely and accurate to avoid penalties at the time of a loss.

Another variation of insurance-to-value provisions is the *monthly limit of indemnity*, used in some business income policies, to cap the insurer's maximum monthly claim payment at some stated fraction of the policy limit. Still another is the provision found in homeowners policies that rewards those who insure to at least 80 percent of replacement cost value by providing replacement cost coverage. Still another approach appears in businessowners policies that include automatic inflation guard and peak season-type coverage.

Insurers also address the insurance-to-value challenge through various underwriting techniques designed to solidify the estimates of property values. These techniques include detailed appraisals and rough appraisals. An insurer may also offer guaranteed replacement cost coverage to a buyer who purchases insurance equal to the full amount of the insurer's estimate.

The closing sections of this chapter briefly explained some of the considerations involved when deductibles, policy limits, and coinsurance might have a bearing on the amount payable following a loss. The often unwritten practice of "absorbing" a deductible was also described.

Chapter Notes

---

1. Although not commonly done, it also is possible to use an annual aggregate deductible with property insurance.
2. In disability income insurance it is referred to as an elimination period.
3. A "corridor deductible" involves a retained gap between two layers of coverage. Corridor deductibles are sometimes found in major medical health insurance policies, where the insured must retain a deductible layer of coverage after the limits of a basic hospital expense policy are consumed before major medical coverage takes over. The term is not normally used in property or liability insurance.
4. J. J. Launie, J. Finley Lee, and Norman A. Baglini, *Principles of Property and Liability Underwriting*, 3rd ed. (Malvern, PA: Insurance Institute of America, 1986), p. 91.

CHAPTER 8

Multiple Sources of Recovery

Often the party who has suffered a loss has the possibility of recovering from more than one outside source, apart from the loss sufferer's own assets. Insurance contracts provide a prominent source of recovery from the financial consequences of a loss. However, insurance may not be the only source of recovery. The loss sufferer may have other rights of recovery grounded in statute, tort, or contract. Also, more than one insurance policy—and more than one insurance company—may potentially provide coverage for the same loss. This chapter deals with the various ways in which actual or potential multiple-recovery situations are handled according to the provisions appearing in various insurance policies. It also examines factors external to policy language that are considered in resolving such situations, which can take on many different flavors.

The chapter begins by cataloging and illustrating *some* situations involving multiple sources of recovery for insured losses. It would be far beyond the scope of this text to attempt to examine all such situations. Emphasis here is on multiple *insurance* sources. Next, the chapter examines the insurance policy language that addresses the issue of multiple sources of recovery—specifically, the policy provisions dealing with other insurance. In this text, these provisions are called "other insurance" provisions, with quotation marks, to avoid any implication that these are simply *"other* provisions relating to *insurance."* The chapter concludes with a brief look at the collateral source rule.

SOURCES OF MULTIPLE RECOVERY

Insurance coverage analysis generally begins with the premise that one insurance policy (or portion of a policy), standing alone, covers a

319

given loss. However, the possibility exists that the insured may have access to additional sources of compensation covering the same loss in whole or in part.

The insured may be the beneficiary of some generous person or entity that would, in the absence of insurance, "take care of" the loss. Such gratuitous sources of recovery are not of concern here. Our focus is on sources to which the insured has some legally enforceable right. The following sources of recovery are considered here:

1. Other insurance in the same policy
2. Other insurance in a similar policy
3. Other insurance in a dissimilar policy
4. Noninsurance agreements
5. Third parties

Other Insurance in the Same Policy

Property-liability insurance policies often overlap internally—between or within sections, parts, or coverage items in the same contract. These coverage overlaps have become more common as a result of increasing flexibility and breadth in the coverage of modern insurance policies. Such overlaps are not the result of some failure on the part of policy drafters. Overlaps usually are clearly recognized, and they may be unavoidable or intentional. Indeed, overlapping coverage is much more desirable for the insured than gaps in coverage.

Fifty years ago a "well-insured" automobile owner carried liability insurance and some coverage for damage to or loss of the car itself. That was it. Other than an occasional question about which of two covered physical damage perils should be regarded as the proximate cause of a loss, the components of the owner's automobile insurance coverage were mutually exclusive. Today, depending on the jurisdiction and buyer preference, an auto policy could include not only liability and physical damage coverages, but also coverage for:

- Medical payments[1]
- "No-fault" personal injury protection
- Uninsured motorists
- Underinsured motorists

Chapter 2 described an approach to insurance policy construction involving "common provisions" and coverage modules for many of the various "lines" of insurance a commercial entity may need. When lines are combined or packaged in one policy, the opportunities for single-policy multiple sources of recovery increase. Policy drafters increasingly have had to direct attention to other insurance in the same policy, as opposed to other insurance generally. A modern commercial package policy may involve numerous overlaps of coverage, including the following:

- Crime insurance and "commercial property" (fire) insurance
- Boiler and machinery insurance and "commercial property" insurance
- Inland marine insurance and "commercial property" insurance
- Boiler and machinery insurance and general liability insurance
- Auto liability insurance and general liability insurance

Multiple sources of recovery can also exist *within the same singular* component or module of a package policy. For example, personal property used to maintain or service a building (such as fire extinguishing equipment, outdoor furniture, floor coverings, or refrigerators) is covered under the "building" coverage of many "commercial property" insurance forms. The same items also qualify for coverage as personal property under another insuring agreement of the same form.

Other examples may include different coverage forms within the same coverage part of a modular policy. For example, *within* the "commercial property" coverage part of an ISO commercial package policy, a building owner may cover the building, using forms specific to that purpose, and also cover the building glass, again using (separate) documents specific to the glass. Since building glass is part of the building, it is covered property under the building insurance. But it is also covered as glass per se.

One might conclude that each of these examples involves a distinction without a difference because the same insurer will pay the loss in any case, but some interesting questions remain.

1. Is there a carve-out provision of some kind, leaving coverage with one, but not both, types of insurance?
2. Do the limits of insurance "stack," giving the insured, if needed, the combined limits of both coverages to handle a large loss?
3. Does a difference in loss valuation provisions or deductibles make it preferable to have the loss paid under one of the coverages? If so, does the insured have the option of selecting which coverage to utilize?
4. Are the building glass, refrigerators, or other items subject to duplicate coverage included in the building coverage's value when applying the coinsurance clause?

It is not our purpose here to answer these specific questions, but rather to itemize some of the questions that inevitably must be raised.

Questions of a similar nature arise in overlaps between components of the same policy. Homeowners policies provide several examples of intra-policy overlap. In Section I, the residential property insurance component of those policies, the insurance provided on the *dwelling* covers by policy stipulation materials and supplies used to repair the dwelling so long as they are on or adjacent to the residence premises. Yet, before being affixed to the dwelling, the materials (such as a bundle of roofing shingles) are personal property. Along with the rest of the insured's personal property, the shingles are therefore covered in the *personal property* component of Section I, which applies to personal property owned or used by an insured.[2]

The phrase "used by an insured," which makes clear that the personal property coverage is not confined to property *of* insureds, introduces another homeowners policy overlap. An insured might be using a friend's camcorder and ruin it by dropping it. Under some homeowners forms, the loss would be covered under Section I.[3] In addition, Section II of this policy—headed "liability coverages"—in an "additional coverage" called "Damage to Property of Others," covers the loss as well, at least up to the modest limit of insurance (usually $500) applying to that coverage.

Other Insurance in a Similar Policy

It is not unusual to see the same party protected by more than one policy of the same general type. The policies may be written on behalf of the same person(s) or entity(ies), but they need not be. The overlap may be by design, transitional, or fortuitous. Consider these three cases:

- A large business has property exposures exceeding the capacity of any single insurer. Two or three different insurance companies issue policies that, together, provide adequate limits of coverage.
- Fred moves to a new home, buys a new homeowners policy, and continues in force the homeowners policy covering the old home while the old home is up for sale. Portions of both policies protect Fred (and other insureds) simultaneously.
- Dot borrows a neighbor's car to take some clothes to the dry cleaners. Dot and the neighbor each carry a personal auto policy. Dot has liability (and possibly other) protection under both policies.

Unlike the single-policy case, other insurance under similar policies usually adds another dimension to multiple sources—multiple insurers. No longer is it merely a question of out of which pocket *the* insurer will pay the claim; now the question is *which* insurer(s) will pay. The policy language that is used should address this possibility. While "similar" policies can be expected to have generally similar policy language, it does not necessarily follow that specifics of the language are in harmony or are consistent with the best interests of the insured. They may be. But as shown later in this chapter, language can create as well as resolve problems in determining the obligations of the insurers involved.

Other Insurance in Dissimilar Policies

Assume Dot's dry cleaner carries a bailees customers policy covering customers' property on the dry cleaner's premises. Chapter 4 made it clear that a bailee has a representative insurable interest in such property, even though the insurance is for the direct benefit of customers. But Dot's homeowners policy covers her personal property anywhere in the world, so she has protection under both that policy and the commercial inland marine policy carried by the dry cleaner—two dissimilar policies. Situations of this type are common:

- Hilda, a homeowners insured, borrows with permission a friend's new twenty-three-foot sailboat for an evening bay sail. Hilda has bodily injury and property damage liability coverage under her homeowners policy and she may also have liability coverage under the boatowner's watercraft policy as a permissive user of the vessel.[4]
- Edwin owns a utility trailer. Under some circumstances, liability claims arising out of the trailer may be covered by both Edwin's personal auto policy and his homeowners policy.
- Gourmet is a catering and party facility. When parties are held at Gourmet, employees park the cars of arriving guests on Gourmet's back lot. This valet parking activity may be covered under both Gourmet's general liability policy *and* its commercial auto liability policy, depending on how the latter is written.[5]
- Gourmet's employee uses her personal automobile to deliver a tray of hors d'oeuvres to a customer. Gourmet's auto-related vicarious liability for the acts or omissions of the employee in this case may be covered under the employee's personal auto policy *and* Gourmet's commercial auto liability policy.

The subject of dissimilar insurance policies arises most frequently in connection with accidents involving bodily injury accompanied by medical expenses and income losses. It is an issue even without considering the financial resources or liability insurance coverage of a third party whose negligence may have caused the injury. Consider an employee injured in an auto accident while on the job. The list of insurance coverages that might apply is not short:

1. The employee's auto insurance
2. The employer's auto insurance

3. The no-fault or medical payments coverage of another driver
4. The employee's individual medical expense insurance
5. The employee's employer-sponsored group medical expense insurance
6. The group medical expense insurance of a spouse or parent
7. The employee's individual disability income insurance
8. The employee's employer-sponsored group disability insurance
9. Workers compensation insurance protecting the employer against a statutory obligation to pay for employees injured on the job

Potential redundancy also results from the intra-policy overlaps possible *within* auto insurance, as mentioned earlier. It simplifies things greatly to acknowledge that workers compensation insurance applies exclusively in most cases involving work-related injuries. But if this accident were not work-related, seven of the first eight items still might apply.

Noninsurance Agreements

Some noninsurance sources of recovery for otherwise insured losses may be available directly to insureds. That is, they might be available without any need to establish fault or cause on the part of another party. Some product warranties or guarantees likewise fall into this category, if they are broad enough to include a replacement or restoration commitment covering fortuitous losses. So, too, do certain types of contractual noninsurance transfers, such as an obligation of a lessee or bailee for the well-being of leased or bailed property without regard to fault. The contract of employment can entitle an employee (and possibly dependents) to benefits under self-insured plans of the employer (such as workers compensation, medical expense, short-term or long-term disability income) that mirror insured plans in the potential for overlap with "insurance" in the literal sense.

Recently, consumer credit card enhancements have created interesting sources of recovery for some losses. Some "premium" cards now protect the cardholder for at least some of the obligations assumed in a car rental contract arising out of damage to or loss of the car, provided the premium card is used to pay for the rental. This feature largely eliminates the need for the renter to pay the substantial daily charge for a so-called collision damage waiver. The coverage may, however, duplicate protection applicable to nonowned autos in the renter's personal auto policy.[6]

Often packaged with the credit card's rental car damage feature are (1) personal effects "coverage," and (2) accident medical expense "coverage." Both are keyed to renting a car with the credit card. Personal effects "coverage" reimburses for damage to or loss of the renter's personal effects while in the rental car; the overlap with homeowners insurance is obvious. The accident medical expense "coverage" overlaps medical expense insurance, possibly several types of auto insurance, and workers compensation. Separately from the auto accident medical expense benefits, some cards provide emergency medical services benefits for illness or accident suffered by traveling cardholders. Finally, in an obvious potential overlap with homeowners policies, some cards provide extremely broad protection for loss of or damage to goods purchased with the card for a limited period after purchase.

Issuers of credit cards with these kinds of enhancements typically do not directly adjust claims. A servicing entity of some sort, often an insurer, usually is involved. In some cases, the benefits themselves are provided to the credit card organization by a policy issued by an insurer. From the standpoint of the claimant, it is not insurance but a contractual agreement of the credit card organization.

Third Parties

As a matter of law rather than contract, an insured may have a legally enforceable right to reimbursement from another for a loss covered in whole or in part by insurance protecting that insured's interest. The "third party" may or may not have liability insurance that would protect it against the financial consequences of such an obligation, actual or alleged. If Ann carries automobile collision insurance and her car is struck by another vehicle negligently operated, Ann has a contractual right to recovery under her own insurance *and* a right under tort law to seek recovery from the other operator.[7] Does the presence of an at-fault party compromise or mitigate Ann's insurer's responsibility to her? Does the presence of Ann's collision coverage compromise or mitigate the extent of the negligent party's obligation to her? In general, the answer to both questions is "no."

The tort-based obligation of another party, with or without liability insurance to cover that obligation, does not affect the nature or extent of a first-party insurer's responsibility to its insured, unless some provision in the contract says otherwise. "Other insurance" provisions simply do not address either tort rights against another or liability insurance protecting that other party. In practice, Ann's collision insurer might pay nothing, but only because the other party (or that party's insurer) steps forward, recognizes the obligation, and discharges it. Or, the collision insurer might pay the loss, then subrogate against the other party.

Generally speaking, a tortfeasor (or the tortfeasor's liability insurance) is not relieved of any burden because of any insurance or noninsurance source of direct benefit to the party wronged by the tortfeasor. As the party primarily responsible, the tortfeasor cannot avoid or reduce consequences of the wrong merely because of collateral sources available to the other party. This notion, as embodied in the "collateral source rule," will be discussed later.

With some perils often covered in first-party coverages, the mere occurrence of the peril equates with a right of recovery against a third party. Vandalism and any version of theft fall in this category—a person found guilty of such a crime may be obligated to restore the victim. Granted, the right of recovery means little in most such cases. An exception is employee dishonesty insurance, a line in which insurer subrogation recoveries may be substantial because the identity of the perpetrator is often known. Of course, no *liability* coverage for the third party is involved for losses arising out of intentional criminal acts.

"OTHER INSURANCE" PROVISIONS

This text uses the phrase "other insurance" provisions in a broad sense to encompass *all policy provisions, regardless of their title, that attempt to specify in advance of a loss how an insurer's obligation will be affected by other insurance applying to the same loss.*

Virtually all property and liability insurance policies contain at least one provision dealing with other insurance. Many property and liability insurance policies contain a section clearly labeled *Other Insurance.* Policy language under many other captions also may deal with other insurance. These provisions too qualify as "other insurance" provisions because of their content, if not their label.

Some health insurance policies contain "other insurance" provisions. In group medical expense insurance the caption *Coordination of Benefits* often is used to identify them. Although this text concentrates on property and liability insurance, some discussion of health insurance is necessary because the question arises whether health coverage might qualify as other insurance under some liability policies, and vice versa.

In the past it was generally safe to assume that "other insurance" provisions were contractual in origin and dealt solely with other *insurance* in the literal sense. Today some "other insurance" provisions are prescribed by statute, and some encompass sources of recovery other than insurance. These points will be examined further as the chapter progresses.

Other-Insurance Situations

An *other-insurance situation* exists when more than one insurance source provides recovery for the same interest, cause of loss, and dollars of loss. Unless some external source of recovery exists, an "other insurance" provision has no effect. But what is other insurance? What situations present duplicate or overlapping coverage between or among different insurance policies or different components of the same policy? A simple two-policy example, later expanded slightly, will illustrate the answer to these questions. The specific "other insurance" policy provisions that resolve these situations will be examined later. For now, a few examples characterize other-insurance situations themselves.

Suppose Erica is an insured under two policies, and an incident, which qualifies under both policies as an insured event, involves adverse financial consequences to Erica. Assume that the insurer that issued each policy has an obligation to her for at least some of the same dollars of loss. With respect to these doubly-covered loss dollars, an "other insurance" situation exists. Two policies duplicate or overlap one another. Erica need not be a named insured, premium payor, or policyowner in either or both policies, so long as she is an insured party.

To put this general principle within the context of some specific policies, assume Erica borrows Bill's auto and uses it with his permission. Erica's own auto liability insurance "follows" her while using a borrowed car. Bill's policy also provides Erica with liability coverage. If the other policy did not exist, each of these two policies would defend Erica and, on her behalf, pay up to its limit any dollar amount Erica might legally be obligated to pay others as damages because of bodily injury or property damage arising out of her use of Bill's car. This is clearly an other-insurance situation, involving the same insured party, the same cause of loss, and the same loss consequences. Each of these two policies, *standing alone*, obligates its insurer to respond to a liability claim against Erica. But these policies do not stand alone. Because other insurance exists, the extent of each insurer's obligation depends on the nature and application of its "other insurance" provisions.

To add another dimension to this example, suppose Erica carries a personal umbrella liability policy which, as is typical, includes liability coverage for auto-related claims. Would the existence of this excess liability policy constitute other insurance that triggers the "other insurance" provision of Erica's and Bill's policies? Not normally. While excess or umbrella policies may cover the same parties and causes, they apply only to *dollars* of loss above a certain layer of coverage. (More specifically, umbrella policies typically apply to dollar losses exceeding either a specified amount or the limits of insurance otherwise available to the insured.) Policy provisions that express this relationship will be examined later.

Taking yet another perspective, what about insurance carried by Mark, who is injured in an auto accident Erica causes? Might not this insurance reimburse Mark for at least some of his losses, thus duplicating some of the dollars that might be paid to him by Erica's liability insurers? Yes, *but* any sources of this sort are *not* other insurance within the context of the "other insurance" provisions in the policies covering Erica's auto liability exposure. Even though Mark might have access to several sources of recovery for some dollars of loss, and even though all of these sources might be "insurance" of some kind, any source directly obligated to an injured third party does not trigger the "other insurance" provisions in the policies protecting Erica. Different interests are involved as, from the perspective of each insured, are different causes and different consequences. Liability policies available to Erica cover claims alleging her legal responsibility to pay damages. Mark's insurance—whether it be auto medical payments coverage, auto no-fault coverage, or health insurance—covers his own financial losses. In the context of applying "other insurance" provisions, this is an important distinction.

Characteristics of "Other Insurance" Provisions

Most property and liability insurance policies contain at least one policy provision dealing with other insurance. Some "other insurance" provisions are obvious and simple, while others are subtle and complex. The following points need to be made before proceeding to a more specific examination of "other insurance" provisions.

- *"Other insurance" provisions are not necessarily limited to those labeled "Other Insurance."* The title may be functional in wording ("excess clause") rather than generic ("other insurance").
- *Provisions that most specifically address the subject of "other insurance" usually are found in the "conditions" section of an insurance policy.*
- *Policies with more than one distinct coverage section often contain more than one "other insurance" provision.* For example, homeowners policies deal with other insurance separately in their property and liability coverage sections, even though both clauses are titled "other insurance." Some commercial package policies, depending on the components included in the policy, may contain ten or more "other insurance" provisions, as well as other untitled provisions relating to other insurance.
- *A single "other insurance" clause may include more than one "other insurance" provision.* The pertinent provision in a widely used general liability coverage form, examined later in this chapter, includes three types of other-insurance language.
- *Any "other insurance" provision of a given type is not neces-*

sarily consistent with another of the same type. Further, literal and mutual application is impossible in many situations—for example, when only two policies provide coverage and each professes to be excess over any other policy.

● *Even consistent "other insurance" provisions can be difficult to apply because of coverage differences ("nonconcurrencies") elsewhere in the policies.*

A later section of this chapter describes some of the ways in which conflicts among "other insurance" provisions are handled.

Types of "Other Insurance" Provisions

"Other insurance" provisions may attempt to accomplish one or more of the following effects:

1. To *exonerate* the insurer from liability
2. To limit the insurer's liability to a *proportion* of the loss
3. To limit the insurer's liability to that part of the loss that is in *excess* of the other insurance
4. To make the insurance *primary* with respect to other insurance
5. To *maintain the principle of indemnity* without indicating any specific position with respect to other insurance

Exonerating Provisions. An "other insurance" provision in some policies may exonerate (relieve or free) the insurer from any obligation if other insurance exists. Coverage including this type of provision sometimes is referred to as *contingent insurance,* and the exonerating language itself sometimes is called an *escape clause.*

Over time, this approach to other-insurance situations has involved at least the following four formats:

1. *Prohibition* of other insurance
2. An *exclusion* of property or activities covered by other insurance
3. A *general disclaimer* of responsibility if other insurance applies
4. An *offset* that reduces the coverage limit by the amount of other insurance

"Other insurance" provisions generally support the principle of indemnity by preventing overpayment or duplicate payment for the same loss. Exonerating provisions, however, are an exception. The principle of indemnity holds that an insured should not profit from a loss by receiving more than the actual loss sustained by that insured. *Exonerating provisions,* as a class, are not concerned with limiting the payment to the actual loss sustained. Indeed, they may well cap the insured's total recovery at something less than the amount lost, depending on the adequacy and terms of the other insurance itself.

Prohibitions. Strict prohibitions of other insurance are largely of historical interest, although they may still be found in ocean marine hull coverage and in direct loss property insurance on "unprotected" rural property presenting a relatively high probability of total loss. A prohibition of other insurance amounts to a policy condition in the most literal sense: It qualifies the insurer's promise of protection by making it contingent upon the absence of other insurance. Breaching this condition can result in a denial of coverage.

For some years homeowners policies used by many insurance companies contained the following prohibition against other insurance:

> Other insurance covering the described dwelling building (except insurance against perils not covered by this policy) is not permitted.

One reason for this provision was that insurers wanted the homeowners policy itself to cover the dwelling in an amount representing a reasonably high percentage of its insurable value. The importance of insurance to value was discussed in Chapter 7. Several related factors also were involved in the early years of homeowners insurance, which offered a single package policy combining, at a lower premium, coverages previously handled through separate policies. First, the problems of inadequate insurance to value were exacerbated under a pricing structure that already reflected a package discount. Second, inadequate insurance to value had traditionally been a problem for household personal property. The homeowners policies attempted to remedy this problem by providing personal property coverage equal to a fixed percentage of the amount of coverage on the dwelling, but this remedy was defeated whenever the dwelling itself was underinsured. The pricing structure and underwriting intent of homeowners policies would be defeated if insurance buyers could purchase separate fire insurance policies on the dwelling (as they had in the past) and use a low-limit homeowners policy as a supplement. In a sense, this "other insurance" provision was an example of underwriting through the policy rather than through underwriting evaluation. At any rate, the times have changed, along with insurance pricing structures and buying habits. Current homeowners forms do not contain this prohibition on other insurance. It is difficult to imagine a situation in which one would intentionally purchase duplicate homeowners insurance, except perhaps during some brief transitional period such as moving from one residence to another or changing one's marital status.

Another prohibition on other insurance appears in directors and officers (D&O) liability policies involving a large retention (deductible). The purpose of the retention is to encourage loss control by making the insured participate substantially in any loss; this purpose would not be served by any device that would eliminate the deductible. The limit of liability provision of one D&O policy includes the following words:

> This policy shall pay only the excess of such retention . . . and such retention shall be uninsured.

Exclusions. Some exclusions clarify insurer intent by eliminating from coverage certain property or activities that may or should be covered by other policies. For example, the liability coverage of homeowners policies excludes coverage for most auto-related losses which, one would expect, should be covered by auto liability insurance. These are not "other insurance" provisions, since they apply even when other insurance does not exist.

In contrast, some policies contain *exclusions* that negate coverage only if other insurance applies. These are "other insurance" provisions in effect, if not in name. As an example, homeowners personal property coverage typically excludes "articles separately described and specifically insured in this or any other insurance." If a homeowners insured bought coverage in a separate inland marine floater—or in an equivalent homeowners endorsement—to cover specific identified items of jewelry with limit(s) available only for the jewelry, the jewelry would no longer be covered under the personal property section of the homeowners policy. The effect is to shift all responsibility for insured loss payment to the policy or endorsement that has generated a premium solely for the jewelry coverage. Note that this exclusion applies even if the specific insurance is inadequate—for example, if the jewelry is worth more than the limit of insurance in the jewelry floater.

(Some exclusionary "other insurance" language contains a "give back" to the extent the other insurance is inadequate. The result is not an exonerating provision in the form of an exclusion but an excess provision expressed as an exception to the exclusion. This approach will be illustrated later.)

General Disclaimers. When used, the disclaimer variety of exonerating provision typically is confined to some aspect of policy coverage rather than to the policy as a whole. It is not unusual to see some fringe or supplemental component of coverage applicable only if no other insurance applies. For example, "commercial property" insurance policies insuring buildings routinely cover any addition to the described building while the addition is in progress, but only if the addition is not covered by other insurance. Some personal auto policies grant automatic coverage on a newly-acquired vehicle provided no other insurance applies to the vehicle. The benefits available under an extended reporting period, or "tail," in claims-made liability coverage may be conditioned on the absence of other insurance covering the same claim.

Some statutory coverages—such as automobile personal injury protection—may be subject to statutes prescribing primacy and exclusive coverage which, in effect, rules out coverage under another policy that otherwise would apply. Consider a state in which the personal injury protection in the policy "on the car" is by statute "first in line" to pay benefits to any occupant of the car, while "stacking" is prohibited. A guest passenger, even though carrying his or her own policy with personal injury protection, would look solely to the insurer of the car (that is, to the policy in which the involved auto is described) for personal injury protection benefits. Even if the passenger's loss exceeded any limit(s) in this policy, the passenger's own insurer may be exonerated from any responsibility.

Offsets. An *offset* is involved when the policy limit of one coverage is reduced by the policy limit of other insurance applicable to the same loss. Two possible scenarios are involved:

- When the limit of the other insurance equals or exceeds the limit in the policy containing the offset provision, the intent is to exonerate the latter policy completely.
- When the policy with the offset provision has the higher limit, it is intended to provide excess insurance—but *only to the extent of the difference between the two policy limits.*

In either case, the sum of both limits is not available. In other words, limits of the two policies cannot be "stacked." Both scenarios may be illustrated by the following uninsured motorists coverage endorsement used in one particular state:

> Any insurance we provide with respect to a vehicle you do not own shall be excess over any other collectible insurance but only to the extent that the limit of liability under this policy exceeds the limit of other such collectible insurance.

This provision could act as either an exonerating provision or a partial excess provision, depending on the limits of any other applicable uninsured motorists coverage. In nearly all cases, it seems the extent of other applicable uninsured motorists coverage would be a matter of chance, and not of advance planning.[8]

A similar approach is taken by some auto insurers in handling cases in which the *same insurer* has issued duplicating policies *to the same entity.* A frequently used provision, perhaps titled something like "Two or More Policies Issued by Us," attempts to make it clear that the insurer's total obligation is not greater than the highest applicable limit in any one of its policies. Again, the limits cannot be stacked, but in this case the limits are in policies of the same insurer issued to the same entity. This clause does not affect the obligation of the insurer in the broader other-insurance context, such as a situation in which the same person is an insured under one insurer's policies issued to two different named insureds. (For example, Erica and Bill purchase their auto insurance from the same insurance company and Erica is driving Bill's car.)

Proportional Provisions. One of the most common types of "other insurance" provisions has the effect of limiting an insurer's obligation to some proportion of the overall loss. These are sometimes called "pro rata" or "contributing" provisions. All involve capping what an insurer will pay at some proportional or fractional share of a loss also covered by other insurance. This is their purpose—*limiting* payment—despite the "loss *sharing*" characteristic frequently attributed to this family of "other insurance" provisions. Loss sharing on a proportional basis may *result* from the application of these provisions, but it is not their *purpose*.

Proportional provisions may take one of the following three forms:

1. Proration by face amounts (or limits of insurance)
2. Proration by amounts otherwise payable
3. Contribution by equal shares

A related provision, also discussed here, is the so-called *apportionment clause*. The bulk of that clause qualifies as a proportional "other insurance" provision. But the rest of the provision is not an "other insurance" provision at all, even though its arithmetic operation is similar to that of a proportional provision and it is usually discussed in the same context.

Proration by Face Amounts. As explained in Chapter 6, all policies contain one or more limits of insurance. These limits usually are expressed numerically, but in a few cases are expressed verbally and converted to quantitative terms after a loss (for example, a loss payment limited to the actual cash value of an auto).

In the typical other-insurance situation, two or more policies—each with its own applicable limit—apply to the same loss. Where it is applicable, *proration by face amounts limits the insurer's maximum obligation to the proportion of the* loss *that the insurer's* policy limit *bears to the sum of all applicable policy limits*. This same concept may be expressed in formula form as follows:

$$\frac{(\text{A's limit})}{(\text{A's limit} + \text{B's limit} + \text{C's limit} + \ldots)} \times \text{Loss} = \text{A's maximum obligation}$$

If two insurers are involved, A's limit is \$10,000, B's limit is \$20,000, and a \$3,000 loss occurs, then A would be contractually obligated to pay no more than one-third of the \$3,000 loss (that is, \$1,000). If B's policy contains a similar provision, its obligation is limited to \$2,000. Notice that the *available* coverage amounts in the policies are not changed by this type of other-insurance provision. Proportional provisions do not subtract coverage. Had the loss been $30,000 or larger, each policy would pay its limit of insurance.

This and other proportional "other insurance" provisions could be viewed as methods for allocating, or apportioning, losses among insurers, rather than as payment-limiting features, but this view would neglect the history of proration by face amounts. Early policies of fire insurance in this country made no reference to other insurance; yet multiple-insurer coverage of the same loss did occur. To the extent that these situations got to court, absent compelling circumstances dictating a different outcome the courts adopted a general rule identical to proration by face amounts, *but* they permitted the insured to recover directly from *any* involved insurer. The paying insurer was then entitled to a contribution from the other involved insurer(s), with the amount of each insurer's contribution based on the proportion of the total insurance provided by that other insurer. The paying insurer had no choice but to assume the task of recovering the other insurer's "share" from the other insurer, that is, to enforce its right of contribution. Obtaining contribution was sometimes difficult, so insurers began solving that post-loss problem through payment-limiting policy language rather than inter-insurer claims for contribution after the fact. Thus, the purpose of these early clauses was to insulate insurers from initially having to pay more than they would end up having to pay after securing contribution from other involved insurers in accordance with the common-law rule. Preserving or reinforcing the principle of indemnity by preventing duplicate payment simply was not an issue, since fire insurance policies were recognized as contracts of indemnity and prohibitions against insureds recovering more than actual loss sustained were uniformly enforced by the courts.

Over the years, proration by face amount as the operative "other insurance" provision has been the norm in fixed-location property insurance. This type of insurance has been called "fire insurance," "fire and allied lines insurance," or, more recently, simply "property insurance." At the heart of this line of insurance for much of the past century have been several versions of the so-called "Standard Fire Policy." These documents have used proration by face amounts.[9] Under the caption of "Pro rata Liability," the 1943 New York Standard Fire Policy reads:

> This Company shall not be liable for a greater proportion of any loss than the amount hereby insured shall bear to the whole insurance covering the property against the peril involved, whether collectible or not.

Later versions of fixed-location property contracts have retained the essence of this position but have been inconsistent on the inclusion of "whether collectible or not" or words of similar import. The recent tendency is to include it. To the extent that a similar provision has been used in other lines such as liability insurance, the application of the provision has usually been qualified by the requirement that the other insurance be "valid and collectible" or "applicable," or the like, but some provisions are entirely silent on the matter. Note the following pertinent excerpts from widely used liability coverages.

> If other valid and collectible insurance is available to the insured for a loss we cover . . . our obligations are limited as follows. . . .

> This condition applies only if . . . the insured has other insurance . . . covering the same obligation to pay. . . .

The first is explicit on the question of valid and collectible; the second is not.

The difference can be important. Insurance may be uncollectible for a variety of reasons—including fraud or misrepresentation in obtaining it, breach of condition, and insurer insolvency, among others. If another insurance policy exists but is of no benefit to the insured, does it qualify as "other insurance" that permits the application of a payment-limiting "other insurance" provision? The "collectible or not" wording enables the insurer to limit its liability to what it would pay if the other insurance had no constraints on its payment. While at first that outcome might seem unfair to the insured, it is part of the agreement between the parties, and the premium charged reflects that agreement. In other words, the insurer would pay some additional loss dollars, and rates would therefore have to be slightly higher if other uncollectible insurance were to be ignored in calculating insurers' obligations. The reduction in premium is the legal "consideration" required for a valid contract to exist.

A slight variant of the above question focuses on the link between collectibility and other phrases common in "other insurance" provisions. The Standard Fire Policy provision quoted above makes reference to "the whole insurance covering the property." Is a policy under which insurance is uncollectible one "covering the property"? The property section of common current homeowners policies reads:

> Other Insurance. If a loss covered by this policy is also covered by other insurance, we will pay only the proportion of the loss that the limit of liability that applies under this policy bears to the total amount of insurance covering the loss.

No mention is made of collectibility, since the "collectibility" phrase was dropped in an earlier policy revision. Is a loss subject to other, uncollectible insurance "covered by other insurance"? Is the other, uncollectible insurance part of "the total amount of insurance covering the loss"? The answer to both questions is probably "no." On the other hand, the obligations of an insolvent insurer often are fulfilled by a state guaranty fund. Is the obligation of a guaranty fund to be considered "other insurance," therefore permitting the application of a payment-limiting "other insurance" provision? Possibly, though the delay inherent in payment by a guaranty fund might also lead a court to conclude that it does not constitute "other insurance."

Proration by Amounts Otherwise Payable. A second form of proportional "other insurance" provision is based on what would be payable under each policy in the absence of other insurance. A policy's *limit* of insurance is *not* involved unless that limit represents what the insurer would have *paid* if it had been the only policy applying to the loss. If, standing alone, a policy would have paid something less than its limit of insurance, that lower amount is the "amount payable" for this purpose. In determining this amount, all pertinent policy provisions—loss settlement, coinsurance, deductible, sublimits—are respected and applied.

Under proration by amounts payable, a policy's obligation is limited to the same proportion of the loss that its amount payable, determined as described above, bears to the sum of that amount and the amount(s) payable, similarly determined, of the other policy(ies) involved. In formula form this can be expressed as follows:

$$\frac{\text{(A's amount payable)}}{\text{(A's amount payable + B's amount payable + C's ...)}} \times \text{Loss}$$

$$= \text{A's maximum obligation}$$

To take an admittedly oversimplified example, suppose a $40,000 loss is covered by Insurer A under a policy with a face amount of $90,000. The loss is also (partly) covered by Insurer B under a policy with a face amount of $10,000. If both policies contained an "other insurance" clause requiring *proration by face amounts*, the approach discussed earlier, Insurer A would pay 90 percent of the loss (or $36,000) and Insurer B would pay 10 percent of the loss (or $4,000). In formula form this would be expressed as follows:

Proration by Face Amounts:

$$\text{A's obligation} = \frac{\$90,000}{(\$90,000 + \$10,000)} \times \$40,000 = \$36,000$$

$$\text{B's obligation} = \frac{\$10,000}{(\$90,000 + \$10,000)} \times \$40,000 = \$4,000$$

Alternatively, if both policies contained a clause requiring proration according to the amount payable by each policy, standing alone, Insurer A would pay $32,000 and Insurer B would pay $8,000. Why? If the $90,000 policy had been the only policy, its insurer would have paid no more than $40,000, the amount of the loss. If the $10,000 policy had been the only policy, its insurer would have paid no more than $10,000, its upper limit of liability. In formula form, this is as follows:

Proration by Amounts Payable:

$$\text{A's obligation} = \frac{\$40,000}{(\$40,000 + \$10,000)} \times \$40,000 = \$32,000$$

$$\text{B's obligation} = \frac{\$10,000}{(\$40,000 + \$10,000)} \times \$40,000 = \$8,000$$

Here, the denominator is not the sum of the two policy faces; it is the sum of the amounts that would be payable if each policy stood by itself and the other policy did not exist.

In the past, proration by amounts payable was routinely part of boiler and machinery policies and of fire insurance policies that could overlap boiler and machinery policies. The language often was called a "joint loss" provision, since it specified that the portion of loss dually covered was a "joint loss." It built a degree of equity into overlapping coverage situations that writers of fire insurance much preferred over proration by face amounts. Under the face amounts approach, a fire insurer with a multi-million dollar policy limit covering the insured's property generally would have been called upon to pay a very large proportion of a loss jointly covered by the fire policy and the boiler policy with (typically) a much smaller limit. The view was that this outcome was unfair to fire insurers since the boiler insurer received a premium for coverage that focused on the boiler or other covered object. Because of coverage modifications reducing the likelihood of overlaps between these two lines of insurance, current standard forms do not provide for proration by amounts payable.[10]

Before the 1984 edition, the workers compensation and employers liability policy used proration by amounts payable. The provision read:

Other Insurance. If the insured has other insurance against a loss covered by this policy, the company shall not be liable to the insured hereunder for a greater proportion of such loss than the amount which would have been payable under this policy, had no such other insurance existed, bears to the sum of said amount and the amounts which would have been payable under each other policy applicable to such loss, had each such policy been the only policy so applicable.

In the typical case involving workers compensation benefits and, say, two policies, the application of this provision resulted in the payment of one-half the loss by each insurer. That would follow since, presumably, each policy standing alone would have paid the same amount—the statutory benefits. The current policy provides for contribution by equal shares, to be explained below. This produces the same result as proration by amounts payable for workers compensation coverage, but not necessarily for the employers liability coverage of the policy.

The approach to limiting, or determining, loss payment embodied in proration by amounts payable has a long history in resolving other-insurance problems. It has been and is a part of some inter-company agreements designed to untie knots in the determination of the liability of insurers when policy language conflicts or operates in a context of multiple meanings or obvious impossibility of application. Its evolution in this role has been under the label of the "limit of liability rule," with the term "limit of liability" having the same meaning as "amount payable" used in this text. Its utility as a breaker of deadlocks is based on a simple fact—it always works.

Contribution by Equal Shares. A third form of proportional "other insurance" provision is a product of the 1960s called "contribution by equal shares." An example found in a general liability coverage form, after introductory language dealing with other valid and collectible insurance, reads:

> If all of the other insurance permits contribution by equal shares, we will follow this method also. Under this approach each insurer contributes equal amounts until it has paid its applicable limit of insurance or none of the loss remains, whichever comes first.

This section of the policy's compound "other insurance" provision also contains additional language dealing with situations in which the other insurance does *not* specify contribution by equal shares.

To illustrate contribution by equal shares, assume a $60,000 claim within the scope of coverage provided by an insured's two general liability policies, Policy A with a $100,000 policy limit and Policy B with a $25,000 policy limit. Both policies provide for contribution by equal shares. The two insurers pay equal dollar amounts until the lower of the two policy limits, $25,000, is reached. At that point, $50,000 of the claim has been paid, leaving Policy A to pay the remaining $10,000 of the claim. Had the claim been smaller—say, $30,000—each policy would have paid $15,000 toward the total. By agreement between themselves, the two insurers usually decide which is to provide investigation and legal services, and the costs of these services would have been divided between them (in the same manner as the claims payments, unless otherwise stipulated in the policy or agreed to by the insurers).

Contribution by equal shares is related to the practice of charging lower rates for successively higher bands or levels of coverage in the same contract, in recognition of the reduced likelihood of larger losses. In other words, the premium increment is less than proportional to a limit of insurance increment. This point is illustrated by the factors shown in Exhibit 8-1, which happen to be used in rating commercial auto

Exhibit 8-1

Relationship Between Premiums and
Liability Limits

Increased Limits Limit	Factor
$ 25,000	1.00
35,000	1.08
50,000	1.16
100,000	1.33
250,000	1.56
300,000	1.61
350,000	1.66
500,000	1.76
1,000,000	1.98

bodily injury and property damage liability on light and medium trucks in one state. Other factors apply to other coverages and other states, but the general pattern is typical. The base premium applies for liability limits of $25,000. That premium is multiplied by the applicable "increased limits" factor for higher liability limits. The point here is that premium increases are not directly proportional to increases in limits of insurance, and they taper off as limits increase, reflecting the decreasing probability of larger losses. $1 million limits are forty times as great as $25,000 limits, but the premium is slightly less than twice as great. Likewise, the premium for a $1 million limit is only 8 percent greater than the premium for a $500,000 limit, although the limit itself is doubled.

Contribution by equal shares tends to put a proportionately greater burden on the policy having the lower limit, but this is equitable. In the above example, Policy A had a $100,000 limit of insurance and Policy B had a $25,000 limit of insurance. While Policy A provides four-fifths of the total coverage, its insurer receives only four-sevenths of the total annual premium (based on the factors in Exhibit 8-1), because the rate structure reflects the fact that losses between $25,000 and $100,000 are less likely than losses under $25,000 in amount. To "allocate" losses according to policy limits would be unfair to the insurer of the $100,000 policy; it would be paying 80 percent of most loss amounts, while collecting 57 percent of the total annual premium for both policies combined. Contribution by equal shares mitigates this inequity by reducing the loss-sharing burden of the insurer with the larger policy limit.

Apportionment. This term has two uses in the realm of other insurance. It has been used in a broad sense to name the process or methodology for allocating ("apportioning") a loss between or among insurers in an other-insurance situation. In a related but more specific use, it has served as the title of the "other insurance" provision in some policies, notably fire insurance policies containing the Standard Fire Policy plus a form that did or could extend the perils covered beyond the fire and lightning of the Standard Fire Policy. The latter use is the focus here.

This concept of apportionment is most readily examined in the light of the ways in which coverage evolved under the Standard Fire Policy. The Standard Fire Policy was expandable as to perils covered. Couple that fact with the once-common practice of covering the same property (for example, a commercial building) under more than one fire policy. These conditions created room for multiple fire policies covering the same property but not the same additional perils.

Consider the following simple example involving two policies and two losses. The policies are as follows:

- Policy A—a $100,000 policy providing building coverage against the perils of fire and lightning only
- Policy B—a $50,000 policy, providing fire and lightning coverage on the same building, but extended to cover windstorm and other perils also

Assume the following independent losses occur:

- Loss 1—a $3,000 fire loss
- Loss 2—a $3,000 windstorm loss

Loss 1, the fire loss, clearly is covered by both policies, each of which would pay according to proration by face amounts. Policy A's insurer would pay $2,000, and Policy B's would pay $1,000. Each insurer's liability is capped, and the insured is made whole.

Loss 2, the windstorm loss, involves an added dimension. The loss is not covered at all by Policy A, but it is well within the limit of Policy B, which provides windstorm coverage. Since no other insurance applies, does Policy B then pay the full $3,000 loss? Not if Policy B contains a provision like the following:

> Apportionment: This Company shall not be liable for a greater proportion of any loss less the amount of the deductible, if any, from any peril or perils included in this policy than (A) the amount of insurance under the policy bears to the whole amount of fire insurance covering the property, or which would have covered the property except for the existence of this insurance, whether collectible or not, *and whether or not such other fire insurance covers against the additional peril or perils insured against hereunder.* . . . [italics added]

This section of the policy's "apportionment" clause reads like an embellished Standard Fire Policy pro rata liability provision except for the phrase italicized here.[11] These words, coupled with the clause's earlier reference to "whole amount of fire insurance," convey that Policy B will limit its obligation *as it would have if Policy A covered the peril of windstorm.* Policy B's payment for the windstorm loss is limited to $1,000.

Obviously, this feature of the apportionment clause is not an "other insurance" provision at all. "Other insurance" provisions generally resolve situations in which two policies would otherwise provide duplicate coverage. Here the insurer's obligation is reduced because another policy *fails* to provide otherwise-duplicate coverage. There would be no penalty if all policies were extended to cover the windstorm peril (or whatever peril causes the loss). Likewise, there would be no penalty with respect to flood or any other peril not covered under a fire policy. The message delivered by the apportionment clause is that one should insure against perils *added to* fire policies as completely as one insures against the basic perils.

In a sense, the apportionment clause encourages the purchase of insurance to value against all perils; it discourages the idea of selecting different limits of coverage against different perils. Without the apportionment provision (and in the absence of a coinsurance clause or other loss-sharing provision), an insured might be inclined to purchase high limits of coverage against the basic perils and smaller limits against other perils less likely to cause a major loss.

This potentially punitive feature of fire insurance policies causes fewer problems than in years past for several reasons:

- The Standard Fire Policy approach to structuring fixed-location property insurance contracts is no longer the norm. Today many policies, both personal and commercial, automatically cover perils at least as broad as those in the Standard Fire Policy with its most common perils add-on of "extended coverage."[12] These perils attach to the same amount of insurance as the peril of fire. This greatly reduces the opportunities for and likelihood of being insured under one policy for fire only and another for fire plus additional perils.
- Increased use of reinsurance by insurers has diminished the need for insurance buyers to purchase multiple policies by obtaining adequate limits of insurance.
- Coinsurance and other practices or coverage incentives encouraging high insurance to value are widely used.
- Paralleling the developments above has been the reduced use of this type of language in fixed-location property coverages.

- Producers and underwriters have become more aware of the possible problems this type of nonconcurrency can create.

One continuing use of this potentially punitive provision is in the ISO dwelling property forms. The current version of these forms contains a clause that reads:

> Other Insurance. If property covered by this policy is also covered by other fire insurance, we will pay only the proportion of a loss caused by any peril insured against under this policy that the limit of liability applying under this policy bears to the total amount of fire insurance covering the property.

While differing in detail from the older "apportionment" clause, the message is the same. The form considers other "fire insurance" and "the total amount of fire insurance" in limiting its liability. For losses from the peril of fire, no potential penalty is involved. But if the dwelling policy covers additional perils not covered in the policy(ies) providing the "other fire insurance," and one of these additional perils causes a loss, this provision calls for the same result as the older "apportionment" clause.

Excess Provisions. Many property-liability policies contain an "other insurance" provision designed to make the coverage "excess over" any other insurance that applies to the same loss. Excess provisions are common in crime, inland marine, ocean marine, auto, and general liability coverages. In the last three of these lines, the excess language is typically part of a compound provision.

Most liability coverage excess provisions apply only if the other insurance is valid and collectible. In policies covering property, a majority are either silent on the matter or affirmatively state that the excess applies even if the other insurance is uncollectible. Compare the following excerpts from two "other insurance" provisions. The first is from a commercial auto policy; the second is from a package policy for small businesses. These excerpts apply to both the property and liability coverages of their respective policies:

> For any covered "auto" you don't own, the insurance provided by this Coverage Form is excess over any other collectible insurance.

> If there is other insurance covering the same loss or damage, we will pay only for the amount of covered loss or damage in excess of the amount due from that other insurance, whether you can collect on it or not.

Like proportional provisions, true excess "other insurance" provisions do not deprive the insured of any of the limit of insurance that would be available in the absence of other insurance. The goal is to avoid being primary—that is, to prevent paying or sharing in any portion of a loss covered by other insurance. Should the loss be large enough to exhaust the other insurance, the entire limit of the policy with the excess provision would be available if needed. Assume Nancy borrows Kay's car. Both Nancy and Kay carry liability coverage under typical personal auto policies. Nancy's limit is $300,000; Kay's limit is $100,000. Nancy strikes a pedestrian and is sued. A $100,000 judgment against Nancy results. By its terms, Nancy's policy is excess over other collectible insurance with respect to autos that Nancy does not own. Its intent is to pay nothing of the judgment. If the judgment is for $150,000, Nancy's policy pays $50,000. If the judgment were $400,000, Nancy's policy would pay $300,000.[13]

If Kay's policy is uncollectible, perhaps due to a breach of policy condition or insurer insolvency, Nancy's policy serves as primary insurance in all three cases. This point shows the difference between coverage subject to an excess "other insurance" clause and an excess insurance policy. An excess "other insurance" provision makes a policy excess only when other insurance applies. Absent other insurance, the policy is primary and the excess provision is simply inoperative policy verbiage. In contrast, a true excess insurance policy is intended to be excess from the outset. It remains an excess policy, subject to a deductible or self-insured retention, even when there is no underlying insurance. Excess and umbrella policies are so common in liability insurance that the primary policy's "other insurance" clause often explicitly recognizes their existence. The personal liability section of the homeowners policy forms illustrates this point:

Other Insurance-Coverage E—Personal Liability
This insurance is excess over other valid and collectible insurance
except insurance written specifically to cover as excess over the limits
of liability that apply in this policy.

Notice the explicit exception referred to in the second half of the quoted sentence. The clause affirms that the homeowners liability coverage is intended to serve as underlying insurance in relation to exposures which also are covered by any excess liability policy.[14]

Most excess "other insurance" provisions make the policy with the provision excess over other insurance regardless of the date when the other insurance became effective. A somewhat different approach is customary in ocean marine insurance, however. When two or more policies are involved, an ocean marine policy is made primary or excess by its relative effective date. For example, suppose two policies are written to cover the same cargo. According to the usual ocean marine "other insurance" clause, the policy with the earlier effective date is primary. The policy with the later effective date is excess over the limits of the primary policy. If a third policy had a still later effective date, it would be excess over the second policy. All policies bearing the same effective date are deemed to be effective simultaneously, in which case the insurers' liability is determined according to proration by face amounts.

An interesting excess provision is found in the ISO personal auto policy. It is part of a compound provision titled "Other Sources of Recovery" that is not confined in its application to other-insurance situations. Instead, as the title indicates, its scope embraces both insurance and noninsurance sources of recovery. The excess portion of the provision reads as follows:

> However, any insurance we provide with respect to a "non-owned auto" shall be excess over any other collectible source of recovery including, but not limited to:
> 1. Any coverage provided by the owner of the "non-owned auto;"
> 2. Any other applicable physical damage insurance;
> 3. Any other source of recovery applicable to the loss.

This provision is one of the few instances of a policy provision dealing with other insurance being worded broadly enough to apply even if another source of recovery is not insurance. Item 3 clearly is broad enough to include the credit card "coverage" described earlier in this chapter. How this excess status fits with the credit card enhancement is an open question. Some cards state that their protection is primary, but a majority apply only to loss not already covered by other means including the auto renter's personal insurance. In most cases, then, the credit card coverage is excess, which obviously does not square with the personal auto policy's excess stance.

Another example of an "other insurance" provision that recognizes noninsurance sources is the workers compensation and employers liability policy, where reference is made to "other insurance or self-insurance."

Primary Provisions. It should be obvious by now that the terms "excess" and "primary" may refer to either different "levels" of coverage or the same "levels" of coverage.

- An excess policy, because of its large deductible, operates at a high "level," placing a "layer" of coverage on top of the upper limits of any primary or underlying policies.
- By virtue of its excess "other insurance" clause, a primary policy may itself become excess over the limits of other primary policies, even though both policies begin at the same "level."
- A given policy may have a clause explicitly stating that coverage is primary. The insurer agrees to pay its limit of insurance before any other insurance policy applies to the loss.

One example of a policy explicitly providing primary coverage is the ocean marine policy that becomes primary by virtue of its effective date. Another may be found in a commercial auto form that contains the following other insurance references:

> For any covered "auto" you own, this Coverage Form provides primary insurance. For any covered "auto" you don't own, the insurance provided by this Coverage Form is excess over any other collectible insurance.

> When this Coverage Form and any other Coverage Form or policy covers on the same basis, either excess or primary, we will pay only our share. Our share is the proportion that the Limit of Insurance of our Coverage Form bears to the total of the limits of all the Coverage Forms and policies covering on the same basis.

Just as two policies cannot simultaneously be excess, neither can two policies simultaneously be primary to one another. Therefore, an alternative arrangement is frequently provided to resolve such conflicts. Here, it is proration by face amounts. In general liability insurance, it is proration by face amounts or, if the other policy contains a similar provision, contribution by equal shares. Notice also the illustration in the second cited paragraph of "other insurance" language dealing with other insurance in the same policy. The reference to any other "Coverage Form or policy" anticipates that the duplication or overlapping of coverage could be with some other component of the same policy *or* with another policy. For example, the auto coverage form from which the quoted material above was taken could overlap with others, including (1) a general liability coverage form in the same policy, or (2) a personal auto policy carried by someone who is also an insured under the commercial auto policy. The coverage intricacies to document these overlaps are beyond the scope of this text, but these intricacies are by design and not the result of sloppy policy drafting or creative interpretation.

With respect to auto no-fault or personal injury protection benefits, "other insurance" provisions invariably reflect the applicable statute. Usually, the intent is to make no-fault auto benefits excess over any comparable benefits payable under workers compensation or compulsory temporary disability insurance statutes. On the other hand, the intent usually is to make no-fault auto benefits primary in relation to voluntary forms of health insurance. Voluntary health insurance may or may not duplicate the no-fault auto benefits, depending on the "other insurance" provision, if any, of the voluntary health insurance in question.

When two or more no-fault auto coverages apply to the same accident, some laws stipulate that the vehicle owner's benefits apply on a primary basis to the owner or the owner's resident relatives, and on an excess basis to all other eligible persons (for example, occupants of the insured vehicle who are not relatives of the owner, or pedestrians who are struck by the insured vehicle). Other states stipulate that the owner's benefits apply on a primary basis to all occupants of the insured vehicle. Under either kind of law, duplications of auto no-fault benefits are avoided. One auto policy invariably provides the no-fault benefits on a primary basis.

Except for true excess policies written subject to a large straight deductible, every policy will provide what is, in effect, primary coverage when it is the only policy that covers a particular loss. This can happen in several different ways:

1. The coverage of a property insurance policy is primary when it is the only policy covering the property.
2. Even if several policies cover the same property, a policy provides primary coverage when it insures against perils, such as earthquake or flood, which are excluded by all the other policies of the insured.
3. The standard workers compensation policy provides primary coverage for statutory benefits when it is the only workers compensation policy applicable, because job-connected accidents and diseases are virtually always excluded or covered on an excess basis by auto and health insurance policies. (In the few situations in which two workers compensation policies apply, the loss is prorated as noted earlier).
4. The coverage of a policy that contains an excess "other insurance" provision becomes primary when there is no other insurance or (in some cases) when the other insurance is not collectible or is not valid at the time of loss.
5. When the "other insurance" clause of a policy calls for proration by amounts payable, the coverage of such a policy becomes primary when no amounts are payable by the other policy(ies).

In each of these five situations, the coverage of a policy is or becomes primary, apart from whether the policy explicitly contains a primary type of "other insurance" clause, because the policy is the only one that covers the loss.

Maintaining the Principle of Indemnity. The primary purpose of some "other insurance" provisions is to maintain the principle of indemnity ("an insured should not profit from a loss"). Consider the following statement in the conditions section of a "commercial property" policy, under the heading "Insurance Under Two or More Coverages":

> If two or more of this policy's coverages apply to the same loss or damage, we will not pay more than the actual amount of the loss or damage.

This provision recognizes that there could be duplication between coverages in the same coverage part or between this coverage part and another coverage part of the same policy. The provision makes it clear that the insurer will pay no more than the actual loss sustained by the insured, regardless of any coverage overlap.

Compound "Other Insurance" Provisions. As mentioned much earlier in this discussion, any given "other insurance" provision does not necessarily describe only one approach to other insurance. Now that the approaches have been discussed individually, it is time to show an "other insurance" provision in its entirety within the context of a policy that includes some additional provisions that, though they are not labeled "other insurance," also address the topic.

This point will be illustrated by using the "occurrence" and "claims-made" versions of the ISO commercial general liability coverage forms. Both variants include the "Other Insurance" provision shown in Exhibit 8-2. In addition, both contain another provision dealing with "other insurance." The claims-made variant also contains an additional "other insurance" provision.

The points of interest in this provision include the following:

1. It is operative only if the other insurance is valid and collectible.
2. By specifying that its home base is "this Coverage Part," it recognizes that another coverage part in the same policy could provide the other insurance triggering the provision.
3. With exceptions noted below, the coverage is primary insurance. If another primary policy applies, a "sharing" approach, to be described later, applies.
4. Exceptions to the primary role, making the coverage excess, are noted. How can this policy be excess to another policy that, by its own terms, is excess or contingent? More on that later.
5. Items b.(1) and b.(2) in Exhibit 8-2 refer to direct loss property coverages that may insure the interest of the same entity covered by the general liability policy. Item b.(3) recognizes that the general liability policy exclusion is not a total exclusion of liability arising out of aircraft, autos, or watercraft.
6. When the policy is made excess by this provision, the "Excess Insurance" section absolves the insurer of a duty to defend if another insurer has a similar duty, unless the other insurer refuses. The paragraph then makes it clear that a deductible in the other insurance, or an amount retained by the insured that is primary to the other insurance, will not be covered by this policy as a portion of the loss that is in excess of that other insurance.
7. The final paragraph under "Excess Insurance" is out of kilter with the title. It is a "sharing" (proration) provision, with no detail on the basis for sharing.

Exhibit 8-2

"Other Insurance" Provision in the Commercial General Liability Coverage Form

---

Other Insurance.

If other valid and collectible insurance is available to the insured for a loss we cover under Coverages A or B of this Coverage Part, our obligations are limited as follows:

a. Primary Insurance

This insurance is primary except when b. below applies. If this insurance is primary, our obligations are not affected unless any of the other insurance is also primary. Then, we will share with all that other insurance by the method described in c. below.

b. Excess Insurance

This insurance is excess over any of the other insurance, whether primary, excess, contingent or on any other basis:

(1) That is Fire, Extended Coverage, Builder's Risk, Installation Risk or similar coverage for "your work;"

(2) That is Fire insurance for premises rented to you; or

(3) If the loss arises out of the maintenance or use of aircraft, "autos" or watercraft to the extent not subject to Exclusion g. of Coverage A (Section I).

When this insurance is excess, we will have no duty under Coverage A or B to defend any claim or "suit" that any other insurer has a duty to defend. If no other insurer defends, we will undertake to do so, but we will be entitled to the insured's rights against all those other insurers.

When this insurance is excess over other insurance, we will pay only our share of the amount of the loss, if any, that exceeds the sum of:

(1) The total amount that all such other insurance would pay for the loss in the absence of this insurance; and

(2) The total of all deductible and self-insured amounts under all that other insurance.

We will share the remaining loss, if any, with any other insurance that is not described in this Excess Insurance provision and was not bought specifically to apply in excess of the Limits of Insurance shown in the Declarations of this Coverage Part.

c. Method of Sharing

If all other insurance permits contribution by equal shares, we will follow this method also. Under this approach each insurer contributes equal amounts until it has paid its applicable limit of insurance or none of the loss remains, whichever comes first.

If any of the other insurance does not permit contribution by equal shares, we will contribute by limits. Under this method, each insurer's share is based on the ratio of its applicable limit of insurance to the total applicable limits of insurance of all insurers.

Form CG 00 01 11 88, Copyright Insuranced Services Office, Inc., 1982, 1988.

8. Where "sharing" is the end result, it will be according to contribution by equal shares or proration by face amounts depending on the "other insurance" provision in the other policy or policies.

The commercial general liability coverage forms also contain two "other insurance" provisions of the exonerating type in the policy section titled, "Who Is an Insured." The relevant provisions are underscored in Exhibit 8-3, which quotes the entire policy section to emphasize the point that "other insurance" provisions may be buried within the context of other policy subject matter.

The first provision relates to highway operation of mobile equipment registered in the named insured's name. Coverage is granted to permissive users and others responsible for their conduct, but *not if any other liability insurance is available to these parties*. The second provision refers to newly formed or acquired organizations owned or controlled by the named insured. With some exceptions, and for only a limited period, such an organization qualifies as a named insured—*but only if no other similar insurance is available to the organization*.

The claims-made version of the CGL contains still another exonerating provision applying to claims covered because of the "tail" coverage under the "basic extended reporting period" of the policy. Any protection afforded under that provision does not apply to claims covered under any subsequent insurance purchased by the named insured.[15]

CONFLICTS AMONG "OTHER INSURANCE" PROVISIONS

By their very nature, "other insurance" provisions attempt to create some degree of order out of the chaos involved in coordinating insurance policies from a variety of sources, written in a variety of styles, each of which focuses on a particular need for coverage. Even in the case of compatible proration provisions, it can be difficult to apply the terms in a way that satisfies all parties because of other differences among the involved policies. The following examples illustrate this point.

- Two policies contain applicable exonerating provisions, presenting an impasse. Does neither policy provide coverage because of the existence of another policy that is exonerated from coverage? Similar results are created by two excess provisions—or, for that matter, two primary provisions.
- One policy is excess over other insurance while the other contains an exonerating provision whereby it provides coverage contingent on the absence of other insurance. Does the presence of contingent coverage trigger the excess provision of the other policy, making it excess over the contingent coverage? Or does the exonerating provision prevail, with the result that there is no insurance to be primary under the excess provision?

Exhibit 8-3
Other Commercial General Liability Coverage Form Provisions Relating to "Other Insurance"

SECTION II - WHO IS AN INSURED

1. If you are designated in the Declarations as:

   a. An individual, you and your spouse are insureds, but only with respect to the conduct of a business of which you are the sole owner.

   b. A partnership or joint venture, you are an insured. Your members, your partners, and their spouses are also insureds, but only with respect to the conduct of your business.

   c. An organization other than a partnership or joint venture, you are an insured. Your executive offices and directors are insureds, but only with respect to their duties as officers or directors. Your stockholders are also insureds, but only with respect to their liability as stockholders.

2. Each of the following is also an insured:

   a. Your employees, other than your executive officers, but only for acts within the scope of their employment by you. However, no employee is an insured for:

      (1) "Bodily injury" or "personal injury" to you or to a co-employee while in the course of his or her employment, of the spouse, child, parent, brother or sister of that co-employee as a consequence of such "bodily injury" or "personal injury," or for any obligation to share damages with or repay someone else who must pay damages because of the injury; or

      (2) "Bodily injury" or "personal injury" arising out of his or her providing or failing to provide professional health care services; or

      (3) "Property damage to property owned or occupied by or rented or loaned to that employee, any of your other employees, or any of your partners or members (if you are a partnership or joint venture).

   b. Any person (other than your employee), or any organization while acting as your real estate manager

   c. Any person or organization having proper temporary custody of your property if you die, but only:

      (1) With respect to liability arising out of the maintenance or use of that property; and

      (2) Until your legal representative has been appointed.

   d. Your legal representative if you die, but only with respect to duties as such. That representative will have all your rights and duties under this Coverage Part.

3. With respect to "mobile equipment" registered in your name under any motor vehicle registration law, any person is an insured while driving such equipment along a public highway with your permission. Any other person or organization responsible for the conduct of such person is also an insured, but only with respect to liability arising out of the operation of the equipment, and <u>only if no other insurance of any kind is available</u> to that person or organization for this liability. However, no person or organization is an insured with respect to:

   a. "Bodily injury" to a co-employee of the person driving the equipment; or

   b. "Property damage" to property owned by, rented to, in the charge of or occupied by you or the employer of any person who is an insured under this provision.

4. Any organization you newly acquire or form, other than a partnership or joint venture, and over which you maintain ownership or majority interest, will qualify as a Named Insured <u>if there is no other similar insurance available</u> to that organization. However:

   a. Coverage under this provision is afforded only until the 90th day after you acquire or form the organization or the end of the policy period, whichever is earlier;

   b. Coverage A does not apply to "bodily injury" or "property damage" that occurred before you acquired or formed the organization; and

   c. Coverage B does not apply to "personal injury" or "advertising injury" arising out of an offense committed before you acquired or formed the organization.

No person or organization is an insured with respect to the conduct of any current or past partnership or joint venture that is not shown as a Named Insured in the Declarations.

- One policy is excess and the other provides for proration. Can the latter limit its liability to a proportionate share? If so, over what is the other policy excess—the other insurer's proportionate share or the other insurer's amount of insurance? If not, respect for the excess provision converts the other policy's proration provision into a primary provision.
- One policy calls for proration by face amounts while the other calls for proration by amounts payable. Depending on the numbers involved, giving full effect to *both* could result in less being paid to the insured than would have been the case had only one policy applied.
- Two policies cover a building. In one, the limit of insurance applies solely to the building. The other policy covers the building *and* its contents on a "blanket" basis, i.e., one limit collectively applying to both items of property. Both policies provide for proration by face amounts. How should the "other insurance" provisions be applied to a loss involving the building *and* contents? Should the insurer covering the building only consider the full limit of the blanket policy in limiting its liability? Or should the amount paid by the blanket insurer for the contents loss first be subtracted from its policy limit?

Efforts to resolve other-insurance conflicts take at least the following five forms.

1. One approach, which should be obvious by now, involves drafting "other insurance" provisions that anticipate possible conflicts.
2. Another common approach, which requires no particular elaboration, simply involves negotiation between or among the insurers involved in a loss.
3. Policy coverage language is drafted in a way that minimizes overlapping coverage and therefore avoids other-insurance situations.
4. Guidelines and procedures are developed by insurers and adhered to by many.
5. Litigation is always available when other approaches are inadequate.

The last three alternatives will now be examined.

Drafting Policy Coverage To Minimize Overlaps

One way to prevent frequent other-insurance conflicts is to prevent coverage overlaps that create other-insurance situations. Policy drafting may have this as one of its objectives. On occasion, it is the paramount objective.

A fertile source of conflict among liability insurance policies has centered on the loading or unloading of vehicles and the coverage of general liability insurance and commercial auto liability insurance. While coverage details are beyond the scope of this volume, auto policies typically have been intended to cover claims arising out of vehicle loading and unloading while general liability policies have been intended to exclude them. Policy language traditionally provided little help on the specifics of "loading and unloading." One dilemma has involved the issue of when—in time, place, or activity—"loading" begins or "unloading" ends. The question is of obvious importance to both the general liability insurer and the auto liability insurer.[16] The answer, or the lack of an answer, could trigger coverage under one, the other, or both policies.

In an effort to isolate coverage to either auto liability or general liability coverage, ISO's current forms incorporate descriptions of these activities. Forms in the two lines contain essentially the same activity descriptions and "dovetail" the two lines by expressing the activity descriptions in the two forms so that each is in effect the reciprocal of the other. The business auto coverage form states that it excludes bodily injury or property damage resulting from the handling of property:

> Before it is moved from the place where it is accepted by the "insured" for movement into or onto the covered "auto"; or. . . .

The commercial general liability forms exclude bodily injury and property damage arising out of the use of autos and then add to the exclusion the clarification that use includes "loading and unloading." In the forms' definitions sections, the term "loading and unloading" is said to include the handling of property:

> After it is moved from the place where it is accepted for movement into or onto an aircraft, watercraft or "auto;". . . .

Both auto and general liability forms refer to "moved from the place where it is accepted." *Before* such movement, the business auto form does not apply. The general liability forms do apply; their exclusion is activated by the conjunction "after," so by inference it does not apply "before."

The intent of this language coordination is to make clear, *in this kind of situation at least*, that the two lines are mutually exclusive but collectively exhaustive—no overlap but no gap. One or the other, but not both, should apply. Other-insurance situations should not occur.[17]

Policy drafting has a number of limitations in resolving other-insurance conflicts. Obviously, there is no single process involving all insurers. Many companies use so-called "standard" forms, but insurers usually are not subject to mandated policy language. So one cannot be certain that a specific fact situation will involve policy language that is coordinated. Further, as mentioned earlier, some *possible* overlaps may be built into, or left in, policy forms because of the diversity of needs the forms meet. Finally, policy drafting is not an exact science, nor is the process one that can involve perfect foresight. Much policy language is reactive or responsive, the example cited above being a case in point. Anticipating what may happen—situations in which policies will be used, what meanings will be placed on policy language by insureds and courts, and the like—is fraught with conjecture.

Industry-Developed Guidelines and Procedures

It probably is accurate to say that most other-insurance conflicts today are resolved through adherence to the *Guiding Principles* or submission to arbitration under the *Special Arbitration Agreement*.

The Guiding Principles. A set of "principles" was promulgated in 1963 as a cooperative effort of a number of insurance industry trade and service organizations. Several earlier, more specific agreements were intra-line (involving fire and allied lines insurance only) or narrowly inter-line (for example, fire insurance and inland marine insurance) in nature. The earlier agreements as a group did not fit well with the expanding use of multiple-line policies that blurred the traditional divisions among lines of insurance.

The *Guiding Principles* deal with property losses generally and with some situations involving bailee and carrier liability coverages that are considered to be inland marine in nature. Their purpose is to eliminate disputes resulting from overlapping coverages. "Other insurance" provisions are set aside to the extent that they conflict with the principles. Adherence to the principles is purely voluntary; there are no signatories. The document states the following provisions:

> These Principles provide for the equitable distribution of available insurance. As among insurance companies, the "other insurance" clause(s) which is (are) contained in a policy(ies) of insurance, and which may include an excess provision, shall be set aside and be inoperative to the extent that it is (they are) in conflict with the purpose of these Principles. Otherwise, these Principles will not change coverage or other conditions under any policy(ies) of insurance. Further, the application of these Principles shall in no event operate to reduce recovery to the insured below that which would have been obtained under any policy or policies covering the risk.

As defined in the *Guiding Principles*, property insurance policies are concurrent if they are of the same general type (that is, both or all homeowners policies), insure the same interest and the identical property, and divide the risk of a specific main hazard between or among policies or companies. The policies may still be concurrent, even if they do not contain identical effective dates or limits, and apart from whether they contain deductibles or coinsurance clauses. Thus, two homeowners policies covering the same insured against loss to exactly the same property are deemed concurrent, even though they have different effective dates.

All situations within the general scope of the *Guiding Principles* involve "nonconcurrent" policies or a combination of three or more policies in which at least one is not concurrent with the others. Policies can be of the same general type, such as fire insurance policies, but be nonconcurrent because they do not cover exactly the same property. As illustrated earlier, Policy A may cover a building and its contents under one blanket amount of insurance, while Policy B covers only contents. In addition, two or more policies of different general types (such as a fire policy and an inland marine policy) are regarded as nonconcurrent.

The operative core of the *Guiding Principles* is found in (1) an order of primacy, and (2) proration by amounts payable. A six-tiered order of primacy is established based on the degree of coverage specificity in identifying property insured and location(s) covered. In decreasing order of primacy are insurance policies covering the following:

1. Described articles or objects at a designated location
2. Specifically described articles or objects without restriction as to location
3. Described groups or classes of related articles or objects at a designated location
4. Described groups or classes of related articles or objects without designating the location
5. All property at a designated location without specifying particular items or related groups or classes of property
6. Property without earlier designation of location or of particular items or related classes of property

If an overlapping policy fits into (1), it is primary to any policy(ies) falling into (2) through (6). Notice that (1) is the narrowest of all on the joint issue of property description *and* location. A policy fitting into (2) is primary as to (3) through (6) but excess as to (1), and so on.

If two or more policies are of the same order of primacy—two policies falling into the (2) category—the principles call for "contribution" by what was described earlier in this chapter as "proration by amounts payable." The *Guiding Principles* call this the "limit of liability rule" and describe it in the following way:

> "Contribution," unless otherwise as specified in General Principle 1-G, shall be on the basis of the applicable limit of liability under each

respective policy or group of concurrent policies as though no other insurance existed, and the limit separately determined under each policy or group of concurrent policies shall be the smallest of the following:
(a) the amount of insurance
(b) the amount of loss, or
(c) the amount payable after applying any policy limitation(s)
The limits so determined of all policies or groups of concurrent policies herein declared contributing shall be added and, if the total amount exceeds the whole loss, each policy or group of concurrent policies shall pay such proportion of the loss as its limit bears to the sum of all the limits, but if the sum of the limits of liability is less than the whole loss, then each policy or group of concurrent policies shall pay its limit of liability. The determined liability of a group of concurrent policies shall be apportioned pro rata among the policies of the group.[18]

Notice that if more than two policies are involved, some of them concurrent and one or more of them not, the concurrent policies are considered to be a "group." Any part of the loss apportioned to a "group" of concurrent policies is shared among those policies on the basis of contribution by the above limit of liability rule.

The principles clarify the application of their limit of liability rule in some situations where policies are not co-extensive as to property covered or dollars of loss covered. For example, assume two policies are subject to the rule but only one has a deductible. The policy without the deductible calculates its limit of liability (amount payable) as though the deductible policy did not exist. The no-deductible policy's limit of liability is charged with the deductible, and only the *remainder* of the limit then enters the calculation to determine the contribution of that policy to the dollars of loss covered in common by the two policies. A similar approach is prescribed when two (or more) deductibles of different amounts are involved. The policy with the lower deductible is charged with the difference between the two deductibles.

In addition to the generic guidelines provided by the hierarchy of primacy and the "limit of liability" rule, the principles lay out some specific types of coverage overlaps and recommend primary-excess relationships to govern insurer liability.[19] The following is taken from General Principle 2-C:

> Coverage for property "used" or "worn" by the insured, for property of servants or guests, and insurance afforded by the "physical damage to property" coverage, shall be primary to any available insurance in the name of the owner of the involved property, except insurance covering a specifically described article or object, whether or not for an express amount, shall be primary.

In a typical case involving homeowners policies, a household guest has personal property coverage under his or her own homeowners policy, and coverage is available under the host's homeowners policy as well if the host's insurer is requested by the host to provide it. In such a case, the *Guiding Principles* recommend that the "other insurance" provisions in the two policies be set aside and that the host's insurance be primary except for articles or objects specifically insured by the guest.[20]

Finally, the principles include a separate section, Part II in the actual document, containing three "Specific Principles." Each deals only with intra-line overlaps—those confined to a specific "line" of insurance.

- The "Casualty-casualty" principle merely affirms that overlaps confined to casualty policies are to be resolved according to the guidelines stated earlier in this section.
- The "Fire-fire" principle does the same but adds certain clarifications to apply when *only* fire policies are involved.
- The "Inland-inland" principle cites specific exceptions to the generic principles when certain inland marine (only) coverages overlap.

None of the specific agreements override the generic principles when the overlap involves different lines, such as fire and inland marine.

To today's property-liability insurance practitioner, accustomed to package policies containing several of the traditional "lines" of coverage, these specific principles may seem archaic. Not so. The foreword to the entire *Guiding Principles* document makes clear that multiple-line policy *components*—casualty, fidelity, fire, inland marine—are to be isolated for the purpose of determining which of the entire collection of principles should apply.[21] Thus, if a package policy's fire coverage (likely called "property" coverage today) overlapped a monoline fire (property) policy, the overlap would be "fire-fire" in nature even though the package policy contained other coverages as well.

No dollar eligibility rules apply to the *Guiding Principles*. They do not specify any loss minimum or maximum as a trigger to their adoption.

Special Arbitration Agreement. Unlike the *Guiding Principles*, which call for arbitration only if insurers fail to agree on the application of specific recommendations, the *Special Arbitration Agreement* is entirely an arbitration device for resolving disputes. The domain of the agreement is liability insurance. Signatories to the agreement may be insurers, self-insurers, or commercial insureds with large deductibles. As signatories, participating entities are bound to submit certain kinds of disputes to arbitration. Problems outside the mandatory class *may* be submitted for arbitration with the written consent of the signatories involved, even if they differ in kind from those subject to mandatory arbitration as described below. Directing and administering the agreement is Arbitration Forums, Inc., a not-for-profit entity supported by the insurance industry.

The Special Arbitration Agreement states its mandatory role as one that applies to disputes involving two or more signatories in which each has issued either of the following:

(a) a policy of casualty insurance covering one or more of a number of parties each asserted to be legally liable for an accident or occurrence out of which a claim or suit for bodily injury or property damage arises, or as a self-insured has been alleged to be legally liable for an accident or occurrence; or

(b) separate policies of casualty insurance to the same party or parties asserted to cover an accident or occurrence out of which a claim or suit for bodily injury or property damage arises;

Paragraph (a) deals with codefendents and may incidentally involve other insurance, while paragraph (b) explicitly deals with actual or possible other-insurance situations. The term "casualty insurance" includes any contract covering bodily injury or property damage liability claims and, primarily relevant to paragraph (b), the following items:

● Personal injury protection (no-fault coverage)
● Uninsured motorists coverage
● Underinsured motorists coverage[22]
● Workers compensation coverage

For an otherwise qualifying dispute, mandatory arbitration is waived under certain conditions. A signatory is not compelled to arbitrate a claim or suit if one of the following conditions applies:

1. Its coverage is subject to retrospective or experience rating.
2. It is or may be vulnerable to payment in excess of its policy limit.
3. The arbitration process might materially prejudice its ability to defend or prosecute a claim or suit based on the same event.
4. In the case of a codefendant controversy, it has raised a defense to coverage under the policy.
5. The policy is one requiring the insured's consent to an out-of-court settlement.
6. The amount in dispute is greater than $250,000.
7. No arbitration panel has been established in the state involved.

In addition, a signatory can petition the board of directors of Arbitration Forums for permission to litigate, rather than arbitrate, an issue if the law on the issue is unsettled and has not been subject to interpretation by courts of the involved jurisdiction.

The Special Arbitration Agreement is an insurance industry sponsored tool. Insurers may also use other means of dispute resolution short of litigation. A number of proprietary "private court" programs exist. In addition, the *American Arbitration Association* has a long history of activity in insurance matters, among others. The Association is an impartial agency dedicated exclusively to negotiation, mediation, and arbitration of disputes in the commercial arena.

Litigation

Court activity involving other insurance has been primarily of the following two types:

1. Multiple policies clearly provide coverage, and the fundamental issue is how much each insurer should pay.
2. The primary issue is whether coverage applies under one or more policies. If coverage is found under more than one policy, the secondary "other insurance" issue must be addressed.

Both legal questions largely involve declaratory judgment actions among insurers, although insureds sometimes have been parties to the litigation.

It would probably be an oversimplification to cite "rules" emanating from court decisions. Different outcomes result even among conflicts presenting essentially the same kinds of policy language. Given the infinite variety of circumstances in which insurance policies function, this diversity is not unreasonable. The following *generalizations* can, however, be made about court decisions on this subject:

- Mutually repugnant clauses—both excess or exonerating, for example—are disregarded and responsibility is allocated proportionally, usually by face amounts, but often by amounts payable.
- Policies with proportional provisions, in conflict with an excess provision, are deemed primary insurance.
- Where some basis exists for making the choice, the policy more specific to the exposure in coverage and premium charge is primary.

OTHER INSURANCE AND HEALTH INSURANCE

Even though this text emphasizes property and liability insurance, a discussion of multiple sources of recovery would be incomplete without some mention of health insurance. Opportunities abound for health insurance to be among the potential sources of recovery for a loss situation to which bodily injury liability, auto or premises medical payments, no-fault personal injury protection coverage, or workers compensation insurance also applies. The discussion under this heading emphasizes those matters of special importance to these potential coverage overlaps.

Individual Health Insurance

While property and liability insurance policy standardization usually involves "standard" policies developed by advisory organizations, standardization in individual health insurance is brought about by regulation. *Uniform policy provision laws* in every jurisdiction reflect a model law developed by the National Association of Insurance Commissioners (NAIC). A number of policy provisions are mandatory; these are unrelated to the present discussion. Several optional provisions, which insurers may include if they so choose, deal explicitly with other insurance:

- *Other insurance with the same insurer.* If an insured has duplicate coverage with the same insurer, the insurer may limit payments to an aggregate amount of indemnity or to the maximum amount payable under one policy.

- *Insurance with other insurers.* This provision is used in *medical expense* policies, where it has an effect similar to the pro rata liability provision of property insurance policies. In general, if duplicate individual coverage applies, the insurer will be responsible only for its pro rata share of benefits payable. This provision typically does not apply to "duplicate coverage" provided under group health insurance, auto medical payments insurance, workers compensation insurance, or recovery as the result of a liability action against a third party.

- *Relation of earnings to insurance.* This provision is used in individual *disability income* policies, where it provides for pro rata payment of benefits under certain circumstances when an insured carries more than one policy. If the total amount of disability benefits payable under all of an insured's applicable policies exceeds either (1) the insured's monthly income at the time of disability or (2) the average of the insured's monthly income for the two years prior to disability, then the total monthly payment is limited to the greater of these two amounts and is made on a pro rata basis by the various policies providing coverage. Unless otherwise stated in the policy, this provision does not apply to benefits that may be payable under workers compensation, employers liability insurance, or group disability income plans.

Most insurers do not use the first two provisions because of the expense and difficulty of enforcing them.

Group Health Insurance

Both group disability income and group medical expense coverages often contain an explicit reference to other insurance. The typical format differs between the two.

Group Disability Income. The benefit statement or formula in group disability income coverage typically is limited to a percentage of the insured's pre-disability earnings, a flat dollar amount, or both. Thus, a group plan might agree to pay a monthly amount equal to 60 percent of pre-disability earnings, or a flat monthly amount such as $1,500, or the lesser of the two. In any case, it is common for these coverages to anticipate the possibility of other sources of disability income and to include provisions that reduce benefits when other sources of income are involved. Most take the form of offsets or, in the parlance of the field, *integration*. In the property-liability context of earlier material in this chapter, this type of language is a subset of exonerating provisions in which payment from another source, or other sources, reduces the *limit of insurance* of the policy with the offset provision. In disability income insurance, the applicable limit of insurance for this purpose is the maximum periodic—monthly, for example—benefit payable.

To illustrate, assume an employer-sponsored plan agrees to pay a maximum of 60 percent of pre-disability earnings, subject to a benefit maximum of $5,000 per month. For an employee earning $3,000 a month, the operative limit is $1,800 per month of disability income. This amount is what the insurer agrees to pay, but *only to the extent it is not paid by specified other sources or programs.* A rather broad set of these other sources might include:

1. Workers compensation and similar statutory programs
2. Automobile "no-fault" laws
3. Any other group insurance plan
4. The employer's retirement plan
5. Any retirement plan basing eligibility on service with the employer[23]
6. Temporary nonoccupational disability benefits law
7. Social security, or similar legislation in Canada

Noticeably absent from the list is individual disability income coverage, which is seldom "integrated" with the group insurance benefit. Depending on the other source(s) of income benefits available and the disabled employee's pre-disability earnings, this type of policy language could result in complete exoneration of the group disability income coverage.

Group Medical Expense Coverage. A *coordination of benefits (COB) clause* usually is contained in group medical expense insurance policies, as well as in the plan provisions of many "self-insured" plans.

The increase in two-worker families creates increasing instances of duplication of benefits. It is not unusual to have a husband and wife covered under both his plan and her plan. Dependents' coverage may also be on a duplicate basis. COB clauses are an attempt to reduce the potential for overpayment of medical expenses and the inappropriate utilization of health care resources encouraged by such overpayment. The importance of this dual objective has been recognized by the National Association of Insurance Commissioners (NAIC), which has attempted to encourage uniformity among the states in dealing with the issue. Guidelines in the form of a "model" COB provision have been developed and periodically revised by the NAIC. Over three-quarters of the states have adopted these guidelines, in some cases with minor variations.

The NAIC model prescribes primary and secondary (excess) relationships between plans. A plan having no COB provision is always primary to one with a COB provision. As between plans each having a COB clause, primary and secondary roles depend on whether the employee or a dependent incurs the expenses and, in some cases, other circumstances. As is the case in the property insurance *Guiding Principles*, a "tie-breaker" is included to handle situations not governed by a more specific guideline. The following orders of priority apply:

- A plan covering a person as an employee is primary to a plan covering the person as a dependent.
- A dependent child has primary coverage under the plan of the parent having the earlier (month and day, not year) birthdate. The other parent's plan is secondary. This birthday rule applies only if the parents are not separated or divorced.
- Dependent children of divorced or separated parents have primary coverage under the plan of the parent with custody. The plan of a stepparent, that is, the spouse of the custodial parent, is secondary. The plan of the parent without custody is, as the case may be, secondary or tertiary.
- Dependent children of separated or divorced parents with joint custody have coverage according to the birthday rule.
- A plan covering an individual as an active employee (or a dependent thereof) is primary to a plan covering that person (and dependents) as an inactive employee, that is, as a retired or laid-off individual.
- For people with coverage under COBRA continuation rights, a plan providing coverage by virtue of employment is primary to coverage continued under COBRA.[24]
- For situations not governed by the guidelines above (for example, dependents coverage and both parents having the same birthday), the plan that has covered the individual for the longer period is primary; the other plan is secondary.

NAIC guidelines provide that a primary plan determine and discharge its benefit payment obligation as if no other plan existed. The secondary plan calculates what it *would have* paid if it were primary, but pays only the allowable expenses not paid by the primary plan to the extent that these do not exceed what it would have paid standing alone. An allowable expense is any necessary and reasonable medical expense covered *in whole or in part* by at least one of the plans involved in the COB resolution. To the extent that the excess status saves the secondary plan money, that amount is recorded as a credit that may be used to finance future claim components, for example, a deductible that would not be covered by either plan.

Because of the broad definition of "allowable expense," a secondary plan could pay for expenses it would not pay for if standing alone. Consider a primary plan that covers within limits certain types of home health care, and a secondary plan that does not. Since the specified types of home health care are covered to at least some extent in one of the plans, the secondary plan could be called upon to pay related charges not covered in full by the primary plan. This is so even though the secondary plan would not have covered such charges *at all* were it the only plan applying. The goal is to limit combined payments to 100 percent of allowable expenses, broadly defined. Another interesting aspect of the COB approach is that a secondary plan might be called upon to fully pay for the expense dollars used to satisfy the primary plan's deductible even if the secondary plan, standing alone, would itself have imposed a deductible.

According to the NAIC model, for COB purposes a "plan" does not include individual or family medical expense contracts but does include any coverage mandated or provided by statute. Thus, automobile "no-fault" benefits coverage could be considered a "plan" according to the NAIC, at least for making the health insurance with COB a secondary plan. However, the essence of "plan" in the guidelines is group protection, not individually-purchased protection.

Some Observations

Several observations can now be made as to how individual and group health coverages relate to other types of insurance.

Relation to Auto Insurance. Several auto insurance coverages provide a recovery source that often duplicates health insurance benefits. In fact, auto medical payments coverage and (no-fault) personal injury protection coverage function as health insurance coverages, even though they appear within a liability insurance policy or coverage. (More precisely, these coverages function as *accident insurance,* a subset of health insurance that also covers against expenses resulting from nonaccidental illness.) Beyond these first-party coverages, uninsured and underinsured motorists coverages pay the damages the *insured* is legally entitled to recover from another, uninsured or underinsured, motorist liable for the insured's bodily injury. And, where another responsible party is insured, that party's auto liability insurance could pay for the injured party's medical expense and income losses.

Where auto "no-fault" laws have been passed, the legislatures generally attempt to make auto personal injury protection coverage primary except with respect to workers compensation coverage or other statutory benefit programs. In at least one state, auto insurance buyers have been given the option to have their medical expense insurance primary to the mandatory personal injury protection benefit.[25]

Where permissible, some individual and group health insurers exclude coverage for expenses payable under auto personal injury protection. The effect is that the health insurance policy includes an excess "other insurance" provision.

Generally speaking, health insurance policies contain no provisions related to the possible duplication of medical payments or uninsured/ underinsured motorists coverage.

Subrogation. Health insurers increasingly attempt to benefit from claims their insureds may have against other parties and, possibly, their liability insurers. The avenues of recovery, however, are a bit involved, as an injured person's health insurance company has no direct right of recovery against the liability insurance company that protects some unrelated party who may—or may not—have been legally responsible for the injury that led to the medical expenses. The bridge between these recovery sources is subrogation.

Historically, the courts have held that health insurers have no inherent or *equitable* rights of subrogation. However, a growing number of courts do permit subrogation under health insurance coverage when it is not specifically prohibited by statute *and* the policy contains an explicit subrogation provision. In other words, many courts now allow *contractual* subrogation in health insurance. Not surprisingly, this trend is reflected in the growing practice of incorporating subrogation provisions in health insurance.

Post-Recovery Reimbursement Provisions. A number of health insurance policies include provisions providing for post-loss *reimbursement of payment* by the insured rather than traditional subrogation references to post-loss transfer of *rights of recovery*. A typical reimbursement provision might read as follows:

Where allowed by law, if you or one of your Dependents:
a. receive benefit payment as described in this policy as the result of a sickness or injury; and

    b. have a lawful claim against another party or parties for compensation, damage, or other payment because of the same sickness or injury; and

    c. receive payment from the other party or parties;

the Company shall have the right to be reimbursed for benefits paid under this policy.

This example could be construed as *broader than* a typical subrogation provision, given its reference to "lawful claim . . . for compensation, damages, or other payment." That language clearly accommodates recovery based on a cause of action against a third-party tortfeasor. However, it might also accommodate a claim by an insured under his or her own auto insurance policy.

THE COLLATERAL SOURCE RULE

Consider an automobile accident in which the injured victim of a negligent automobile operator is insured under a major medical expense policy and a disability income policy. Assume that coverage under both policies is triggered by the injury and that the insurers pay benefits in accordance with their terms. How, if at all, do these insurance payments affect the extent of the negligent operator's (the tortfeasor's) obligation to pay damages to the victim? Do these reparations sources reduce the tortfeasor's burden, or are they irrelevant to that issue?

The Rule

As a general rule, *a tortfeasor is liable for the damages sustained as a result of the tortfeasor's wrongful act or omission without regard to the actual or possible existence of other sources of benefits or compensation available to the party wronged.* Thus, in the scenario above, the monetary obligation of the negligent driver would be unaffected by the fact that some of the victim's losses were covered by the two policies. The two policies are examples of *collateral sources,* or sources other than the tortfeasor. A collateral source may be, and often is, insurance, but numerous other sources, such as employment-related sick leave or salary continuation plans, could be cited. In an action by the victim against the tortfeasor, the collateral source rule in effect bars the tortfeasor from introducing evidence of payments from collateral sources in an effort to reduce the amount for which he or she is liable. And the tortfeasor's liability insurer is in precisely the same position.

Using the word "collateral" in a broad sense, this entire chapter has involved collateral sources. But in the context of the legal doctrine known as the "collateral source rule," an other-insurance situation as described earlier is not a good fit. Other-insurance situations involve one interest directly protected by more than one insurance policy, or more than one coverage in the same policy. Like an other-insurance situation, a case involving the collateral source rule involves multiple sources of recovery. But in the latter, the obligation of one source is grounded in tort rather than in contract. Even if the tortfeasor has liability insurance, the contractual obligation in the policy runs to the tortfeasor-insured and not to the victim. The victim is not "covered by" that policy.

The rationale of the collateral source rule is straightforward—a wrongdoer should be fully responsible for the consequences of his or her wrongful act and should not be spared any part of that burden because of any collateral sources of benefits available to the party wronged. But the rule is controversial. Its application clearly can result in double recovery for some dollars of loss suffered by a claimant or plaintiff. Some view this as simply a wasteful application of resources in our overall reparations "system." Further, the rule may create an incentive for claimants to "run up" medical bills or income loss covered by collateral sources, since that enlarges the windfall included in the damages payable by the tortfeasor or that party's liability insurer. In addition, the dollar amount of general damages, such as payment for pain and suffering, is often related, albeit crudely and informally, to the size of the special damages involved—payments for medical expenses, income loss, and the like. Since the collateral source rule bars reducing these special damages by amounts available from collateral sources, it can be argued that damages for pain and suffering, and the like, tend to be larger than would be the case in the absence of the rule. Finally, "system costs," such as attorneys' fees, are increased, at least where such costs are a function of the size of the damages awarded or payable.

Some Insurance Considerations

One relatively common question for liability insurers has been the status of medical payments coverage included as an adjunct to liability insurance in the same policy. What if our injured victim in the opening paragraph of this section had been a passenger in the negligent operator's car and was paid medical payments by the operator's auto insurer, then sued the operator for damages covered under the liability portion of the same policy? In the context of any damages due the victim, is the medical payments coverage a source within the scope of the collateral source rule? Some courts have held that medical payments benefits in a defendant's policy are not a collateral source, that is, medical payments coverage for this purpose is not separate from and irrelevant to the amount of damages to be paid by the defendant's liability coverage in the same policy. That view seems reasonable, given that the defendant, in most cases at least, is hardly a stranger to the contract providing *both* sources of recovery for the victim. In contrast, it would seldom be the case that the defendant would have any linkage at all with other possible collateral sources.

Recently, insurers have been addressing this issue in personal auto contracts by specifically dealing in the contract with the relationship between medical payments coverage and liability coverage. It is now common to see an offset requirement imposed on insureds under medical payments. Consider the following excerpts from the "limit of liability" section of the medical payments coverage in the ISO personal auto policy:

> B. Any amounts otherwise payable for expenses under this coverage shall be reduced by any amounts paid or payable for the same expenses under Part A or Part C.
> C. No payment will be made unless the injured person or that person's legal representative agrees in writing that any payment shall be applied toward any settlement or judgment that person receives under Part A or Part C.

Part "A" of the policy is liability coverage; Part "C" is uninsured motorists coverage. In either case, the goal is to make it clear that medical expenses are to be paid for just once, at least insofar as this policy is concerned. Since even a medical payments insured who is a stranger to the contract—for example, a guest passenger—is subject to the terms and conditions of the coverage accruing to his or her benefit, this kind of policy offset requirement effectively removes the matter from the possibly unpredictable realm of the collateral source rule.

Some states' no-fault insurance laws have in effect partly negated the collateral source rule. These laws preclude an injured person from seeking as damages from a responsible party the dollars of loss paid or payable by the no-fault personal injury protection coverage applicable to that injured person. Thus, the liability insurer of the responsible party is spared paying the injured person the medical expenses and lost income, among other things, payable by the personal injury protection covering the individual.

Are workers compensation benefits a collateral source within the purview of the collateral source rule? In general, compensation benefits do not mitigate the tort-based obligation of a party (other than the employer) responsible for the compensable injury or death of an employee. So the collateral source rule still applies. However, in most states the outcome differs because the payor of workers compensation benefits, whether the employer or the employer's insurer, either has a lien on the proceeds of any tort recovery by the claimant-employee or is subrogated to the rights of the claimant (or the claimant's employer), in both cases to the extent of the compensation benefits paid. Thus, in most states the claimant-employee cannot recover twice for the elements of loss paid as compensation benefits.

The collateral source rule is not restricted to damages due to injuries or death. The same potential for double recovery exists in cases involving damages payable because of damage to property. However, as indicated earlier in this text, any insurance-based windfall is usually avoided via the property insurer's right of subrogation in such cases. True, many property insurance policies permit insureds some leeway in waiving rights against others, possibly making subrogation moot, but a waiver by the insured destroys the insured's rights as well. Double recovery, then, is not an issue.

SUMMARY

This chapter deals with the many types of situations in which a party who has suffered a loss has access to more than one source of recovery for that loss. These situations are, in part, addressed by "other insurance" provisions within insurance policies. However, policy provisions could not possibly address specifically all of the various situations in which multiple sources can be involved.

The chapter began by examining the nature of other sources of recovery. They include other insurance in the same policy, other insurance in a similar policy, other insurance in a dissimilar policy, noninsurance contracts, and third parties.

Discussion then moved on to examine the "other insurance" provisions found in property-liability insurance policies. It was noted that many policy provisions deal with "other insurance" issues, even if they do not bear the caption "other insurance."

"Other insurance" provisions generally attempt to accomplish one or more of the following five results:

1. To *exonerate* the insurer from liability
2. To limit the insurer's liability to a *proportion* of the loss
3. To limit the insurer's liability to that part of the loss that is in *excess* of other insurance
4. To make the insurance *primary* with respect to other insurance
5. To *maintain the principle of indemnity* without indicating any specific position with respect to other insurance

Samples of each type of provision were analyzed and some of the reasoning behind each was examined.

Not surprisingly, "other insurance" provisions may conflict with one another, and conflicts need to be resolved when a claim is handled. Conflicts are avoided by policy drafters who draft policy language designed to minimize overlaps in coverage, as well as "other insurance" provisions that clarify how the most common other-insurance situations will be addressed. When policy provisions alone do not suffice to resolve a problem, industry guidelines are used. The *Guiding Principles* are used to resolve many property insurance issues, while the *Special Arbitration Agreement* is used in settling many liability insurance issues. A last resort in all cases is litigation.

Health insurance occasionally provides coverage for the same elements of loss as general or auto liability, medical payments, workers compensation, and no-fault personal injury protection coverages. The chapter briefly examined the ways in which health insurance addresses "other insurance" issues and made some observations relating to auto insurance, subrogation, and post-recovery reimbursement provisions.

Finally, this chapter briefly examined the collateral source rule. While other principles in the chapter generally involved adjustments being made to allow for multiple sources of recovery, the collateral source rule tends to preclude any such adjustments on the premise that a tortfeasor should not benefit from other benefits available to an injured victim. From the standpoint of insurers, it can be argued that this rule tends to increase the overall costs of the reparations system.

Chapter Notes

---

1. In some states auto medical payments coverage is not sold because of the mandatory medical expense benefits in personal injury protection coverage.
2. This might appear to be a distinction without a difference, since there is coverage in any case. But the dwelling limit of insurance might be exhausted by damage to the dwelling itself, leaving building materials uncovered otherwise.
3. The camcorder owner also may have property insurance covering the loss; that is outside the scope of this discussion.
4. To complicate things, the liability coverage in the homeowners policy of the boatowner also covers Hilda.
5. This could also be a one-policy case if both coverages are contained as modules or parts of a package policy.
6. One word—caution—sums up the situation involving a car renter's responsibilities and the handling of them. Our purpose in this chapter is merely to illustrate a possible overlap.
7. This conclusion requires qualification in any jurisdiction, such as Michigan, that includes property damage in its no-fault law.
8. The term "excess-escape" is sometimes used in describing this type of provision.
9. Some have contained additional "other insurance" references as well, for example, a prohibition of any other fire insurance not declared in the policy, or a warranty of no other insurance except as noted in the policy.
10. Overlaps are still possible in this historically knotty area. Some insurers (fire, and boiler and machinery) voluntarily use an endorsement known as a "loss adjustment endorsement" in their policies. Its application is contingent upon the other policy(ies) being similarly endorsed. To the extent that insurers disagree, the endorsement provides for (1) first paying the insured (each insurer pays half of any amount in dispute), and (2) then submitting the inter-insurer issue to arbitration.
11. The unquoted portion of the provision dealt with other insurance that was not "fire" insurance and called for proration by amounts payable.
12. In the context of fire (property) insurance, the precise meaning of "extended coverage" has changed modestly over time. This fact does no violence to the point made.
13. These examples assume no conflict with the "other insurance" provision in the owner's (Kay's) policy. If Kay's policy is typical, it provides for proration by face amounts in situations involving Kay's car. In practice, this provision is disregarded and the owner's policy serves as primary insurance.
14. The discussion of excess liability insurance assumes a "true" excess policy in order to minimize complexities. Actually, most homeowners who buy excess liability insurance have a personal umbrella policy. An umbrella policy usually provides true excess insurance over (1) the minimum underly-

ing limits the policyholder is presumed to carry or, if larger, (2) the actual underlying limits carried by the policyholder. However, the usual umbrella policy goes one step further. It also covers some losses that are not covered by the underlying policy, but subject to a stipulated, and usually small, deductible.

15. If the optional "supplemental extended reporting period" endorsement is made applicable, still another provision—found in the endorsement—is operative, adding the protection under this "forever tail" to the list of excess situations cited in the "other insurance" provision of the coverage form.

16. What if both coverages are with the same insurer? The question still may be important for a number of reasons including (1) possibly differing limits of insurance for the two coverages, (2) the status of an aggregate limit in the general liability coverage, and (3) the possible need by the insured for the limits of both coverages if the loss is large.

17. This capsule merely illustrates policy drafting designed to avoid overlaps and is not a complete version of how these two coverages handle loading and unloading of vehicles.

18. General Principle I-6 incorporates this rule by reference, then clarifies how it is to be applied when (1) different deductibles are involved, or (2) the policies differ *in part* on the scope of loss covered.

19. These situations all involve coverage secured by one party that inures to the benefit of another.

20. By inference, then, the host's insurance is to be excess on specifically insured property of a guest or residence employee. But earlier we saw that such property is excluded altogether in the typical homeowners policy. Some insurers, at least, disregard the exclusion and pay on an excess basis.

21. The term "casualty" is restricted to first-party casualty coverages, such as crime insurance.

22. In some states uninsured motorists coverage applies to property damage as well.

23. As compared to (4), this accommodates multiple-employer plans, for example, a single statewide plan for public school teachers.

24. The Consolidated Omnibus Budget Reconciliation Act (COBRA) was signed into law in 1986. Among other things, COBRA imposed on certain employers the obligation to make available the continuation of group insurance to terminated employees and/or their covered dependents.

25. This is no longer a part of the applicable Pennsylvania law.

CHAPTER 9

External Factors Affecting Insurance Policy Analysis

Most questions involving the rights and duties of the parties to an insurance contract can be answered by analyzing the provisions in the written document known as an insurance policy. However, various factors outside the insurance contract may also need to be considered. This chapter examines a wide-ranging number of these external factors. The common thread that weaves together these wide-ranging topics is this: Each major topic discussed within this chapter directly or indirectly involves something not written into insurance policies themselves that may affect the way in which the information in a policy is interpreted.

ROLE OF THE COURTS

Many of the external factors affecting insurance policy analysis are based on court decisions.

Two issues that courts commonly address in resolving insurance-related claims involve (1) determining whether insurance coverage applies to a given claim, and (2), with respect to liability insurance claims, determining whether the insured is legally obligated to pay damages.

Coverage and liability are different concepts that often are confused by insurance students, insurance practitioners, and members of the insurance-buying public. For example, a mentally-ill patient escaped from an institution one night and set fire to the building housing an auto repair shop that contained a customer's truck. The repair shop owner filed a claim with its insurance company for damage to the truck. An insurance company representative stated that the repair shop was not liable for the damage to the truck. The repair shop owner became angry with this response. Although the adjuster had said, "You are not liable," the owner interpreted this to mean, "You are not covered."

The distinction is as follows:

- Questions of *coverage* involve the *insurer's* contractual obligation to the insured. In the case of property insurance or some other first-party coverage, the insurer may have a contractual obligation to pay claims to the insured. Under a liability policy the insurer may have a contractual obligation to the insured to defend claims and, if necessary, to pay damages on behalf of the insured.

- Questions of *liability* involve the *insured's* obligation to pay damages to a third-party claimant. These questions are outside of, or external to, the relationship between a liability insurer and its insured.

Confusion arises from two sources. First, the term "liability" also is used (accurately) to refer to the insurer's contractual obligations to the insured ("The insurer's liability under this policy. . ."). Second is the practice, slowly being phased out, of referring to an insurance policy's "limits of liability." Many recent policies substitute the less-confusing phrase, "limits of insurance."

When there is some question about liability or coverage or both, it may require a court to resolve the issue. Courts hear two kinds of cases: civil and criminal. *Criminal cases* involve people accused of committing wrongs that society has decided to punish, either by fines or imprisonment. All other cases are *civil cases,* decided by civil courts. It is in the civil courts where issues dealing with insurance are addressed.

Civil cases involve the alleged breach of some private duty owed to a member of the community. These duties are either imposed by the common law or civil statutes, or voluntarily assumed by contract. A person or business entity that breaches some such private duty is subject to an action at law for damages.

It is entirely possible for the same act to constitute both a crime and a civil wrong with the offender being subject to both criminal sanctions and civil liability. For example, a person who strikes another may be charged with the crime of assault and battery and also be subject to civil liability for damages toward the victim. Similarly, a motorist who causes death in an auto accident may be subject to punishment for vehicular homicide (a crime) and liable for damages in a civil suit. In each of these examples, the offender is answerable to the public for having committed a crime and answerable to private parties for a private civil wrong.

A civil action for damages is tried in a civil court, and a criminal action is tried in a criminal court. Each remedy involves a separate trial.

The burdens of proof are very different in civil and criminal cases. In a civil case a plaintiff can win only by proving the case by a *preponderance of the evidence.* In a criminal case, however, the state must sustain a much more difficult burden of proof that requires proof of guilt *beyond a reasonable doubt.* Therefore, an accused may be found innocent by a criminal court but lose the case in a civil court. The opposite result also is possible, though unlikely. Alternatively, the accused could win or lose both cases. It is commonplace for an injured plaintiff to win a civil case for damages against a defendant who is found innocent of criminal charges. An insurance policy can cover the damages in a civil action, but an insurance policy cannot cover criminal penalties. Such coverage would violate public policy.

PROCEDURES TO RESOLVE COVERAGE DISPUTES

When an insurer is notified of a claim or suit, it has four options. These options are not explicitly described in the insurance policy although the first two are implied:

1. *The insurer can accept the claim or defend the suit.* If a liability claim is involved, it pays the claim or agrees to defend the insured against the allegations of the suit and to pay damages up to the policy's limits. If a property claim is involved, it agrees to pay the claim.
2. *The insurer may completely disclaim any obligation under the insurance policy.* In doing so, the insurer takes the risk that it might later be sued by the insured, and it might ultimately be found to have breached its duties under the insurance contract.
3. *If there is some question of liability or coverage or both, the insurer may issue either a reservation of rights letter or, less commonly, a nonwaiver agreement.* In electing either procedure, the insurer agrees to investigate the claim and, for liability cases, provide defense but *reserves* its *rights* to disclaim coverage under the policy if the insurer later discovers through investigation that certain coverage does not apply.
4. *The insurer may seek a declaratory judgment.* In other words, the insurer may ask the court to rule upon or "declare" the parties' rights without actually awarding any relief.

Although it is desirable to handle claims promptly, an insurer must be extremely careful that claims-handling decisions are not made in haste. A premature decision in either direction can have undesirable results for the insurer.

- If the insurer makes the premature decision to provide coverage—or even implies that coverage applies, the insurer may be prohibited from disclaiming coverage later. It all depends on the circumstances. By its actions or representations, the insurer may waive its right to later assert some reason for denying protection. (Waiver and estoppel are discussed more fully later in this chapter.)

- If, on the other hand, the insurer denies coverage, then the insured may be forced to resolve the issue at its own expense. If he or she still believes coverage should apply, the insured then has the right to sue the insurer in an attempt to recoup the costs as well as the damages.

The insurer, in denying coverage, loses some of its policy defenses. For example, after denying that coverage exists under a property insurance policy, the insurer cannot later defend itself on the basis that the insured failed to file a proof of loss. The insurer that denies a claim also is open to subsequent allegations of bad faith and a judgment for punitive damages (discussed later).

Suit by Insured

Following an insurer's denial of coverage, both named insureds and additional insureds may file a suit against the insurer to recover money they have spent to resolve the original claim. The insurer needs to respond to such a suit to avoid a default judgment. However, the insurer may be able to have such a suit dismissed if the named insured or additional insured has not met the duties imposed by specific policy provisions.

Significant differences exist between property and liability policies with regard to their suit provisions. A property condition of homeowners forms, titled "Suit Against Us," states that "no action can be brought unless the policy provisions have been complied with and the action is started within one year after the date of loss." The liability portion of the homeowners policy contains the same stipulation about compliance with policy provisions, but it is not subject to the time limitation for filing suit. The reason is that liability policies also stipulate that no suit can be brought against the insurer until the obligation of the insured has been determined by final judgment or agreement; both can involve lengthy delays.

A policy provision saying that suit against the insurer depends on the insured's compliance with policy conditions does not mean that certain breaches by the insured will nullify its chances of enforcing coverage. When an insurer denies coverage outright, the insured is free to do whatever is necessary to resolve the claim, and the insurer generally loses its rights under the policy. For example, suppose an insurer denies that coverage applies to a given claim, the insured negotiates a settlement with the claimant by accepting some liability for the claimant's loss, and the insured then sues the insurer to enforce the coverage that originally was denied. In responding to this suit by the insured, the insurer cannot raise the defense that the insured breached the "duties after loss" condition of the policy by admitting its liability in order to settle the claim.

As a general rule, a third-party claimant cannot file suit against the insurance company of the tortfeasor (insured). However, there are exceptions in which a few states allow direct suits by claimants against insurance companies. The laws of the jurisdictions that permit such actions are referred to as "direct action statutes."

Preserving the Insurer's Rights

Reservation of rights letters and nonwaiver agreements should be recognized as a strong signal to the insured—and possibly others—that there is a potential coverage problem. By introducing either, the insurer raises the issue that it is unclear whether coverage applies to the claim.

Reservation of Rights Letter. When an insurer issues a reservation of rights letter to its insured, it in effect is handling the claim but subject to the possibility that coverage may be denied. The insurer specifies the nature of the dispute and states that it will investigate the claim or suit and provide a defense if necessary; however, it reserves its rights to deny coverage later in the event that the insurer's investigation shows that coverage does not apply. A reservation of rights letter has the following two purposes:

1. *To protect the insurer* so that it may deny coverage later, if conditions warrant, without being subject to an accusation that its earlier actions waived its right to deny coverage
2. *To inform the insured* that a coverage problem may exist and provide the insured an opportunity to protect his or her own interests

The issuance of a reservation of rights letter implies that there is a conflict between the interests of the insured and "the interests" of the insurance company. As long as the insurer is handling the case, the insurance company must appoint an attorney to defend the insured against the claimant at the insurance company's expense. In light of the potential conflict of interests, an insured sometimes prefers to select its own legal counsel, at the insurer's expense, to protect its interest.[1]

Regardless of who ultimately pays for the insured's defense, it is important that the reservation of rights letter clearly set forth the insurer's position. It must be specific and concise, and it must refer specifically to, and quote, the pertinent policy language. It also is important that the reservation of rights letter be sent to the insured as soon as the claims person recognizes a potential problem. An unreasonable delay could leave the insurer vulnerable to an action in bad faith.

As the insurer's investigation continues, the insurer may modify its position on certain possible defenses and acknowledge protection under the policy, or the insurer may deny coverage for additional reasons.

Nonwaiver Agreement. Although both a reservation of rights letter and a nonwaiver agreement signify that the insurer does not waive its rights to later deny coverage, there is one major difference between them. While a reservation of rights is signed by only the insurer, the nonwaiver agreement must be signed by both the insured and the insurer.

Nonwaiver agreements are not used as often as reservation of rights letters for at least two reasons:

- *The insured can refuse to sign a nonwaiver agreement.* When that happens, the insurer might deny a defense and ask a court to resolve the coverage question through a declaratory judgment action.
- *There is some authority to the effect that a nonwaiver agreement might be unenforceable because of the lack of consideration.* The insurer that promises to provide the insured a defense following acceptance of the nonwaiver agreement may not be giving the insured anything more than what the insured was owed by the insurer anyway.[2]

The "lack of consideration" argument is based on the reasoning that the duty to defend a suit is broader than the duty to pay. Even if some of the plaintiff's allegations are not covered by the policy, the insurer still has the obligation to defend all such allegations; it can presumably limit the payment of *damages* to those resulting from the allegations that are covered. So when the insurer presents a nonwaiver agreement rather than issuing a flat denial of coverage, it may signify that at least part of the action is covered.

Declaratory Judgment Action

In a declaratory judgment action, the insurer presents a *coverage* question to the court and asks the court to determine ("declare") the rights of the parties under an insurance policy. This kind of action could involve questions such as whether there has been an "occurrence," whether a given exclusion applies, or whether the insurer has the obligation to defend the insured against a specific set of allegations. The purpose of a declaratory judgment action is to resolve questions of *coverage* apart from questions regarding the insured's *liability*.

These actions are particularly useful when an insurer is confronted with a substantial third-party claim that involves a serious coverage question. If handled promptly, a declaratory judgment provides a decision on the coverage question before the third-party claim is litigated. If the court declares that coverage applies under the policy, the insurer can then decide how best to conclude the action. On the other hand, if the court declares that the insurer has no duty under the policy, the claim is closed so far as the insurer is concerned.

A declaratory judgment action may be used in addition to a reservation of rights letter or a nonwaiver agreement, or it may be used as a substitute. If an insured refuses to sign a nonwaiver agreement or rejects a reservation of rights letter, a declaratory judgment action may be the only method by which the insurer can avoid waiver and estoppel.

Declaratory judgment actions commonly are viewed as procedural devices used by insurance companies. However, insureds also can request declaratory judgments. Declaratory judgment actions are permitted by the laws of all but two states.[3]

LEGAL DOCTRINES

This section summarizes some of the major legal doctrines and principles that have influenced the courts in reaching their ultimate decisions with respect to the interpretation of insurance contracts. The same doctrines and principles are applied when negotiating claims outside the courtroom setting.

Contract of Adhesion Doctrine

As mentioned in earlier chapters, insurance policies are contracts of adhesion. Ambiguities in a contract of adhesion are interpreted against the party that drafted the agreement. Whether ambiguities in an insurance contract must be interpreted against the insurer depends on (1) who actually drafted the policy provision and (2) the insured's degree of sophistication in insurance matters.

In the most common insurance transactions a sophisticated seller, the insurance company, has drafted the insurance policy that is sold to an unsophisticated buyer who has had little or no say in the actual wording of the contract. Typically, then, any ambiguities are interpreted against the insurer. In some cases, however, the insurance contract is drafted, in whole or in part, by the insurance buyer or its representative, or it is negotiated between the insurance company and a sophisticated insurance buyer. In these cases the contract of adhesion doctrine may be applied somewhat differently.

Insurer Prepares Agreement. The insurer usually drafts the insurance contract. If there is any doubt about the policy's meaning, a court will interpret the policy against the insurer—and in favor of the insured. This is deemed to be the fairest approach because the insurer, who selected the language and terms of the agreement, presumably had every opportunity to serve its own best interests.

In some cases, the court rules that the policy or its terms are ambiguous. The term "ambiguity" has two meanings:

- It may mean that a provision of the contract can reasonably be interpreted in more than one way.
- It may mean that after using all of the tools of interpretation the court cannot determine the meaning of the language used.

In either event, the policy usually is construed for the insured's benefit. In other words, the insured is given the benefit of any doubt.

Insured Prepares Agreement. Many larger entities have their own risk management departments. Others are represented by knowledgeable and experienced insurance brokers, or by risk management and insurance consultants, who may draft manuscript insurance provisions. These professionals often have the same degree of sophistication, if not more, as the underwriting departments of some insurance companies.

When a risk manager, broker representative, consultant, or other party acting on behalf of the insured writes a policy provision that ultimately is not clear in intent, the provision could very well be construed against the insured (who may, in turn, have recourse against the broker or consultant).

Sophisticated Insured Rule. A growing body of law holds that the degree of sophistication of the insured or its representative should be taken into consideration in determining the intent of policy language that may be unclear—even if the provision in question was drafted by the insurance company.

In one case the insurer of a building destroyed in a fire brought an action against the city alleging negligence on the part of the fire department. The city's liability insurer denied protection to the fire department on the basis that coverage (1) did not apply, and also (2) was not intended to be provided. While the policy was in part ambiguous, it was not construed against the insurer. The reason, according to the court, was that the city that purchased the insurance was represented by an insurance advisory committee, a city attorney, and an experienced insurance producer. Because of the city's expertise on the matter of insurance, the court held that both the city and the insurer stood on an equal footing.[4]

Whether an insured is determined to fall within the so-called "sophisticated insured" rule depends on the circumstances. The courts often take into consideration the following factors:[5]

1. Size of the insured
2. Insured's employment of a professional risk manager
3. Involvement of counsel on insured's behalf
4. Insured's retention of a sophisticated insurance broker
5. The use of a manuscript policy
6. Relative bargaining power of the parties

While the ignorant insured may have a stronger legal position with respect to the resolution of ambiguities in the insurance contract, ignorance is not recommended.

Reasonable Expectations Doctrine

Although not all courts recognize the doctrine of "reasonable expectations," it serves at times to balance the rights of insureds with those of insurers. The reasonable expectations doctrine is triggered not by an ambiguity in the policy, but by the insured's surprise in the way the policy provisions are said to apply. When the *reasonable expectations doctrine* is applied, an insurance policy is interpreted to provide the protection that the insured might reasonably have expected, even though that expectation is not clearly expressed in or supported by the policy.

This doctrine sometimes is applied to renewal policies. When a renewal policy is issued, the insured can "reasonably expect," unless there is some kind of oral or written explanation accompanying it, that the provisions of the renewal policy are the same as those of the expired contract. Even though it normally is the insured's obligation to read the policy, if the policy provisions are amended without calling the changes to the attention of the insured, the insurance company may be bound by the terms of the earlier policy.

Unconscionable Advantage Doctrine

The courts rely heavily on general maxims of equity, which are necessarily vague so that their nets can expand or contract as the court thinks necessary. Although there are no well-defined limits to the principle that one cannot take unconscionable advantage of another, the courts have come to the aid of the insured in cases where the insured is trying to preserve the contract but finds some clause objectionable, difficult, or almost impossible to perform. Some court opinions candidly recognize the principle of unconscionability. Whether or not it is explicitly recognized, it often is the only rationale for a decision.

In one case an insured sent written notice of a fire loss, including detailed inventories of items lost in the fire. The information was more complete than that required by the proof of loss. (Like many other property insurance policies, this one required that the insured submit a signed and sworn "proof of loss," which usually is done by completing a form provided by the insurer.) The insurer never requested a completed proof of loss form, despite inquiries about the status of claim from the insured. In the meantime, the insurer proceeded to pay the mortgagee its interests under the policy, without any proof of loss form, and it then denied the insured's claim for failure to file the proof of loss form. A court prevented the insurer from taking unconscionable advantage of this insured.

There is an implied covenant of good faith and fair dealing in every insurance contract. This covenant demands that the insurer deal fairly with all of its insureds.

Substantial Performance Doctrine

Closely related to the concept of reasonable expectations is the equitable doctrine of "substantial performance." This doctrine recognizes that although policy conditions must be met, there are circumstances under which something short of literal performance may be acceptable. The doctrine may be applied to those insureds who presumably have undertaken to perform their contracts in all material and substantial particulars in an honest and faithful manner. Whether they have indeed done so becomes a factual question to be evaluated from all of the circumstances surrounding a case. The insured must be able to demonstrate that there was no willful omission or departure from the contract.

At one time, strict compliance with all insurance contract conditions was required. In more recent times, however, this requirement has been relaxed by legislative intervention, competitive business practices, and judicial interpretation. Today, the doctrine of substantial performance is used, instead of literal compliance, as the minimum standard that must be met by the insured. As long as the insured is acting honestly and in good faith, substantial compliance with the policy provisions usually is adequate, and the insurer will not be allowed to deny liability on the grounds of the insured's failure to abide by a narrower interpretation of the policy requirements.

Doctrines of Waiver and Estoppel

The concepts of waiver and estoppel are closely related. The terms themselves need to be defined before moving on to an explanation of how they may be applied.

- *Waiver* is the voluntary relinquishment of a known right.
- *Estoppel* exists when a party's present claimed position cannot be enforced because it is inconsistent with that party's past conduct.

Waiver and estoppel often are combined. Suppose, for example, an insurer accepts a policyholder's renewal premium twenty days after the due date, when coverage normally would have terminated. The insurer waives (voluntarily relinquishes) its right to terminate the policy for nonpayment of the renewal premium. Now, suppose a year later, the insurer refuses to pay a claim for an event taking place ten days after the premium was due, on the basis that coverage had terminated. The insured, however, insists that it intended to maintain continuous coverage by paying the renewal premium within the twenty-day period allowed last year. By *waiving* its rights to terminate the policy when it accepted the late premium one year (past conduct), the insurer may be *estopped* from enforcing the termination (present claimed position) during a subsequent year.

Collateral Estoppel. Simply stated, collateral estoppel means that the determination of an issue by litigation between two parties is binding in a subsequent suit involving essentially the same parties; the same issue will not be tried again. As one court phrased it, "collateral estoppel is the doctrine that renders conclusive in a subsequent action on a different claim, the determination of issues actually litigated in a prior action."[6]

Application of this doctrine requires the following three elements:

1. There must be identity of issues in the successive cases.
2. There must have been a determination of these issues by a valid final judgment.
3. The parties must be identical, or in privity, or the party estopped must have refused an opportunity to participate. This is known as the rule of mutuality of estoppel.

The doctrine is based upon the theory that parties should not be permitted to litigate the same issue more than once, provided there has been a full and complete determination of the issue.

Insurers have frequently invoked this doctrine to defeat a suit by other plaintiffs where the first suit was decided in favor of the insurer. A common example is an auto accident after which several passengers file separate suits against the driver. Most courts hold that once a driver is found to have been free of negligence, this issue cannot be relitigated in subsequent suits by other passengers. However, not all jurisdictions apply the doctrine in this way.

Judicial Estoppel. This doctrine holds that when someone argues a certain way or takes a certain position, he or she is bound by the original stance and cannot later take the opposite position on a subject involving essentially the same issues. If an insurer interprets its insurance policy in a certain way and wins one case, it cannot later interpret the policy in another way in order to avoid coverage—given the same set of circumstances.

For example, in litigation involving asbestosis, an insurer argues that its liability policy is "triggered" only at the time of the manifestation of the bodily injury (which was well after its insurance policy had expired). Suppose that later, in an entirely different case, the insurer attempts to argue that its policy is "triggered" at the time of the initial exposure to asbestos by a person (in this case, the initial exposure period was long before its policy was issued). Under the doctrine of judicial estoppel, the insurer that argues one way about how its policy applies and wins its argument will be estopped from later maintaining the policy's application in a contradictory way in order to avoid coverage of another claim.

EXTERNAL FACTORS INVOKED BY
POLICY PROVISIONS

Some very pertinent rights and obligations are not spelled out in the language of an insurance policy itself, although they may somehow be called upon or "invoked" by the policy. Included in this category are provisions under which the contract may be modified by the provisions in subsequent revisions of the same policy or by unnamed, applicable statutes. Some similar "external factors" have been mentioned in earlier chapters. For example, workers compensation insurance pays the benefits stipulated in the state workers compensation law. Likewise, some insurance policies refer to the insurer's rules and rating manuals as the basis on which premiums will be computed, although the rules and manuals themselves are not attached to the policy.

The contract provisions discussed here are mentioned elsewhere in this book. Because of their importance in invoking external factors that ultimately affect policy interpretation, they need to be reexamined here from a somewhat different perspective.

Coverage Automatically Expanded by Policy Revisions

Many insurance contracts contain a liberalization clause. A liberalization clause has the effect of taking documents that are outside the policy and incorporating them into the contract.

The Insurance Services Office (ISO) commercial property conditions form includes the following provision:

LIBERALIZATION

If we adopt any revision that would broaden the coverage under this Coverage Part without additional premium within 45 days prior to or during the policy period, the broadened coverage will immediately apply to this Coverage Part.

Because of this clause, an insured may be the recipient of an extra-contractual right that was not contemplated when the policy was written.

The liberalization clause comes into play whenever an insurer introduces policy form revisions that broaden coverage without an additional premium charge. Before liberalization clauses came into use, insurers that improved their policies would receive a number of requests to cancel and rewrite outstanding policies using the new, broader form. Those insureds whose policies were not reissued did not then receive the benefit of the changes.

The liberalization clause automatically amends an existing policy, as of the effective date of the new policy form, to incorporate its broadened features into the existing contract. However, this clause works in only one direction—it does not automatically invoke any new restrictions in coverage. This clause has tended to give insureds the opportunity to have their cakes and eat them, too, but that unilateral advantage may not continue. The liberalization clauses in a few recent policy editions state that they do not apply to general program revisions that involve both broadenings and restrictions in coverage. It is too early to judge whether this will become the general approach.

It is impossible for most insureds to recognize when they are entitled to the broadened coverage of a new policy edition they have never seen. Because insurer claims representatives naturally become most familiar with the outstanding policies that have been in use for a while, as opposed to brand new policy revisions, it also is difficult for them to remain abreast of the fine points of recently introduced forms changes. It may be even more difficult to recognize their effect on claims under existing contracts. However, the terms of the liberalization clause provide contractual *rights* to which insurance buyers are entitled, even though they are based on documents external to the contract in which the liberalization clause is contained. It is an ethical obligation of insurance company representatives to provide policyholders with *all* the benefits to which they are legally entitled.

Coverage Modified in Conformity With Statutes

For many years, it was common for policies to incorporate a specific *conformity with statute* provision. A typical clause read as follows:

> The terms of this policy which are in conflict with the statutes of the state wherein this policy is issued are hereby amended to conform with such statutes.

Often, laws are passed affecting a relatively minor part of an insurance contract. Even without a conformity provision, state statutes control insurance policies. However, the presence of the clause reassures some regulatory agencies that might otherwise be concerned by insurance contracts that were out of compliance with current statutes.

Printing a special one-state version of a policy or a one-state amendatory endorsement to reflect the quirks of that state's laws is done at some expense that eventually must be paid by policyholders. The conformity to statute clause enables insurers to use a countrywide form despite conflicting state statutes.

The conformity with statute clause has been dropped from use by the Insurance Services Office. But the American Association of Insurance Services still utilizes this clause in its personal and commercial property forms. Whether or not the policy contains an explicit "conformity to statute" provision, insurance policyholders are entitled to the benefits applicable under any current statute.

COVERING THE UNKNOWN

Many policy provisions provide coverage to unnamed insureds, or on nonowned property, or for unidentified exposures or undefined perils. Too, there is the problem of delayed policy issuance, which creates a time period during which some assumptions must be made concerning the specifics of the contract.

Unnamed Insureds

As a general rule, only a party named in a contract can maintain an action to enforce it. However, the interests of some unnamed parties are insured under property and liability insurance policies because some policy provision includes them by reference. Unnamed insureds include, for example, those who fall into a generic class description or those who serve as a legal substitute for a named insured. Coverage for additional insureds, either by name or with generic descriptions, may be added by endorsement.

Chapter 4 discussed these various approaches to specifying the parties insured under a given insurance contract. They are mentioned briefly here as a reminder that the identities of those parties insured under any insurance contract may not readily be ascertained by examining only the insurance policy itself.

Nonowned Property

Many situations exist where nonowned property can be the subject of a covered loss. In some cases, the legal obligation for indemnifying against loss or damage to nonowned property arises out of a relationship between the named insured and the property owner. In others, it is based on an obligation assumed under a contract. Among the various categories of nonowned property are the following:

- *Bailed property*—dry cleaners, laundries, warehouses, and repair shops that have within their care, custody, or control the property of customers for which they may or may not be legally liable
- *Leased property*—autos, computers, and other equipment leased under written contracts that prescribe the respective responsibilities of the parties
- *Property on consignment*—property belonging to others on the premises of distributors and retailers awaiting sale, generally subject to a written contract between the parties specifying who is to be responsible
- *Employees' property*—items such as tools and clothing, owned by employees, situated on the premises of their employers. Some union contracts make the employer responsible for loss of such tools where accountability may not otherwise exist.

It often is not necessary that an owner of property be named in the insurance policy in order to protect its insurable interests. Various property policies offer various degrees of protection to unnamed persons, or beneficiaries, sometimes subject to the approval of the named insured.

- The property section of homeowners forms commonly covers loss to personal property of others in the care, custody, or control of the insured.
- Homeowners forms generally also cover, at the named insured's option, personal property owned by a guest or domestic employee while such property is within the premises occupied by the insured.
- Some inland marine floaters written for dry cleaners or other bailees will cover loss to customers' goods even without regard to the bailee's liability.

- The standard building and personal property coverage form of ISO, under "your business personal property" coverage, covers leased property that the named insured has a contractual obligation to insure. An additional coverage applies to personal effects and personal property of others for a limited amount. Coverage on personal property of others in the named insured's care, custody, or control also may be arranged under a separate insuring agreement.

Unidentified Exposures

Automatic coverage commonly is granted when a new exposure arising during the policy period is covered without immediate notification to the insurer. In some cases automatic coverage applies until the end of the policy period, at which time the new exposure must be reported. In others, the exposure automatically is covered and the insured is given a specified number of days within which to report it to the insurer so that it can be added to the policy. This automatic coverage sometimes is spelled out in policy provisions, but in other cases it is a matter of custom or practice developed, in part, to minimize paperwork.

One such example concerns newly acquired autos under the personal auto policy. This policy includes as a covered auto an additional auto acquired by the named insured or resident spouse during the policy period so long as the named insured asks the insurer to cover it within thirty days after the named insured becomes the owner.[7] Assume that after the policy has been in force for three months, the named insured buys a new (additional) private passenger auto. Two weeks after she buys this vehicle, she still has not reported it to her insurance company and she is involved in an auto accident in which she is at fault and causes damage to the other car. The named insured is covered here because the accident took place within the thirty-day period.

Commercial property insurance policies also commonly offer automatic coverage for a certain period. This extension may encompass newly constructed as well as newly acquired buildings and structures. Generally, these new additions are subject to limitations as to insurance amounts, time within which the insurer must be informed about these new exposures, and, for new construction, the location of the construction. However, if a newly acquired building is partially damaged during the policy's automatic coverage period, the insured may well be protected if the loss is otherwise covered by the policy.

Commercial general liability policies also commonly include various forms of protection for new exposures that arise after the policy is issued, subject to an additional charge when the policy is audited at expiration. If an insured with a CGL policy, for example, conducts business as a convenience store and during the policy period adds an automatic carwash at the same premises, general liability coverage should apply without notice to the insurer for the duration of the policy, whether or not the carwash is necessary or incidental to the store's operation.

However, some limitations must be heeded when new exposures arise under a CGL. If the named insured forms a partnership or a joint venture (which is a partnership for a limited purpose), this needs to be reported to the insurer immediately, because many policies specify that only those partnerships and joint ventures that are declared to the insurer are deemed to be covered. Any other organization in which the named insured acquires ownership or majority ownership during the policy period may need to be reported within, say, ninety days of such acquisition. If injury or damage takes place after such acquisition and during the ninety-day period, the named insured will be protected subject to the policy terms. But if the acquisition is not reported, the insured is on its own after the specified reporting period.

Undefined Perils

Fire is one of the most serious and common of property perils. It is listed as a named peril in most named-peril property insurance policies (except those specifically designed to cover flood, burglary or robbery, or some other specific peril), and it is not excluded from "all-risks" policies (except plate glass policies and those using a difference-in-conditions approach). However, while property policies do not say so specifically, some fires are not considered to be a covered cause of loss or peril. While the courts have made exceptions in some unusual cases, the general rule is that no coverage applies under the "fire" peril to loss of covered property by a *friendly* fire—a fire that remains within its intended place. If some valuable item were to be accidentally dropped onto a heated stove or into a fireplace, many insurers would not pay for the resulting damage or destruction of the property even though the policy does not contain any written exclusion to that effect.

However, a *hostile* fire, which is one that is accidental or leaves its intended place, generally is considered a covered peril. Thus, if sparks from a lighted fireplace set a house on fire, a hostile fire has occurred and the damage would be covered by the policy. Again, there is nothing specific within the typical property policy's provisions that makes this distinction.

Delayed Policy Issuance

Often, a complete, written insurance policy is not formally issued until after its effective date. To provide insureds with peace of mind and the assurance that protection applies despite the lack of a complete, written contract, insurers commonly issue binders. A binder is a temporary contract that signifies that a certain kind of coverage exists. The problem is that binders generally are only one page long, and they do not contain all the provisions ultimately appearing in the complete written insurance contract, although they may refer to specific form names or numbers. So when a loss occurs before the actual policy is issued, there may be some misunderstanding about the actual coverage that was agreed upon.

There is no rule on which one can rely in the event of problems; each situation must be considered on its own merits. Decisions often are influenced in part by how state statutes define insurance binders. Generally speaking, the terms of a policy prescribe the extent of coverage even when the policy has not yet been delivered. Thus, in one case, the terms of a fire insurance policy governed the coverage provided to an insured even though the policy had not been delivered before the fire occurred. Under the policy provisions for replacement cost coverage, the insured was not entitled to replacement cost because it elected not to replace the building and equipment destroyed by fire. The insured therefore could recover only the actual cash value of the property.[8]

In another case, an accident occurred before the policy was issued, and the binder did not mention that any deductible was applicable. The insured argued that the deductible did not apply. However, the court upheld the application of the deductible because the deductible was a common condition of the policies issued by this insurer for the type of risks in question.[9]

UNWRITTEN RIGHTS TO CONTINUE PROTECTION

Numerous occasions arise when protection under an insurance policy does not end or lapse when one might expect it to. In some cases insureds are accorded continued protection because a given statute mandates it; because of insurance company procedures dealing with billing cycles, delays in renewals, or policy issuance timing practices; or because of the way an insurance contract is structured.

Statutory Protection

When underwriting results began to suffer in the mid-sixties, particularly in private passenger auto insurance, insurers embarked on a wave of policy cancellations that created considerable ill will among consumers. Shortly thereafter, legislation was introduced in many states to limit insurers' cancellation and nonrenewal rights. Originally these statutes applied only to auto liability insurance, but now many also apply to property and liability insurance covering both individuals and commercial entities.

The majority of states currently impose restrictions on insurance companies that desire to terminate coverage.[10] The laws give insurers a certain number of days in which to investigate new submissions during which they may reject applicants for any valid reason. Once this so-called "look-see" period has passed, the policy may be canceled only for certain specified reasons.

As mentioned earlier in connection with "conformity to statutes," the applicable law always takes precedence over policy provisions. The personal auto policy of ISO reflects this in the following policy condition:

> If the law in effect in your state at the time this policy is issued, renewed or continued:
> a. requires a longer notice period;
> b. requires a special form of or procedure for giving notice; or
> c. modifies any of the stated termination reasons;
> we will comply with those requirements.

In some cases, policies include cancellation or nonrenewal conditions that are more liberal to the insured than the requirements of currently prevailing laws. In such cases, the policy provision, which favors the insured, would prevail, but that is not the point here. The point is that if the insurer fails to follow at least the statutory provisions or provides late notice, the insurer will likely be required to continue insurance for the full term or another term.

Cancellation Practices

Sometimes insureds can obtain coverage that otherwise might not apply because of insurance company practices of handling cancellation notices. For example, when a premium installment is not paid, one might intuitively expect that coverage has terminated. However, laws or policy provisions often require the insurer to provide a certain number of days' advance notice to the insured before any cancellation takes effect. Until that time period has elapsed, the insurer is obligated to fulfill its promises just as though no notice of cancellation had been issued.

It can complicate matters when the insurer rescinds the notice of cancellation, continues coverage, and later issues another notice of cancellation. If the insurer produces a pattern of notice and reinstatement, it could be estopped from denying coverage later. In one such case, for example, an insurer was precluded by a court from canceling a policy for late payment of a premium where, over a period of years, it had engaged in the practice of canceling the insured's policy, accepting late premium payment, and then reinstating the policy.

Briefly, the facts of this case indicated the following:

(a) December 14, 1981—policy canceled
   January 8, 1982—premium received, policy reinstated
(b) November 15, 1982—policy canceled
   November 17, 1982—premium received, policy reinstated
(c) January 24, 1983—policy canceled
   January 26, 1983—premium received, policy reinstated
(d) September 20, 1983—policy canceled
   September 24, 1983—premium received, policy reinstated
(e) December 8, 1983—policy canceled
   December 14, 1983—premium received, policy reinstated
(f) December 30, 1984—policy canceled
   January 7, 1985—premium received, policy reinstated
(g) March 20, 1985—policy canceled
   April 1, 1985—premium paid, policy *not* reinstated

Initially the insurer accepted the premium payment that was due on February 27, 1985. The insurer deposited it on April 1 and refunded it on April 11, 1985. It was a day later, on April 12, that the named insured's daughter was involved in an accident. Even so, the insurer was held to be responsible under its policy, because there was a uniform course of dealing by the insurer that was relied on by the parties. The court stated that the conduct of the insurer of consistently reinstating the insurance policy after notifying the insured of cancellation had established a uniform conduct of doing business so as to allow the insured to rely on it.[11]

The foregoing may be an unusual circumstance, but it is not unusual for insurers to reinstate coverage after a cancellation notice has been issued. This practice enables all parties to effect continuous coverage, without a gap.

BURDEN OF PROOF

Generally, the burden of proof is on the *insured* to show that coverage applies under a policy. For example, if a claim is made against the insured because of bodily injury or property damage stemming from the insured's products, it is necessary for the insured to show that it had purchased products liability insurance. The burden of proof then shifts to the insurer, which, to preclude coverage, must show that one or more exclusions apply. It is not always easy for an insurer to establish that an exclusion applies. The use of an "all-risks" property insurance policy, rather than a named perils policy, shifts the burden of proof of causation to the insurer—even though the policy does not say so.

The difference is as follows:

- *Named perils policy.* When property is covered on a named perils basis, it is the burden of the *insured* to show that loss to covered property was proximately caused by one or more of the named perils. If the insured can sustain this burden of proof (assuming the other elements of an insured event are present), there is a presumption that the loss is covered and the burden then shifts to the insurer. Only then, if coverage is to be precluded, must the insurer be able to show that a specific exclusion or some other barrier to coverage in the policy clearly applies to the claim.
- *"All-risks" policy.* When a property policy is written on an "all-risks" basis—with or without the "all," the policy does not say so, but the insured has the burden to show only the existence of an "all-risks" policy and loss to covered property. The insured is not required to establish the cause of loss. Indeed, it can be much easier to establish the damage or destruction of property than it is to show its cause! Once the insured fulfills these minimal requirements, the *insurer*, if it wishes to preclude coverage, must then prove that the claim is excluded from coverage.

Sometimes an insurer simply points to one or more exclusions as the basis for denying a loss under an "all-risks" policy. This is not enough. The insurer must also show that the loss was *proximately caused by the excluded peril.* This places an especially heavy burden on the insurer because the contract of adhesion doctrine suggests that exclusions in the policy usually will be given the interpretation that is most beneficial to the insured. To sustain the burden of proof, it is not enough for the insurer merely to offer one reasonable interpretation under which the loss is excluded.

Thus, there is an important difference between named perils and "all-risks" coverage insofar as the burden of proof is concerned. With a named perils policy, the primary burden is on the insured to prove that loss was caused by a named peril. With an "all-risks" policy, on the other hand, the heaviest burden is on the insurer to prove that the loss was caused by an excluded peril. In both instances, this burden is not specifically addressed in the policies.

OVERLAPPING SOURCES OF RECOVERY

An insurance company is not necessarily aware of all the other insurance or noninsurance sources of recovery that may be available to a policyholder. Even the policyholder may not be aware of possible overlapping sources of recovery until after a loss—if then. As discussed in Chapter 8, various provisions in each insurance policy clarify how *that policy* will respond following a loss for which multiple sources of recovery exist. However, a provision in one policy cannot directly clarify the responsibility of an insurer that issued another policy external to the insurer's own insurance contract.

The entire topic of "other insurance" was examined in detail in Chapter 8. The following point must be emphasized here: *The external factors affecting an insurer's obligation under its insurance contract may include other insurance policies, other noninsurance sources of recovery, and external formal agreements as to how other-insurance situations will be reconciled.*

Subrogation by Insurer

It is not necessary that the insured pursue a claim against its own insurance company and relegate recovery to that insurer. The insured may bypass its own insurance company and attempt to recover directly from the third party responsible for the injury or damage. These alternatives are not explicitly described in most policies.

The subrogation provision in most property-liability policies provides that, when an insurer makes payment for loss to, or on behalf of, an insured, the insurer takes over the rights that the insured may have had to collect damages from any other party responsible for the loss. The insurer is "subrogated" to the insured's right of recovery. Subrogation shifts the ultimate cost of a loss to the party most responsible for causing the loss.

Bases of the Legal Actions. The insurer's right to subrogation is independent of policy provisions. In fact, the courts have uniformly upheld the right of the insurer to implement subrogation under all indemnity-type coverages, as well as under all property coverages, even when these policies did not contain an express subrogation clause. Yet, nearly all property-liability policies contain subrogation provisions for reasons that include insurers' general concern that failure to include an express provision might be interpreted as a voluntary waiver of subrogation rights.

The broad sources of the right of subrogation are statutes and common law. However, once the right of subrogation is established, the legal actions can be based upon any appropriate area of private law, according to the dictates of the particular situation. That is to say, the nature of the insurer's subrogation action will depend on the rights and remedies that the insured has against the tortfeasor. The insured's right to recover money damages from the other party could be based on negligence, strict liability, intentional interference, breach of contract, or failure to discharge the legal duties of an agency relationship. Likewise, the basis of the insurer's subrogation action is limited only by the extent to which the insured has a right to indemnity from the other party.

When the insured suffers property damage, the insured may or may not have the right to recover from another party. If not, there can be no subrogation by the insurer. If so, the insured's right of recovery is most often based upon the negligence of the other party. In property insurance also, the usual subrogation action is based on negligence.

Targets of Subrogation. Despite the general rule that an insurer cannot sue its own insured for recovery of loss or damages, there have been increasing attempts to do so. These attempts are especially prevalent with property insurance. In one commonly cited case, the court upheld the insurer's right to recover against a subcontractor even though the subcontractor was an insured under a builders risk policy. The court maintained that the insurable interest of the subcontractor was limited to the value of its own work and not to the work of others that was damaged.[12] A number of other cases involving builders risk policies have followed, with mixed results.

In another property insurance case, a corporation's insurer did not have the right of subrogation against a corporate officer whose negligence caused the fire in question even though the officer was not specifically named in the policy. The corporate officer was considered an additional insured under the policy on the basis of having up to $2,500 of coverage of his personal effects at the insured premises. Because the executive was an insured, the insurer could not obtain any reimbursement of its loss payment from this executive.[13]

It is relatively rare for an insurer to successfully subrogate against an insured under a liability policy. In fact, being named as an additional insured is a technique used to prevent subrogation attempts by insurers. But insurers nevertheless will try on occasion if the circumstances appear to be warranted. In one case in which the insurer succeeded, the court held that an insurer was entitled to subrogation from a partner of an insured partnership who intentionally, and for personal reasons, set a fire that caused covered losses under the policy.

These cases of subrogation against insureds are still relatively small compared to the number of cases in which surrogation is pursued against third parties.

"Self-Insurance" Sources

The question of whether self-insurance that takes the form of a formal funding arrangement, unfunded retention, or a deductible is deemed to be a form of insurance is frequently raised in litigation. The purpose for raising the question is to obtain another source of recovery. The underlying problem is that many liability insurance policies refer to "other *insurance*," which leaves open the question of whether a retention arrangement of some kind is actually a form of insurance.

In one case, for example, an insurer issued a liability policy for an association of nurses that promised payment of up to $200,000 per claim only after a member's other valid and collectible insurance was exhausted. A hospital that also employed one of those nurses maintained a similar liability policy subject to a limit of $500,000. Under its provisions, however, the payment of damages was subject to a $100,000 self-insured retention with the additional condition that the policy was to apply in excess over any other applicable insurance. A suit arose when the employed nurse negligently performed her duties and caused injuries to a patient that led to $375,000 in damages. Both insurers and the hospital paid the damages and then took to court the question of the share each should ultimately bear.

The trial court held that the hospital's self-insured retention of $100,000 constituted "other insurance" under the excess insurance provision of the association's liability policy. The court also ruled that the other two insurers were to share equally the difference of $275,000. On appeal, the court reversed the decision. In doing so, it held that the $100,000, characterized as a self-insured sum in the hospital's liability policy, was merely a deductible and did not constitute "other insurance." The insurer of the association policy therefore had to pay the $100,000 that was advanced by the hospital, and then both of the insurance companies had to share the remaining sum on a pro rata basis.[14] On the other hand, there have been cases where the courts have held that a deductible is considered "other insurance" for purposes of determining collateral sources.[15]

As a result of the growing number of cases on this issue, many insurance policies—particularly those that are manuscripted by captives, pools, risk retention groups, and specialty-line insurers—include references to the terms "self-insurance" and "self-insured retention or deductible" within the other insurance provisions of their contracts. Doing so will likely enhance these insurers' ability to maximize the other sources of recovery.

EXTERNAL NONINSURANCE CONTRACTS

Another type of external factor that can influence the payment of loss under an insurance policy involves the side agreements that shift liability from one party to another. Such agreements are made under countless types of contracts, entered into on a daily basis. These contracts are widely referred to as "noninsurance contracts" because, while they resemble insurance in that they involve some transfer of risks, they are not insurance contracts. Construction contracts, lease of premises agreements, easements, equipment leases, purchase order and sales agreements, and elevator maintenance agreements are among the noninsurance contracts that commonly include a transfer of risk.

Two common types of noninsurance contracts affecting liability insurance are exculpatory and hold harmless agreements. Pre-loss waivers, discussed shortly under a separate heading, are a type of exculpatory agreement commonly affecting property insurance situations.

- *Exculpatory agreements.* In an exculpatory agreement, one party says to a second party, "I will not hold you responsible for what you do to me." An exculpatory agreement therefore relieves the other party of its liability.
- *Hold harmless agreements.* In a hold harmless agreement, one party says to a second party, "I will be responsible for claims brought against you by a third party." Under the hold harmless agreement, the tortfeasor's legal liability to the third party is not affected. However, one party to the hold harmless agreement agrees to pay damages for the benefit of (and defend) the second party, who may become liable to pay damages.

Noninsurance contracts specify which party will pay for losses. However, the general intent underlying most noninsurance contracts is not to force one party to retain the loss, but rather to indicate in advance of any loss whose insurance company is expected to cover it.

For example, when Party A agrees to hold harmless and indemnify another contracting party for specified kinds of losses, Party A generally intends to see to it that Party A's own insurance company will respond on behalf of Party A if the agreement must be fulfilled. If Party A maintains contractual liability insurance, it is possible that all or part of the financial consequences of the contract, as agreed to by Party A, will be handled by its insurer. Much will depend on the nature of the underlying contractual provision and the extent to which an insurance policy covers the contractual obligation.

Exculpatory Agreements

Generally, an exculpatory agreement is any kind of contract provision that by nature or purpose seeks to absolve, relieve, or excuse a contracting party from the defense and/or consequences of an alleged fault, blame, or guilt the party would otherwise bear by the operation of law. In other words, the word "exculpatory" refers to a broad class of contract provisions that seek to transfer loss exposures from at least one contracting party to another.

Hold Harmless Agreements

A hold harmless clause in a contract is an agreement whereby one party (indemnitor) agrees to hold harmless another party (indemnitee) for certain liabilities to third parties that may be imposed upon the indemnitee by law. Such assumption of liability can vary from the broad assumption of the indemnitee's sole fault, to the comparative fault of both the indemnitee and indemnitor, to a more limited agreement whereby protection of the indemnitee is contingent on the sole fault of the indemnitor.

Pre-Loss Waivers

Property insurance policies commonly include a subrogation provision that provides for the transfer or automatically transfers to the insurer, following a loss, the insured's rights to recovery from any third party who is responsible for the property damage. The subrogation provision of many property policies also forbids the insured from doing anything after a loss that would adversely affect the insurer's right of subrogation against others. If this condition is breached by the insured, the insurer may be released entirely from any obligation under the policy. To preserve the insurer's rights of subrogation, the typical subrogation provision prohibits the insured from waiving any of its rights of recovery *after a loss*.

After a loss the insured would, in effect, be waiving not its own rights, but the insurer's. Before the loss, the situation may be different. Pre-loss waivers are explicitly permitted in the typical property insurance policy provision, and such waiver agreements are common. Within the context of this chapter, therefore, it is relevant to examine the nature of such pre-loss waivers which, although they are external to the insurance contract, can have a bearing on the various parties' rights of recovery under the insurance contract.

A pre-loss waiver sometimes is referred to as a waiver of subrogation. Its purpose is to prevent an insurer from exercising its right of subrogation against someone whom the insured may have released from liability. An example could be a lessee or tenant of a building. The landlord (lessor) may give the tenant (lessee) a waiver only to the extent that the lessor's property policy provides coverage. In other words, both parties agree that the tenant is not responsible (is exculpated) for any damage to property covered by the landlord's insurance. Often these are mutual waivers; that is, the tenant gives the lessor a waiver and the lessor does the same for the tenant.

The following are two examples of subrogation provisions. The first is the typical clause found in property insurance that contains the pre-loss waiver. This provision commonly forms a part of the policy condition titled *transfer of rights of recovery against others to us*. It reads as follows:

> If any person or organization to or for whom we make payment under this Coverage Part has rights to recover damages from another, those rights are transferred to us to the extent of our payment. That person or organization must do everything necessary to secure our rights and must do nothing after loss to impair them. But you may waive your rights against another party in writing:
> 1. Prior to a loss to your Covered Property or Covered Income.
> 2. After a loss to your Covered Property or Covered Income only if, at time of loss, that party is one of the following:
>   a. Someone insured by this insurance;
>   b. A business firm;
>   (1) Owned or controlled by you; or
>   (2) That owns or controls you; or
>   c. Your tenant.
>
> This will not restrict your insurance.

The second type of subrogation clause, found in a builders risk policy, is uncommon and not so obvious, particularly to the parties insured under this policy who seldom actually see the policy provisions. It reads as follows:

> **Impairment of Recovery Rights:** Any act or agreement by the Insured before or after loss or damage whereby any right of the Insured to recover in whole or in part for loss or damage to property covered hereunder against any carrier, bailee or other party liable therefor, is released, impaired or lost, shall render this policy null and void, but the insurer's right to retain and recover the premium shall not be affected.

This policy provision is unusual, but it helps to make an important point. There is a tendency to assume that all policy provisions of a given type are identical—but one should not judge a clause by its caption. *Most* property insurance policies permit waivers of subrogation prior to loss, but it could be dangerous to assume that *all* policies do. According to the terms of this policy, breach of the above provision nullifies the entire policy. Pre-loss waivers are *not* permitted under this particular policy. The existence of an external contract containing a pre-loss waiver could void this policy—an important piece of information that would not come to the attention of one who has merely scanned the subheadings within the policy!

UNLISTED SETTLEMENT OPTIONS

While most insurance policies contain specific language that explains how claims will be settled, there are instances when settlements agreed to by the parties do not directly conform to any of the alternatives cited by policy provisions. Three examples of such unlisted insurance settlement options are negotiation, structured settlements, and rehabilitation.

Negotiation

Negotiating a settlement often involves give and take, making a concession here and getting a concession there. When auto physical damage insurance is purchased, for example, the insurer agrees to pay for the loss in money or to repair or replace the damaged or stolen property minus any applicable deductible. Since no dollar amount is specified in the policy to represent the auto's value, the insurer will have to consider the make of the auto, its age, its condition, the extent of the damage, and, possibly, any diminution in value following repair to structural damage. The amount the insurer ultimately pays will likely hinge on negotiation if the insured is reluctant to accept the insurer's first offer. Such circumstances are especially likely when the cost of an auto's repairs exceeds the difference between the auto's value immediately before the loss and its value immediately after the loss. In these situations, vehicles are normally considered "constructive total losses." The insurer pays for the full value of the auto (less any deductible) and takes title to the damaged vehicle to be sold as salvage. Some negotiation might be involved before insurer and insured come to an agreement on the value of the now-totaled vehicle—especially if there is something unusual about the vehicle or if the insured wishes to keep the salvage.

The same kind of negotiation may take place with respect to liability insurance. It is not unusual, for example, for the insurer's claim representative to negotiate with a third party over the amount of damages that will be paid. In more serious cases, much of the negotiation occurs between the attorneys representing both parties.

Structured Settlements

Structured settlements (sometimes referred to as "periodic payment settlements") serve as an alternative to the traditional lump-sum payment of damages to an injured claimant. Under a structured settlement, the insurer provides periodic future payments for damages, either for the life of the injured person or for a stated period. Typically, the insurer arranges the funding by purchasing an annuity. Structured settlements have become particularly popular in bodily injury and wrongful death cases involving large verdicts. The technique could be said to be an adaptation of the weekly or monthly payment provisions of state workers compensation laws.

Scheduled lump-sum payments, often at five- and ten-year intervals, may be included. The claimant may use these lump-sum payments to pay for anticipated medical or rehabilitation expenses. Considerable flexibility and creativity may be exercised, depending on the individual needs of the claimant.

Rehabilitation Services

Rehabilitation has been defined as "the restoration of an injured or diseased person to his or her optimum physical, mental, vocational and economic usefulness."[16] Rehabilitation programs, such as those now provided under workers compensation laws of many states, are thought of as a means to reduce the seriousness of disabling injuries. They meet that purpose, in part, by providing vocational or physical assistance to the injured so that they can return to some form of gainful employment.

The interests of disabled persons generally favor starting rehabilitation as soon as possible. In fact, rehabilitation is considered an integral part of complete medical treatment, but it may go much farther and include such things as vocational training, training to drive a specially equipped auto, and so on.

While the cost of an extensive rehabilitation program can be large, and there is no guarantee of success, the opportunity for long-term savings has made rehabilitation an important method of loss control for insurers—and one that is not prescribed in most insurance policies. (Some "no-fault" personal injury protection endorsements to auto insurance policies explicitly provide for rehabilitation expenses.)

FACTORS AFFECTING AMOUNT PAYABLE

It is probably the exception rather than the rule that the property or liability insurance policy, alone, includes enough information to dictate what precise dollar amount of loss is payable by the insurance company. Whether they cover property of the insured or liability of the insured, insurance policies normally rely on external information to determine in whole or in part the amount that will have to be paid.

Valuation of Property Losses

While property insurance generally is written subject to a certain specified *maximum* dollar limit of insurance, the insurer is not necessarily required to pay that amount—even in the event of a total loss. It may turn out that the insured is carrying inadequate limits of insurance and therefore must retain part of the loss. Another factor that may limit the amount of recovery for a property loss is the extent of the insurable interest possessed by insured parties. Insurable interests were examined extensively in Chapter 3, and this chapter will not attempt to repeat that material. The point here is that the nature and extent of a party's insurable interest in property at the time of the loss is external to the property insurance policy, but it can have a profound effect on the amount of recovery provided under a policy.

The measure of damages in a personal property loss ordinarily is actual cash value. Actual cash value is not defined in most policies, but it customarily means replacement cost now less depreciation. The many external factors typically considered in determining the depreciation of property were explained in detail in Chapter 6. When the value of property is determined after a loss, the valuation also affects the loss payable because of coinsurance clauses or other loss-sharing provisions.

The external factors mentioned above have been analyzed in earlier chapters. One external factor that has not been mentioned is the effect, in some states, of valued policy laws.

Valued Policy Laws.   Valued policy laws, or so-called total loss statutes, apply only to fixed-location property policies. They apply principally to loss by the peril of fire (although some states also include windstorm). These are not to be confused with valued policies, which are policies that set in advance of loss the dollar value of property and agree to pay that amount in the event of loss.

Valued policy laws were enacted by some states in the late 1800s and early 1900s, mainly to give insureds "what they had paid for." In general, these laws provide that in case of total loss to an insured's property, primarily real property, from one or more certain specified perils (usually fire), the amount stated in the policy declarations is conclusively presumed to be the value of the structure at the time of the loss and is payable in full without any deductions. If the "actual" value of the property is less than the limit of insurance in the policy, a valued policy law precludes the insurer from arguing that a lesser sum should be paid. It is for this reason that valued policy laws are said to favor the insured.

As noted earlier, the general rule is that policy provisions that are in conflict with a statute, including valued policy laws, are void. Thus, for example, coinsurance clauses, pro rata clauses, and the option to repair or replace are invalid in the event of total loss. However, a valued policy law does not ordinarily override such policy provisions as the suit clause or notice of loss.

There are many peculiarities to these laws. As they apply in a minority of states, none of them needs to be mentioned here. The point is that a valued policy law is an external factor that might have to be taken into consideration following loss to property. If it does, it may affect the amount payable regardless of any specific policy provisions to the contrary. These are not the only laws that have an effect on the amount payable. Whether the policy says so or not, the applicable law always takes precedence over the policy language.

Valuation of Liability Claims

When bodily injury is involved, the value of a liability claim often depends on medical records and the reports and opinions of attending physicians. The determination of a claim's size requires proper evaluation of medical information.

While the determination of the amount of damages in a property damage claim is similar to a property insurance loss, a bodily injury liability claim is significantly different. Bodily injury may involve not only special damages, but also general damages. Punitive damages may be involved in both bodily injury and property damage claims.

In short, the amount payable under an insurance policy often is difficult to determine until various external factors are taken into consideration in valuing the loss or damage.

Special Damages. Specific out-of-pocket expenses and income losses are known as special damages. In bodily injury cases, these usually include hospital expenses, doctor and miscellaneous medical expenses, ambulance charges, prescriptions, and lost wages for time spent away from the job during recovery. Because they are specific and identifiable, special damages are easier to calculate than general damages. Still, it is not always easy to determine a proper level of medical treatment, proper charges for that treatment, the appropriate length of a disability period, or the extent and duration of future medical care.

General Damages. Examples of general damages include compensation for pain and suffering; disfigurement; loss of limbs, sight, or hearing; and loss of the ability to bear children. Because these items are not tied to specific measurable expenses, to estimate their dollar value from a claims-paying standpoint requires considerable experience, and even then it becomes somewhat arbitrary.

Punitive Damages. In some states, when the court finds the insured's conduct to be particularly reprehensible, it may award a third type of damages referred to as punitive damages. The object of punitive damages is to punish the wrongdoer. Some states that recognize punitive damages do not allow insurers to pay punitive damages on behalf of an insured because that would tend to insulate the insured from the intended punishment. Some policies specifically exclude the payment of these damages even if they are otherwise insurable in a given jurisdiction.

Defense Costs.   Most liability policies place no dollar limit on the defense costs payable by the insurance company. (Exceptions include excess or some umbrella liability policies, as well as a few other policies that include defense coverage "within policy limits.") The insurer is not obligated to provide further defense once the entire policy limit has been paid for damages. But the point is that defense costs seldom have any relationship to the policy limit and are payable in addition to the policy limits.

There are practical limitations, however, that tend to keep defense costs in line. For example, an insurer is not likely to spend $100,000 defending a suit for $10,000 in damages. But it is not unheard of for an insurer to spend $100,000 or more in defense costs for a suit seeking $1 million in damages. The cost of providing defense is becoming so overwhelming a factor to insurers that many have proposed various limitations or provisions to share the costs by both insureds and insurers. To date, however, few of these proposals have been implemented.

A major reason behind the spiraling costs of legal defense is that the duty of the insurer to defend is broader than the duty to pay damages. This means that, so long as there is a potential for liability and coverage, the insurer has the obligation to defend the insured even if some of the allegations are groundless, false, or fraudulent and even if some of the allegations are not covered by the policy. In other words, if some allegations are covered, the insurer must defend all allegations— whether covered or not—but ultimately is obligated to pay damages on only that liability for which coverage is provided by the policy.

Treble Damages.   Treble damages may be awarded against an insurer under either the Racketeer Influenced and Corrupt Organizations Act (RICO) or antitrust statutes.

RICO.   The Racketeer Influenced and Corrupt Organizations Act (RICO)[17] was enacted by Congress in 1970 after several Congressional investigations into organized crime. It provides for both criminal penalties and civil remedies for prohibited conduct. The broad civil remedies part has special interest to insurance companies because any damages awarded are *mandatorily trebled* (tripled).

While RICO legislation was introduced as a tool for fighting organized crime originally, RICO has been applied in practice to a diverse group of suits involving, among others, accountants, banks, bankruptcies, corporation takeovers, landlords and tenants, intra-church disputes,

and dishonest employees. It was little used in insurance until the early
1980s. It is now common in lawsuits dealing with insurance matters.
The civil remedy section of this act reads as follows:

> Any person injured in his business or property by reason of a violation
> of Section 1962 of this Chapter may sue therefor in any appropriate
> United States district court and shall recover three-fold the damages
> he sustains and the cost of the suit, including a reasonable attorney
> fee.

The important point about this law is its imposition of treble damages plus other costs of litigation. Such trebled damages are not discretionary; they must be awarded if in fact any person is injured by reason
of a violation of this law. Given that incentive to plaintiffs, the concerns
of defendants are whether such damages can be covered by liability
insurance.

Whether a liability policy must protect an insured against whom a
violation of this federal law is alleged depends on the circumstances.
Many professional-type liability policies, including directors and officers
liability policies, commonly are amended with exclusions that specifically
preclude punitive damages, as well as trebled damages as may be mandated under RICO, Sherman Anti-Trust, and Clayton Acts. Both kinds
of damages are usually specifically excluded, because it is still open to
question whether the treble damages are punitive in nature. According
to one source, there are three differences between punitive and RICO
treble damages:[18]

> Under common law, imposition of punitive damages requires a finding
> of malice or outrageous conduct on the part of the offender. With
> RICO, there is no such requirement; the damages are automatically
> imposed if the statutory preconditions are met.

> Under common law, a defendant's wealth is generally admissible to
> provide the basis for assessing the amount of punitive damages, for
> the idea is to make the damages large enough to punish that particular
> individual and to deter others. With RICO, trebling is automatic and
> the defendant's wealth or lack of wealth is irrelevant.

> Common law punitive damages are assessed at the discretion of the
> jury; the plaintiff has no absolute entitlement to them. RICO damages
> are assessed whenever statutory standing is met, and juries may not
> even be told that the damages they find will be trebled.

In the absence of these exclusions of RICO and other federal acts,
there may be sufficient room for maintaining that "damages," if not
otherwise defined in the policy, may be payable if the policy otherwise
covers the alleged liability of the insured and the damages are otherwise
insurable at law. Even if these kinds of damages are not covered for
some reason, the insurer still may be required to defend an insured
against whom RICO violations are alleged. The duty to defend is broader

than the duty to pay. If one of the allegations is potentially within the policy's coverage, the insurer must defend all such allegations whether or not they are covered by the policy. In the final analysis, an insurer might not have to pay the trebled damages imposed by RICO, but it may have to defend such an action to its conclusion.

Anti-Trust Laws. Treble damages can also be assessed against violators of anti-trust laws. The Sherman Act, which was enacted in 1890, holds that "Every contract, combination . . . or conspiracy, in restraint of trade . . . is declared to be illegal." Unlike the RICO act, a number of cases have dealt with the issue of coverage, under liability policies, of anti-trust violations. In one case, a liability insurer had a duty to defend an anti-trust action against its insured in which there were also allegations of common law business torts. The court found the policy between the parties to be ambiguous because one clause of the policy insured against intentional torts or acts and another clause attempted to exclude from coverage these same acts. Specifically, the umbrella liability policy insuring agreement referred on the one hand to the coverages of personal injury and advertising offenses, which are intentional torts. But on the other hand, the policy conditioned coverage of such offenses on an "occurrence," which is a contradiction because the latter term requires that injury must neither be expected nor intended from the standpoint of the insured. The insurer therefore was required to defend the insured.[19]

However, in another case involving an anti-trust action, the court ruled against defense of the insureds, because the alleged price-fixing scheme could be characterized only as causing a loss of profits to the plaintiff, and therefore failed to constitute "property damage," as that term was defined in the policy. Both the primary and umbrella insurers therefore were held to have no obligation to defend the insureds in the anti-trust action.[20]

The Application of Policy Limits

The fact that an insurance policy declarations page stipulates a maximum limit of insurance does not necessarily mean that all loss payments will be less than or equal to that limit. Some policies provide additional or supplemental coverages that not only expand the scope of protection but also provide additional coverage limits.

The homeowners forms, for example, provide numerous additional coverages and limits. A "$100,000 homeowners policy" that provides $100,000 coverage on the dwelling building normally also provides coverage in the amounts of $10,000 on appurtenant structures, $50,000 for personal property, and $20,000 for loss of use. Limited additional insurance is provided on loss to trees, shrubs, plants, and lawns on the residence premises. Generally, debris removal expense is included as part of the coverage amount applying to the damaged property. If, however, damage to covered property plus the expense of removing debris exceeds the limit on the property, the policy provides an additional amount of insurance of 5 percent toward the cost of debris removal. Yet another example of a coverage that is payable beyond the policy limit is credit card forgery and counterfeit currency. The amount payable is generally limited to a maximum of $500 in any one loss.

Both property and liability losses may result from a single incident. For example, the homeowner whose negligence starts a fire on his own property might also be legally responsible for property damage to a neighbor's property to which the fire spreads. A business might also have liability under workers compensation statutes for employees injured in a fire or other property-damaging incident.

Most modern business liability policies are written subject to aggregate limits. Once the aggregate amount specified in the policy has been paid in damages because of one or more occurrences, further protection ceases. At any given point in time, the amount of protection remaining, if any, under an aggregate limit is not specified in the policy.

Even if an aggregate limit applies to a policy, it is still possible for an insurer to end up paying several times that limit if more than one policy was in force (or if the same policy was in force for several policy periods) during the time when coverage was triggered. This can happen when the loss is said to have been caused by the "continuous or multiple" trigger theory. According to this theory, coverage is triggered (or activated) from the time of the claimant's initial exposure to the harmful condition or substance through the time injury or damage becomes manifest. This means that the occurrence limit of each policy year during this entire period of the continuous trigger would become at risk and possibly payable. If there is no aggregate limit applicable to such occurrence, the amount of damages payable during the policy could end up to be some multiple of the occurrence limit.

DAMAGES OR OTHER PENALTIES ASSESSED AGAINST THE INSURER

Although most insurer payments are limited by provisions within insurance contracts, several considerations outside the insurance contract may greatly expand the amounts payable by an insurer. Sometimes these external factors raise the ante to the extent that the insurer's ultimate payment far exceeds the applicable policy limit(s). The nature of these damages and penalties, and the rationale behind them, are especially relevant to the insurance professional.

Compensatory Damages

Compensatory damages may be awarded against an insurer if the insurer has breached its contract or delayed the payment of a claim.

Breach of Contract. The general rule in the United States always has been that damages for breach of a property insurance contract are limited to the recovery prescribed by the policy, plus interest. Because of perceived abuses of insureds by insurers, there has been a movement in recent years to find ways to enhance recovery beyond this limit. One of these is the adaptation to insurance of the general rule prevailing in general contract law that permits recovery of compensatory damages for breach of an implied covenant of good faith and fair dealing.

Note that the covenant of good faith and fair dealing is *implied*. It therefore is not expressly stated within the policy provisions. Such a covenant, furthermore, applies to both the insurer and the insured. Thus, the insured owes a duty to give the insurer truthful underwriting or claims information; the insurer, in turn, has the obligation to be fair and reasonable in handling claims.

In many such instances the insured has been able to show that a definite financial loss was brought about by the insurer's breach of the contract. Suppose an insurer improperly fails to pay a $100,000 property claim when business property is destroyed, and the business fails as a result. The business owner might demonstrate that, as a result of the insurer's failure to fulfill its obligations under the insurance policy, the insured not only lost the $100,000 value of the building, but also the ability to generate another $400,000 in future income that would have been earned had reconstruction of the building been financed on a timely basis. In such cases, based on the common-law rule, courts have been awarding damages in excess of the recovery prescribed in the policy (for example, the actual cash value of the property up to policy limits). This is said to be justified on the grounds that the suit is not on the policy itself but on the breach of the policy created by the insurer's failure to pay the claim. Thus the policy provisions are not controlling as a cap on the damages payable by the insurer.

Prejudgment Interest. When an insured event occurs, some party generally suffers an *immediate* financial loss. To the extent that the loss is not immediately paid by an insurer, the claimant experiences an additional financial loss resulting from the time value of money. In other words, there is a period of time during which that party goes without either the asset or the money to restore that asset. The claimant may be compensated for the time value of lost money if it is awarded prejudgment interest.

Prejudgment interest is interest allowed on the amount of a claim from the time it is liquidated to the time it is paid. A claim is *unliquidated* if the amount of damage cannot be computed except on conflicting evidence, inference, or interpretation. In property insurance, a claim becomes liquidated at the time that the damages become fixed in a definite amount or can be accurately computed by reference to well-established market values. In liability cases, a claim is liquidated if a jury, in effect, awards a dollar amount of damages as of a date prior to the judgment; prejudgment interest will bring the amount of the award up to date in terms of the value on the date of the judgment.

Prejudgment interest places the injured party in the same financial position he or she would have been in if the defaulting party had performed properly. It reflects the injured party's loss of use of money wrongfully withheld by the other party. The awarding of such interest is usually within the discretion of the trier of fact. Many states have laws on the matter.

Under property policies, most prejudgment interest suits arise when it is alleged that the amount of the underlying property claim was definitely set at a certain time and the insurer wrongfully withheld payment. Interest may be awarded even if the insurer acted in good faith if it can be shown that in fact the claim was liquidated. However, it has been held that a property insurer is not liable for such interest where it puts the total payment in excess of the policy limit unless there is bad faith or arbitrary delay.

Under liability policies, a claim for such interest can be handled in one of two ways:

- If prejudgment interest is awarded against an insured in the underlying tort suit, the liability policy will pay such interest as part of the damages and subject, therefore, to the limits of insurance applicable to damages. This is the traditional approach.
- The ISO commercial general liability coverage form, under supplementary payments, provides that the insurer will pay the prejudgment interest on that part of the judgment it pays, *in addition* to the policy limit.

This CGL is broader than umbrella liability policies, which generally limit prejudgment interest as part of the payment of damages.

Punitive Damages for Bad Faith

As mentioned earlier, punitive damages are damages awarded *against an insured* not to compensate the plaintiff for actual damages, but rather to punish the defendant. It was mentioned that the claimant under a liability insurance policy might be awarded both compensatory and punitive damages, and that both compensatory and punitive damages are payable by a liability insurer in many jurisdictions.

Punitive damages may also be awarded *against an insurer.* Once an insured has proven that the insurer is guilty of fraud, malice, or oppression, he or she may be entitled to punitive damages. These damages frequently bear no relationship to the compensatory damages. Because the purpose is to punish the defendant, it is permissible to put the wealth of the defendant into evidence. The plaintiff's attorney can paint for the jury a picture of a big, wealthy insurance company versus a small, poor insured—an image that cannot help but sway the jury.

On the one hand, it can be argued that awarding punitive damages against insurers raises their overhead costs and therefore tends to drive up insurance rates. On the other hand, the reality and the threat of punitive damages awards benefit the public to the extent that such awards may discourage insurers from giving even the appearance of bad faith.

While punitive damages are usually in favor of the insured (as in bad faith cases against insurers), there have been attempts by insurers to ask for punitive damages against their insureds when they feel a claim is fraudulent or otherwise patently unjustified.

Penalties Under Unfair Claim Settlement Practices Acts

Unfair claims practices acts address many aspects of claims handling, including insurers' responsibility for prompt communications with their insureds, adequate investigation, detailed explanations of coverage denials, and so on. Generally, such laws require that insurers handle claims promptly, which means prompt investigations, evaluation and, where warranted, prompt settlement. Ordinarily, if an insurer is found to have violated a provision of an unfair claims practices law with such frequency as to indicate a general business practice, penalties can be assessed against it by the state insurance department.

Unfair claim practices acts generally do not allow a claimant to sue an insurer for violation of the act, but this does not leave the wronged party without a civil remedy in those states that permit a separate tort action for bad faith against the insurer.

Most unfair claim practices acts cover some or all of the following:[21]

- Misrepresenting pertinent facts to claimants
- Misrepresenting policy provisions relating to any coverage at issue to claimants
- Failing to acknowledge and act reasonably promptly upon communications with respect to claims arising under insurance policies

- Failing to adopt and implement reasonable standards for the prompt investigation and processing of claims arising under insurance policies
- Failing to affirm or deny coverage of claims within a reasonable time after proof of loss requirements have been completed and submitted by the insured
- Not attempting in good faith to effectuate a prompt, fair, and equitable settlement of claims in which liability has become reasonably clear
- Compelling insureds to institute litigation to recover amounts due under an insurance policy by offering substantially less than the amounts ultimately recovered in similar actions
- Attempting to settle a claim by an insured for less than the amount to which a reasonable person believed he or she was entitled by reference to the written or printed insurance policy
- Attempting to settle a claim by an insured for less than the amount that a reasonable person would believe he or she was entitled by reference to written or printed advertising material accompanying or made a part of an application
- Attempting to settle claims on the basis of an application that was altered without notice to, or knowledge or consent of, the insured, his or her representative, or agent or broker
- After payment of claim, failing to respond to insured's or beneficiary's inquiry of the coverage under which payment has been made
- Engaging in the practice of appealing, without proper cause, arbitration awards in favor of insureds or claimants for the purpose of compelling them to accept settlements or compromises less than the amount awarded in arbitration
- Delaying the investigation or payment of claims by requiring an insured, claimant, or his or her physician to submit to a preliminary claim report, and then requiring the subsequent submission of formal proof-of-loss forms if both submissions contain substantially the same information
- Failing to settle claims promptly, when liability has become apparent, under one portion of the insurance policy coverage in order to influence settlement under other portions of the insurance policy coverage
- Failing to provide promptly a reasonable explanation of the basis relied on in the insurance policy, in relation to the facts or applicable law, for the denial of a claim or for the offer of a compromise settlement

- Directly advising the claimant not to obtain the services of an attorney
- Misleading a claimant regarding the statute of limitations

SUMMARY

While the previous chapters in this volume have concentrated on analyzing the types of information found within insurance policies, this chapter focuses on a wide range of factors external to the policies themselves that affect policy analysis.

When a dispute over the interpretation of an insurance policy arises, the dispute may ultimately be resolved in a civil court. One possible procedure involves a suit by the insured. Like everyone else, insureds have a right to bring suit against anybody, including the insurer. However, the suit provision of the insurance policy may make it easy for the insurer to have such a lawsuit discharged unless the insured has complied with other policy provisions. When faced with a claim for which coverage is not clear, the insurer may issue a reservation of rights letter or a nonwaiver agreement before proceeding. In some cases the insurer—or the insured—may seek a declaratory judgment action to determine questions of coverage before proceeding to litigate the underlying questions of the insured's liability.

Legal doctrines affecting insurance policy interpretation include the contract of adhesion doctrine, the reasonable expectations doctrine, the unconscionable advantage doctrine, the substantial performance doctrine, and the doctrines of waiver and estoppel. Courts may rely on any or all of these doctrines when asked to resolve a dispute concerning the interpretation of an insurance contract; they may also be considered in out-of-court negotiations or settlements.

Some policy provisions call upon or "invoke" external resources. For example, the liberalization clause may bring into an existing policy those broadening provisions of the insurer's new policy edition. And, although statutes always take precedence over contract provisions, many policies contain a provision specifically stating that the policy is thereby altered, if necessary, to conform to any applicable statute.

Insurance policies may cover a number of "unknowns." Unnamed insureds may be covered because of some relationship to named insureds as described in the policy. Nonowned property may be covered. Newly arising exposures may be covered automatically or for a limited time period during which they must be reported. Covered perils may be undefined. And, when the issuance of a policy is delayed, binders may provide coverage that is not completely specified until the written policy is produced. All these situations provide some opportunity for dispute.

Policyholders may have some unspecified rights to continue their protection under a policy. Statutes may limit the number of reasons for which an insurer may cancel or specify the number of days of advance notice an insurer must give before cancellation can become effective. In addition, insurers' cancellation practices—such as the practice of routinely accepting late premium payments—sometimes provide loopholes.

Insurance policies say nothing about the concept of a "burden of proof," but it can have an important effect on the way coverage is applied to a loss. In named perils property insurance, for example, the burden is on the insured to show that the loss was caused by a covered peril. With "all-risks" coverage, the insured is presumed to have met that burden of proof unless the insurer can show that the peril was not covered.

Other sources of recovery, external to an insurance policy, may have a bearing on the amount payable by that policy. Examples include situations involving other insurance or subrogation. A question not addressed by many policies is whether a "self-insurance program" of some kind qualifies as other insurance.

Noninsurance contracts entered into by the insured, such as exculpatory agreements or hold harmless agreements, can have an important effect in determining the responsibilities of an insurer who has provided contractual liability coverage. Likewise, insureds' pre-loss waivers of liability can affect the subrogation opportunities available to property insurers. Like other external factors, these noninsurance contracts are not a part of the insurance policy itself.

Settlement options not listed in the policy often are available. Negotiation commonly is involved in arriving at the value of a claim. Structured settlements may involve periodic payouts to seriously injured claimants rather than the more traditional lump-sum settlement. And, in some cases, rehabilitation services may be provided to restore injured claimants' productive capacity, even where the insurer has no contractual obligation to pay rehabilitation expenses.

The amount payable under a property insurance policy depends on a wide range of factors that must inevitably be considered in establishing the value or repair cost of damaged property. In some states, valued policy laws may dictate the way in which a total property loss is to be computed, whether or not that methodology agrees with that of the policy. The amount payable under a liability policy normally involves special damages and/or general damages awarded by a court or arrived at through an out-of-court settlement. In some cases, however, punitive damages also are claimed; in some states, liability insurance is held to cover punitive damages. Treble damages may also apply and be covered in cases where RICO or anti-trust laws have allegedly been violated. In any case, certain defense costs must be handled.

Last, but not least, suits against the insurer may result in a finding that the insurer is liable for damages that do not arise directly out of the insurance contract. Compensatory damages may be awarded against the insurer if the insurer is shown to have breached its duties under the insurance contract. Prejudgment interest may be charged against the insurer if a delay was involved in handling a claim. And penalties may be assessed if the insurer has violated any unfair claim settlement practices acts.

Generally speaking, insurance policy analysis involves an educated examination of the provisions written into an insurance policy. But analysis of the written provisions alone does not tell the whole story. One must also consider external factors, such as those dealt with in this chapter, that determine how the written provisions may be interpreted and applied in practice.

Chapter Notes

1. *50 American Law Reports 4th* 932.
2. Allan D. Windt, *Insurance Claims and Disputes*, 2nd ed. Section 3.18, Shepard's/McGraw-Hill, Inc., 1988.
3. Windt, Section 8.02.
4. Industrial Risk Insurers v. New Orleans Public Service, Inc., 666 F.Supp. 874 (1987).
5. Stephen M. Hoke, "Contract Interpretation in Commercial Insurance Disputes: The Status of the Sophisticated Insured Exceptions and Alternatives to the Ambiguity Rule," *Federation of Insurance & Corporate Counsel*, Quarterly/Spring 1990, p. 264.
6. Huck et al. v. Gabriel Realty Co., 136 N.J. Super 468 (1975).
7. Slightly different rules apply if the vehicle is a replacement vehicle rather than an additional vehicle.
8. Mamou Farm Services, Inc. v. Hudson Insurance Co., 488 So. 2d 259 (1986).
9. Auto-Owners Ins. Co. v. Jensen, 667 F2d 714 (1981).
10. The reasons behind this development and its impact are discussed in depth in Robert B. Holtom, *Restraints on Underwriting: Risk Selection, Discrimination and the Law*, The National Underwriter Company, 1979.
11. Clinton E. Miller, *How Insurance Companies Settle Cases* (Santa Ana, CA: James Publishing Group, rev. 1, 2-90), Sec. 1521.1, pp. 15-8 and 15-9.
12. Paul Tishman Co., Inc. v. Carney Del Guidace, Inc., 320 N.Y.S.2d 396 (1971), aff'd 359 N.Y.S.2d 561 (1974).
13. Fireman's Insurance Co. of Newark, N.J. v. Wheeler, 1991 C.C.H. (Fire and Casualty) 8539.
14. American Nurses Association v. Passaic General Hospital, 484 A2d 670 (1984).
15. See Eric Hollowell, "Self-Insurance Against Liability As Other Insurance Within Meaning of Liability Insurance Policy," *American Law Reports 4th* 707-724.
16. Evelyn R. Hartman, "Insurance Rehabilitation—Who, What, When and Why?," *The Weekly Underwriter*, June 27, 1981, no. 24, vol. 224, p. 16/ADJ.
17. 18 USC 1961 et seq.
18. Alvin K. Hellerstein and Elizabeth A. Mullins, "The Likely Insurance Treatment of Treble Damage RICO Judgments," *The Business Lawyer*, vol. 42, November 1986, pp. 132-133.
19. Tews Funeral Home v. Ohio Casualty Co., 832 F.2d 1037.
20. L. Ray Packing Company v. Commercial Union Ins. Co., 467 Atl.2d 832 (1983).
21. Miller, Sec. 1521.1, pp. 15-8 and 15-9.

Bibliography

Anderson, Ronald A. and Kumpf, Walter A. *Business Law*. 10th ed. Cincinnati, OH: South-Western Publishing Co., 1976.

Black, Henry Campbell. *Black's Law Dictionary*. 4th ed. St. Paul, MN: West Publishing Co., 1968.

Brooks, Harry F. and Malecki, Donald S. *Insuring the Lease Exposure*. 2nd ed. Cincinnati, OH: The National Underwriter Company, 1989.

Cozen, Stephen A. and Bennett, Richard C. "Fortuity: The Unnamed Exclusion." *The Forum*, vol. XX, no. 2, Winter 1985, p. 225.

Daynard, Harold S. *Between the Lines: A Guide to Property and Inland Marine Insurance Policy Interpretation*. Hartsdale, NY: BTL Publishing Co., 1986.

Gibbons, Robert J. *Principles of Premium Auditing*. Vol. I. 2nd ed. Malvern, PA: Insurance Institute of America, 1986.

Hartman, Evelyn R. "Insurance Rehabilitation—Who, What, When and Why?" *The Weekly Underwriter*, vol. 224, no. 24, June 27, 1981, p. 16/ADJ.

Hellerstein, Alvin K. and Mullins, Elizabeth A. "The Likely Insurance Treatment of Treble Damage RICO Judgments." *The Business Lawyer*, vol. 42, November 1986, pp. 132-133.

Hoke, Stephen M. "Contract Interpretation in Commercial Insurance Disputes: The Status of the Sophisticated Insured Exceptions and Alternatives to the Ambiguity Rule." *Federation of Insurance & Corporate Counsel*, Quarterly/ Spring 1990, p. 264.

Hollowell, Eric. "Self-Insurance Against Liability As Other Insurance Within Meaning of Liability Insurance Policy." *American Law Reports 4th*, pp. 707-724.

Holtom, Robert B. *Restraints on Underwriting: Risk Selection, Discrimination and the Law*. Cincinnati, OH: The National Underwriter Company, 1979.

Launie, J. J.; Lee, J. Finley; and Baglini, Norman A. *Principles of Property and Liability Underwriting*. 3rd ed. Malvern, PA: Insurance Institute of America, 1986.

Lees, Paul K. and Werkown, Marlas. "Confronting Employment-Related Claims for Emotional Distress." *Defense Counsel Journal*, October 1989, pp. 454-459.

Keeton, Robert E. and Widiss, Alan I. *Insurance Law*. St. Paul, MN: West Publishing Co., 1988.

Knight, K. G., ed. *Lloyd's Survey Handbook.* 4th ed. Colchester, United Kingdom: Lloyd's of London Press, 1985.

Lorimer, James J.; Perlet, Harry F.; Kempin, Frederick G.; and Hodosh, Frederick R. *The Legal Environment of Insurance.* Vol. I. 3rd ed. Malvern, PA: The American Institute for Property Liability Underwriters, 1987.

Magee, John H. *General Insurance.* 3rd ed. Homewood, IL: Richard D. Irwin, 1952.

Malecki, Donald S. "Careful Research Pays Off When Offering Earthquake Coverage to Commercial Clients." *Rough Notes,* November 1990, p. 60.

————. "New ISO Builders Risk Form Is Not for Everyone." *Rough Notes,* March 1989, p. 36.

Miller, Clinton E. *How Insurance Companies Settle Cases.* Santa Ana, CA: James Publishing Group, rev. 1, 2-90.

National Association of Insurance Commissioners. "Personal Lines Property and Casualty Insurance Policy Simplification Model Regulation," 1986.

Smith, Barry D. *How Insurance Works: An Introduction to Property and Liability Insurance.* Malvern, PA: Insurance Institute of America, 1984.

Wiening, Eric A. "An End to All-Risks Insurance?" *The Risk Report,* vol. VI, no. 6, February 1984.

Windt, Allan D. *Insurance Claims and Disputes.* 2nd ed. Colorado Springs, CO: Shepard's/McGraw Hill, Inc., 1988.

Index

D

E